CARRIERS AND COACHMASTERS

Trade and Travel before the Turnpikes

Engraving from an undated handbill for the Canterbury coach.

CARRIERS AND COACHMASTERS

Trade and Travel before the Turnpikes

Dorian Gerhold

Phillimore

2005

Published by
PHILLIMORE & CO. LTD
Shopwyke Manor Barn, Chichester, West Sussex, England

© Dorian Gerhold, 2005

ISBN 1 86077 327 3

Printed and bound in Great Britain by
MPG BOOKS LTD
Bodmin, Cornwall

CONTENTS

LIST OF ILLUSTRATIONS

Frontispiece: Engraving from an undated handbill for the Canterbury coach

Maps

ACKNOWLEDGEMENTS

I am grateful to a number of people for advice and references, including John Armstrong, Robin Bush, Peter Edwards, Peter Gerhold, David Harrison, Negley Harte, Nicholas Kingsley, Chris Lewis, Robert Peberdy, Leslie Pressnell and Kate Tiller. David Harrison and Robert Peberdy kindly read and commented on an earlier version of the conclusion. I would also like to thank those who have accommodated me during my tours of Record Offices, especially Nicholas and Mary Kingsley, Chris Lewis and Xanthe Brooke, John and Melinda Palmer, Robert Peberdy and my parents.

I would like to thank the following for their permission to use the following images: Corporation of London Records Office, frontispiece, 2, 60, 64, 65; The Bodleian Library, 1 (Douce DD 119, p. 385), 12 (Gough Oxf. 31), 63; Dorian Gerhold, 3, 42, 66, 70, 71, 74; English Heritage, NMR, 6, 11; The National Archives, 7, 10, 33, 34, 40, 54, 61; © Oxfordshire County Council Photographic Archive, 8, 45; Oxfordshire Record Office, 9; Lowther Family, 13; Cambridge City Council, 14; By permission of the British Library, 17, 27, 38, 46, 48, 53, 56, 57, 72, 73, 75, 76, 77, 78 (Burney 130B, 269B, 17B, 44A; Thomason Tracts, E912(1); PP 1349a.37(4)8; Burney, 344B (two), 149B, 368B, 373B, 392B, 445B, 518B); Robert Peberdy, 18; Guildhall Library, London, 19, 20, 22, 31, 36, 50; London Metropolitan Archives, 21; Oxford University Press, Map 5; Bristol Record Office, 23; Keeper of the Archives, University of Oxford, 29; Ernest Hinchliffe, 37; The Devon & Exeter Institution, 39; Sherborne Castle Estates, 43; By kind permission of the Dean and Chapter of York, 44; Liverpool Record Office, 49; By permission of the trustees of the Will Trust of Sir Richard Hamilton, 52; Photo George Plunkett, 55; Kress Collection, Baker Library, Harvard Business School, 59; Record Society of Lancashire and Cheshire, 62; © Crown copyright, NMR, 67; © John Sibbick; reproduced by permission of Chrysalis Books Group Plc, 68; Suffolk Record Office, Ipswich, 79; City of York Libraries, York Reference Library, 80; Reece Winstone Archive, 81, 82.

INTRODUCTION

The traditional picture of roads in the horse-drawn era – impassable in winter, vehicles hopelessly bogged down in mud, travellers drowning in deep ruts, irregular and expensive road services, most goods haulage by packhorses prior to turnpiking and all significant traffic passing by river or coastal vessel – was long ago swept away by detailed research,[1] although much history is still written as if it had not been. There is now much greater appreciation of the vital role of the common carrier and of how thoroughly the country's main industry – textiles – and other producers of high-value goods depended on the carrier's services. The operation of one 19th-century firm, Russell's of Exeter, has been examined in detail.[2] Stage-coaches after the establishment of the mail-coach system in 1784 have of course always received admiring attention.

However, much of the research, like that on Russell's and on mail-coaches, has dealt with the period after the 'turnpike mania' of 1751-72 created a dense network of turnpike roads. The earlier carriers and coachmasters have remained mysterious, and none of their business archives is known to survive. This is even truer of stage-coaches than carriers, and little has been written about *any* coachmasters other than a few celebrities from the very end of the coaching era. Early stage-coaches have little of the romance attached to their successors, and have been presented as so slow and unreliable that it seems remarkable that anyone used them. Can there possibly have been regular coach, waggon and packhorse services, especially over long distances and in winter, before any turnpikes had been established? Can we get closer to that world of mud and ruts and straining horseflesh, and at the same time learn more about the economics and the quality of road services and of their value to a country beginning to industrialise?

That we can is in large part due to an unlikely figure, Thomas Delaune. Delaune was born near Cork to Catholic parents in about 1635. At 16 he began work as clerk to the owner of a pilchard fishery. His employer persuaded him to become a Baptist, and this caused him so much trouble that he moved to England, where he obtained a living through literary work and by keeping a school. However, his *A plea for the non-conformists* of 1683 was deemed seditious, and, being unable to pay the fine imposed, he spent the rest of his life in Newgate Prison, where he died in 1685.[3]

of LONDON. 385

An Alphabetical Account of all the Carriers, Wagoners, and Stage-Coaches, that comes to the several Inns in London, Westminster, and Southwark, from all Parts of *England* and *Wales*, with the respective days of their Coming in, and Going out.

A.

Abington.

WIlliam Perton *Wagoner, comes to the* Bell *in* Friday-street *on Wednesdays, and goes out on Thursdays.*

Edward Perton *with Coach and Wagon the same days, to and from the* Sarazens-head *in* Friday-street.

Aylesbury.

John Christmas *Wagoner, comes to the* George *by* Holbourn-Conduit *on Wednesdays, goes out on Thursdays.*

Mr. Webb *Coachman, comes to the* Crown *in* Holbourn *on Mondays, Wednesdays and Fridays, and goes out on Tuesdays, Thursdays and Saturdays.*

Mr. Fryer's *Coach comes to the* Black Swan *in* Holbourn, *on Tuesdays, Thursdays, and Saturdays, and goes out on Mondays, Wednesdays and Fridays.*

Andover in *Berkshire.*

Roger Bird *Wagoner, comes to the* King's-Arms *in* Holbourn-Bridge *on Wednesdays, and goes out on Thursdays.*

Haverhill in *Suffolk.*

William Swan *Carrier, comes to the* Four Swans *in* Bishops-gate *on Wednesdays, and goes out on Thursdays.*

Mr. Ashton, Townes *and* Cole, Edward Onyon

S   Car-

1 *The first page of Delaune's list of carriers and stage-coaches in 1681.*

In 1681 Delaune published *The present state of London, or memorials comprehending a full and succinct account of the ancient and modern state thereof.* Appended was a list of the carriers and coachmen serving London, which he had employed six people to compile.[4] The book was reissued in 1690, after his death, as *Angliae metropolis: or, the present state of London,* with a similar list, thoroughly revised. (For convenience, those in both lists are referred to here as Delaune's carriers and coachmasters.)

These were the first lists of coach services but not the first of carriers. That distinction belongs to John Taylor's *Carriers cosmographie* of 1637. And Delaune's were certainly not the last such lists. What makes his work so valuable, and in some respects unique, is that he included the full names of the carriers and coachmen – a total of 645 carriers and 212 coachmen, making 805 in all (since some were both carrier and coachman). In contrast, every other list of carriers until 1786 provided only destinations, London inns and days (and occasionally times) of arrival and departure. As for coachmasters, no other lists prior to the 1830s ever provided names.[5] Delaune's names have been the key for identifying records relating to carriers and coachmasters.

Though centred on Delaune's carriers and coachmasters of 1681 and 1690, this book covers a longer period, from the 1650s, when the stage-coach network came into existence, to the 1750s and 1760s, when turnpike roads began to affect road services significantly. It examines the *public* part of road transport – scheduled services available to anyone. And it is largely concerned with services to and from London. All the carriers and coachmasters discussed in this book served London unless the contrary is indicated. London then dominated England more than ever before or since, having in about 1700 one-ninth of its population, three-quarters of its foreign trade, nearly half its merchant fleet, a dominant position in its inland trade, its largest concentration of industrial workers and its seat of government, and was the home of the majority of its professional people and the centre of upper-class social life for half the year.[6] London's proportion of England's population rose from 7.2 per cent in 1650 to 11.7 per cent in 1750.[7]

Sources for carriers and coachmasters

Two types of document are especially important for carriers and are useful too for stage-coaches: records of the Courts of Chancery and Exchequer and probate inventories. Many carriers became involved in Chancery and Exchequer suits. Sometimes the records provide just incidental information, such as where the carrier lived and what land he owned, but sometimes the case related directly to a carrying business, covering the sale or inheritance of the business, liability for lost or stolen goods, whether a carrier was liable for his partner's debts or accounts between a carrier and his warehousekeeper or innkeepers. The latter in particular sometimes resulted in detailed accounts being set out, as discussed below.[8] It is largely the bills and answers presenting the parties' arguments which have been used here, but sometimes also depositions by witnesses and in one case exhibits, consisting of accounts relating to waggons, packhorses and coaches between London and Birmingham in the 1730s and 1740s. The difficulty with Chancery and Exchequer records is to find relevant cases, and for this Delaune's names have been crucial. Some Chancery records are now indexed on the internet – a number of them by subject and place as well as by name.[9] Other legal records include the proceedings of the Old Bailey, now available on the internet.[10]

Probate inventories[11] list the possessions of a deceased person, including any horses and vehicles, and again Delaune's names have been crucial for finding them, since most collections are not indexed by occupation, and anyway carriers and especially coachmasters were not always recorded as such. Moreover, the information in carriers' and coachmasters' inventories is far more useful if something is known about the service they were providing (see Appendices 2 and 7). Occasionally each horse and vehicle is itemised, but the information is usually more of a summary. Inventories also indicate the carrier's or coachmaster's other interests, such as farming. Similar information on stock is sometimes available from Chancery and Exchequer records, from newspaper advertisements (especially those offering a business for sale) and wills. The defects of probate inventories are of course well known. In particular, items may be omitted, for example if seized by creditors, and this may be misleading if only *part* of the stock was seized;[12] also a business might decline during its owner's final illness. However, enough inventories have been found to make it unlikely that the overall picture is seriously distorted.

These sources have proved less plentiful for coachmasters than carriers, partly no doubt because there were fewer of them, but for coachmasters there is also abundant evidence from advertisements and diaries. Advertisements for stage-coaches start to appear in London newspapers in 1653, and such newspapers multiply from the 1690s.[13] Regional or local newspapers start to become available in 1706 – the *Norwich Gazette* being the earliest surviving.[14] The advertisements vary in fullness, but usually give destination, days of operation, time of departure, inns and owner, sometimes adding the fare and occasionally providing miscellaneous other information, such as the number of teams used. Some coachmasters rarely advertised, except to announce a change of ownership, whereas others did so regularly, often advertising the start of both summer and winter schedules. A few carriers also advertised their services, usually when the owner or inn changed. Other types of advertisement include those relating to the sale of stage-coach or carrying businesses and the sale or theft of horses, which often indicate the type and size of the horse. Few newspapers have been indexed, but in this period advertisements were relatively few and nearly always gathered together on the last page, so searching is reasonably fast. There were also handbills, which are occasionally found among family papers.

Diaries vary greatly in how fully coach journeys were recorded. Some diarists indicated only where they lodged, or just the start and end of the journey, but some listed the dining and lodging places and other stops, and the best diaries sometimes give times of departure and arrival (thereby indicating miles per hour). They are crucial as a check on the timings given in advertisements, for providing information about coaches in winter (when advertisements were relatively rare) and, since they often make it possible to work out where teams were changed, for indicating how the teams were organised. They also provide much other information, for example on passengers and how they passed the time. They do not always state the means of travel, but in the case of stage-coaches this is often indicated by the presence of strangers. Several bibliographies of diaries exist,[15] but some of the unpublished diaries can be found only through indexes at libraries or county record offices.[16]

There are several other important sources. For stage-coaches there are pamphlets relating to an attempt to suppress them as a nuisance in 1672.[17] For carriers there are orders of the justices of the peace setting maximum rates of carriage from 1692,[18] summaries in the *House of Commons Journals* of evidence from witnesses on the size of teams and petitions from carriers and their customers, and a few manuscript or published lists of carriers serving places other than London.[19] Letters can provide much information, but only published or indexed collections have been used for this study; the most useful have been those of tradesmen and those between gentlemen and their estate stewards.[20] Personal and household accounts have also been little used here.

Many other sources, such as wills and deeds, can provide personal details about carriers and coachmasters. In fact almost any collection of papers may provide relevant information, and much remains to be discovered. The study of carrying and stage-coach services depends not on finding a specific source and exploiting it but on assembling scattered information from a variety of sources and using it together, for example using diaries to verify the advertised journey times of coaches, as in the present study. Together, the sources make possible an analysis of the carriers and coachmasters and their businesses and their effectiveness in linking local communities with London. They also allow for the first time a description of the origins of the stage-coach network.

2 A list of carriers using seven London inns in 1692. Recording their rates of carriage, which was the purpose of the exercise, seems to have been quickly given up as too difficult. This list provides valuable confirmation of Delaune's accuracy (see Appendix 1). (Corporation of London RO, Misc. MSS. 31.6.)

Carriers, coaches and roads

Carrying and coach services differed greatly: the former were much longer established, were considerably more numerous, travelled more slowly and had dozens of customers for each journey, including many regular ones, instead of just a few. Carrying was a more complicated business, requiring much more continuous attention. However, there were three major similarities between the two types of business. Both provided relatively expensive services which relied for their custom on their relative speed and reliability, as discussed later. Both depended utterly on the horse, either as a hauler of vehicles or a beast of burden, and the horse largely determined their operating practices, their economics and the very nature of the services provided. And both used the same roads.

Historians and contemporaries have generally been united in criticising the state of the roads before turnpiking. The only maintenance was provided under the system of statute labour, instituted in 1555, whereby occupiers of land had to provide vehicles and cattle and householders had to provide labour for six days a year for repairing the roads of their parish. Parish highway rates were permitted from 1654, but few parishes imposed them. One turnpike road was established in 1663, on the Great North Road between Wadesmill and Stilton, but the next

3 *Part of the main Bristol road at Beacon Hill near Sandy Lane, turnpiked in 1714 but superseded in the 1750s by other routes. Nothing appears to have been done by the trust in charge of this road to widen stretches of 'hollow-way' or reduce the gradient. This was one of a number of early turnpike roads abandoned in favour of better routes.*

was not created until 1695, and the system developed slowly, so that not until the 1720s was a significant proportion of the roads used by London carriers and coaches turnpiked.[21]

Making individual, often rural, parishes responsible for heavily-used trunk routes had obvious disadvantages, and there is also no doubt that statute labour was inefficient.[22] But the question which matters is not whether statute labour was efficient: it is what that system achieved or failed to achieve in terms of keeping the roads in repair. Contemporary comments are of limited assistance. Macaulay made much of a passage from Ralph Thoresby's diary for May 1695 relating to a flood on the Great North Road near Ware, 'which raised the washes upon the road to that height that passengers from London that were upon the road swam, and a poor higgler was drowned, which prevented our travelling for many hours'.[23] But was this a common situation on that stretch of road, and was that road (covered, in part, by the first turnpike) a typical one? Some roads, especially on low-lying clay, as in parts of the Great North Road, were extremely difficult to maintain, whereas others, especially on chalk, needed little maintenance. The state of the roads varied not only from place to place but also from one year to another and (obviously) from one season to another. Moreover, the standard of judgement varied according to what sort of road use the observer had in mind and what comparisons he was making. Wheeled vehicles needed a better road than packhorses and riding horses. Defoe in the 1720s, having seen what the better turnpikes had done, was less inclined to describe a road as good than Ogilby 50 years earlier.[24]

Roads are of course a means to an end: what matters is not roads themselves but the traffic they bear. In the past, pre-turnpike roads have often been assumed to have been dreadful, and road services have therefore been regarded as inevitably inefficient and unreliable. A more rational approach is to examine what sorts of road services were possible in the 17th and early 18th centuries and, equally important, what sorts were not possible, and to derive conclusions about the state of the roads and their effects on economic development from that assessment. In this respect Delaune's carriers and coachmasters are highly informative, and they are highly informative too as regards the impact of the early turnpikes.

PART ONE

CARRIERS

CHAPTER I

THE CARRYING NETWORK

In the 1680s about 205 waggons and 165 gangs of packhorses entered and left London every week,[1] carrying about 460 tons of goods each way and performing a vital service for the country's burgeoning industries and for many other users. Direct services extended as far as Richmond and Kendal in the north,[2] Denbigh, Oswestry and Monmouth in the west and Bideford and Exeter in the south-west. The network was densest close to London, especially north of the city, although within about twenty miles of London there was probably so much casual carrying that a list of regular services was pointless, and Delaune records only one Middlesex carrier at each date. Beyond about eighty miles from London direct services became much fewer (Map 1). However, they connected with regional and local services, making the carrying network all-pervasive. Some counties, such as Norfolk and Devon, had relatively few London services because carrying tended to be concentrated in a few large firms based in the county town, sometimes sending several waggons at a time, whereas in others, such as Lancashire, more places had their own carrier.[3]

The network of London carriers was long-established. A London carrier is first recorded in 1398, at Oxford, and in the 15th century they existed at least at Exeter, Bristol, Gloucester, Worcester, Coventry, Cambridge, Colchester, Norwich and Higham (Norfolk).[4] The increase in cloth exports through London in the second half of the 14th century, London's growing control over England's internal trade in the mid-15th century and its dominance over the cloth export trade from the early 16th century, together with political centralisation from the late 15th century onwards, must all have contributed greatly to the development of the London carrying network.[5] In fact, the cloth industry, the London carrying trade and metropolitan dominance over the English economy clearly grew together. How soon an extensive network comparable with that of the 1680s was in place is unclear, but it certainly existed by 1637, when John Taylor published his *Carriers cosmographie*. Taylor's work was inferior to Delaune's, with no personal names and more omissions, but in some areas, such as the West Country, the pattern of London services was almost identical to that in the 1680s.[6] By the 17th century growth may have been reflected in larger packhorse gangs and the sending of several waggons at a time rather than extra services.

The one major development in the 17th century had been the replacement of two-wheeled carts by four-wheeled waggons. Carts rather than packhorses had been the country's dominant form of carriage since at least the 14th century,[7] despite the persistent myth to the contrary.[8] London carriers were among the users of carts, and in the 1590s carriers' carts were sometimes drawn by five or six horses. However, from the 1560s, some carriers began to replace their carts by waggons (introduced from Flanders), and Stow, writing in 1605, stated that they 'now come to London from Canterbury, Norwich, Ipswich, Glocester &c., with passengers and commodities'. Their use seems to have spread slowly at first, but from the second decade of the 17th century they became general for London services using vehicles, perhaps because of some technical improvement in the waggon, and by the 1620s waggon services to London appear to have been as numerous as in the 1680s.[9] Carts disappeared from London carrying, but there is no evidence in the 17th century of waggons replacing packhorses, and thus of an increase in wheeled transport. London carriers were probably more inclined towards packhorses than other road users because the packhorse's greater speed was more valuable to them, and in both 1681 and 1690 there were almost as many packhorse services to London each week as waggon services.[10] Moreover, almost every county and many towns and cities had both types of service, and there were even some carriers using both, as discussed later.

Map 1 *Carrying services to London in 1681. The few caravans and coach-waggons are included. The varying size of the circles reflects the number of services per week from each place, but not necessarily the quantity of loading, since a weekly waggon service with two or more waggons each time has the same weight here as a weekly packhorse service with a mere four horses. No attempt is made here to correct any omissions by Delaune. (Source: Delaune 1681.)*

Table 1. Numbers and capacity of carrying services, per week, 1681

Distance covered from London (miles)	Pack-horse services	Waggon services	Total services	Miles	Capacity – tons (each way)	Packhorse ton-miles	Waggon ton-miles	Total ton-miles
15-50	48	96	143	8866	157	1631	7847	9478
51-100	61	74	135	18552	169	5678	17748	23426
101-150	30	26	55	13517	78	6729	12082	18811
Over 150	27	3	31	11681	59	19898	2418	22316
Total	166	198	364	52616	463	33936	40095	74031

Source: Delaune 1681.

Notes: Numbers are rounded to the nearest whole number, so may not add up. No adjustment is made here for Delaune's omissions (see Appendix 1). 8½ coach-waggons and one caravan per week are included as waggons. Where the type of carriage is unknown services have been divided equally between packhorses and waggons. Tons per service (which determine the figures in the last four columns) are as follows: packhorses for the four distance categories 0.5, 0.7, 0.9, 1.9; waggons 1.4, 1.7, 2.0, 2.0. Numbers of services in 1690 were similar – 160 packhorse and 202 waggon services per week, with a similar breakdown by distance. Eight services covering less than 15 miles were listed in 1681 and three in 1690.

Packhorse firms

The carrying network is best understood by looking at individual firms or partnerships. The one with the longest route (263 miles) was that at Kendal, with four partners. All were local men, though based near rather than in Kendal – in 1681 Samuel and Thomas Briggs at Stainton, Richard Greenwood at Milton and John Yeats at Holmescales. At the time of his death in 1686 Yeats had 13 packhorses (as well as five other horses probably used for farming), and this was no doubt typical of his colleagues, indicating a total of 52 packhorses. In about 1700 the total stock was said to be 60 horses (Fig. 13). The most important loading must have been cloth and stockings from Kendal, but when Greenwood was robbed in 1665 (probably on his way back from London) the thieves took 'all the choyce wares ... being silk, tabby, taffata, ribbon, lace, cambrick, holland, diaper, stuffs, hats, some plate, and many other mercers and haberdashers wares and gentlemens goods'. There was no other direct service between Kendal and London, though goods could be sent from London slightly cheaper, but slower and less reliably, via Liverpool, or more expensively and slower via Preston or Wigan.[11]

Each week one of the four carriers set off for London, passing through Keighley, Wakefield and Northampton, though in 1711-17 two of the four were travelling instead via Lichfield and Towcester (Map 2).[12] They were engaged in the typical form of carrying partnership: each partner paid all the costs and kept all the income from his own journeys. There was no common property and no joint accounts,

4 *Packhorses in Gloucestershire, from a view of Bradley Court in Sir Robert Atkyns,* Ancient and present state of Glostershire *(1712). Note the driver following behind, and the fact that the horses were not tied together.*

KEndal Carriers are removed from the White *Horfe* without Cripple-Gate, to the Caftle Inn in Great Wood ftreet, who carry to Wakefield, Bradford, Kighley, Skipton, Settle, Kirby-Lonfdale, Lancafter, Kendal, and all adjacent Places: As alfo to all Places in Cumberland, and to all Parts in Scotland. They come in every Thurfday, and fet out every Friday.

5 *Carriers rarely advertised, except to announce a change of inn or owner. Even then they often provided very limited information. Here the Kendal carriers announce a change of inn.* (London Gazette, *19 June 1693.*)

so it was not strictly a partnership at all, simply four distinct businesses with a co-operative arrangement over timings and perhaps over places for depositing goods. The partners can only ever have met each other on the road, at the inns which were their regular lodging places. Two of the partners of 1681 had been replaced by 1690, all of those of 1690 by about 1700, and all but one of those of about 1700 by 1714, but the service continued in the same manner with new partners until about 1750.[13]

The Kendal packhorses arrived in London on Thursdays and left on the Friday following at noon. In Kendal they arrived on Tuesday or on Wednesday at noon and set off again the following Monday.[14] The journey therefore lasted ten or 10½ days (excluding Sundays), and there were 4½ or five days of rest at Kendal between journeys. The horses averaged 25 or 26 miles per day of travel. In 1712-16 one of their customers, Joseph Symson of Kendal, was confident enough about their regularity to tell his correspondents not just the days they would be at towns on the route but also the hours: 'He'll be at Mr Mattock's at Holme Chapel on Thursday the 18 instant exactly by ten in the forenoon that day'; 'be sure [to] meet the carrier exactly at the time. He will be at Towcester as above on Tuesday the 18 instant by 8 in the morn'.[15]

Map 2 *The Kendal carriers' route, 1690. Only Welford and Wakefield are specifically recorded as overnight stops. The dashed line indicates the alternative route which two of the four Kendal carriers were following in 1711-17. (Sources: C 8/404/18; Symson, Nos. 26, 580, 839, 1466, 1571.)*

6 *Blease Hall, Old Hutton, about four miles from Kendal. In 1700, William Bateman of Blease Hall was one of the four Kendal carriers. Carriers were often based just outside the main town served, as in this case, and many transport centres of this sort remain to be identified by local historians.*

7 *Extract from Nicholas Barry's accounts with his innkeeper at the Swan Inn, Egham, in 1706-9, covering January-February 1708. They were attached by the innkeeper to his answer to a Chancery suit begun by Barry. The usual pattern was: Thursday, up waggon; Friday, up packhorses; Saturday and Sunday, down waggon and packhorses (resting on Sunday). (C 6/381/3.)*

More detailed information survives about the Exeter carrying firm, which had a single owner. From 1676 to the 1690s it belonged to Thomas Morris of Exeter. Services to London were weekly, and he and his son appear to have conducted alternate ones. His account with his innkeeper at Bridport survives for August 1687 to January 1688 among the records of the Court of Chancery. Since hay was paid for per horse, the account indicates how many packhorses lodged at the inn on each night. Morris usually sent eight to ten horses, but occasionally as few as six or as many as fourteen. Thirteen were sent during most of December, the time of Exeter's St Nicholas Fair. The account also covers his fortnightly Exeter to Oxford service. It shows that the London and Oxford services were indeed conducted weekly and fortnightly respectively without fail. The only irregularity was a slippage from Monday, Wednesday and Friday to Tuesday, Thursday and Saturday for two periods of a fortnight or so. There can have been little difference between Morris undertaking regular packhorse journeys between Exeter and London in the 1680s and William Naynow and Michael Sweetlady doing the same in the 1460s, since neither packhorses nor roads are likely to have changed much between those dates.[16]

Morris's business was sold by his son to Nicholas Barry in 1704, and three years of accounts between Barry and his innkeeper at Egham from October 1706 to November 1709 have survived, again among the Chancery records (Fig. 7). Barry's packhorses were at Egham twice a week every week throughout those three years (a total of 163 weeks), again demonstrating the reliability of carrying services. They arrived and left a day early twice and a day late apparently six times. Their journeys probably took 5½ days each way, covering 33 miles per day, as they did under Barry's son in 1722, but on Saturdays they covered 42 miles (from Egham to London and back). The business was larger than under Morris, probably having absorbed one or more of the other Exeter firms. The weekly number of packhorses ranged from 11 to 26 (apart from one week with only seven) and averaged 17 to 18. In 1707 Barry added a weekly waggon, while retaining the packhorses.[17]

Barry's was one of the largest packhorse firms recorded, probably having about 70 packhorses.[18] In probate inventories the largest holding was Joseph Naylor's 101 horses for Leeds and Wakefield in 1718; if, as seems likely, he was then sole proprietor of this service, about a third of these would have set off for London each week. The next largest holding was John Frost's 25 at Lightcliffe near Halifax in 1713. Frost was almost certainly conducting every third journey, as in 1690, so the total number of horses for this Halifax service was about seventy-five. The smallest London firms recorded had just four packhorses, including Thomas Bass at Abbotsley (Huntingdonshire) in 1685 and Margaret Mussell at Horsham in 1693. Long-distance firms tended to have more horses per service than short-distance ones, though the size of the place served was also significant (Appendix 2).

Waggon firms

An example of a large firm using waggons is that of Richard Hales junior, Trowbridge carrier in 1707-9. Hales had 45 horses and six waggons to perform a weekly service.[19] His father, Richard Hales senior, had owned the almost equally large Frome firm for about thirty years. The Trowbridge firm is another one well recorded in accounts with an innkeeper – at the *Red Lion*, Staines, from April to October 1709.[20] Each week 14 horses were stabled at the *Red Lion*,[21] indicating two teams and waggons each time, which reflects the importance of Trowbridge's cloth industry and also the carrier's preference for sending several waggons at a time rather than single waggons more frequently. Again not a single week was missed, for 27 weeks. The account covered a period of summer, but other accounts (discussed later) indicate similar reliability in winter.[22]

The size of each business is indicated by the number of horses rather than waggons, for, while surplus waggons could be kept in store without incurring costs, horses were expensive to feed even when there was no work for them.[23]

8 *Engraving of a waggon by David Loggan in 1675. In this case the waggoner had a pony to ride.*

Hales's Trowbridge firm is the largest waggon firm recorded, and the three next largest in inventories were also at major cloth towns: those of Richard Hales senior at Frome in 1710 (39 horses), John Whitmash at Taunton in 1723 (30 to 32 horses) and Robert Beecroft at Norwich in 1663 (28 horses). Henry Warren at Stamford had 34 horses in 1681, but only 21 of these were specifically described as waggon horses (the others included six 'old horses', four 'old sadle horses' and a nag). Other large firms served Cambridge, Portsmouth and Warwick (24, 22 and 21 horses respectively). But most waggoners had only one or two waggons and teams, typical examples being John Roberts's 13 horses and two waggons at Evesham in 1690 and Henry Harwood's six horses and a waggon at Aylesbury in 1689 (Appendix 2).

Trading areas

Carriers nearly always lived at the provincial destination given by Delaune. Thirty-two per cent of Delaune's carriers have been identified from other records (205 out of 645), and, of these, 172 lived at the place listed or just outside it, or, where two or more places are listed, at one of them or between them. In a further 12 cases there were evidently two or more main destinations close together, such as Warrington and Leigh and Macclesfield and Congleton, of which Delaune listed only one.[24] No Londoners have been identified among Delaune's carriers: the carrying services of the 17th century were locally-organised services, without London involvement.

There were probably two reasons for this. First, as Delaune's days of arrival and departure show, the horses always had their rest away from London (keeping horses in London being relatively expensive) and, since they were the carrier's main asset, it made sense to live where it was possible to keep an eye on them. Secondly and more importantly, the carrier needed to keep in touch with his customers and to look out for possible loading. The observation of a Plymouth carrier in 1817 was just as valid in previous centuries: 'the persons who order the goods are the persons who say how it shall be sent to them & they are the best judge who serves them well. It's not for the London or the Exeter houses to send by whom they please.' For goods sent *to* London, especially cloth, Londoners appear usually to have paid for carriage (though heavier items such as malt were at least sometimes supplied to London carriage-paid),[25] but attempting to seek loading in London for a particular town was hardly feasible. There were a few London-based owners of carrying firms in the first half of the 18th century, serving Exeter, Bristol and Norwich, but the Bristol carrier had a partner in Bristol and the Exeter carriers always had agents in Exeter who were either already established as carriers' agents there or were family members.[26]

Of the 21 exceptions to the rule that Delaune's carriers lived at or near the place listed, four appear to result from Delaune lumping together two loosely-connected partnerships at different places.[27] Three were Thomas, Barnard and Silvester Keene, brothers and substantial farmers at Wroughton, Garsdon and Minety respectively in north Wiltshire, who were part of a partnership of four Bristol waggoners.[28] They were presumably each sending a waggon at least once a month to make up a weekly service, and differed from many other farmers using their horses for carrying only in that they provided a regular service.

9 *The probate inventory of John Jordan of Banbury, 1689. Jordan had a weekly waggon to London in 1681, and his widow the same in 1690. As in most other carriers' inventories, the horses and waggons are dealt with in a single entry; however, most provide far more detail about household goods than this one. (Oxfordshire RO, MS Wills Oxon Peculiar 44/1/9.)*

All but two[29] of the remaining 14 cases involved what may be described as an 'extension service', whereby the carrier of a particular town also served a larger town or city further from London. For example, in 1690 Henry Whiffen and Robert Seager of Dorchester, recorded as Exeter carriers, had waggons from Dorchester to London and also separate waggons from Dorchester to Exeter (all goods being unloaded at Dorchester).[30] The service could be described as an Exeter to London one and sometimes functioned as such, even though most goods probably began or ended their journeys at Dorchester. The three Norwich carriers in 1690 included Robert Cooke of Bury St Edmunds and Roger Hurst of Cambridge, and other examples are a York carrier at Doncaster, three Portsmouth carriers at Petersfield, an Oxford carrier at Watlington and the Rye carrier at Hawkhurst. In the case of Norwich there were also goods conveyed by carriers listed by Delaune at other places: Matthew Lancaster of Cambridge was described in 1687 as a carrier from Cambridge, Norwich and Lynn to London, and James Swan of Saffron Walden also carried Norwich goods to London, although he did not himself carry them from Norwich or claim to be a Norwich to London carrier.[31]

In general, however, the places listed by Delaune provide a reliable indication of the area from which the carrier obtained his loading. Several examples are available of the trading areas of London carriers. The executor's account for Thomas Bass of Leicester show that he was owed money for carrying by 47 people in 1693; of these, 38 lived in Leicester, six others within four miles of Leicester, two slightly further out (at Kibworth and Wistow), and the other was the Earl of Stamford. A different picture is suggested by a journey by Richard Greenwood from London to Kendal in 1687 (described in Chancery proceedings), during which he received £1 7s. 0d. 'for carrying of short packs to Northampton', 18s. for carrying goods to Rotherham and £2 2s. 0d. for goods carried to Bradford. In fact these are two halves of the same picture: the carrier had a regular connection

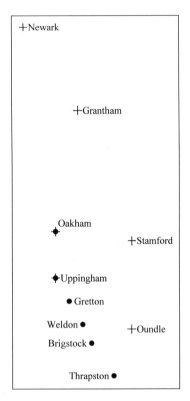

Map 3 *Trading areas (all at the same scale) indicated by advertisements for (top left) the Stamford carrier in 1728 (crosses) and the Thrapston carrier in 1735 (circles), (above) Chester carriers in about 1720, and (lower left) the Sheffield and Chesterfield carriers in 1687-8. (Sources:* London Gazette, *12 September 1687, 28 June 1688; handbill on wall of agent's office, Erddig, Clwyd;* LEP, *16 November 1728; Fig. 26.)*

at his home base, which provided the bulk of his loading and where credit might be given, as in Bass's case, but also, unless fully loaded, he would accept goods for anywhere else en route, and in these cases would usually require cash on receipt or delivery. In 1693 the Kendal carriers claimed to serve towns on their road from Wakefield through Bradford to Kendal, as well as Lancaster and the whole of Cumberland and Scotland, though these last were reached through forwarding by other carriers.[32]

The main difference between the Leicester and Kendal carriers was the size of the area served. This tended to be smaller the closer to London, where London carriers were more numerous. It was typically a town and the area immediately around it, or several towns along a stretch of road, as in the Thrapston area (Map 3).[33]

The carrier's 'connection' of regular customers, even more than his horses and other stock, was the basis of his business and extremely valuable. Consequently the business was usually worth about twice as much as the stock. For example,

James Swan purchased the waggon and horses of a Saffron Walden carrier in 1690 for £110, at least £50 more than he considered the stock was worth. Abraham Clavey bought Richard Hales's Frome business in 1710 for £600, although he claimed the stock was worth no more than £250.[34] In such transactions the purchaser was obtaining a going concern with regular customers, information about potential loading and usually an undertaking by the vendor (and in the Frome case the vendor's son and son-in-law) not to act as a carrier on the road or at the town in question. The importance of local connection meant that competition could be muted, with regular customers not investigating potential competitors. Carriers themselves probably tended to avoid competition and its attendant risks where possible, by not soliciting customers known to be served by other carriers. When Hales's son-in-law refused to accept the agreement with Clavey and set up as a Frome carrier himself, the charge for carrying wool from London fell from 10s. per pack to 9s.[35]

Given the value of connection and the ability to pass it on to a new owner, and the consequent difficulty of establishing new firms, it is not surprising to find considerable continuity, with businesses passed on from one generation to another or from vendor to purchaser (as recorded in advertisements and Chancery suits). The families of at least two of the carriers listed in 1690, John Whitmash of Taunton and Samuel Tanner of Rodborough near Stroud, were still carriers in the 19th century on the same roads.[36] Much more often, families changed but firms continued right up to the railway age, as in the case of the Exeter firm which belonged to Thomas Morris and Nicholas Barry.[37] References to wholly new businesses are rare.[38]

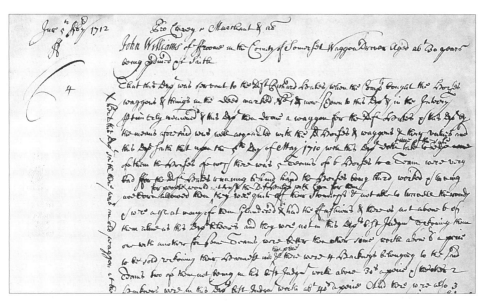

10 *Part of a deposition made in Chancery in 1713 by John Williams of Frome, one of the waggon drivers of Richard Hales and then Abraham Clavey. Williams describes the stock taken over by Clavey when he acquired the Frome carrying firm in 1710, indicating its condition and value. The writing in Chancery depositions is less easy to read than that in the bills and answers. (C 24/1325, No. 16.)*

11 *The* Waggon and Horses *inn, Frome. On taking over the Frome carrying service in 1710, Abraham Clavey also acquired from his predecessor the lease of Frome's tithe barn, which was probably his warehouse, and almost certainly the adjoining* Waggon *and* Horses *inn.*

Local and other carriers

The carrying trade included not just London carriers but also local and regional carriers, specialised carriers and casual carriers. Carrying links between major towns and cities were sometimes as long-established as the London ones. The first common carriers recorded, from Oxford to Winchester and to Newcastle in 1394-5, pre-dated by several years the first serving London, and carriers from Bristol to Exeter and to Buckingham were recorded in the late 15th century.[39] Defoe remarked in the 1720s that the Bristol wholesalers had such a great inland trade 'that they maintain carriers just as the London tradesmen do, to all the principal countries and towns from Southampton in the south, even to the banks of the Trent north'. Norwich in 1728 had about 55 services per week, including about 14 to places outside Norfolk. Other places with significant carrier networks of their own included Oxford, Cambridge, Exeter and Kendal,[40] but there were undoubtedly more. Some of the longer links were infrequent – for example, from Oxford in 1703, only once a month to Shrewsbury and thrice a year to

Westmorland (Fig. 12); in the latter case it was often more convenient to send goods from Kendal via the London carriers to Northampton, from which another carrier could take them to Oxford.[41]

The regional firms were sometimes larger than many of the London ones. For example, in about 1700 at Kendal there were firms with 24 horses to Lancaster, Liverpool and Manchester and the same to York and Hull (Fig. 13), and a gang of 18 Halifax to Norwich packhorses was advertised for sale in 1727. The more local carriers tended to be comparable in scale to the smaller London firms. Examples in Gloucestershire inventories between 1689 and 1706 include five with from five to nine packhorses, one with only three packhorses, one with six horses and a waggon and one with four horses and a waggon. There were some carriers who served the whole area around a town rather than a fixed route, such as one who operated within five miles of Maidenhead in 1660-85.[42]

Goods were often transferred between London and regional or local carriers, enabling the London carriers to serve places off their route. John Taylor noted in 1637 that

Carrier	Inn	comes in	goes out
Banbury	Star	{ Tuefd. Friday	Wedn. Saturd.
(hamp.			
Cov. by South-	Flower de luce	Thurfd.	Friday
Bath & Briftol	Ship	once in 2 weeks.	
Birmingham	Star	once in 2 weeks	
Cambridge			
Dorfet			
Exon	Catherine wheel	once in 5 weeks	
Glocefter	Roe-buck	Thurfday	Saturd.
Chippingnorton.	Plough	Thurfday	Saturd.
Devizes	Crofs-Inn	Tuefday	Thurfd.
Northampton.	Maiden-head	Wednefd.	Thurfd. Saturd.
Hamfhire by } Reading, and } to Petersfield }	near the Angel.	Tuefday	once in 2 weeks
Salisbury	Caftle-Inn	Thurfday	Friday
Shrowesbury	Catherine-wheel	once in a month	
Chefter			
Wolverhampton			
Winchefter	Blew-boar.	Thurfd.	Friday
Windfor	Holy-well	Tuefday	Thurfd.
Warwick	Star	Munday	Wedn.
Wales N.S.	Ship	once a Quarter	
Worcefter	Star	Wedn.	Thurfd.
Wefimorland	Angel	thrice a Year	
Wilts. Marlb.	Crofs Keys	Wedn.	Thurfd.

12 *The first published list of a carrier network other than London's – for Oxford in 1703. (The Oxford Almanack (1703), p. 17.)*

15

If a carrier of Yorke hath a letter or goods to deliver at any towne in his way thither, he serves the turne well enough, and there are carriers and messengers from Yorke to carry such goods and letters as are to be past any waies north, broad and wide as farre or further than Barwicke: so he that sends to Lancaster, may from thence have what he sends conveyd to Kendall, or Cockermouth, and what a man send to Hereford may from thence be passed to Saint Davids in Wales, the Worster carriers can convey any thing as farre as Carmarthen, and those that goe to Chester may send to Carnarvan: the carriers or posts that goe to Exeter may send daily to Plimouth, or to the Mount in Cornewall.[43]

Sometimes goods passed from carrier to carrier more than once, as in Cumberland in the 1690s, where goods brought from London to Kendal for Whitehaven passed to the Kendal to Cockermouth carrier and then to the Cockermouth to Whitehaven carrier. When a London carrier handed over goods at Kendal to the Penrith carrier, he expected the latter to collect and pay him his share of the carriage money, even if it was not received, since 'by the constant practise custome or agreement between the London carriers and the Penreth carriers the Penreth carrier upon his acceptance of the goods from the London carrier was and is oblidged to answer and pay the London carrier'.[44] However, over short distances London carriers might undertake delivery themselves, or customers might pick up their own goods, thereby avoiding the risk of loss or damage and the divided liability which resulted from the transfer of goods between carriers.[45] A sergemaker of Milverton whose packs of wool were brought from London to Taunton, eight miles away, sometimes arranged for a local carrier to collect them and sometimes sent his own horses. Lord Fitzwilliam noted in 1701 that the Peterborough carrier delivered goods directly to his house at Milton (three miles from Peterborough) only once or twice a year: small parcels and boxes had been fetched instead, or brought by a tenant's waggon on market day.[46]

The carriers discussed so far were common carriers, the word 'common' indicating that, having made their services available for general hire, rather than by individual agreement, they had become legally obliged to provide their services to all who required them. However, there were also specialised and casual carriers to whom this did not apply. Most specialised carriage was probably short-distance, but the exceptions included the packhorses conveying lead from Yorkshire and Derbyshire mines to the coast,[47] cheese waggons from Cheshire to London, and packhorses carrying fish from various places to London. The cheese waggons might carry other goods as back carriage: Sir John Lowther of Whitehaven noted in 1698 that at Chester and Liverpool were 'cheese waggons which return for the most part empty, so wil carry anything for a smal matter'.[48] The gangs of packhorses carrying fish to London from Newcastle upon Tyne, Workington, Carlisle, Lyme Regis, Hastings, Colchester and elsewhere from the 16th century to the 18th were the fastest form of land carriage of goods, and the first which continued through the night without stopping, but there is no evidence of them carrying goods other than fish. The fish gangs from Hastings

13 *A rare example (opposite page) of a manuscript list of carriers, covering those serving Kendal in about 1700. Note that two services are listed more than once to different destinations; in particular, Whoely and Wakefield appear to have forwarded their London goods from Manchester rather than carrying all the way to London themselves. (Cumbria RO, D/Lons/W1/34.)*

From Kendall Carriers Names	To London	Price of Carriage thither	Days going out from Kendall	Price of Carriage back	Days setting out home again	Lodging	Days coming into Kendall	Number of Horses Imploy'd
Wm Bateman Arthur Dixon Jos. Dixon Jno. Meel		if pack 6 8 21 to 26	Moundays	26 to 28	Fridays	Castle Inn in Wood Street	Wednesdays	60
Ralph Wholly Tho. Wakefield	By way of Lancast. to London	20 to 25	Thursdays & Satturdays	24 .. 20	Fridays	Ditto & Swan with 2 Necks Lad Lane	Thursdays & Satterdays	24
Jno. Winder	To Newcastle	7 .. 8	Satturdays sometimes Moundays	8 n 10	Satterdays sometimes Moundays		Fridays	
Ralph Wholy Jno. Wakfield	To Liverpool	8	Thursdays & Satturdays	8			Thursdays & Satturdays	
Jno. Wakefield	To Manchist.	7 .. 8	Satturdays	8			Thursdays & Satterdays	
Wm Wadd	To Leeds & Wakefield	8 10	Moundays	10	Friday	Talbot at Wakfield	Tuesdays	10
Jno. Holme Rowd Tatum	York & Hull	10 14	Satturdays & Wednesday	10 14			Satterdays & Wednesday	24
Wm Wadd	Norwich & Linn	26 .. 28	Moundays	32 .. 34			Fridays	12
Mich. Tyson	To Cockerm.	4	Wednesdays & Satturdays					
Jno. Holme Rowd Tatum	To Settle	4	Wednesdays & Satturdays					
Pet. Bilboe	Kirkby Stev.	2 .. 6	Satturdays	2 .. 6				
Guy Warwick Tho. Wilson	To Deal Richmond Sedbar	6 4 .. 6 .. 1 .. 6	Satturdays					
Ja. Halhead Jno. Turner	To Penrith	3 .. 3 .. 8 to 8	Moundays & Thursdays	8 .. 3 2 .. 8 to 8	Wednesday & Friday		Wednesday & Fridays	20

17

and Folkestone reached London in 12 to 15 hours, indicating speeds of about five miles per hour. Defoe explained that, from Workington and Carlisle, 'with horses, which, changing often, go night and day without intermission ... the fish come very sweet and good to London, where the extraordinary price they yield, being often sold at two shillings and sixpence to four shillings per pound [£14-£22 per cwt], pay very well for the carriage'. Geese were brought from East Anglia in vehicles which also travelled day and night.[49] Many tradesmen carried their own goods. For example, in 1699 there were said to be 200 lace dealers in Buckinghamshire, of whom about 150 came to London every week, selling lace and buying thread and silk.[50]

Casual carriers undoubtedly conveyed a much greater tonnage of goods than common carriers did, especially over short distances but sometimes for long distances too. For example, many farmers performed an occasional journey when they happened to have teams and waggons available, sometimes (allegedly) neglecting their farms in order to obtain ready money in this way. In 1729 it was claimed that, prior to legislation of 1718 which required waggons hired for carriage to have wheels at least 2½ inches wide, 'many farmers, who had not constant employ for their teams, would at leisure times carry goods from London, and other places, for hire, whereby they kept down the exorbitant demands of common carriers'; these included farmers in the Birmingham, Dudley and Leicester areas carrying to London. The 'professional' carriers listed by Delaune differed from these not in that they were not farmers (since many were) but that they provided regular, scheduled services. Others also engaged in carrying. John Rowlatt of Stanyon, Northamptonshire, a trader in woad, sometimes had woad carried to London in his own waggons in the 1670s, and sometimes brought back goods for Gilbert Stoughton, the Kettering carrier, when the latter was overloaded; at other times Rowlatt sent his goods by Stoughton. In October 1683 John Bold of 'Rockaden', Shropshire, with a cart and four horses, was loaded with calicoes and groceries at the *Castle and Falcon*, Aldersgate Street, for delivery at Newport and Chester; more than two months later nothing more had been heard of him or the goods. London carriers might themselves undertake casual journeys where there was sufficient incentive: Henry Warren, Stamford carrier, took a waggon to Beverley Fair for 25 years up to 1676.[51]

One of the problems facing casual carriers was to obtain back loading, but London innkeepers and their bookkeepers apparently helped in this. In 1728 a London innkeeper stated that

> It is usuall & customary for the book keepers & persons dealing in the same way to go out on the road in order to meet waggons which are usually called by waggons or jockey waggons[52] & who do not use any particular stationed inne but usually or frequently go with those who meet them as aforesaid & promise them the best loading home againe.[53]

The London carriers were therefore part of a much larger transport system.

CHAPTER II

CARRIERS, INNKEEPERS
AND WAREHOUSEKEEPERS

The carrier's role

There is plenty of evidence of carriers travelling, and it would be easy to assume that they actually drove their horses and waggons. A Chancery suit between two of the Kendal partners shows that this was not necessarily the case, even though their schedule provided for each partner to take his gang of horses to and from London every four weeks. In June 1687 the two partners, Samuel Briggs and Richard Greenwood, stayed at the same inn in Welford, Northamptonshire, the former heading for London and the latter for Kendal. However, Greenwood was certainly not driving. He had taken horse at the *Black Swan*, Holborn (not the inn his packhorses stayed at), and it was only at Stony Stratford that he 'overtooke' his packhorses. Later, at Wakefield, he had time to dine and start counting some money before his packhorses arrived at the gate of the inn. Greenwood refers to 'his man', who presumably drove.[1] There is also plenty of evidence of waggon users employing drivers, even for short routes such as Uxbridge and Baldock to London.[2]

Nor was it the role of the carrier to stay at home keeping the accounts, as they tended to do in the 19th century. Of 66 London carriers whose wills have been examined, almost half (32) provided a mark rather than a signature. Robert Fearey of Peterborough, being illiterate, had to have the accounts at his inn at Biggleswade read to him or inspected on his behalf. For the same reason, the accounts of Daniel Want, Devizes carrier, at his inn in Maidenhead had to be settled by his wife, and those of Thomas Morris of Exeter at Bridport by Morris's son.[3] Several carriers employed a bookkeeper in their home town, such as the apothecary used by Thomas Southgate in Norwich.[4] Female members of the family were sometimes employed on the accounts, such as Nicholas Barry's daughter at Exeter around 1710, or 'to look after ye concernes at home in takeing in & dellivering out goods and other household affayres', as in the case of Jane Rogers' daughters at Ludlow in the 1690s.[5]

What Delaune's carriers generally did was to oversee the driving of their packhorses or teams, making sure the horses were looked after and seeing to business along the road by visiting customers, horse dealers and others, usually staying at the same inns overnight. Even though not themselves driving, they were constantly on the road. A snowstorm on Salisbury Plain in 1684 trapped the

14 *The only known portrait of a 17th-century carrier, though somewhat earlier than those discussed in this book. It is of Thomas Hobson, Cambridge carrier (by cart and later by waggon) from 1568 until his death in 1631. Hobson's longevity and the fact that he served Cambridge made him extremely well known. His refusal to allow his hackney horses to be taken outside their proper turn gave rise to the expression 'Hobson's choice', i.e. 'this or none'. The portrait survives at Cambridge Guildhall because Hobson was a benefactor to the town.*

Shaftesbury, Yeovil and Taunton carriers and the son of the Exeter carrier with their packhorses. In 1695 it was claimed that several carriers on the western roads were unable to attend a parliamentary committee because 'their business is so confined to particular stages, that they could not attend to give their evidence, without great prejudice'.[6] It was not necessary slavishly to follow their horses, as the case of Greenwood indicates: instead they shadowed them. The carrier was the organiser and risk-taker, not the driver or bookkeeper.

Some carriers may have travelled in more than usual comfort. The possessions of Matthew Bakewell of Burton upon Trent in 1690 included 'one gee who coach', named after the biblical King Jehu, who 'drives furiously'.[7]

Some of the more substantial carriers may not even have shadowed their horses, especially if family members or trusted staff were available to do it for them, and many had no alternative to using such people because they had more than one team or gang on the move at a time. For example, two of Lawrence Standish of Warwick's teams in 1689 were called Lawrence's and Thomas's (after his sons); John Hilton of Leigh's two gangs of packhorses in 1698 were described as 'one gang of horses yt. James Wright goes with' and 'Ye other gang of horses James Hilton followes'; and in 1704-14 Nicholas Barry of Exeter employed his son, son-in-law and another man as 'outriders', whose duties were described as 'aiding and overseeing the said carriage drivers and servants'.[8] When Henry Church of Hereford died in 1703 his widow Mary, lacking health and strength to take on the whole management herself, employed Thomas Weale 'to manage the

Advertiſement.

THeſe are to give notice, That *Edward Bartlet Oxford Carrier*, hath removed his Inn in *London*, from the *Swan* at *Holborn-Bridge*, to the *Oxford-Armes* in *Warwick lane*, where he did Inn before the Fire. His Coaches and Waggons going forth on their uſual days, *Mondays*, *Wedneſdays* and *Frydays*. He hath alſo a Hearſe, with all things convenient to carry a Corps, to any part of *England.*

15 *A change of London inn by an Oxford carrier and coachmaster in 1672. (London Gazette, 10 March 1672.)*

travelling part' of the business, taking up goods on the road, receiving payment for their carriage and paying charges on the road; he received £10 a year plus his diet and 10s. per fortnightly return journey. John Stiles of Cambridge around 1680 entrusted the whole management of his firm to his former apprentice, Charles Tine, as his 'agent'.[9]

Remote management carried risks, illustrated by the 'very considerable robbery' carried out upon one of Barry's successors by an outrider and the fact that Tine set up his own Cambridge carrying service.[10] There are several reasons for believing that, apart from using family members, it was unusual. First, the most common form of carrying partnership involved having as many separate carriers as there were teams or gangs on the road at once, as in the Kendal case. Secondly, carriers tended to retire and pass on their business in old age, like Richard Clavey, Wells carrier, 'haveing great concerns on his hands and being grown sickly and infirm that he could not go through with or manage the same'.[11] Thirdly, carriers are frequently recorded on the road. Even a wealthy man such as William Clarke senior, Yeovil carrier, was among those trapped by snow on Salisbury Plain in 1684.

SAmuel Whibben, John Barratt, and John Hoſey, Briſtol Carriers, who formerly lodged at the Three Cups in Bread-ſtreet, and lately at the Bell in Friday-ſtreet, are now return'd to the ſaid Three Cups, where any Perſon may be furniſhed with Hackney-Horſes, or have any Goods carried to the ſaid City, parts adjacent, or any places on that Road, at Reaſonable Rates. They come in on Tueſdays and Fridays, and ſet out Wedneſdays and Saturdays as uſual.

16 *A change of London inn by the Bristol packhorse carriers in 1693. This is an example of other evidence exactly confirming an entry in Delaune's lists (apart from Hosey becoming Delaune's 'Hosier'). (London Gazette, 31 August 1693.)*

Other occupations

Many carriers also pursued other occupations, though usually in a related line of business. The most common of these was farming. Of 60 London carriers for whom probate inventories are available, just over half (32) can be regarded as farmers,[12] owning ploughs or substantial farming stock, and a further five had more than just a few cows or pigs (for example Francis Bacherler of Stonehouse, Gloucestershire, in 1686, with three acres of wheat and barley, two acres of beans and two pigs). In 1685 Silvester Keene, Bristol carrier, had 102 sheep and lambs, six oxen, a cow, a heifer and farming equipment, together worth £56, compared with £36 for his carrying stock; in that case and three others the farming stock was over half the total value of the inventory. More often, the farming stock was less valuable than the carrying stock (even in the case of Robert Beecroft of Norwich, who had 76 acres of crops in 1663). However, since crops would be harvested and then sold, the inventory values must sometimes understate the importance of farming, especially as hay, oats and beans have been excluded from the figures unless clearly being grown.

Combining farming and carrying had several advantages. First, the carrier had pasture for his horses during their rest days, though not much land was needed for this purpose. Secondly, if the cost of provender rose, this could be offset by the extra price received for the farmer's own produce, thereby reducing a significant risk. Thirdly, and probably most importantly, a farm could provide work for the horses when they were not employed in carrying, for example where a weekly journey to London and back was less than a full week's work for them. This was probably more significant for waggon users, since packhorses, being smaller, would have been less useful than waggon horses for farm work such as ploughing.[13] Waggon users were more likely than packhorse users to have farming stock (62 per cent compared with 43 per cent) and it was also on average of greater value (£98 compared with £49).[14] The reasons for combining farming and carrying ought to mean that carriers, especially waggon users, were biased towards arable rather than pastoral farming, but the inventory evidence is not clear enough to be certain.[15]

B Ingham Waggon inns at the Chequer Inn in Holbourn, sets out from Bingham on Tuesdays and comes into London on Saturdays, and returns on Mondays to Bingham through New-Market, Milden Hall, Brand, Moundford, Hilborough, Swaffham, Castleacre, Rutham, Little Raynham, Great Raynham, Hempton, Fekenham, Burnham, Holkham and Walsingham to Bingham, and carries to Holt and Wells, and all places adjacent, carefully performed by John Saffany, who served Mr Hooks and Rickards the former Carriers 24 years. N. B. All persons that are pleased to employ him, are desired to give their Correspondence this notice to prevent Mistakes. J. Legg, Book-keeper in London.

17 Advertisement by the carrier of Burnham Market, Norfolk, in 1705, probably on taking over the business. Saffany had spent 24 years serving its previous owners. (Post-Man, 10 April 1705.)

18 *Waynes Close, Burford, headquarters of Richard Mills' waggon service in the 1680s. In 1685 Mills had ten horses and two waggons for a weekly service to London. Very few carriers' headquarters have been identified so far.*

Whatever the benefits, being both carrier and farmer clearly did not confer such a competitive advantage that all or most carriers had to be farmers. It must have caused certain difficulties, and probably required someone trustworthy, such as a wife, to stay at home looking after the farm. One way round that problem is suggested by a Chancery suit involving Arthur Dixon, Kendal carrier. In September or October 1705, being obliged to go to London, 'by meanes whereof [he] could not possibly attend the reaping and getting in several cropps of corne and grain which was then groweing on several lands & closes in or near Kendall', he either sold the crop, according to his own account, or let the land on a one-year lease, according to his opponent.[16] The other problem was that carrying services needed to be regular, whereas farms required horse labour irregularly, with peaks typically in April and October,[17] and might need it when the horses were required for carrying.

Three other types of business were sometimes engaged in by carriers. The first was stage-coaching, especially long-distance coaching, as discussed later.[18] However, only a small minority of carriers were also coachmasters. The second was innkeeping. Definite innkeepers among Delaune's carriers were Gilbert Stoughton of Kettering, Thomas Jaques of Petersfield, Samuel Locker of Derby, Roger Bird of Andover, Michael Minchin of Salisbury and Arthur Palmer of Chelmsford, and there are other probable cases where it cannot be proved that both carrying and innkeeping were engaged in at the same time.[19] Even so, the number of innkeeper-carriers was small, and the link was nothing like as strong as between innkeeping and coaching. Coaching was more likely to bring trade to an inn, and also required less attention than carrying, which made it easier to combine with innkeeping. Significantly, four of the six innkeeper-carriers just listed were also involved in coaching.

The third type of business was trade in the sorts of goods conveyed by carriers, notably cloth. The carriers' commercial information and business contacts presumably gave them an advantage here, though it is not usually clear whether carrying or the other trade came first. Abraham Voale of Colchester, baymaker (making a type of cloth called bays), purchased a Colchester carrying business in 1668 and continued both trades, together with stage-coaching by 1690.[20] Richard Mills of Burford was both clothier and carrier, as was Henry Whiffen of Dorchester and probably also John Lockett of Dorchester.[21] At Stansted Mountfichet in Essex the connection was with poultry: John, Thomas and George Peacock, sons of a poulterer, were carriers from Stansted in 1681; at least two of them had been poulterers in the 1660s, and in 1696 one was a poulterer and two were innkeepers.[22] John Newcome of Lincoln was a fellmonger (a dealer in hides). John Harrison of Sundridge, Chiddingstone carrier, evidently used his journeys to keep his shop stocked; in 1696 it contained linen, hosiery, haberdashery, groceries, salters' goods, cheese and butter. In the 1720s several Norwich carriers traded in hops brought from London, and in the 1730s a Stamford carrier traded in brandy, rum and clover and trefoil seed from London. Carrier-coachmasters who were also involved in another trade included Voale (mentioned above), John Cromwell of Gloucester, a dealer in pins, in the 1670s and Onias Phillippo of Norwich, a soapmaker, in 1693.[23]

However, it is significant how few examples there are of carrying being combined with another trade, except farming or coaching. This reflected the time and attention required to run a carrying business. Delaune's carriers usually described themselves as carriers, common carriers or waggoners, and there is no doubt that in most cases carrying, with its non-stop operation and insistent routine, occupied the bulk of their attention.

Wealth

Carrying businesses of any size involved substantial expenditure on horses and provender, and London carriers were usually men of substance. Most wills indicate at least some land owned or leased (most often a few acres of meadow at their provincial base), and in 49 inventories listing rooms, only eight dwellings had fewer than five rooms, and 15 had nine or more.[24] Twenty-four out of 61 inventories record plate. Those carriers described by Delaune as 'Mr' (49 in 1681) probably included the most prosperous, though not all those so described were well-off: among them were Mr Richard Merchant of Chesterfield, who described himself as a gentleman, Mr William Clarke of Halstock (Dorset), Yeovil carrier, a substantial landowner, Mr Henry Whiffen of Dorchester, Exeter carrier, who was variously described as carrier, clothier and gentleman, and several carriers who were also coachmasters. Several inventories indicate large amounts of ready money, such as Henry Warren of Stamford's £660 in 1681.[25] These carriers were, however, somewhat exceptional. At the other end of the scale, inventories record some much poorer carriers, such as Henry Harwood of Aylesbury (total value £31) and George Elmes of Melton Mowbray (£27). Six of the seven carriers whose goods amounted to £46 or less died before 1690, and it may be significant that only two of their businesses appear to be recorded in that year. Even an apparently healthy financial position indicated by an inventory, or by large bequests in a will, might of course be offset by large debts.[26] There were clearly some carriers who lived a hand-to-mouth existence, and customers were sometimes nervous of trusting them with money.[27]

The proportion of a carrier's wealth tied up in his horses and other carrying stock varied greatly. In 33 out of 59 examples carrying stock accounted for 23 to 45 per cent of the total.[28] Differences among carriers largely reflected whether they had farming stock: those above that range mostly had little or none. In two cases carrying stock exceeded 80 per cent of the total. The capital needed to acquire the stock for a carrying service was typically between £30 and £150, though sometimes up to £250 and in one case (Warren of Stamford) more still. However, these figures would have to be doubled to give the approximate cost of purchasing an existing firm with its connection. The £30 to £150 range was low by comparison with what was needed to establish a business in London (a minimum of £100 in most trades),[29] but was probably more impressive in relation to businesses in provincial towns.

Female carriers

Ten female carriers were listed in 1681 and 15 in 1690. Almost all were described as widows or are known to have been widows of carriers, and were perhaps waiting for sons to grow up or an opportunity to sell the business. William Woollett of Cranbrook left his carrying stock to his wife in 1720, requesting her to take his son into partnership when he was 22. William Webb of Maldon, Essex, left his property in 1696 to his wife Susanna, 'whom I advise not to keep up the waggon longer than she needs'. Elizabeth Martin of Cambridge, widow, employed her son-in-law to travel to and from London in 1704-11, in return for £10 (later £20) per year and the income from goods taken up or set down on the road. Mary Church of Hereford, widow, who employed a man for the 'travelling part' of the business in 1703-8, later claimed that he took advantage of 'her want of a full and perfect knowledge & understanding of her affairs by reason she was not able to undertake journeys herselfe for the inspecting her concerns'. However, Mary Church appears to have been in poor health, and Jane Rogers, widow of a Ludlow carrier, having subsequently married a Leominster carrier, travelled fortnightly to London for about four years. After her death in about 1701 her husband took over the Ludlow business but one of her daughters 'sometimes went along with his carryadges to Worcester & often to London'. Only two women are listed both in 1681 and 1690: widow Sayward or Seyward, waggoner of 'Bradford' and 'Berkshire' in 1681 and of Reading and Newbury in 1690, and widow Margaret Mussell of Horsham, still carrying and farming at her death in 1693.[30]

Innkeepers

The carrier's most important business relationships were with his innkeepers and his London warehousekeeper. Chancery proceedings indicate that carriers made agreements with particular innkeepers, rather than simply stopping where they happened to be at the end of the day, and they therefore covered the same stretch of road on the same day of each journey. The description of waggons as 'stage-waggons' itself indicates regular stages, just as for stage-coaches. However, carriers sometimes used more than one inn in a town, perhaps to promote competition.[31] Usually there was an agreement to pay certain prices per bushel of oats and beans and per night per horse for hay, although Nicholas Barry of Exeter apparently agreed nothing more precise at Egham than 'kind & good entertainment both for man & horse att very reasonable rates'.[32] There was sometimes also a fixed sum for the ostler to look after the horses (where services terminated) and in one case a charge for lodging and feeding the carrier's drivers.[33] At the *Bull Inn* in Bridport, Thomas Morris of Exeter paid the same prices from 1680 to 1688 'without regard to the prices of beanes and oates in the markett of Bridporte'; effectively the innkeeper bore the risk of short-term fluctuations in provender prices. However, the innkeeper had the option of terminating the agreement, and there may well have been an expectation that a serious and sustained rise in the cost of provender would result in higher charges: Nicholas Barry, despite his vague agreement, paid the same prices for hay and beans for over three years, but the charge for oats increased from the normal 2s. per bushel to 2s. 6d. from November 1707 to April 1708. Nicholas Rothwell of Warwick paid the same prices for two years in London in 1743-5.[34]

Innkeepers not only provided provender and shelter, but also collected and delivered out goods and, where there was considerable loading, might provide a separate warehouse. In effect they were local agents. At Dorchester, where Jacob Weare, Exeter carrier, divided his route, with separate teams in each direction, the innkeeper was making out way bills in 1724 and receiving 5s. a week in return, though this was exceptional.[35] Carriers and innkeepers served each other by transmitting money, usually by drawing bills on each other: carriers might make payments for the innkeeper in other places, or might draw a bill on the innkeeper for payment to the carrier's creditors in the innkeeper's town.[36]

Although London carriers only occasionally acted as innkeepers, it was common for them to purchase inns, as at least five of the West Country carriers of 1690 did.[37] They could thereby not only ensure good service for their horses and men, but also use their own valuable custom to obtain a higher than usual rent. In the early 1680s Gilbert Stoughton, Kettering carrier, rented out the *Bakers Arms*, Bedford, for £24 per year, £18 'being the old rent' and £6 'for the said complainant's [i.e. Stoughton's] custome'. Sometimes the carrier rented out the inn but kept its stables for his horses, as Thomas Southgate of Norwich was doing at Thetford and Littlebury in 1707.[38]

Warehousekeepers

The duties of the carrier's warehousekeeper in London (well recorded in Chancery proceedings) were to receive and look after goods at the beginning or end of their journeys, and to receive and account for money brought to London or paid in London for carriage.[39] When a waggon or packhorses arrived, the warehousekeeper first received the bill of loading and then, according to a Stamford carrier's warehousekeeper, 'this deponent stands in his warehouse door & sees by his bill that the porters bring all the goods therein mencoed into the warehouse'; or, according to a carrier, 'their method is, to unload the goods by the waggon side, and deliver every parcel single, to the book-keeper, who sits in the ware-house to take an account of them'.[40] Sums in the bill of loading were immediately charged against the warehousekeeper, chiefly any cash sent to be paid out in London and carriage money to be received in London upon delivery. The warehousekeeper also charged himself with any money received or to be received in London for carriage of goods down, and had to make good any bad debts resulting from his giving credit. Even the carrier himself had to observe certain procedures: when

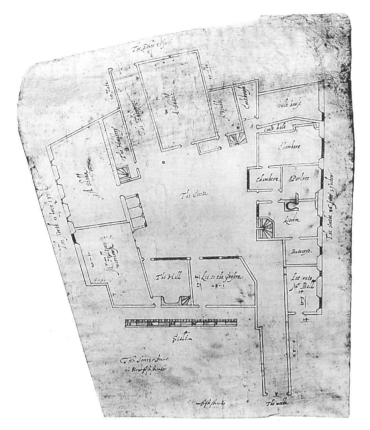

19 *Plan of the Star, Fish Street Hill, in about 1700, showing its stables, warehouse and other rooms arranged around a courtyard. In 1690 it was used by Mr Varnham, Canterbury and Maidstone coachmaster, and John Adcock, carrier of Ashford in Kent.*

20 *The Oxford Arms, Warwick Lane, as rebuilt after the Great Fire. In 1690 it had five waggons a week to destinations in Berkshire, Hampshire, Northamptonshire and Oxfordshire and Edward Bartlett's thrice-weekly Oxford coach.*

21 *The* King's Head, *Southwark, towards the end of its life in the 19th century. In 1690 it accommodated eight packhorse services and the Leatherhead coach.*

Andrew Hart of Cambridge delivered goods himself in London, he marked the warehouse book with 'a long stroke' and handed over the carriage money to his warehousekeeper.[41] The warehousekeeper was discharged of responsibility for goods collected in London when he had entered them on the bill of loading and delivered the bill to the carrier. The warehousekeeper might also handle other business in London for the carrier, including the organisation and payment of porters and carmen, arranging for the greasing and repairing of waggons and agreeing compensation for damaged goods.[42] Probably he also looked out for loading for the carrier. He usually accounted weekly.[43]

The warehousekeeper's bill of loading, together with the bill compiled at the other end of the route, were the basis of carriers' accounting. Mary Church gave her servant Weale at the start of each journey 'an up bill of parcels of all goods & money up to London taken out & from her warehouse booke at Hereford', which Weale delivered to the warehousekeeper in London 'being his order & directon to deliver out the goods & pay the money'. In London Weale similarly received a down bill compiled from the warehouse book:

> And in every of the said up bills & down bills the said Weale was to add to & enter down all such goods & money as he should from time to time receive & take up at Ross Gloucester & onwards upon the road up and down from London which addiconal up bills & down bills were to be respectively entered into the severall warehouse books ... that thereby every weekes carriage of goods & returns of money from the severall places ... might appear to [Church] at the end of every journey ... And the said warehouse books were to be a check in the ballance of the said Weales accounts.[44]

This system was still in use in the 19th century, except that by the 1720s, at least in some firms, bills of loading (or way bills) were sent by post and goods and receipts from places along the route were added to them subsequently from 'road books' carried by the waggons.[45]

Warehousekeepers were usually employees of carriers rather than innkeepers, though there is also an example from 1721 of an innkeeper contracting with two men who were to act as warehousekeepers 'providing goods and loading for all carryers resorting to the said inn'. While some warehousekeepers worked for all the carriers at a particular inn, such as Susan Walthew at the *Swan*, Holborn Bridge, in 1695, who 'belongs to thirteen or fourteen carriers', carriers at the same inn might have different warehousekeepers.[46] Partners usually shared a warehousekeeper. Thomas Morris of Exeter's warehousekeeper in 1692 was also a factor at Blackwell Hall (London's cloth market), and could therefore handle much of Morris's loading up to its final sale.[47] A few warehousekeepers later became innkeepers, in at least one case (James Fry at the *Bell*, Friday Street in the mid-1720s) continuing to act as warehousekeeper.[48] Wages varied, as did the amount of work. Among the Cambridge carriers, Matthew Lancaster paid £30 a year in 1684-6, Robert Ridgwell 10s. per week in 1688 and Nathaniel Sayer £10 a year and 4s. in the pound on money received for letters and parcels in 1694-5.[49]

22 *The* White Hart, *Southwark, as rebuilt after a fire in 1676. In 1690 it was used by several packhorse services from Sussex, including widow Mussell's Horsham service, and Arthur Goldring's coaches and waggons from Portsmouth.*

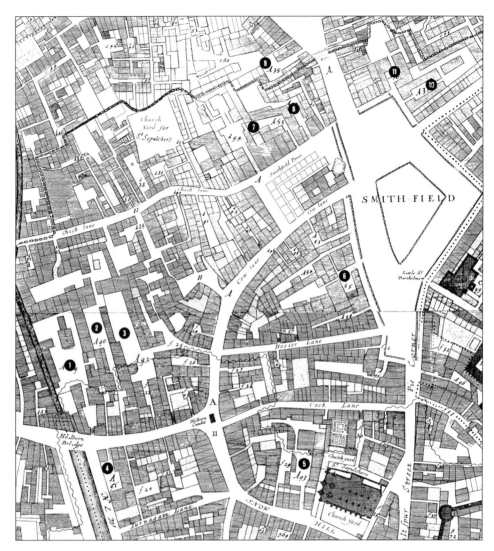

Map 4 *Inns around Smithfield and Holborn Bridge in 1676, as shown on Ogilby and Morgan's map. The inns marked are:* 1. White Swan, *Holborn Bridge;* 2. King's Arms, *Holborn Bridge;* 3. George, *Holborn Bridge;* 4. Rose, *Holborn Bridge;* 5. Saracens Head, *Snow Hill;* 6. George, *Smithfield;* 7. Rose, *Smithfield;* 8. Ram, *Smithfield;* 9. Castle, *Smithfield Bars;* 10. Bell, *Smithfield;* 11. Bear and Ragged Staff, *Smithfield. In 1742 the* King's Arms, *Holborn Bridge was advertised as having a shed under which 20 waggons could be loaded at the same time.*

As already indicated, carriers also employed drivers and sometimes outriders and bookkeepers. At least one carrier employed an ostler at his provincial headquarters, though not necessarily full-time.[50] Some appointed porters in London, but in other cases portering was delegated to the warehousekeeper, who might hire porters casually.[51] In terms of staff, carrying firms were very small organisations.

CHAPTER III

LOADING

Some road users had the option of water transport, by river or coastal vessel, and the number of rivers made navigable was rising,[1] but substantial areas of England were still more than 15 miles from navigable water in 1700 (Map 5). The greater the distance from navigable water, the more water transport lost its advantage of lower charges through the cost of carriage to and from the wharf. Even where navigable water was reasonably close, it might offer only circuitous and slow routes to London, as in the West Country and the West Midlands. Coastal services could be fast where the route was reasonably direct,[2] especially along the east coast, but in general they were slower than road transport and above all much less reliable, being dependent on the wind. Also, time was often lost while vessels waited for full loads, though from the 1720s some on the east coast were beginning to advertise regular departures (Norwich and – in 1736 – Yarmouth) or at least a maximum waiting time in London (King's Lynn and Hull).[3] Moreover, goods were more likely to be damaged and in war-time there was greatly increased risk. River transport was less dependent than coastal vessels on the wind, but still tended to be slow and indirect. On the other hand, water transport was usually considerably cheaper than road transport. Where reasonably direct water transport was available, road transport relied on its speed and reliability to attract custom for its relatively expensive service.

Rates of carriage by road and water

Identifying what rates of carriage were by road is hampered not just by the scarcity of information but by variations in charges between different types of loading. Carriers tended to charge higher rates to gentlemen and wealthy institutions (precisely the customers for whom records are most likely to have survived), and they might also vary their charges between different types of goods and between up and down goods (particularly if goods in one direction were regarded as back carriage).[4] For example, between Norwich and London in 1697 the up charge was 13 pence per ton-mile while the down charge was 9 pence, but 11 pence for silk, which was especially high-value and easily damaged. The Newcastle upon Tyne carriers emphasised in 1744 that 'it hath never been customary to carry gentlemen and tradesmen's goods on the same terms'.[5] Small consignments sometimes paid a much higher rate per ton-mile. Charges also varied between packhorses and

Map 5 *Areas more than 15 miles from navigable water in 1700. (Source: T.S. Willan,* River navigation in England *(1936), p. 32.)*

waggons. They may have varied too from year to year as provender prices rose or fell, though carriers were to some extent protected from such fluctuations by their agreements with innkeepers and there was no long-term trend in provender prices in this period.[6] Provender prices also varied from one region to another and this may have affected charges.

The available evidence is collected in Appendix 3. Given the variety of influences on charges, no great consistency could be expected. Trade rates by waggon were usually from 8 to 13 pence per ton-mile, and those by packhorse from 9 to 18 pence, while gentlemen typically paid from 15 to 21 pence (sometimes much more). These ranges are consistent with the general statement from 1720 – by waggon 10 to 12 pence, by packhorse 12 to 14 pence. That statement makes carriage by packhorse about 20 per cent dearer than by waggon, but the range of packhorse charges in Appendix 3 is much wider, indicating rates anything from 12 to 40 per cent dearer than by waggon.[7]

A more confusing picture is presented by the maximum rates of carriage specified by justices of the peace under an Act of 1692. These ranged from 5 to 28 pence per ton-mile. The justices employed many different ways of specifying rates, varying by season, by size of package, between heavy and light goods and between waggons and packhorses. Probably all of these variations reflected actual charging practices, except that the distinction between heavy and light goods may have been a disguised way of charging more to gentlemen than tradesmen. The first requirement is to disregard rates specified per lb in cases where a rate per cwt was also set; in these cases the rate per lb was the parcel charge and therefore higher and unrepresentative, though where *only* a rate per lb was set this was evidently intended to apply to all carriage, as in West Yorkshire.

Justices in different counties may have had different aims. The Act of 1692 stated that 'diverse waggoners and other carriers by combination amongst themselves have raised the prices of carriage of goods in many places to excessive rates to the great injury of trade'. Despite the reference to trade, the particular combination objected to may well have been the assumption among carriers that gentlemen could be charged higher prices. When charges were regulated at Oxford in 1674 this was made explicit: the Oxford to London carriers, while exacting what rates they pleased, had 'aggravated this their unreasonable practice by requiring greater summes from scholars, than towns-men'.[8] To resolve this problem, the justices needed only to aim approximately for the trade rate, which is what they seem normally to have done.[9] The Newcastle upon Tyne carriers responded defiantly to exactly that aspect of the justices' rates in 1744, saying they would insist on 50 per cent more from gentlemen, but they are unlikely to have succeeded in this.[10]

In some counties, such as Lincolnshire, the justices may have pegged rates at the packhorse level, whereas a few counties had only waggons and in some counties separate rates were set for packhorses and waggons. Also, since the justices' rates were a ceiling rather than a floor, no harm was done if justices who were unconcerned about

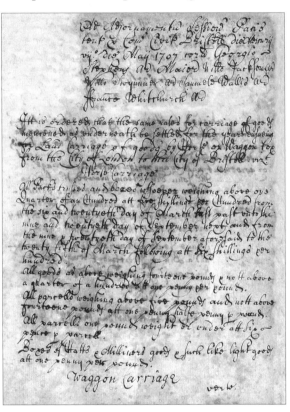

23 *Rates of carriage set by the justices of the peace at Bristol in 1707. This was a more detailed assessment than most. (Bristol RO, JQS/D/3.)*

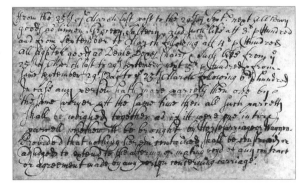

carriers' charges set a relatively high rate. Only in a few counties (Dorset, Hampshire and the West Riding) at certain periods is there clear evidence of the rates being periodically reconsidered and minor adjustments made, though many counties made occasional changes (Appendix 3).

Furthermore, until 1748 the justices' rates applied to down carriage (from London) only, whereas up carriage was sometimes dearer, and this may account for some of the lowest figures, such as to Cheshire and perhaps Shropshire, where the availability of the cheese waggons (whose owners regarded down carriage as back carriage) may have distorted the charges; in fact the Cheshire justices, apparently unaware that their powers applied only to down rates, *did* make up rates higher than down ones in 1693. At Norwich, up charges might have been expected to be higher than down charges, because cloth being sent to London was the most important loading, but the justices may themselves have contributed to the difference by controlling only the down charges. In 1697 at Norwich, the actual down charge was the same as the justices' rate set the previous year (except for silk), but the up charge was much higher. In places lacking much industry, or much industry which sent its produce by road to London, it was down loading which was most plentiful, as at Kettering,[11] so down charges may sometimes have exceeded up charges.

Taking these considerations into account, the justices' rates are reasonably consistent with actual charges. Most of the rates set were within the range 8 to 17 pence, including 18 out of 23 in 1692-9 (and four more partly so) and 27 out of 29 in 1700-47 (and the other two partly so); in 1748-51, 16 out of 22 were from 10 to 14 pence per ton-mile.[12] In the few counties where separate rates were specified, the waggon rates were generally 6 to 11 pence per ton-mile and the packhorse ones around 10 to 13 pence per ton-mile, the packhorse rates being generally from 17 to 43 per cent higher. The justices' rates are more helpful than other evidence as regards seasonal variation. Where this was allowed for, carriage was from 13 to 33 per cent dearer in winter than in summer in 17 out of 23 cases.[13]

Goods could be carried much cheaper by casual carriers or as back carriage by the cheese waggons of Cheshire. Lord Cardigan's regular carrier was warned in 1725 that he was 'not to expect the carriage of any considerable quantity of goods at a time', as his Lordship then hired a waggon casually – at 3s. 4d. or 3s. 6d. per cwt instead of 6s., but slower. William Stout of Lancaster, a shopkeeper, found in 1689 that he could have goods by the cheese waggons to Standish for 3s. to 5s. per cwt in summer (3.5 to 5.9 pence per ton-mile), carriage thence to Lancaster costing a further 1s. 6d. (9.4 pence per ton-mile). Similar prices to Standish (3s. 6d. or 4s. per cwt) prevailed in 1690, 1693 and 1702, thanks to war, which caused the carriage of cheese to be shifted from sea to land and thus increased the availability of waggons and carts from London.[14] However, casual carriage was not always available, particularly during busy times of the farming year or for small quantities.

Charges for river carriage were usually as low as one penny per ton-mile for bulk cargoes over long distances (albeit sometimes higher on small rivers and on upper reaches), but the average for goods may have been about 2.5 pence per ton-mile.[15] Coastal transport could be even cheaper – for example from 0.3 to 0.8

pence per ton-mile for coal, grain or lead from Hull, Goole, York or Newcastle to London in 1739 (rising to the higher figure in war-time – 12s. per ton at Hull compared with 10s. in peace-time). Freight charges by coastal vessel from Boston to London in 1745 were 16s. per ton (1.7 pence per ton-mile), though like the other figures this probably excluded wharf charges.[16]

However, bulk cargoes of tons at a time are not a fair comparison with the smaller consignments sent by waggon. One of the few direct comparisons available is for goods between Oxford and London, where the Vice-Chancellor specified in 1674 a maximum of 3s. 6d. to 4s. per cwt by road and 1s. by water (4.1 pence per ton-mile), though there were possibly wharf charges to be added to the latter. John Haynes, who wanted water carriage of wool prohibited, argued in 1706 that, taking into account all the costs of water carriage, it was not much cheaper than land carriage: 11s. per pack compared with 13s. from London to Exeter, 3s. 6d. compared with 4s. 6d. to Colchester, and 12s. compared with 15s. to Selby (for Leeds and Wakefield), added to which were the cost of insurance (or the risk) and damage to the wool 'by the fogs, wet, &c.' (In 1720 it was said that 'the clothiers in Yorkshire would rather give double the price for land carriage than have their wool brought by sea where it receives so much damage'.) The difference was therefore much less than for bulk cargoes, though water carriage was still generally cheaper. Water transport also lost some of its advantage over short distances: in 1741, a ton of wool sent from Halifax to Wakefield (17 miles) cost 9s. by water and 15s. by land (6.5 and 10.8 pence per ton-mile respectively).[17]

One of the most important comparisons was not between land and water on the same route but, for those in north-west England, between direct land carriage to London and a combination of land and water carriage making use of vessels on the east coast. In 1716 a Kendal mercer, Joseph Symson, was sending packs by land for 23s. to 25s. per pack or by land and sea via Newcastle, the latter costing 7s. or 7s. 6d. per pack by land to Newcastle, 1s. 6d. per pack for 'shipping', a small amount for freight, 2s. 2d. per pack for pack cloths and cords (supplied by the carrier in the case of direct land carriage) and a charge for repacking at Newcastle. In 1718 he wrote that 'In summer we frequently send them [linseys] by the sea from Newcastle and find with pack sheets lessens the price of carriage near one half, but they are sometimes longer and more uncertain in going that way.' There was also the risk of shipwreck.[18]

Loading

Only scattered evidence is available concerning what was conveyed by Delaune's carriers, chiefly from Chancery proceedings, advertisements concerning lost goods and Old Bailey proceedings, but it is enough broadly to confirm the picture obtained from more detailed records for the 19th century.[19]

The goods carried can be divided into seven categories. Undoubtedly the most important was manufactured goods, especially textiles, being sent to London for further processing, export or distribution inland. A few carriers defined their role primarily in relation to textiles: Abraham Voale in 1668 undertook 'the imployment of carrying and conveying bayes and sayes and other goods wares & commodities' from Colchester to London, and Lawrence Holbrooke, Wells carrier, was engaged in the 1680s in 'the carrieing of broade clothes wosted hose

24 *Advertisement concerning Canterbury silk stolen by highwaymen from the Dover waggon in 1682. (London Gazette, 18 December 1682.)*

& other comodities and merchandises' between Somerset and London.[20] Other manufactures carried included silk from Canterbury in 1680-2, gloves from Worcester in the 1690s, canvas from Manchester in the 1720s, buttons from the Birmingham area in 1735, earthenware from Staffordshire in the 1740s and stockings from the Kidderminster area in 1748.[21] Leather goods and higher-value metalwares were probably also carried.

Secondly, industrial raw materials were sent to London, the greatest manufacturing centre in the country.[22] Examples include woad in 'great quantities' from Northamptonshire in the 1670s, leather and calf skins from various places in the mid-1680s, malt from Baldock in 1676 and Saffron Walden in 1690 and hops from Sussex in the 1710s.[23] Some of the textiles could be placed in this category, being finished and turned into clothing or furnishing fabrics in London.

Thirdly, examples of foodstuffs sent to London include cheese from Uttoxeter and Newcastle-under-Lyme, substantial quantities of butter from Cambridge, Peterborough, Silsoe and Dorchester at various dates, venison from Kettering, Peterborough and Stamford likewise, 12 stone of bacon from Hampshire in 1688, oysters from Colchester in 1699, ducks from Peterborough in 1705, cider from Herefordshire in the 1720s and poultry from Huntingdon in 1730.[24] The oysters were warranted good for four or five days carriage from London, and many were taken out of London again by carriers, for example to Derby in the early 18th century.[25] Venison was sent from Peterborough to Lord Fitzwilliam in London around 1700 and, when some arrived stinking, Fitzwilliam observed that the carrier used to lay it out every night to cool and to pepper it to season and preserve it; on one occasion he believed the carrier had swopped his buck for a worse one. The types of foodstuffs most likely to be sent are indicated by those Lord Cholmondeley obtained from his Cheshire estate around 1700: garden produce, game, poultry, cheeses, cooked meats such as game pies, jars of honey, boxes of fruit and vegetables and beer and cider.[26] They were generally perishable or of high value, and did not include low-value staples such as grain, except over short distances (though the latter probably contributed to the large number of short-distance services north of London). Possibly the single most important item was cheese, though it was sometimes sent in dedicated waggons. In the late 17th century cheese worth £500 was sent to London by carrier every week from the great cheese market at Uttoxeter, and in 1751 over 2,000 tons was sent by land to London from Gloucestershire, Wiltshire and Berkshire, 'being a perishable commodity, and while new not bearing water-carriage to London'.[27]

Fourthly, industrial raw materials sent *from* London (sometimes having been imported) included hops to Cambridge and Norwich in the 1690s and Dorchester in the 1720s, steel and whetstones to a Gloucester ironmonger in the 1670s when urgently needed (otherwise by sea), brass wire from Southwark to Gloucester for a pinmaker at Mitcheldean in 1689 (3 cwt in a single consignment), wool to Somerset, Wiltshire and Colchester at various dates and tanned sheep skins in 1724.[28]

Fifthly, shop goods (sometimes London's own manufactures but sometimes already carried to the city) were sent from London all over the country by carrier, including draperies, hats, haberdashery, groceries, tobacco, wine, drugs and books. For example, medicinal pills and drinks were advertised in 1682 with the observation that 'You may write for any of these, and have them sent by a carrier to any town in England', and a Kendal apothecary in about 1700 was obtaining drugs by carrier from London with liberty to return them if damaged or no longer needed. A box sent from Westminster to Blandford in 1721 contained 'ffifteene yards of silk called lutestring thirty yards of sattin a silk gown and petticoat one quilted pettycoat one pair of stayes one cloth wastcoat a girdle buckle and thirty yards of ribbon of the value of fforty pounds and upwards'. The Lancashire people expecting goods from London by the Manchester carrier on one journey in 1704 included a chapman, four grocers, a dyer, two mercers and a haberdasher, and a Bristol waggon destroyed by fire in 1716 had contained £3,000 of 'mercers and salesmen's goods'.[29]

Sixthly, there were gentlemen's goods. Gentlemen often sent a stream of items between their London and country homes and occasionally full waggon-loads of furniture and pictures. A good example is provided by the letters of Lord Fitzwilliam in London to his steward, Francis Guybon, at Milton near Peterborough

25 *Advertisement relating to haberdashery goods lost by Richard Newcomb, Stratford-upon-Avon carrier, in 1684. (London Gazette, 22 January 1685.)*

LOft between London and Stratford upon Avon in Warwickſhire, the 22. of October laſt, a Parcel directed to Mr. William Hunt, 33 Yards of Black Tiffeney for Mourning Scarves, two half Pieces of Figured Ribbon 4 d. broad, half a Piece of 20 d. Pink Colour Taffity Ribbon, a Groce of Gimp Lace mixt with Tincy, a Groce of Silk Buttons, a Dozen of Jett Necklaces, three Remnants of Hair Shag all of them containing 17 Yards 3 quarters. About Nov. 21 2 Pieces of Stript Silk Norwich Crape, and two Pieces of mixt Norwich Sick Crape not Stript, directed to Mr. Will. Hunt aforeſaid ; Whoever gives notice of the Goods to Mr. Richard Newcomb at his Warehouſe at the Ram Inn in Weſt-Smithfield London, ſhall have 40 s. reward.

WHEREAS DANEL ADCOCK, of Titchmarsh, in the County of Northampton, has lately purchas'd the Stage-Waggons from Oakham, Uppingham, and Thrapston, to London, commonly call'd, or known by the Name of the Gretton Stage. This therefore is to give Notice, That the said DANIEL ADCOCK intends to keep the same Stages as heretofore. And sets out from Gretton every Monday Morning at Two o'Clock ; from Weldon at Five, and at Ten from the White Hart Inn in Thrapston; lies at the George Inn in Bedford the same Night ; goes from thence every Tuesday Morning at Four; lies at the Saracen's Head Inn in St. Alban's the same Night; goes from thence every Wednesday Morning to the Bear and Ragged Staff Inn in Smithfield, London, by Two in the Afternoon the same Day : Returns from thence every Thursday Morning at Nine, and lies at St. Alban's the same Night ; at Bedford the next Night ; and at Thrapston on the Saturday Night ; delivers Uppingham and Oakham Goods every Monday or Tuesday at the same Towns : And takes in Goods for London at the Bell Inn in Oakham every Saturday ; and at the Royal Oak Inn in Uppingham the same Evening.

And for the Conveniency of Gentlemen and others, who have Occasion to send Venison, or other perishable Goods, to London, constant Attendance will be given at Gretton every Wednesday Night at Twelve o'Clock ; at the King's Arms Inn at Weldon at Two on Thursday Morning ; at the Duke of Montagu's Arms in Brightstock at Three, and at the White Hart Inn at Thrapston at Five. And the same shall be deliver'd at the Bear and Ragged Staff in Smithfield, London, every Friday Morning by Five o'Clock ; to continue from the 18th of June, all the Venison Season, (if GOD permit) by

D. ADCOCK.

N. B. Constant Attendance shall (Personally) be given by the said DANIEL ADCOCK, for the Taking in, and Delivery of Goods, Parcels, and Passengers, at all the Times and Places above-mentioned.

26 *An unusually detailed advertisement by a new carrier in 1735, providing plenty of evidence that he intended to keep regular hours. A separate and faster service was provided for venison. See Map 3. (Northampton Mercury, 23 June 1735.)*

in 1697-1709. Fitzwilliam reckoned to send a large quantity once or twice a year, such as nearly a waggon-load to Milton in 1701 including hampers of wine, boxes of china, pictures and cabinets. His letters refer most frequently to conveyance of money or venison to London (the latter often by coach). Other consignments to London included partridges, pheasants, honey, several dozen Newington peaches and his own portrait. Goods sent to Milton included wine and brandy, brooms and brushes to clean the house, mourning and paper escutcheons to hang in the chancel on the death of Fitzwilliam's son, pictures, a great copper cistern for putting bottles in, stone bottles of oil, a large watering pot for the garden, a box of glass lanterns for the house, a light carriage called a calash, a box of grafts of pears (covered in horse dung and earth), six pairs of bowls and two jacks for the bowling green and a horse. Servants were also conveyed by waggon.[30] Well-to-do tradesmen might order similar types of goods from London, such as the buttons, silk, shoe lace, tea, coffee, snuff and books which Joseph Symson of Kendal obtained from London by carrier in 1711-20.[31] Symson's books and the books, pamphlets and newsletters which one of the Verneys in Buckinghamshire was obtaining from London by carrier in the 1670s provide a glimpse of the cultural importance of the London carriers.[32]

Seventhly, no description of carriers' loading could avoid having a miscellaneous category. Examples include bags and boxes of writings, bundles of trees, a box of tulips and the occasional dog or horse – the latter attached to the back of the waggon or driven with the packhorses. A London wainscoter had materials down to Yeovil in 1706 for work in the area (presumably wood and tools). The stock of a Cambridge milliner, in a box weighing 1 cwt and said to be worth £275, was carried to London in 1674.[33] There are a few examples of goods imported at ports other than London finding their way to the city by carrier – cloves from Dordrecht via King's Lynn and St Ives in 1662 and silks, spices and linens from Harwich and other Essex ports.[34]

As the examples above indicate, the higher cost of road carriage meant that goods conveyed by road tended to be of high value in relation to their weight, and therefore able to bear that higher cost. Around 1700, for example, conveying West Country serges to London by road cost only about 2 to 4 per cent of their value, and brass wire was sent by carrier from London to Gloucester in 1689 for only 3.2 per cent of its value. Even between Kendal and London, sending linseys by carrier in 1711-20 cost only 6 to 8 per cent of their value.[35] London carriers never, or virtually never, carried minerals, timber and the heavier and less perishable agricultural items such as grain. Heavy items had to be carried by water or not at all, except over short distances (as in the case of malt) or if there was particular urgency. In the West Country in the 19th century, items for which the cost of road carriage to or from London exceeded about 3 per cent of their value were not usually conveyed in any quantity unless there were reasons for urgency, such as perishability, but this was for an area with good coastal transport. In the 17th and early 18th centuries there were many more areas lacking good water access

27 *Advertisement of a change of London inn by the Stamford, Grantham and Newark carrier in 1729, warning of nefarious practices by his former innkeeper. The impressive list of names, including two Mayors, indicates the importance attached to the carrier's services. (LEP, 20 February 1729.)*

Jan. 28, 1728-9

STAMFORD, GRANTHAM, and NEWARK, &c. STAGE-WAGGON being removed from the Bell Inn in Wood-street, London, sets out every Monday, as usual, from the Castle Inn in Wood-street, and every Thursday from the Old Castle, Smithfield-Bars, London, carries Goods and Passengers to and from the abovesaid Places, and Places adjacent, at reasonable Rates. Peform'd (if God permit) by JOHN NEWBALL.

P. S. Whereas the extravagant Demands of JOSEPH HARRISON, Landlord, at the abovesaid Bell Inn, did oblige me to remove my Waggon from his House on the 11th of November last : And on my not complying to his Impositions, did (in a malicious Opposition to me) persuade or admit other Carriers to send a Waggon into the aforesaid Bell Inn, and advertise that the Stamford, Grantham, and Newark Carrier is yet continued at the Bell Inn : And whereas since my Removal there hath not (to my Knowledge) been any Waggon gone from the aforesaid Bell Inn to the abovesaid Places : But it hath been the unjustifiable Practice of the said JOSEPH HARRISON to receive and detain several Parcels of Goods, sent thither by Persons not knowing of my Removal, and to deprive me of my Carriage, have sent the said Parcels, &c. by the York, Richmond, or other Carriers, to the Detriment and Disappointment of several Gentlemen and Tradesmen in and near the abovesaid Places.

To prevent such Abuses for the future, and to acquaint the Public of it, I beg the Favour of every Gentleman, Tradesman, &c. who, at any Time, send for, or send Goods to the abovesaid Places, to write, or cause to be wrote under the Direction of each Box, Parcel, &c. To be sent by JOHN NEWBALL, Carrier, at the abovesaid Castle Inns.

We certify that the said JOHN NEWBALL is our Carrier, and to our Knowledge, since his Removal from the abovesaid Bell Inn, no other Stage Waggon from London hath been sent to the abovesaid Places, though other Carriers have pretended and advertised to oppose him : We therefore, in Justice to his Character, have suffered our Names to be hereunto set.

STAMFORD.

John Blackwell, Mayor	John Spencer	Robert Taylor
Leo. Thorogood	Richard Nevison	Isaac Savery
Francis Willcox	Thomas Moore	Benj. Berresford
John Seaton, Sen.	Francis Moore	Edward King
Geo. Denshire	Tho. Black	Henry Wright
John Rogers	Tho. Morris	Mathew Judd
John Goodhall	Tho. Alcock.	William Smith
Henry Butcher	Rob. Franklin	Robert Watts
Peter Simons	Mar. Newark	R. Wooldray
John Seaton, Jun.	John Taylor	Edward Baker
Charles Shipley		

GRANTHAM.

Henry Short, Alderman	Benjamin Town	John Charmbury
Francis Fisher	Thomas Stevens	Henry Johnson
Rawson Hart	Thomas Langley	Richard Wells
William Kirke	Thomas Garner	John Cheetam
Thomas Rawlinson	William Coddington	Lewis Steward
Simon Grant	Henry Stokes	Richard Linthwaite
John Fisher	John Swan	Thomas Sharpin
Ralph Clarke	Thomas Chippindale	John Sharp

NEWARK.

John Milnes, Mayor	Christopher Buckells	Matthew Cumberland
Samuel Raftall	Benjamin Fransworth	John Twentyman, Jun.
John Lund	Edward Eastland	Edward Smith
John Herring	William Green	William Gascoyne
William Hyes	William Twigg	

to London, and carriers in such areas sometimes conveyed articles for which road transport was not well-suited, such as Staffordshire earthenware,[36] so the distinction between goods carried by land and by water was probably much less clear than in the 19th century. When, in war-time, William Stout the Lancaster shopkeeper had to obtain goods from London by cart or waggon, instead of by sea, costing about 5s. 6d. per cwt, items worth less than 23s. per cwt continued to go by sea convoy; in other words, in exceptional circumstances, Stout was willing to pay transport costs amounting to 24 per cent of the goods' value, but not more.[37]

While there were many heavy items almost invariably carried by water, there were probably few which were nearly always carried by road. Where water transport was available and there was no urgency, there was little point in paying the extra charge for road transport, except to reduce the risk of damage. Apart from silk, which was easily damaged, it was probably cloth which came nearest to being conveyed exclusively by road. Prior to the 1680s virtually all West Country cloth sent to London went by road, though thereafter substantial quantities by coastal vessel, and in the 1720s Defoe wrote that Taunton and Exeter cloth came to London 'chiefly by land', as did all the cloth and other textiles from Wiltshire, Gloucestershire, Worcestershire, Shropshire, Yorkshire, Manchester and Coventry.[38] Articles normally sent in small quantities, such as books and medicines, probably also went by road as a matter of course.

Road and water transport were of course often complementary, and some goods were conveyed to or from London using both modes. Usually this involved provincial carriers taking goods to the coast or to the Thames or its tributaries for onward transmission to London, for example from the north-west to Newcastle, Hull or Bawtry for carriage along the east coast, or from the west to Lechlade or (in the 18th century) Newbury for carriage along the Thames, but London carriers were directly involved in such mixed journeys around the Fens, where there was good river transport but not to London. Thomas Johnson of St Ives stated in 1662 that he was 'often intrusted to receive goods att St Ives … which were sent to him from Lynn Regis by divers marchants ffactors and tradesmen resideing there and to carrie the same to and deliver the same att London'. In January 1673, 18½ tons of iron was sent from London by water to Guildford and then waggon to Portsmouth. Some London carriers apparently themselves used the boats between London and Gravesend, since the Canterbury, Ashford and Lenham carriers lost goods when one sank in 1732.[39]

Carriers conveyed passengers as well as goods, either hiring them hackney horses[40] or accommodating them in waggons.[41] Passengers were probably more advantageous to carriers by waggon, since each passenger was only a small addition to a waggon-load and they would sometimes walk rather than ride, though they occasionally damaged or stole the goods. Fares by waggon or packhorse were generally around 1.0 pence per mile, compared with about 2.4 pence by stage-coach.[42]

Unlike local carriers, London carriers do not normally seem to have undertaken errands for their customers. John Christmas of Aylesbury bought lead for an Aylesbury glasier and Roger Goldring of Petersfield sold hogsheads of brandy for a customer,[43] but there are few such examples. Particularly in London their time was limited, and concentration on their main task was an aspect of their professionalism.

Letters

One source of carriers' loading was under threat in Delaune's time. Carriers had inevitably conveyed letters when there was no official public postal service and there were few other forms of regular communication, apart from a few municipal foot-posts carrying letters. No doubt many carriers simply took letters on their regular journeys, but some made special arrangements. In 1632 the Norwich Assembly, seeking to prevent Sunday travel, set out times for the letter carriers employed by the Norwich carriers distinct from those for the waggons: whereas the waggons took four days, the letter carriers on their return journey were to leave London by 2 p.m. on Tuesday and reach Norwich by 8 a.m. on Thursday.[44]

The government's postal service was made available to the public in 1635, with a monopoly of the inland carriage of letters, but 'common known carryers' were exempted and remained so until 1711. Not until long after 1635 were most towns served by the official posts. However, carriers were soon encountering trouble, and in 1638 a proclamation specified that carriers could still convey letters with their vehicles or packhorses on their 'ordinarie known journeys', but that (unless they were university carriers) their letters must not arrive more than eight hours before those vehicles or packhorses nor depart more than eight hours after them. In 1660 the eight-hour concession was withdrawn. Carriers were occasionally prosecuted, such as John Slyer of Tewkesbury in 1669. Slyer conveyed letters by means of Thomas Evans of Uxbridge, who travelled all night to London, delivering the letters more than 12 hours before Slyer's goods reached the city.[45]

Conveyance of letters by carriers and coachmasters was well-organised, as the following report of 1680 makes clear:

> Tuesday last a gentleman coming from Bedford in ye stage coach lay that night at St Albans. There was that night two stage coaches that came thither from Bedford towne. Three more from other parts of that country. And also 7 waggon carryers from those parts. All these had great store of letters. Each put his letters into his owne bagg and sealed them up. Then all their baggs with many baggs more belonging to other carryers then in that towne were put into a great male. And sent up by horseman to London that night so that they were delivered by the carryers severall porters Wensday morning before the post letters went abroad. There were not so few as 200 letters among ye Bedford carryers.[46]

Around the same time the Post Office considered a plan whereby it would contract with the carriers and coachmen to convey their letters for them at only one penny per letter, as was already done in Sussex (where John Barnes was both carrier and postmaster at Chichester). The aim was to encourage people to send their letters direct to the Post Office and thus to gain the carriers' trade. In response, Thomas Gardiner noted of the carriers that:

> The advantage of comming and bringing letters before their horses (which letters are therefore seizable) is purely to quicken their return, and thereby lessen their expenses in London, and their stay after their horses especially for advantage by letters, each one bringing two pence at least.[47]

Since the majority of carriers' letters were taken up within 60 miles of London, especially on days when the Post Office provided no service from the places concerned, he proposed instead a daily service to places within 60 miles and to agree with the carriers only for places beyond 60 miles. The Post Office continued to do battle with the carriers: in 1686 fines of £440 were levied on John Warren, Stamford carrier, and his London porter for conveying letters and packets. From 1711 carriers were permitted to convey only letters relating to goods they were carrying and which were not paid for separately.[48] Nevertheless, letters long continued to be sent by carriers.

Money

Carriers were an important means of conveying money from one part of the country to another, and had been so since the early 16th century or before.[49] Sometimes they included this in their description of their role: Thomas Jaques of Petersfield described his waggons and coaches in 1679 as 'for the carriage of moneys goods wares merchandizes & passengers', and Mary Church of Hereford's business in 1703 was not just conveying goods 'but alsoe in returning great summes of money & negociateing inland bills for such returns'.[50] Carriers might physically convey cash or bills of exchange, or, probably less commonly, they might simply balance receipts and payments in different places and not have to move anything at all. As gentlemen increasingly resided in London, they had more and more need to convey money to the city, and the carriers were their main way of doing so.[51] Tradesmen and tax collectors also used the carriers to move cash.

The main alternative to the carrier was returns of money, by which the requirements of people in different places were balanced so that cash did not have to be moved. For example, drovers received money in London and needed it in the country, whereas gentlemen generally received it in the country and needed it in London; thus the gentleman's steward might pay the drover in the country in return for a payment by the drover to the gentleman in London.[52] The problem was that suitable returns were not always available, and then the carrier usually had to be resorted to. At Norwich in 1697, following the recoinage of the previous year, it was reckoned better to send money by carrier than by bills of exchange (or returns), 'in regard that bills at London have been soe badly paid and the difficulty of getting of good bills in Norwich'.[53]

The sums conveyed by carrier could be extremely large. Thomas Morris of Exeter sometimes carried £5,000 to London in a single journey in the 1680s, and he carried £9,710 for one of the farmers of the hearth taxes in five months in 1680. His son carried over £50,000 in sealed bags from London to Exeter for one firm of Exeter and London money changers in six years in the 1690s. In about 1700 Joshua Guest's Stamford waggons sometimes carried £1,300.[54]

Sometimes the money conveyed was to pay for goods carried in the opposite direction, or on credit for goods to be carried in future. For example, in the 1680s, a London merchant, sending wine to a Cambridge vintner by Charles Tine, would draw bills upon the vintner payable to Tine, which sums Tine would receive and pay to the merchant in London. Similarly, Roger Bird, Trowbridge and Frome

ON the 20th inftant between Enfield and Edmunton 3 Men fet upon William Martyn, the Cambridge Carrier, and feveral others; one of them upon a light brown Nag, another upon a dark brown Nag with a mealy Nofe, and the other upon a dark grey Horfe, taking from him a Portmanteau, in which were feveral Bills of Exchange, payable to him to the value of between 5 and 600 l. together with feveral Parcells directed to Cambridge, efpecially one, a Canvas Bag of Writings, and another a white parcel of Writings, both directed to Cajus College, Cambridge, and an Hanger with a fhagged Handle, a parcel of new Hofe, and Gloves, and a Book, in which was fet down a particular account of Monies paid and received by the faid William Martyn. Whoever gives Notice of the Bills and Parcels, fo as they may be recovered, to Mr. Samuel Lowndes, Bookfeller, over againft Exeter Exchange in the Strand, fhall have 3 Guineas Reward.

28 *Advertisement concerning a theft from one of the Cambridge carriers in 1693.* (London Gazette, 27 February 1693.)

carrier, stated in 1716 that 'it is usual for the persons for whom … Bird carrys cloths and other goods to draw bills for payment thereof upon account upon the persons they trade withall in London or to receive for such clothiers use payable to … Bird or his servants'.[55] However, the cash was frequently unrelated to goods carried.

Cash was often concealed from the carrier. Customers would hide it in packs or boxes of goods, or even in a meat pie or a firkin of soap,[56] or would declare less than the full amount, in order to avoid the much higher rate of carriage for money. An estate steward warned in 1663 that this was 'not a safe way. It begins to be common', but it remained popular.[57] Following Southcote's case in 1601 it had become established that carriers were always liable in case of theft, unless by the King's enemies (the justification being that they might otherwise collude with thieves), and in 1648 it was established in addition that they were liable even for cash or valuables not declared to them. However, it was becoming recognised in the mid-17th century that the carrier could limit his liability.[58] In 1692 Thomas Southgate of Norwich, 'haveing found that many people who sent packs boxes or trunks by your orator's [Southgate's] wagon did usually hide plate jewells money or other rich treasure in such packs trunks or boxes among their other goods and conceale the same from your orator with an intent to putt the hazard of looseing such plate jewells money or treasure by robbery or otherwise upon your orator without his knowledge and without allowing him any thing for such hazard and charge', advertised extensively that he would not be answerable for loss in such cases. This did not prevent him being taken to court over the loss of a box said to contain £46, his opponent claiming that no-one had asked what was in the box and that such advertisements were ineffective when the Norwich justices had set a maximum rate of 4s. per cwt. Witnesses on behalf of Southgate reported sending thousands of pounds secretly by his waggon, claiming that they would have considered themselves liable for any loss.[59] In the case of Tyly v. Morris in 1699, Thomas Morris of Exeter escaped liability for the £350 out of £850 stolen on Hounslow Heath which had not been declared and paid for at the special rate.[60] However, how far carriers could limit their liability remained unclear in law.

Many customers did declare money, and paid a rate per £100 conveyed. For example, the driver of an Amersham waggon in 1738 carried a purse in his waistcoat pocket containing £19 10s. 0d. from an Amersham grocer to a London cheesemonger (and lost it). In such cases the carrier was indisputably responsible for its safe delivery. However, he might well be unable to make good a loss of hundreds of pounds, so some risk remained. A man sending a trunk containing £500 in Anthony Rush's waggon to Bedford in 1680 took the precaution of riding in the waggon with it. The other risk was that the carrier might convert the money to his own use, as Arthur Dixon, Kendal carrier, did with part of £153 entrusted to him to deliver to London in 1701. This was a reason for selecting one member of a partnership such as the Kendal carriers and not trusting the others. Mary Church of Hereford claimed in 1710 that her returns of money business had been much reduced through her servant failing to arrange for the payment of bills due, 'the said business altogether depending on a good creditt and reputation & an exact and punctuall discharg of such bills as are drawn from time to time'.[61]

Unless cash was handed to the carrier packed with other items or in sealed bags, he simply received money in one place and paid it in another. Such transactions tended to be called returns of money, although this was strictly correct only when money was not actually moved.[62] Sometimes the carrier did not have to move the money physically because it was balanced by money consigned in the opposite direction. For example, in 1705 Lord Fitzwilliam, wanting money in London, thought Robert Fearey, Peterborough carrier, might supply a return of money, as he was often receiving cash in London for ducks and so on; however, he was not willing to take a bill on Fearey's poulterers in Newgate Market, having 'no occasion to run about adunning people for my owne'. In 1693 Thomas Briggs, Kendal carrier, was contracted to carry excise money from Cumberland and Westmorland to London; a Kendal man who was owed money in London arranged to borrow £400 from him in Kendal in exchange for bills to that amount payable by a goldsmith in London. Unfortunately the bills were not honoured.[63]

Probably in most cases the carrier did have to move the money, and what may have been the most common mechanism was set out in 1725 by Mary Pearce, widow of the Dorchester innkeeper of Jacob Weare, Exeter carrier:

> When persons had occasion to send any sumes of money to London by the said Weare's waggon ... they applyed to the said Christopher Pearce as employed by the said Jacob Weare for that purpose and payd him the said sums at Dorchester and the said Christopher Pearce thereupon gave bills for the same payable at London which he drew upon the said Jacob Weare or his book-keeper there and sent the said money he so received by the next waggon to the said Jacob Weare or his book-keeper at London who thereupon paid the said bills deducting only the money allowed for the remittance.[64]

Sometimes the carrier made payments before he received the sum involved,[65] and it was a short step from this to making short-term loans as a matter of course, as Nicholas and John Barry, Exeter carriers, were doing in the early 1720s.[66]

The charge for conveying money to London appears to have varied from place to place and from time to time. At Exeter in the late 17th and early 18th centuries it was usually 10s. per £100, but sometimes only 7s. or 7s. 6d. At Norwich in the 1690s the usual rate was 20s. per £100. From Kendal the charges recorded are 33s. in 1675, 25s. in 1687 and 20s. in 1693 (suggesting a gradual reduction). Where payments to the carrier in London enabled him to avoid having to move cash, there might be no charge: in 1728 John Newball, Stamford carrier, advertised that money consigned to his innkeeper in London would be paid without charge at Stamford, Grantham or Newark.[67]

Carrying large amounts of cash, and being known to do so, made carriers vulnerable to robbery, and some major robberies by highwaymen are recorded in the late 17th and early 18th centuries. The carrier often lost hundreds of pounds (£1,100 in one case in 1699).[68] In 1697 Thomas Southgate of Norwich was said to have caused two or three highwaymen to be hanged, and to have 'beene way laid and threatned to be murdered by some of their gang for soe doeing'.[69] Carriers' inventories virtually never record firearms,[70] carriers sometimes travelled in the hours of darkness,[71] and sometimes they even left waggons in the street overnight (though usually with a man to watch).[72] The carrier's main defence was that the cash was hidden among the goods, and therefore had to be searched for, costing the highwayman precious time, unless he had inside information. Also carriers sometimes travelled in convoy (with seven or eight waggons in one case in 1726).[73] When Henry Warren, Stamford carrier, was robbed by four men on horseback on his return from Beverley Fair in 1676, he had over £10,000 in the waggon. The robbers unloaded much of the waggon and cut open several casks containing money without finding it, but eventually came upon £1,870 in a cask belonging to a London mercer. This robbery took place during the day, so Warren was able to claim the sum from the unfortunate hundred in which the robbery took place.[74] A heavily loaded waggon probably required a large gang to search it quickly enough, and the number of robbers recorded was usually from four to eight, though a Maidstone carrier was robbed in 1697 by two unmounted men.[75] Theft at inns and pilfering by passengers were probably at least as serious as highway robbery, and pilfering was said to be common.[76] The possibility of highway robbery must always have been a worry, but it did not usually stop carriers agreeing to convey large sums of cash or their customers being willing to use the carrier for this purpose.

CHAPTER IV

WAGGON OPERATION

Waggon costs

The cost structure of waggon operation explains many of the decisions made about the organisation of services. Two sources are available. Executors' accounts for Robert Ridgwell of Cambridge (set out in a Chancery suit) cover a short period in January 1695 – probably no more than a week or so. The payments were for oats, beans and hay for the horses (£9 13s. 0d.), shoeing (11s. 3d.), wages of two waggon drivers (£1 7s. 0d.), damage to hops (8s. 3d.), farrier and paper (2s. 8d.), 'for letters & unloading ye waggons & expence' (3s. 8d.), a smith for 'lints capps & clouts' for the waggons (10s.), mending horse collars (1s. 6d.), a farrier curing the horses (£1 8s. 9d.), a porter (2s. 6d.), straw (6s.), a man clouting two waggons (1s.), and 'for toll for passage of the waggons grease for waggon wheels, charges to porters & others for unloading waggons and working about goods brought up to London and carryed from London to Cambridge' (£1 5s. 8d.).[1] These accounts obviously ignore the cost of replacing horses and waggons, but this can be estimated. The figures are useful chiefly for showing the dominance of horse costs – 60 per cent for provender alone and 82 per cent for all horse costs.

29 *A breakdown of the costs of an Oxford carrier in about 1700, almost certainly drawn up as part of an appeal to the university authorities to permit higher rates of carriage. (Bodleian Library, University Archives, Chancellor's Court, 134/1/1.)*

The other source is a breakdown of costs between Oxford and London in the early 18th century (Fig. 29).[2] It survives among the records of the Chancellor of the University of Oxford, and almost certainly formed part of an appeal for higher rates of carriage. The carrier may therefore have exaggerated his overall costs, but this is unlikely to have affected significantly the proportions for the different items, and the costs stated appear reasonable.[3] As with Ridgwell's account, the few missing costs can be estimated.[4] The result is consistent with Ridgwell's account: provender costs were a higher proportion (69 per cent) but total horse costs were almost the same (81 per cent) (Table 4). Assuming an average load of 1½ tons, costs were 5.8 pence per ton-mile.

Map 6 *Debts of John Goldring relating to his Portsmouth waggon, 1718, as listed in Chancery proceedings. Debts to Londoners are not recorded. (Source: C 11/2303/30.)*

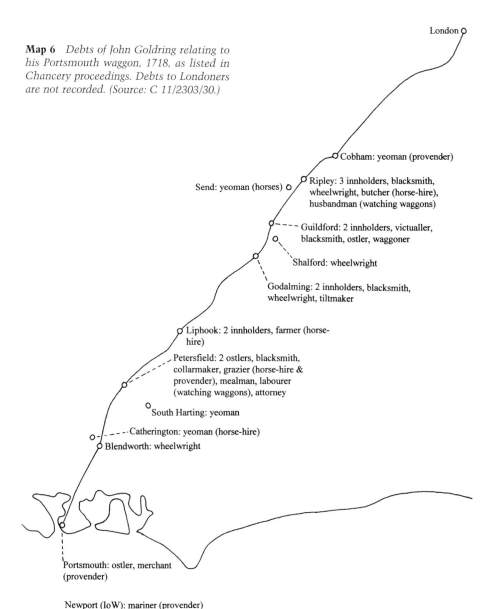

London

Cobham: yeoman (provender)

Send: yeoman (horses)

Ripley: 3 innholders, blacksmith, wheelwright, butcher (horse-hire), husbandman (watching waggons)

Guildford: 2 innholders, victualler, blacksmith, ostler, waggoner

Shalford: wheelwright

Godalming: 2 innholders, blacksmith, wheelwright, tiltmaker

Liphook: 2 innholders, farmer (horse-hire)

Petersfield: 2 ostlers, blacksmith, collarmaker, grazier (horse-hire & provender), mealman, labourer (watching waggons), attorney

South Harting: yeoman

Catherington: yeoman (horse-hire)

Blendworth: wheelwright

Portsmouth: ostler, merchant (provender)

Newport (IoW): mariner (provender)

The main consequence of the dominance of horse and especially provender costs was that, since horses had to be fed even when not working, it was essential to obtain the maximum possible work from them. This forms the background to the following sections. Another consequence was that increases in provender prices were a significant risk, though this was limited by agreements with innkeepers for fixed provender prices and by the fact that many carriers benefited as farmers from provender being dear. In contrast to horses, waggons were a minor cost. Most expenditure on them was for repairs and maintenance rather than new waggons. In the 13 inventories which provide sufficient information, waggons accounted for 12 to 37 per cent of the carrying stock, and horses and harness for 63 to 88 per cent.

Horses, waggons, teams and loads

Before the mid-18th century there were very few large horses. Whereas present-day riding horses are generally between 14½ and 17 hands and horses employed by the Metropolitan Police between 16 and 18 hands, medieval horses in London were generally between 12½ and 15 hands. Even the much-discussed military 'Great Horse' seems to have been typically 14 to 15 hands, and the horse armour now in the Royal Armouries would sit comfortably on horses of 15 to 16 hands. Henry VIII's regulations on horse-breeding stipulated a minimum size for stallions of only 15 hands.[5] The quality of English horses certainly improved between the mid-16th and mid-17th centuries, especially through imports of Flanders and Frisian horses,[6] but the impact on size is unclear. In the few horse markets where height was recorded in the late 17th century, there were scarcely any horses over 15 hands.[7] These markets were not necessarily where carriers obtained their horses, but early 18th-century newspaper advertisements suggest that, apart from coach horses, horses over 15 hands were still rare, even in the Fens,[8] and even stallions offered for 'leaping' were usually only about 15 hands.[9]

The largest horses in the 17th century were usually described as 'coach horses', and, as discussed later, were almost always between 15 and 16 hands. Coach and

30 *A waggon in Gloucestershire, with an unmounted waggoner, from a view of Bradley Court in Sir Robert Atkyns,* Ancient and present state of Glostershire *(1712). Whether the waggoner had a pony or not probably reflected the number of miles covered per day.*

31 *A waggon in Piccadilly in 1707, from a view of Burlington House drawn by Knyff and engraved by Kip.*

waggon horses had a similar task in this period – dragging a heavy vehicle along roads frequently rutted or covered in mud – and therefore may well have been of similar size. This is supported by evidence on feeding: Gregory King assumed for his calculations about horses that coach and other draught horses had the same feed,[10] and in the few available examples the rations actually given to coach and waggon horses were indeed similar (Appendix 5). In the case of Nicholas Rothwell's Birmingham horses in 1743-5, the coach horses were given less hay and beans but more oats than the waggon horses, and cost sometimes slightly more and sometimes slightly less to feed than the waggon horses, depending on whether the coach was following its two-day or three-day schedule. Using similar horses would have enabled carriers who ran both waggons and coaches to switch their horses between them as required. However, given the rarity of horses exceeding 15 hands, the fact that 'coach horses' were normally distinguished from other draught horses and the evidence from inventories that waggon horses were slightly less valuable than coach horses (averaging £4 17s. 0d. compared with £5 8s. 0d.),[11] a reasonable conclusion is that carriers' waggon horses were slightly smaller than coach horses and typically about 15 hands.

There was certainly regional variation, brought about by the suitability of different horses on different roads rather than variation in availability: in 1719 a petition from merchants and others of Lancashire and Cheshire explained that 'the horses used in those counties are small and not able to draw by one third the same weight as those of the Midland counties nor can any other horse be made use of for that the rough stony roads in those parts would quickly batter and destroy such heavy strong horses, should they attempt there to draw with such'.[12]

Only five inventories indicate the type of horses, although some others may have used 'horse' in the technical sense of a gelding more than six years old. Trowbridge and Warwick carriers had both geldings and stoned horses (i.e stallions), though with two mares (perhaps ponies for riding) in the Warwick case; a Newbury carrier had horses and geldings; and the same Warwick firm at a later date and a Melton Mowbray carrier had horses and mares.[13]

There is no evidence of carriers using oxen,[14] despite their extensive use in other countries. In the Middle Ages, oxen (or bullocks) could draw larger loads than horses and were cheaper to keep, but could work fewer hours per day, so horses were able to perform more work in a given time. In the 19th century, when horses were stronger, oxen could still compete in places where free provender was available and commercial provender was expensive and poorly distributed,[15] but neither of these conditions applied in 17th- and 18th-century England. It was the slowness of oxen which made them particularly unsuitable for carriers.

Very little is known about the waggons used. The particular advantages of the type of waggon introduced from Flanders in the mid-16th century have not been identified, nor is it clear why its use became widespread in the 1610s, though the introduction (from Germany) of a swivelling front axle with an adequate turning arc is a possible reason.[16] The waggons had narrow wheels, which kept friction to a minimum but could damage road surfaces; legislation requiring broader wheels was in force from 1662 to 1670 (stipulating four-inch wheels) and from 1719 (stipulating 2½-inch wheels).[17] Axles were probably of wood rather than iron, though William Iliff, Exeter carrier, had at least one iron axle in 1739.[18] In 1744 it was said that empty waggons required two horses to draw them, which suggests a weight of about 18 cwt.[19] A few inventories list waggon equipment. For example, Matthew Glover of Hitchin had a drag chain (used to restrain one wheel when descending hills), two tilts (for covering the waggon) and two ropes.[20] Oddly, no lanterns are mentioned, though waggon journeys were certainly not confined to daylight hours.[21] Bells on the horses to warn other road users seem to have been normal, at least by 1747.[22]

Waggon teams drew at length (i.e. with the horses in single file), unlike stage-coach teams. In 1748 the traveller Pehr Kalm observed that English waggon teams were harnessed in 'quite a peculiar manner':

> I have once seen as many as eight such horses spanned all in a row after one another, nevertheless, it is rare to see so many. Commonly five or six horses are used for one of the large baggage wagons ... They are bound to and after one another with strong iron chains, one of which goes on each side of the horse, and where it comes sometimes to rub against the horse's side it is covered with leather, so that it may not gnaw the horse. The weight and thickness of these chains is such that any other than English horses would with difficulty be able to support it ... By the collars, the horses drew the load or the wagon, which is fastened on to these iron-chains; and the chains are supported by straps, four inches broad, which lie across the horse's back. There are seldom any reins used in the whole length of this long row of horses, but they were accustomed to be steered wherever he wished, or to stop or go faster, only by the various and particular calls of the driver.[23]

Horses drawing at length are less efficient than horses drawing in pairs, since they pull more effectively when close to the load being drawn. The reason for drawing at length was that the roads were not usually wide enough for horses in double file *and* a waggoner riding or walking beside them. Following legislation of 1696 requiring waggoners to harness their horses in double file and draw with double shafts or a pole between the wheel horses, the carriers petitioned the Commons, stating that 'upon trial and experiment thereof, they have found it impossible to travel the narrow roads, passes of streets, and gateways of inns, for that they are not broad enough to contain the same'. The petition indicates that most justices of the peace regarded the provision as impractical, and the committee which heard the carriers' case agreed, though it was not repealed until 1707;[24] probably it was never enforced. Its purpose had presumably been to prevent the wear caused by the horses' feet being concentrated in a single track. From the 1750s, when turnpike trusts became widespread and many roads were widened, no more is heard of drawing at length.

The size of teams was controlled by law, this being, in the absence of reliable weighing machines, the best way of regulating the weights carried and thus protecting the roads. (A weight restriction imposed in 1662 was temporary, and no further attempt to control weights directly was made until 1742.) The limit in 1662 was seven horses, of which six were to draw in pairs; in 1670 five horses drawing at length and any greater number to be in pairs; in 1696 eight horses in pairs; in 1707 six horses; in 1715 five horses at length; and in 1718 six horses 'either at length or in pairs, or sideways', after which there was no further change until 1753. A provision of 1707 that waggoners could use as many horses as necessary on hills designated for this purpose by the justices was repealed in 1710 as having given 'opportunity of drawing in other places with more than six horses or beasts'; instead waggoners were permitted to borrow horses from another waggon travelling the road.[25] Undoubtedly the law on team sizes was routinely ignored. Philip Bridle of Taunton, using more than five horses at length in the 1670s, had horses seized on the road at the instigation of a previous owner of the business. There was more systematic activity around London in the 1690s and 1700s by informers, especially by John Littlehales, who had held office until 1687 under the Surveyor-General of His Majesty's Highways, but who continued long afterwards to demand protection money from carriers.[26] The prevalence of informers near London was perhaps why Richard Hales nearly always left two horses behind at Staines on his way to London in 1709, reducing his teams from seven horses to six.[27] One restraint against prosecutions by the parishes responsible for maintaining the roads was that the carrier might retaliate by informing against them concerning the state of their roads, which, according to an MP, 'terrifies them from doing it'.[28]

Larger teams were less efficient, because it is harder to ensure each horse pulls its weight and because horses pull less effectively the further they are from the load being drawn, but the marginal cost of adding an extra horse was often less than that of putting on an extra waggon and paying for an additional driver.[29] The largest teams recorded in evidence given to a House of Commons committee in 1695 consisted of nine horses at length, used by four carriers, one of whom had also employed teams of 13 horses in double file.[30] The largest teams in carriers' accounts with innkeepers were also of nine horses, with the possible exception of Nicholas Barry's. However, teams were usually smaller: in the five accounts, teams ranged from five to nine horses (or possibly ten), but the most common size in all but one was seven horses; in the other (Nicholas Rothwell's) it was six horses. The 15 teams listed in the inventory of William Iliff, Exeter carrier, in 1747, while mostly of eight horses, included three of nine and two of ten.[31] In the five other inventories where the teams are separately described, nine of the 15 teams had six horses and four had seven;[32] some carriers had only

Upon the Petition of the Northern Carriers :

Mr. *Johnson* said, That, within Three Years last past, upon Discourse with *Littlehale*, who pretended to be a Surveyor of the Highways, the Informant asked him by what Authority he acted, and distrained the Waggoners Horses; who said, He had a Deputation for it from Justice *Lawrence*, which cost him 20 *l*: And further asked, What he had done with the Money arising by such Distresses, which belonged to the Poor, and Highways; and by what Law he demanded quarterly Payments of the Waggoners, and took their Geese, Turkeys, and Ducks, without paying for them; to which he said, That what he received of the Waggoners was for Gratuities, for to suffer them to go without making Distresses on them; and, as to the Poor, he was ready to answer to those to whom it belonged to demand it: And *Littlehale* then told Mr. *Johnson*, That he had distrained upon one *Thom. Smith*, Carrier of *St. Ives*, when he had only Pack-horses, for Six Offences committed by him, a Quarter of a Year before, when he drove a Waggon; and made him unload his Pack-horses in *Shoreditch*, and pay 12 *l*. 10 *s*. before he could have his Horses and Goods to go on his Journey.

John Guest, of *Stamford*, Waggoner, said, that he bought of Mr. *Warren*, formerly *Stamford* Carrier, his Waggon and Horses, and has followed the Employment of a Waggoner ever since; and that, the first Time of the Informant's coming to London, *Littlehale* demanded 8 *l*. a Year of him; and said, his Predecessors paid him after that Rate: That the Informant paid him after that Rate for 3 Quarters of a Year; but *Littlehale* afterwards raising his Rent, from 8 *l*. a Year to 12 *l*. and from thence insisting on 20 *l*. a Year, the Informant refused to pay him any thing; though, had he stood at his old Rate of 8 *l*. a Year, the Informant believes he had still paid it him; whereupon *Littlehale* procured 12 Warrants, of 40 *s*. each, which were served on the Informant by a Constable at *Barnet* as for so many Offences committed by the Informant, for driving on the Road, contrary to Law; and paid 24 *l*. 13 *s*. thereupon; and afterwards brought his Action, and had Judgment against the said Constable, for the said 24 *l*. 13 *s*.; but, he proving poor, the Informant lost his Money:

And said, His Predecessor was under an Agreement with *Littlehale* to pay him 40 *s*. a Quarter to draw his Waggon with as many Horses as he pleased; but the Informant had not transgressed the Law when *Littlehale* demanded the first 40 *s*.; nor ever was convicted of any Offence; but paid his Money upon producing of the Warrants against him.

Samuel Meager, Waggoner, said, That, at *Coney*, as he was driving to *London*, *Littlehale* demanded 10 *s*. of him; which the Informant refused to pay; but, as the Informant was returning into the Country, *Littlehale* seized Two Horses out of Five; and, the Informant proceeding on his Journey with the Three Horses that were left, it killed them all; whereby he is quite undone; and knows not for what Reason *Littlehale* should demand the 10 *s*. or seize his Horse; for that he never travelled with more than Five Horses:

And says, *Littlehale* has taken from him, at *Newgate* Market, Butter, Cheese, &c. without ever paying for them.

32 *Evidence given by carriers and others to a House of Commons committee in 1696 concerning protection money being demanded of them for using teams with more horses than the law allowed. (House of Commons Journals, vol. 11, 1693-97, p. 512.)*

five or six horses in total. (One, Michael Whiteing of Cokethorpe, had only three, but Cokethorpe was a very small place.) Pehr Kalm in 1748 regarded five or six horses as normal,[33] and pictorial evidence, generally in engravings by Kip or Loggan, is usually of teams of five at length.[34] A reasonable conclusion is that teams were generally of six or seven horses, regardless of the state of the law, but that there were sometimes larger teams of up to nine horses at length, and occasionally smaller teams for short-distance services. In some cases there was also a pony for the waggoner to ride, but sometimes the waggoner had to walk.

Evidence from the early 17th century indicates that a reasonably heavy load per waggon horse, excluding the weight of the waggon, was about 6 cwt,[35] at least in southern England and the Midlands, and there is no reason to assume a different figure in the second half of the century. Undoubtedly loads per horse were somewhat smaller in winter than summer – only 84 per cent of the summer load in the case of a Portsmouth carrier in 1619.[36] Waggon horses could of course draw more for short distances, or if the carrier was willing to risk wearing them out prematurely, so 6 cwt is not a maximum figure but an indication of the largest loads per waggon horse regularly hauled. Given teams of six or seven horses, loads of up to about 6 cwt per horse indicate waggon loads of about two tons, and this is consistent with the little 17th-century evidence for waggon loads.[37]

However, this was not necessarily the capacity of each waggon service listed by Delaune, since some carriers, such as Hales at Trowbridge, regularly sent more than one waggon at a time. Delaune recorded several carriers as using two waggons per weekly service (in 1690 at Colchester, Leighton Buzzard and Stamford), but probably did not do so consistently.

In 1684 Gilbert Stoughton of Kettering stated that he had for many years lodged at the *Bakers Arms*, Bedford, with 'for the most part two waggons att a time', and other carriers sending more than one waggon per journey included Robert Seager of Dorchester in 1689-91 and Thomas Huff of Gloucester in 1707.[38] Also, inventories of carriers at Frome, Norwich and elsewhere reveal more teams than were needed for a weekly service.[39] Probably most services did consist of a single waggon and team, but not all.

Waggon accounts

As indicated earlier, carriers' accounts with their innkeepers, set out in Chancery proceedings, provide a detailed glimpse of waggon firms in operation.[40] Five have been found. That for Hales's Trowbridge teams at Staines has been discussed already.[41] That of Daniel Want, Devizes carrier, at the *Bull*, Maidenhead, in August to November 1693 is particularly informative, though it is for a somewhat atypical service.[42] Want's teams were at Maidenhead weekly without fail during the 15 weeks covered, usually on Tuesday and Thursday nights, but twice on Monday and Wednesday, once on Wednesday and Friday and once on Tuesday and Friday (Table 2). Want's stock at the end of that period was ten horses (including

Table 2. Daniel Want's waggons and teams at Maidenhead, 1693

Dates	Days	Waggon horses	Teams	Ponies
Aug 8/9	T/W	10	2	0
Aug 15/17	T/Th	7	1	1
Aug 22/24	T/Th	5	1	1
Aug 29/31	T/Th	6	1	1
Sept 5/7	T /Th	12	2	2
Sept 11/13	M/W	7	1	1
Sept 18/20	M/W	8	1	1
Sept 26/28	T/Th	11	2	1
Oct 3	T	7	1	0
Oct 10/12	T/Th	7	1	1
Oct 17	T	8	1	1
Oct 24/26	T/Th	8/9	1	1
Nov 1/3	W/F	7	1	1
Nov 7/9	T/Th	7	1	1
Nov 14/17	T/F	8/7	1	1

Source: C8/556/7.

Notes: Where only one day is given, this seems to include the return journey from London two days later. The 8/9 Aug entry is presumably an error. The number of teams is indicated by the 'diet' of the waggoners: 1s. per man and therefore per team. The number of waggoners' ponies is indicated by the difference between the number of horses specified and the number incurring a payment of 6d. for hay (hay was provided free for the ponies at Maidenhead). In 1690 Delaune listed Want as reaching London on Wednesdays and setting off on Thursdays.

a waggoner's pony) and three waggons.[43] Therefore most of his horses came to London every week, and the journey to and from London had to be completed between Monday and Saturday in time for at least some of the same horses to set out for the following week's journey. This and the 29 miles covered in one day between Maidenhead and London indicate that the journey took three days each way. The teams therefore covered the astonishing total of 182 miles per week. Yet the provender given was apparently less than Hales's horses received (Appendix 5). What may have made this possible was lighter loads, and Want's service was perhaps more like a caravan than a waggon, proving greater speed at higher cost. The Wiltshire cloth towns certainly seem to have placed a high priority on speed.[44]

33 *Extract from Nicholas Rothwell's account with his London innkeeper in 1743-5 for the feeding of waggon horses, packhorses and coach horses. (C 104/218, Cremer v. Rothwell.)*

Unlike Hales, Want varied the size of his teams from week to week, presumably in response to the quantity of loading or the state of the roads. Three times he sent two teams and waggons, with ten, 12 and 14 horses in total, indicating hiring of horses in the two latter cases. Probably there was some rotation of horses to allow an occasional week's rest, as well as occasional hiring, to compensate for the high number of miles per week.

The third account was between the widow of Jacob Weare, Exeter carrier, and her innkeeper at the *George*, Dorchester, from March to October 1724.[45] This service was exceptional in a different way, in that Weare had divided his route at Dorchester, with separate teams thence to London (resting five days at Dorchester) and to Exeter (resting three days at Dorchester). Again the waggons and teams came and went in every one of the 24 weeks. The only irregularities (other than in the final fortnight) were one London team departing a day late in May and another arriving a day late in September and making the Exeter team a day late for one journey. Team sizes varied only occasionally: those to London normally had seven horses (possibly including a driver's horse) but once five, twice six and once eight. Teams to Exeter sometimes had six horses and sometimes seven (and once eight). Weare's teams were somewhat faster than was usual, the London ones covering 31 miles per day, and this appears to have been reflected in higher provender rations.

The fourth account is that of Nicholas Barry of Exeter with his innkeeper at the *Swan*, Egham, discussed earlier as regards Barry's packhorses (Fig. 7).[46] In September 1707 Barry added waggons to his existing packhorse service. The criteria for reliability are somewhat different in this case, since not sending a waggon in a particular week did not mean there was no service; when there was little loading the packhorses may have been sufficient, as perhaps during the longest gap – five weeks without a waggon in May-June 1708. What is particularly impressive is the way the weekly waggon normally continued uninterrupted during the winter: without a break from November 1707 to March 1708 and with only two weeks missed from November 1708 to February 1709. Teams varied from five horses (twice) to ten horses (twice), though the latter was perhaps two teams. This variation had a clear seasonal pattern, especially in the first year, when teams were of seven in September-October 1707, eight to ten in October-December, eight in January-March 1708, usually seven in April-June and six in July-October. In 1709 there were seven weeks with 12 to 15 waggon horses, indicating two teams, and there were sometimes additional waggons on other days of the week.

The fifth account also covers a long period, from July 1743 to July 1745. It relates to Nicholas Rothwell of Warwick's Birmingham to London waggons (as well as his packhorses and coaches) at the *George*, Aldersgate Street, London (Fig. 33).[47] Teams were always of six horses, except three times when seven were sent, and there were no waggoners' ponies. In summer there were generally two waggons a week, the ordinary waggon leaving London on Saturdays and what Rothwell's advertisements describe as the 'constant waggon', leaving London on Thursdays.[48] 'Constant waggon' almost certainly meant flying waggon, running all night or nearly all night, and it ran only in summer, from April until October or November, being replaced in winter by packhorses. In the 56 weeks when it was operating it arrived in London regularly every Wednesday and left the following day, except one week when it arrived and set off a day late.

In summer 1743 Rothwell's ordinary waggons were irregular (about every fortnight). Loading was evidently poor, and, since the constant waggons were the premium service, it made sense to concentrate the loading in them. However, loading clearly improved thereafter, and for 87 weeks from November 1743, including two winters, a waggon arrived every Friday and set off every Saturday, apart from five weeks when it departed early or late.[49] From October 1744 to March 1745 there was an additional fortnightly waggon also leaving London on Saturdays.

The accounts prove that waggon services were generally reliable, even in winter, but this does not mean that services were *never* interrupted or late. Just as with present-day transport, severe snow could halt services, though only a few examples are recorded.[50] Flooding probably also sometimes disrupted services, and plague certainly did (for the last time) in 1665-6.[51] However, goods were more likely to be held up because the carrier had too much loading, especially at intermediate places, than because his waggons were delayed. Even when the accounts indicate waggons travelling a day late, they were still using the same inns, suggesting that the reason was a decision to travel a day later, perhaps to accommodate a specific consignment, rather than casual delays on the road.[52]

Waggon operation

Some waggon proprietors used the same system of alternate journeys as the Kendal carriers. For example, Henry Whiffen and Robert Seager of Dorchester described in Chancery proceedings in 1690 how their Dorchester and Exeter service operated (Fig. 34). One week Whiffen sent his waggon or waggons from Dorchester to London, paying all the expenses and keeping all the income from that journey; the next week Seager did the same, 'and so the waggons returne back from London to Dorchester aforesaid by turnes'. They had separate warehouses in Dorchester, though the same warehousekeeper in London. However, Whiffen and Seager were unusual in that they were genuine partners between Dorchester and Exeter: on that road they 'in partnership betweene them keep one wagon and eight horses which trant from Exeter to Dorchester and so back'. According to Whiffen, 'the charges of the horse-meate and other charges about the waggon on the roade travelling betweene Exeter and Dorchester … being commonly the same one journey as the other are paid equally betweene … Seager and this defendant'. Nevertheless, they were still responsible for alternate services: in their own week they paid the wages of 'the servants travelling with the said waggon', kept the horses at their own charge at Dorchester and retained the profits, 'without giving any accompt'. According to Seager the cost of servants was also shared, as well as the cost of a bookkeeper at Exeter, and the surplus of carriage money over costs was divided between them from time to time.[53]

34 *Henry Whiffen's answer in Chancery in 1690, explaining how he and Robert Seager organised their waggon service between London, Dorchester and Exeter. (C 5/67/33.)*

Whatever the case, sharing waggons and horses was extremely unusual, since it exposed carriers to potentially imprudent purchases of horses and provender by others. Only two other examples have been discovered: Arthur Goldring of Petersfield had a share in the Portsmouth waggons and horses in 1690, and John Goldring of Petersfield and Edward Jaques of Ripley jointly owned a waggon and horses serving Chichester in 1717.[54] Most waggon proprietors, covering relatively short distances, had no need for partners at all.

The evidence for miles covered per day is set out in Appendix 4. There were some impressive journeys, of up to 31 miles a day in the 17th century and 34 miles a day in the 18th. However, much of the evidence relates to exceptional services, such as Want's 31 miles per day from Devizes. Of the few carriers who advertised, some had a particular interest in passengers and therefore in speed. The Norwich waggons of the early 17th century were on the level roads of East Anglia; the Coventry waggon of 1675 may have been a coach-waggon; and some waggons in the 18th century may have been changing teams and travelling overnight, or at least stopping for fewer hours overnight.[55] From 1735 Appendix 4 is selective, omitting all flying waggons and therefore including only the slower services, which are more likely to have resembled those of the 17th century. Appendix 4 suggests that a typical day's journey in the 17th and early 18th centuries was 20 to 25 miles, though occasionally more. This is the same distance as for carts in the 14th century and for four-wheeled vehicles around Paris in the 15th,[56] reflecting the fact that it depended much more on the capabilities of the horse than on the quality of particular roads.

The theoretical maximum number of miles per week (with six-day weeks) was therefore 120 to 150 miles. Some evidence for actual miles per week can be assembled from Delaune's lists by analysing the numbers of partners in jointly-run services and services which were less than weekly. For example, two partners for 258 miles per week between Dorchester and London suggests 129 miles per week per team.[57] Of course partners and services were not always related in this way,[58] and Delaune sometimes omits partners, but there should be a clustering of services near the actual maximum mileage. In fact there was a reasonable number up to and including the 120s, though most were well below this, mileages in the 90s being the most common.[59] This was probably because waggon services tended to be relatively short-distance, and the potential number of miles was therefore limited except where more than one journey per week was possible. The inventory evidence indicates only two or three carriers with teams exceeding 105 miles per week.[60] Many waggon users must have needed other work to keep their horses fully employed. Probably 120-130 miles per week can be taken as the maximum for normal waggon loads and about 100 miles per week as typical.[61]

No direct evidence is available concerning miles per hour on the road, but 17th-century waggons are unlikely to have been faster than 19th-century ones. Russell's Exeter waggons in 1816-21 averaged just over 1.8 miles per hour (regardless of season), close to the two miles per hour used by one of the proprietors as a rule of thumb.[62] The speed was determined not by the state of the roads but by the speed at which waggon haulage was cheapest, and so the comparison is not affected by the improved state of the roads in the 19th century. On the other hand, Russell's waggons used relatively hilly roads, which did affect speed, so two miles per hour rather than 1.8 may well have been typical in the 17th century. On that basis, 20 to 25 miles per day took 10 to 13 hours, plus two hours or so in the middle for feeding the horses.

In winter, while the cheapest waggon speed remained the same, the poorer state of the roads meant that more horses were required to move the same loads at the same speeds. Different strategies were adopted in response. Team size could be increased, as in the cases of Barry and of a Newbury carrier in 1621 who used six horses in summer and seven in winter.[63] Or the same team size could be continued, as in Rothwell's case, presumably with reduced loads or slightly lower speeds. There is a small amount of evidence, all from the 18th century, of longer journey times in winter (Appendix 4), though the seasonal difference was much less than for stage-coaches.

The waggon proprietor wanting shorter journey times had several options. One was to use packhorses, as discussed later. Another was simply to work the teams more miles per day, as in Want's case, possibly with smaller loads. The third method, also discussed later, was the flying waggon. Flying waggons changed teams at intervals in order to travel throughout the night, but the first is not recorded until 1720.[64]

Carriers had to cope with variations in loading. Packhorse users were at first sight better off than waggon users in this respect, since they could simply add horses to their gangs, but they had exactly the same problem as waggon users in deciding whether to maintain horses which would be needed only occasionally or to rely on hiring them. Carriers sometimes carried for each other when loading was heavy, and Gilbert Stoughton of Kettering sent whole waggon-loads from London by a woad producer for whom such loads were back carriage.[65] Much more common was the hiring of teams or individual horses from farmers and others. Creditors of John Goldring, Portsmouth carrier, in 1717 included a yeoman of Catherington in Hampshire for a team for one journey from Portsmouth to London, a Liphook farmer for a team of six for one journey from Liphook to Portsmouth, a Petersfield grasier for use of a team several times and a Ripley butcher for use of a mare four times between Ripley and London. In 1689-91 Robert Seager of Dorchester, 'being sometimes overladen & haveing two great carriages for his owne horses to draw', borrowed horses from a yeoman of Winterbourne Monkton. According to the latter, between Trinity and Michaelmas 1689 he sent his waggon with six horses and a man nine times from Dorchester to Exeter, for which he reckoned he deserved 30s. per journey in addition to the cost of the provender. He later provided horses to help draw Seager's own waggons, for which he claimed 10s. per horse plus provender to Exeter and 15s. plus provender to London.[66] Occasional hiring of horses was undoubtedly cheaper than keeping more horses than were regularly required (the latter costing about 15s. per week per horse),[67] though it was necessary to own the horses which *were* regularly used in order to ensure the reliability of the service. The cost of such hirings and the availability of horses for hire at different times of the year must have had a considerable influence on the economics of carrying and the quality of service. Hiring of horses undoubtedly contributed to the high quality of service carriers by waggon were able to provide.

CHAPTER V

PACKHORSE OPERATION

Packhorses and their loads

Packhorses were smaller than waggon horses, and were drawn from the smaller breeds such as galloways, a name which tended to be applied to any horse under 14 hands.[1] According to Blundeville, writing in 1565 but setting out criteria which must also have applied a century later, purchasers looked for three things in a packhorse besides strength: 'first, that he be a good traveiler, secondlye, that his hoofes bee so good as he nede not to bee often shod, thirdlye that he be no unreasonable feader, for the avoyding of expences'. Markham emphasised a good stride, for 'he which takes the longest strides goes at the most ease and rids his ground fastest'.[2] The inventories suggest that, despite their smaller size, packhorses were only slightly less valuable than waggon horses (£4 13s. 0d. compared with £4 17s. 0d.) and were far more valuable than small horses in general.[3] The stock needed for a packhorse service was consequently much more valuable than that of a waggon service with similar capacity.

The inventories generally refer only to 'horses', but four are more informative, listing horses and mares, packhorses and mares and (twice) geldings and mares. Blundeville had argued that packmen generally used geldings, 'which lacking ye fervent heat that stoned horses have, cannot consume so much meate as they do, but chiefly perhaps because the gueldings are more easy to rule by the waye then horses'.[4] It was common in at least some other periods and other countries to place a mare at the front of the gang, which encouraged the others to follow, and this may also have been done in England.[5] There is no evidence of carriers using mules, despite their toughness, longevity and suitability for hilly areas.[6]

35 *Engraving of packhorses, from David Loggan's view of All Souls in* Oxonia illustrata *of 1675.*

36 *Yorkshire clothiers conveying cloth by pack-horse in the early 19th century (from George Walker,* The costume of Yorkshire *(1814)).*

In the 17th and 18th centuries the typical packhorse load was about 240 lb, or one horse-pack, though packs varied a little from one place to another; in Kendal they were 256 lb. This can be compared with the waggon horse's load of about 6 cwt, or 672 lb.[7] Presumably the size of packs had been determined by what a packhorse could bear.

The inventories provide a little information about packhorse equipment, which varied according to the type of loading. Pack saddles, hampers and pack cords are self-explanatory. Pack cloths were for protecting the goods, and so probably were surplices. 'Wantyes' were leather bands around the horse's belly, used to secure the pack, and 'garthes' (or girths or sursingles) were the part which passed around the horse's leg.[8] Loading packhorses, ensuring an evenly balanced load and that the goods did not harm the horse or each other, was clearly a skilled task. John Frost, Halifax carrier, had 'an olde ringe of bells', no doubt to warn approaching travellers and to help the horses follow each other, and Elizabeth Yeats, Kendal carrier, had a lantern, the only example found of artificial lighting.

There is nothing to suggest that the horses in a gang were tied together, and pictorial evidence indicates that they were not.[9] Even so, the driver might leave them at times to make their own way, as indicated by the following evidence given at the Old Bailey in 1752 by the driver of George Glover's Preston packhorses:

> I was the driver of these packhorses; my master and I set out on the 24th of July from Lad-lane; he left me at Islington and went back. When I came to Highgate, I had all my horses and packs; one horse carried a woman, and 15 with packs; I stopped and drank at the Wrestlers, and there told the horses over [i.e. counted them]; it was then dark and a rainy night. I turned them before me, and did not stay above five minutes after them, and kept with them all the way till I came about a quarter of a mile beyond Brown's Wells, sometimes on the side and sometimes behind them on foot. Near the six mile stone, but it was so dark I could not see it, in telling them over I found the bald mare with her halter about her feet, and no pack on. ... Then I got upon her and looked about backwards and forwards for almost an hour, but could not find any thing; then I rode on and over-took the rest of the horses on this side Barnet; I believe it was then betwixt 10 and 11.[10]

The most common collective term for packhorses, at least in northern England, was a gang, but there is one reference (from Kendal) to a 'gate' of packhorses. However, Samuel Whibben, Bristol carrier, had two 'drifts' of packhorses in 1714, and in 1718 the Derbyshire justices decided a horse bridge was needed at Alport ford for the 'great gangs of London carriers' horses, as well as great drifts of malt horses and other daily carriers and passengers'.[11] The largest gangs specifically recorded as such were of 20 horses from Frome and Wells in 1682 and Manchester in 1749, 21 from Wigan in 1757 and 22 from Lancaster and Preston in 1747.[12]

Inventories specify the number of horses for 20 of Delaune's packhorse users (Appendix 2).[13] For seven packhorse users travelling 152 or more miles to London (excluding the exceptional case of James Naylor),[14] the average number of horses available for each journey was 17, ranging from 12 at Kendal to 25 at Halifax. For seven carriers travelling between 105 and 146 miles to London, the average number of horses available per journey was lower, at nine. For the five short-distance packhorse users (from 30 to 54 miles to London) the average number of horses was only five.[15]

Using the 240 lb figure, average capacity was 36 cwt for the longer-distance packhorse services, 19 cwt for the intermediate ones and 11 cwt for the short-distance ones. There are not enough inventories for these figures to be wholly relied on, but there clearly was some relationship between length of journey and number of horses. On the other hand, any tidy relationship between distance

37 *The packhorse bridge at Thornthwaite, North Yorkshire. Most existing packhorse bridges date from between about 1660 and 1760, though there are some earlier ones. The survival of over a hundred of them appears to indicate an extensive network of packhorse carriage, but in fact they are virtually all across minor rivers and streams. The largely medieval bridges which served the London carriers were nearly all wide enough for wheeled vehicles.*

WHereas the Hereford and Monmouth Car-
riers have fuftain'd many Loffes by reafon of their Goods being
brought to their Inns, both in London and in the Country, fo late
that they were obliged to Travel much in the Night; to prevent fuch
Inconveniences for the future, this is to give Notice to all Gentlemen,
Tradefmen, and Others, that from and after the 2d Day of Dec.
1720, they will take in no Goods at London, but what fhall be brought
on Friday before 10 at Night, nor none at Hereford and Monmouth
but what fhall be brought before 6 on Monday Morning. Note, The
faid Carriers will not be accountable for any Money, Plate, Jewels, &c
that fhall be pack'd up in any Box or Parcel, without their Knowledge. Hereford Carriers Inns at the Saracen's Head in Friday-ftreet.
Nath. Drew, John Gibfon. Monmouth Carriers at the Bell in
Friday-ftreet. John Watkins, James Hughes,

38 *Advertisement by the Hereford and Monmouth carriers in 1720 requiring goods to be delivered to them by certain hours (making clear that it could be customers who caused delays). (Evening Post, 15 December 1720.)*

and capacity was disrupted by the varying amounts of loading at different places. Services at towns making cloth or other high-value items, such as Halifax, were obviously likely to have the greatest capacity. These two influences were of course themselves related: small places without much loading were more likely to have their own carrier the closer they were to London.

Packhorse operation

Like waggon operation, packhorse operation can be observed in detail in the accounts of carriers with their innkeepers. Two such accounts, relating to the same Exeter firm, have been discussed earlier.[16] Both demonstrate the extreme regularity of services, as well as the variation in the number of horses from week to week.

The other account relates to Nicholas Rothwell's Birmingham packhorses. They reached London every Wednesday night and set off on Thursday morning for 20 weeks in winter 1743-4 and 23 weeks in winter 1744-5, apart from being a day late once each winter. In summer they were replaced by the 'constant waggon'. Usually there were just two packhorses and a pony (a 'titt'), but a few times three or four packhorses (almost always in late December or early January). The journey took three days, so they covered 40 miles a day. An odd feature is the large rations they received – about as much oats as Rothwell's coach horses and more beans (Appendix 5). A possible reason is that Rothwell simply used a few of his coach horses, for a purpose for which they were not well suited but at less expense than buying and selling packhorses twice a year, and three out of four times the coach service ended and the packhorse service began, or vice versa, at exactly the same time.[17] It may have been common, especially in the 18th century, for waggon proprietors to operate just a few packhorses: in 1710 Richard Hales's Frome waggon business, with five waggon teams, included three packhorses, one of which was seized by a creditor when it 'was loaded at From to go for London'.[18]

Examples of miles per day covered by packhorses are set out in Appendix 4. They indicate a range from 33 miles per day from Exeter in 1722 to only 22 miles per day from Shrewsbury in the 1620s, apart from the 40 miles per day of the Birmingham packhorses in 1743-5. The miles per day, except for Birmingham, are similar to those in 14th- and 15th-century Burgundy (25 to 31 miles per day),[19] which suggests that this range was primarily determined by the packhorse's capabilities. The range overlapped that of waggons, the fastest waggons outpacing the slowest packhorses recorded, but packhorses were always faster *on the same roads*. For example, the 5½ days of John Barry's Exeter packhorses in 1722 compares with eight days up and six days down by his waggons (Fig. 39). Probably pack-horses were worked faster (and were

> ### JOHN BARRY,
> The *Exeter* Carrier from *London*,
> WHO for many Years past has Lodg'd at the *Saracene's-Head* in *Friday-street*, LONDON, has for a Twelve-month since been removed to the *Bell-Inn*, in the same Street; from whence he sets out with his PACK-HORSES every Saturday, and reaches EXETER every Friday following; and takes in Goods and Passengers for *Salisbury*, *Blandford*, *Dorchester*, or any other Places on the Road from *LONDON* to *EXON*, as also for any Part of *Devonshire* or *Cornwall*,
> Likewise, His WAGGON sets out from the aforesaid Inn every Monday Morning at Ten a-Clock, and arrives at *Exeter* every following Saturday, and carries Goods and Passengers to any of the Places above-mentioned.
> N. B. His Pack-Horses set out for *London*, from his Father's House, without *Southgate*, *Exon*, every Monday, and enter *London* every Saturday; and his Waggon, setting out every Friday, reaches *London* the Saturday of the following Week: Both which convey Goods or Passengers to the Towns before-named, or other Places on the Road.

39 *Advertisement by John Barry of Exeter for his packhorses and waggons, 1722, showing that his packhorses had shorter journey times than his waggons.* (Post-master, or, The Loyal Mercury, *20 July 1722.)*

more expensive to use) when competing with waggons for the more urgent goods than when providing the basic carrying service in areas without waggons, and this may account for the wide variation in packhorse charges noted earlier. Miles per hour are unknown: the only example – three miles per hour for packhorses (or carts) from Stamford to London in summer 1728 – is little use on its own because there is no way of knowing how typical it was and whether it depended on changes of horses, as the five miles per hour achieved by fish gangs from the south coast certainly did.[20]

How then were the rapid journeys of the Birmingham packhorses achieved? They are a unique example for the period covered here,[21] but were matched in earlier periods. In the 15th century Bristol packhorses reached London in three days (41 miles per day, compared with 31 in 1714) and Norwich packhorses did so in three days or just over (up to 37 miles per day).[22] Either more miles per hour or more hours per day were required, and little information is available about the trade-offs involved here, between the benefits of faster journeys (such as a higher rate of carriage) and disadvantages such as smaller loads, longer rest periods for the horses, larger rations and horses worn out more quickly, though Table 3 suggests a link between more miles per day and more rest days. Changes of horses would have been difficult to organise for a weekly service, but Rothwell could have stationed his horses in the middle of the route, with horses working out and back each week, so that they would have had to cover 40 miles per day on only two days a week.

Table 3. Packhorses' miles per week and rest days, 1680-1753

	Kendal 1680s	Bristol 1714	Hereford/ Monmouth 1720	Exeter 1722	Halifax 1725/Leeds 1729	Birmingham 1745	Lancaster 1753
Miles per working day	25-6	31	27-8	33	27-8	40	23
Days in cycle	28	14	14	21	21	14	28
Days work per cycle	20-20½	8	10	11	14	6	21
Days rest per cycle	7½-8	6	4	10	7	8	7
Rest days per 28 days	7½-8	12	8	13 ⅓	9 ⅓	16	7
Miles per week overall	132	122	133-8	121	128-31	120	120

Sources: see Appendix 4.

Notes: The length of cycles for Bristol, Hereford/Monmouth, Exeter and Birmingham are assumptions (but supported in the Hereford/Monmouth case by the fact that each firm had had two partners in the 1680s): longer or shorter cycles in each case would have resulted in improbable numbers of rest days or miles per week, with the latter far outside the 120-150 mile range. The Liverpool firm of 1753 also served Wigan and Lancaster, and it is assumed here that each gang went to Lancaster every journey, taking 1½ days each way between Liverpool and Lancaster. Sundays are included.

As for the horses' miles per week, the best indication can be obtained from Delaune's entries for carriers who were either in partnership or operating a less than weekly service, since this usually (though not always)[23] indicates how often each carrier's gang set off to London. The number of miles per week derived by this method ranges widely, but 42 of the 94 examples fall between 120 and 149 miles per week.[24] 120 to 150 miles per week therefore appears to have been typical, mileages in the 120s being the most common.

All the long- and intermediate-distance services covered by inventory evidence fell within the 120-150 mile range, apart from those of Chesterfield (152 miles) and Stroud (105 miles). However, none of the short-distance services exceeded 108 miles per week. Short distances to London must often have made it impossible to use the packhorses' labour to full effect in London carrying alone, and other horse-work probably had to be found. George Holder of Stroud (105 miles a week) also carried from Stroud to Bristol. Thomas Bass of Abbotsley (108 miles) also had a cart, which may have been used locally. Margaret Mussell of Horsham

(72 miles) and John Harrison, Chiddingstone carrier (30 miles), had substantial farms.[25] Packhorses would not have been ideal for heavy farm work, but perhaps the size of horses in these cases was a compromise.

Packhorses and waggons compared

Delaune provides two examples of carriers using both packhorses and waggons – at Ashbourne in 1681 and Cambridge in 1690, and a partnership at Lincoln in 1690, for which Delaune does not indicate the type of carriage, included both a packhorse user and a waggon user.[26] More examples are available in the following century: firms at Exeter from 1707 to 1739, Frome in 1710 and 1737, Bristol in 1714 (with two drifts of packhorses and two waggon teams – Fig. 40), Boston in 1737, Sherborne and Yeovil in 1739, Warwick and Birmingham in 1743-5 and Chester at some time in the first half of the century. A local carrier between Taunton and Exeter was using both in 1727.[27] As already indicated, some waggon firms, such as those serving Frome in 1710 and Birmingham in 1743-5, kept just a few packhorses.

Equally significant is that almost every county in 1681 and 1690 had both types of service to London (Map 7), the exceptions being a few with only waggons (Norfolk in 1681; Hampshire and Berkshire in 1690) and a few with only packhorses (Yorkshire, Lancashire and Herefordshire at both dates). Also, many towns and cities had both types of service. Even in Lancashire, waggons were specially organised between London and Standish in summer in the war years of 1689-95 and 1702.[28] The last London packhorses recorded, in 1758, were not at some remote town with execrable roads but at Bristol, which had had waggons to London for at least a century and which had a wholly turnpiked road to

40 *Extract from the relatively detailed probate inventory of Samuel Whibben, Bristol carrier (but living just outside the city at Barton Regis), of 1714, recording his ownership of both packhorses and waggons. (PROB 3/18/131.)*

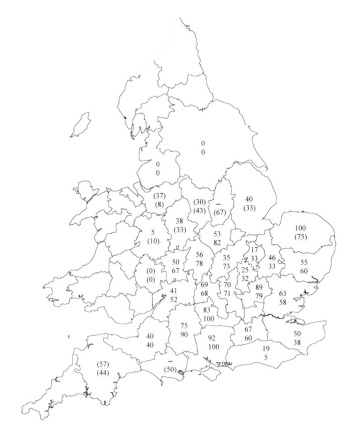

Map 7 *Proportions of services by waggon in each county, 1681 and 1690. The overall figure at both dates was 55%. The upper figures relate to 1681, the lower to 1690. Uncertain cases are excluded. Figures are in brackets where they relate to fewer than five services; no figure is given where there were fewer than two. (Sources: Delaune 1681, 1690.)*

London.[29] There are even examples in the late 17th century of carriers changing from waggons to packhorses: Roger Hurst, Norwich carrier, did so between 1681 and 1690 (though he perhaps used both in 1690), and so did a St Ives carrier in the mid-1690s.[30] If packhorses were really as inefficient a method of carriage as has usually been claimed, surviving only because waggons were incapable of passing along the roads (especially in winter), packhorse services should have disappeared wherever waggon carriage was possible.[31]

Waggons had several clear advantages: they could carry larger objects;[32] they could carry objects varying in size and weight without these having to be made up into packs of similar weight;[33] they could carry passengers more easily; they provided greater protection from the weather; waggon horses could more easily be switched between carrying and farm work than packhorses; and less capital was required for a waggon and team than for a gang of packhorses of equal capacity.[34] Above all, horses could draw a greater load in a vehicle than they could carry on their backs – based on the figures of 6 cwt (672 lb) per waggon horse and 240 lb per packhorse, nearly three times as much,[35] though these figures obviously varied according to the quality of roads and horses.

However, the comparison of weights is misleading, for three reasons. First, the comparison is not of like with like: as already discussed, packhorses tended to be smaller horses, and they consequently required less feed (Appendix 5).

Secondly, packhorses tended to cover more miles per week – a maximum of about 150 compared with 120, or a typical 125 compared with 100.[36] Thirdly, the packhorse was much less seriously affected than the waggon horse by poor roads and especially by hills, which could reduce and even eliminate the difference in capacity.[37] Fourthly, packhorses usually travelled faster than waggons (typically 25-33 miles per day compared with 20-25),[38] which meant that a higher price (around a fifth to a third higher)[39] could be charged for a superior service. Other advantages were that packhorses could be used where there was insufficient loading for waggons, that the cost of waggons and waggon repairs was saved and that packhorses did not give rise to trouble from informers over illegal team sizes.

A rough cost breakdown can be assembled based on the Oxford waggon's costs discussed above, adjusted to reflect the costs of conveying the same loads by packhorse (Table 4). It obviously provides only an illustration, since the comparison will have varied from road to road and depends on a number of assumptions. On the basis of Table 4, it cost almost 50 per cent more to convey a given weight by packhorse than by waggon. This was more than the extra price which could be charged for packhorse carriage, but the comparison is highly sensitive to the assumptions made, especially concerning the differences in loads and provender consumption. For example, substituting the 256 lb of a Kendal pack for the 240 lb used in the comparison reduces the cost differential to 40 per cent. Also,

Table 4. Costs of waggons and packhorses compared

Cost	By waggon (%)	Adjustments	By packhorse (conjectural)	%
Provender	68.6	x 2.8 x 0.8 x 0.71	109.1	73.4
Harness & shoeing	7.1	x 2.8 x 0.8	15.9	10.7
Depreciation of horses	2.3	x 2.8 x 0.8	5.2	3.5
Horsekeepers	3.4	x 2.8 x 0.8	7.6	5.1
Drivers	6.2		6.2	4.2
Bookkeepers & porters	3.7		3.7	2.5
Waggons	7.8	x 0	0	0
Rent	0.9		0.9	0.6
Total	100.0		148.6	100

Source for waggon percentages: Fig. 29.

Notes: Costs have been added to those in Fig. 29 as indicated in the notes to chapter 4 to produce the waggon percentages. Assumptions are: that each waggon horse conveyed 2.8 times as much loading as a packhorse, that packhorses could cover 150 miles per week compared with the waggon team's 120, that packhorses cost only 71% as much to feed as waggon horses, that spending per horse on harness and pack saddles was comparable, and that depreciation per horse and spending on shoeing per horse and on drivers per ton carried was comparable in the two cases. As regards provender, there was great variation among waggon horses (Appendix 5); here the comparison is between Barry's packhorses and Hales's waggon horses.

packhorses probably conveyed the majority of the small parcels, for which the justices sometimes specified disproportionately high rates of carriage.

Clearly the merits of packhorses and waggons could be finely balanced, and they were to some extent complementary, one being relatively fast and the other relatively cheap. Hence the decision by some carriers to use both, or to keep a few packhorses for urgent goods. However, the differences in cost and speed were not enormous, and packhorse carriage was probably cheaper on some roads than waggons would have been. On the basis of Table 4, the waggon lost its cost advantage completely if bad roads reduced the loading per waggon horse from 2.8 to 1.8 packhorse loads. Another conclusion is that Delaune's lists probably include two types of packhorse user: users by necessity, because of poor roads or insufficient loading for a waggon, and users by choice, because of the packhorse's greater speed. The latter were likely to provide faster services, as the Bristol, Exeter and Birmingham examples in Table 3 suggest.

Some attempt can be made to explain the geographical variation shown in Map 7. The quality of roads was certainly significant, mainly through the effect of bad roads on the economics of waggon carriage, by increasing the draught required and ruling out use of the most powerful waggon horses,[40] rather than by physically preventing the use of waggons, although the latter may sometimes have been the case in northern England. Level roads in East Anglia clearly contributed to the importance of waggons there, whereas hills and also high rainfall (hence muddy roads) in the north and the Welsh Marches and clay soils in Sussex contributed to the rarity of waggons there. However, road quality was only one of the factors. Inadequate loading probably accounts for many of the short-distance packhorse services, and counties with many services from small towns, such as Kent, tended to have a smaller proportion of waggon services than those with services mainly from substantial towns, such as Wiltshire. The types of loading may have been influential, waggons tending to be used for goods which were bulky (probably including barrels of imported wine in Hampshire), were awkwardly shaped for packhorses (butter from Cambridgeshire), needed weatherproof carriage (broadcloth in Wiltshire), or were of relatively low value (grain and malt from Hertfordshire), and packhorses tending to be used for goods which were of high value (cloth from Yorkshire and Devon) or perishable. The packhorse's greater speed was more important for long journeys than short ones.[41] The relationship between carrying and farming was probably also significant, short-distance carriers often needing farm work to keep their horses fully employed (and therefore being more likely to use waggons), and predominantly pastoral areas having less farm work to employ draught horses than arable areas did. In the 18th century this complex balance of advantages and disadvantages was swept away as the advantage shifted decisively towards waggons in all areas.

CHAPTER VI

THE DEVELOPMENT OF CARRYING

Whereas there may have been little to distinguish the carriers of 1650-1750 from those of the 15th century, except the replacement of carts by waggons, from the mid-18th century the carrying trade changed significantly, becoming both larger and more efficient. Increased efficiency resulted partly from better roads but also from better horses, larger firms and new ways of reducing journey times.[1] To what extent were these influences operating before 1750 and beginning to affect rates of carriage and journey times?

Turnpikes, better horses and larger firms

The most easily examined change is the spread of turnpiking, which increased from 12 per cent of a sample of major London routes in 1714 to 55 per cent in 1730 and 71 per cent in 1750,[2] though its impact on road users is much harder to identify. The speed of carrying services was determined by the speed at which horse-drawn carriage was cheapest rather than the quality of the roads. Carriers virtually never sought to provide greater speed at the higher cost which would have been necessary, and there is no evidence in any period of turnpikes causing carriers to increase the travelling speed of their waggons.[3] Instead, the main impact of better roads should be looked for in terms of increased loads per horse and consequently lower rates of carriage, though improved roads were not the only cause of this. Tolls were probably a relatively small cost: even in the 19th century, they formed only from 8 to 16 per cent of carriers' total costs.[4]

In 1730 waggons from Colchester to London, on a fully turnpiked road, were said to be drawn by six horses and to carry 80 to 90 cwt of cloth, indicating 13 to 15 cwt per horse, far more than the typical 6 cwt of the 17th century. However, this was on the road Defoe regarded as the best in England, and such weights per horse were not usual in southern England until the 1830s. Typical loads in the 1750s and 1760s appear to have been 8 to 10 cwt per waggon horse, an increase of between a third and two-thirds since the 17th century, but there is no direct evidence from before 1750.[5] Legislation of 1742 laid down prohibitive tolls if loading and waggon together exceeded three tons, which, assuming teams of six and waggons weighing about a ton, indicates $6\frac{2}{3}$ cwt per horse, but how this related to actual loads carried is unclear. There is no evidence before 1750

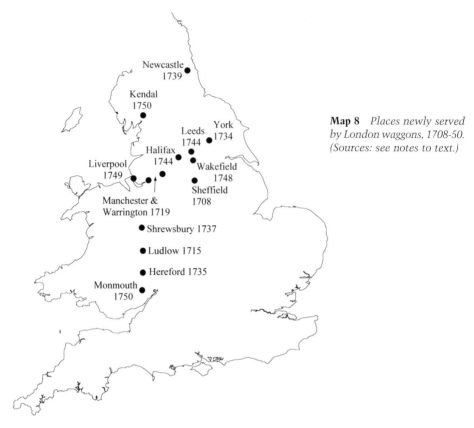

Newcastle
1739

Kendal
1750

Leeds   York
1744   1734

Halifax
1744

Liverpool
1749   Wakefield
                    1748

Manchester &   Sheffield
Warrington 1719   1708

● Shrewsbury 1737

● Ludlow 1715

● Hereford 1735

Monmouth
1750

Map 8 *Places newly served by London waggons, 1708-50. (Sources: see notes to text.)*

of increased use of horses in double file, as occurred with the wider roads and larger waggons of the 1750s.[6]

In so far as they increased the load per waggon horse, turnpikes would have increased the advantages of waggons relative to packhorses, and there is evidence of packhorse services disappearing and waggon services spreading to new places in the first half of the 18th century, though in the case of Newcastle upon Tyne the high rate of carriage suggests that the advantage of waggons there was at first very limited (Appendix 3). The new waggon services are shown on Map 8.[7] However, some of these examples are too early for turnpiking to have had much impact, and in the West Country packhorses disappeared completely from London carrying in advance of any turnpiking, so there were clearly other influences at work too.[8]

One such influence was probably better waggon horses, needing less provender and having greater strength. This is the most difficult change to assess, but a clue is provided by Rothwell's provender account in the 1740s. The ration of oats per horse was considerably less than for any of the waggon horses in earlier accounts, though more beans were given (Appendix 5); the overall saving on provender (at constant prices) was about a quarter.[9] However, it would be unwise to make too much of a single example. As for greater strength, there is no direct evidence. Nevertheless, better waggon horses could well have been the major cause of the spread of waggon services, at least until the 1740s or 1750s.[10]

Larger firms were important for several reasons: they were likely to be able to make better use of capacity and they could take in hand activities hitherto contracted out, such as smiths' and wheelers' work and the purchase of provender. The latter cut out an innkeeper's margin of perhaps 40 per cent, at the cost of exposing the carrier more directly to fluctuations in provender prices.[11] The only inventory recording stock for smiths in the 17th century is that of Andrew Hart of Cambridge, who was both carrier and coachmaster (with 34 horses), whereas in the 19th century it was common for carriers to employ their own smiths and wheelers.[12]

Growth in loading overall helped firms to become larger,[13] but the disappearance of smaller firms and mergers and takeovers were also important. Delaune's lists indicate some disappearances between 1681 and 1690, at places such as Ledbury which never again had their own London carriers. Such disappearances were sometimes connected with the death of the proprietor, as at Abbotsley and Cokethorpe. As for takeovers, in 1710 Abraham Clavey, Wells carrier, purchased the nearby Frome firm and Roger Bird the younger, Andover carrier, purchased the Trowbridge firm.[14]

However, bringing firms into single ownership did not necessarily result in merger. In about 1688 Richard Rogers, Leominster carrier, married Jane Miles, widow of a Ludlow carrier. In 1690 Rogers was listed as sole proprietor of both the Leominster and Ludlow firms, but his wife continued to manage the firm at Ludlow, and apparently travelled to London fortnightly. Her children later claimed that Rogers seldom came to Ludlow,

Preservation of public Roads. A Petition of the several Merchants and Tradesmen of and within the City of *York*, whose Names are thereunto subscribed, was presented to the House, and read; setting forth, That the Petitioners have, for several Years past, experienced the great Advantage, in their way of Trade, of Stage Waggons from that City to *London*, and so back again, which go and return every Week; whereby the several heavy and cumbersome Commodities the Petitioners deal in, are, with great Security and Certainty, brought and carried to and from *York* to *London* without any Loss, Damage, or Delay; which Advantage to the Petitioners, as well as to the Trade in general in this Part of the Kingdom, would be greatly disturbed and incommoded, in case any Restraint, beyond what the Laws now in being have provided, should be laid upon the Waggons, as to the Number of Horses necessarily employed in the conveying of those heavy Goods, which the Necessity of the Petitioners several Trades requires, and more especially at this time, when the Difficulties and Dangers of bringing those Goods by Sea are so very great, that, without a Convoy, the Petitioners cannot hazard so considerable a Property; and which they, in order to have the Security of, have of late been frequently obliged to wait several Months for, although their Merchandize and Goods have been as long shipped, and thereby daily perishing; and that as the Waggons for the Conveyance of such Goods are obliged to be made, to answer such Purposes, very substantial and strong, the very Draft whereof, when empty, is sufficient for, and is as much as, Two Horses can well draw; therefore, if the Number of Horses was to be confined to less than Three or Four, more than sufficient to draw the said Waggons when empty, the small Quantity of Goods, to be brought by such Waggons, could not possibly defray the Expence of the Waggoner; who therefore must necessarily be obliged to lay down his Waggon; whereby the Petitioners, and the Consumers of those Goods they severally deal in, will, by the Increase of the Price of such their Commodities, through the Scarcity and Hazard of removing them, as in Times of Peace, be greatly injured, and Trade in general greatly suffer thereby: And therefore praying, That the House will take the Premises into Consideration, as not so far to restrain the Waggoners in their Carriage of Goods, as may either totally oblige them to desist from further carrying the same, or else, by increasing the Rate of Carriage, load those Goods with Charges insupportable either by the Merchant or the Consumer.

Ordered, That the said Petition do lie upon the Table.

41 *A petition to the House of Commons from York merchants and tradesmen in 1744, referring to the advantage gained 'for several years past' from waggons, pointing out the difficulty and danger of carriage by sea in war-time and objecting to a proposed reduction in the permitted size of teams. (House of Commons Journals, vol. 24, 1741-45, p. 798.)*

but [he] continued the same imploye from Leominster to London as formerly he had done onely they and theire respective gangs of horses and wagons severally mett as they went for London in ye Cytty of Worcester, but kept distinct innes warehouses and lodgeings in London, the sayd [Rogers] not at all takeing or demanding any account of the said Jane and her servants.

42 *The Great House, Corve Street, Ludlow, from which Jane Rogers and then Richard Rogers operated a packhorse service to London from 1688 to 1714. The house continued to be occupied by carriers until 1780. There was a warehouse in the yard behind, and a shop and carriage office on the right run by one of Jane Rogers' daughters.*

They added that if Jane had not continued as a carrier she would have starved, as Rogers would not allow her any other maintenance. Upon Jane's death in about 1701, Rogers took over the Ludlow firm, but one of his stepdaughters 'tooke care of his whole concerne of Ludlow carryadge and sometimes went along with his carryadges to Worcester & often to London', accounting fortnightly. This ended after a quarrel with Rogers' new wife four years later.[15] In this case both Ludlow and Leominster retained their own carrying firms until the 19th century.[16] The probable reason is that towns valued having their own carrier, who could be spoken to regularly and who could be relied on to give their goods priority rather than favouring goods from a destination further from London because they paid better. In the 18th and 19th centuries this preference would gradually be overridden, at least on the longer routes, as carrying firms

> CLAVEY's Flying FROOME Waggon
>
> SETS out with Goods and Paffengers from *Froome*
> for *London*, every *Monday* at One o'Clock in the
> Morning, and will be at the *King's-Arms* Inn at
> *Holborn-Bridge* the *Wednefday* following, by Twelve
> o'Clock, at Noon ; from whence it will continue to
> fet out for *Froome*, and Parts adjacent, every *Wednefday*
> Night at Twelve o'Clock, and will be there on *Sa-*
> *turday* by Twelve at Noon.
>
> And whereas the Difficulty of getting Horfes at
> *Froome* has been frequently found inconvenient for
> Paffengers, who come down in this Waggon, and
> want to go farther than *Froome* ; for the future all
> fuch Perfons may be fure of being fupply'd with able
> Horfes at the moft reafonable Rates to go to any place
> beyond the faid Stage, by the Proprietor of the faid
> Flying-Waggon ; and all Paffengers may depend upon
> being well accommodated at the *Bell* Inn in *Froome*.
> N.B. *The other Waggons keep their Stages as ufual.*
> Attendance is conftantly given at the *King's-Arms*
> aforefaid, to take in Goods and Paffengers Names ;
> but no Money, Plate, Bank Notes, or Jewels, will be
> infured, unlefs delivered as fuch.
>
> *Perform'd, if God permit, by Abr. Clavey.*

43 *Advertisement for Abraham Clavey's flying waggons between Frome and London, 1737. (Sherborne Mercury, 21 June 1737.)*

72

increasingly achieved economies of scale, but in the first half of the 18th century significant reductions in the number of firms occurred in only a few areas, notably Cambridgeshire and Northamptonshire (from 18 to nine firms and from 24 to nine firms respectively between 1705 and 1738) and Devon and Dorset (from 12 firms in 1705 to four in 1738 and two in 1765). In the latter area the declining number did result in one exceptionally large firm – that of William Iliff, Exeter carrier, with 128 horses in 15 teams in 1747. Overall, the number of London carrying firms remained almost constant while the number (as well as capacity) of London carrying services increased, from about 345 per week covering 20 or more miles in 1681-90 to 420 in 1738 and 490 in 1765.[17]

Flying waggons

The other cause of increased efficiency was the flying waggon, which provided greater than packhorse speed at waggon cost, and thereby contributed to the replacement of packhorses. Although waggon services were spreading to new places in the first half of the 18th century, introduction of waggons did not necessarily mean the disappearance of packhorses. Some packhorse services continued into the 1740s and 1750s (Map 9).[18] Some of these, especially in northern England, were large gangs; others were just a few packhorses supplementing a waggon service.[19] When the shorter-distance packhorse services disappeared is unknown.

Map 9   *The last references to London packhorse services, 1737-58 (Sources: see notes to text.)*

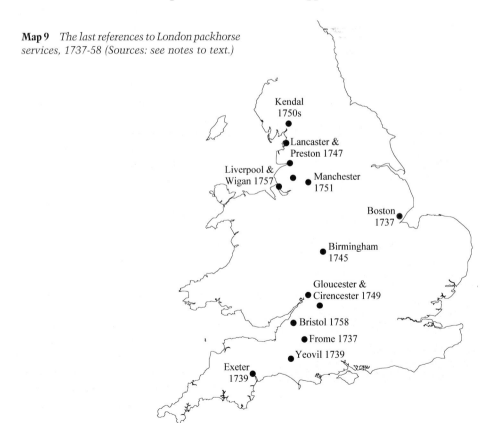

Several different processes caused the disappearance of packhorses. Better roads and better waggon horses improved the economics of waggon carriage relative to packhorse carriage. Recalling the distinction made earlier, packhorse users by necessity must gradually have abandoned packhorses as roads were improved and as the smaller firms disappeared or grew. But for packhorse users by choice, more was needed: they had to replicate the packhorse's greater speed. What made this possible was the flying waggon, which changed teams at intervals and travelled all night, although there were occasionally so-called flying waggons which merely shortened their overnight stops.[20] The first overnight services (other than packhorses carrying fish) were probably waggons or carts from Northamptonshire carrying venison, possibly as early as 1708. The first flying waggons specifically described as such served Northampton in 1720. The next were from Frome in 1737 and Bath in 1738.[21] At these places, together with Norwich, goods transport tended to be fast, due to the requirements of those sending venison, broadcloth, gentlemen's goods and worsted respectively, whereas in some areas, such as Shropshire, it tended to be slow.

The Northampton flying waggon (in summer only) took two days for 67 miles, leaving Northampton at 5 a.m. Allowing time for feeding the horses it may have run all night, though it could possibly have stopped for a few hours at night. However, the times specified for the Frome flying waggons in 1737-9, indicating 42 to 46 miles per day (more than the 39 miles per day of the Exeter flying waggons in the early 19th century),[22] leave no doubt that they ran all night. Other places listed in 1738 as having waggons travelling overnight (and therefore probably with flying waggons) were Cirencester, Tetbury, Buckinghamshire and Frimley, and there were flying waggons to London from Derby by 1742, Birmingham and Leicester by 1743 and Salisbury by 1750; advertised times suggest flying waggons also to Stamford in 1743 and Wakefield and York in 1748.[23]

At first flying waggons seem to have replaced packhorses only in summer, as on the Frome route in 1737-44 and the Birmingham route in 1743-5. Waggons

THIS gives Notice to all Merchants, Shopkeepers, and others, that the *London* Carrier Warehouse for the Reception and Delivery of Goods to and from Thence, is kept at *Thomas Butterworth's*, at the Sign of the *Griffin*, on the back of the Shambles in *Leeds*; where constant Attendance is given for Mr. *Samuel Fenton*, Mr. *Samuel Haggas*, and Mr. *Matthew Lee*; one of whom goes out every Wednesday, and another returns every Friday. N. B. All Goods and Merchandizes are carried with great safety, and cheaper than by any other Carrier to and from *London*, *York*, *Newcastle*, *Richmond*, *Rippon*, *Beedal*, *Bradford*, *Skipton*, *Otley* and other Places adjacent. They also receive and deliver Goods for *Nottingham*, *Leicester*, *Northampton* and other Road Towns, and go to the *White Horse* without *Cripplegate*, *London*, every Wednesday, and comes out on Friday following.

44 *Advertisement by the packhorse carriers of Leeds in 1729. (Leeds Mercury, 5 August 1729.)*

running overnight (but not waggons as such) do seem to have required better roads to operate all year, perhaps because of the danger of traversing ill-maintained roads in darkness. Once flying waggons could travel all year there was no further need for packhorses. Cirencester's flying waggons were summer only in 1748-9, but all year in 1750-1, this change coinciding with the last mention of Cirencester's packhorses in 1749, and the directory which last recorded packhorses from Bristol in 1758 listed flying waggons from Bristol in 1760.[24] Customers could then use a service faster than packhorses had been at a rate not much above the old waggon rate.[25]

London carrying transformed

Defoe claimed in the 1720s that, as a result of turnpiking, rates of carriage were 'abated in some places, 6d. per hundred weight, in some places 12d. per hundred', and there perhaps were reduced rates on the Essex road, but there is no confirmation of this.[26] Despite claims that the justices' rates demonstrate the effectiveness of turnpikes in the first half of the 18th century,[27] none of the justices' rates so far located were reduced until 1743 (except that for the North Riding, cut from an unreasonably high level by 1726 and then unchanged for at least 25 years), and only two by 1750 (Northamptonshire and the West Riding), while in three counties (Holland in Lincolnshire, Shropshire and Somerset) the rates had increased by 1750 (Appendix 3). In the West Riding the separate winter rate was reduced significantly in 1744 and abolished in 1745, and the all-year rate was cut substantially in 1750, albeit to a level common elsewhere much earlier. Here the reduction may have reflected the replacement of packhorses by waggons (and in turn the improvement of roads around Leeds in the 1740s),[28] bringing reductions in rates of carriage not available in areas already using waggons.

In the 1750s, unlike the 1740s, the evidence for increased efficiency resulting in lower rates of carriage becomes plentiful, with at least nine counties reducing rates of carriage, despite a small rise in the cost of inputs such as provender since the 1730s.[29] In the Leeds to London case, between about 1700 and 1838 the cost of carriage fell to about 31 per cent of what it would have been but for productivity improvements in the intervening period, and by far the greatest growth in productivity took place in the 1740s and 1750s. Leeds to London may have been an extreme case, but evidence for other routes suggests the cost of carriage there fell between the 1690s and 1830s to about 44 per cent of what it would otherwise have been.[30] One consequence was that, except over the shortest distances, casual carrying largely disappeared, and regular, professional carriers virtually monopolised road transport. London carrying firms became much larger.[31] From the 1750s the carrying trade continued on a trend of rising productivity and (despite the creation of a canal network) growth in the number of London services – from about 420 in 1738 to 490 in 1765 and 1,095 in 1838.[32] However, judging by the justices' rates, together with the timing of the disappearance of packhorses, the crucial period, with the greatest growth in productivity, was the late 1740s to the 1760s. As more rivers were made navigable and canals were built, road transport increasingly specialised in what it was best at, and it came to serve those needing rapid conveyance of high-value, low-weight items more effectively than ever.

PART TWO

STAGE-COACHES

CHAPTER VII

THE STAGE-COACH NETWORK
AND ITS ORIGINS

The network in 1681-90

Stage-coaching, unlike carrying, was a fairly new industry in the 1680s, when Delaune provides the first overall view of the network, but it was already a substantial one. Delaune lists about 130 coachmasters at each date, providing about 410 services a week. However, there are certainly some omissions from his lists, as discussed in Appendix 1, and the number of services was probably somewhere between 450 and 480, employing about 1,450 horses,[1] at least in summer (many coaches were less frequent in winter). Short-distance services, often running daily, were predominant (Map 10), much more so than in carrying. There were only about 25 to 28 services per week extending beyond 130 miles, though they accounted for a significant proportion of the miles per week. The furthest places served directly were Exeter, Chester and York, but there were linked services from York to Newcastle (weekly) and Edinburgh (fortnightly).[2] In London the stage-coaches' inns were in or close to the City or in Southwark, apart from a few at Charing Cross.

Only a few counties (other than the most distant) lacked London coach services of their own (Map 10). In practice, coach passengers usually had to ride horses to reach their final destination anyway, and coaches consequently served areas well beyond their terminus. When Adam Ottley wished to travel from London to Pitchford in Shropshire in 1725 and found the Worcester coach fully booked,

45 *Engraving of a coach from David Loggan's view of All Souls in* Oxonia illustrata *of 1675. This was possibly a stage-coach, since it is undecorated and in 1669 the first flying coach departed from outside All Souls, but even if not it probably differed little from a stage-coach. Note the driver with both reins and whip and the postilion.*

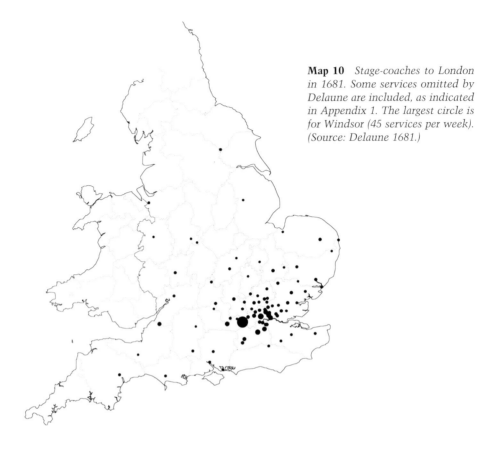

Map 10 *Stage-coaches to London in 1681. Some services omitted by Delaune are included, as indicated in Appendix 1. The largest circle is for Windsor (45 services per week). (Source: Delaune 1681.)*

he took the Lichfield coach instead and continued from Lichfield on his own horses.[3] There were few if any provincial services until about 1700.

Few places had more than a single coach firm, and fewer still more than two, although sometimes there were both a town's own coaches and others passing through. Six places in 1681 and eight in 1690 had three firms, and only Windsor in 1681 with nine and Oxford in 1690 with five exceeded this. The only places over 100 miles from London with competing services at both dates were Bristol, Worcester and Norwich.

Before the stage-coaches

Hackney coaches existed by the mid-1620s,[4] long before the first stage-coaches, for hire both within London and for longer journeys. Stage-coaches differed from these in two main ways: they had regular schedules along fixed routes, and passengers shared them with strangers. However, these were characteristics not only of the stage-coaches but also of the coach-waggons or waggon-coaches which had plied England's roads since the 16th century and a few of which still operated in the 1680s. These coach-waggons were an important precursor of the stage-coach, providing the first public passenger services operating over long distances to regular schedules, and therefore demand some attention here.

As already discussed, carriers began using four-wheeled waggons in the 1560s and these became widespread in the 1610s. The fact that their use at first spread only slowly and only to large towns suggests that initially their main advantage over two-wheeled carts was that, being less likely to overturn, they were more suitable for passengers.[5] Probably only a minority would have been described as coach-waggons, but there are certainly many references to waggons conveying passengers in the early 17th century. For example, an Oxford waggon had eight passengers when robbed in 1613. Most of the passengers in Thomas Hobson of Cambridge's waggons in the 1620s were said to be 'schollers, woemen, or children', and in 1617 Fynes Moryson claimed that, because of the long hours per day, 'none but women and people of inferiour condition, or strangers (as Flemmings with their wives and servants) use to travell in this sort', though there were also some better-off travellers by waggon.[6]

John Cressett, an opponent of stage-coaches, described the coach-waggons or 'long coaches' as follows in 1672 (probably referring to York, Exeter and Chester only because he was seeking to make comparisons with the stage-coaches to those places):

> The first stage-coaches were long coaches in the middle of the waggons, that travelled with their horses one before another, about 20 or 25 miles a day, were a week or eight dayes going to York, Exeter, and Chester, and so proportionably to the other stages. These travelled easy, carried sick and antient people, journeys suitable to their strength, and were not above one to a place, in one week, so did no great hurt.[7]

They had from four to six horses, harnessed 'one before another' rather than in pairs, and carried 20 to 25 people.[8] In other words they were operated in a similar way to waggons, and at similar speeds. Coach-waggon fares were little or no different from waggon fares (Appendix 10).

What then turned a waggon into a coach-waggon? There was sufficient difference in the vehicle for the appraisors of the goods of Henry Warren of Stamford in 1681 to distinguish between his 'long wagons' and his 'coach wagons'.[9] Probably a coach-waggon was basically a waggon but had some physical adaptation, such as seats,[10] and travelled at the upper end of the range of miles per day by waggon. There may sometimes have been a separate compartment for passengers, since in 1657 Mr Martin, proprietor of a 'wagon coach' from Ipswich, stated that 'each passenger payes in the coach 10 shillings, and 8 shillings behind' (Fig. 48). Probably the vehicles varied in character, as suggested below.[11]

The main difference between the coach-waggon and the stage-coach was the latter's greater speed, dependent on changes of horses (at least in summer) and on carrying relatively few passengers. Changes of horses were crucial. The horses had to be compensated for higher speed by reduced loads, reduced miles per week, shorter stages or a combination of these. Consequently stage-coaches charged more – typically 2.4 pence per mile, compared with 1.2 to 1.7 pence per mile for coach-waggons in the 1650s (Appendix 10).

Stage-coaches and coach-waggons can be distinguished by their speeds and fares, but not always by the terms used for them. 'Coach' is a Hungarian word, originally referring to an unsprung four-wheeled vehicle whose body rested directly on its axles,[12] and, appropriately, it was used in England for the unsprung coach-waggon before it was applied to the stage-coach. Even after the introduction of the stage-coach some people long continued to describe the coach-waggons as coaches. In 1657, for example, advertisements for stage-coaches and coach-waggons were mixed together under the heading 'Coaches' in the *Publick Adviser* (Fig. 48). In 1681, whereas both Henry Warren's appraisors and Delaune recorded his coach-waggons, Warren himself referred in his will to his 'horses waggons and coaches'. The Newcastle-under-Lyme and Coventry coach-waggons were both described as coaches in the late 17th century.[13]

Consequently, not all references to 'coaches' can be taken as meaning stage-coaches. For example, the origins of stage-coaching have sometimes been dated to 1629 on the basis of the following letter sent from Cambridge to Sir John Coke in December 1629:

> Your son had order given in his letter to come in the coach, which he had no mind to do, partly by reason of the tedious and wearisomeness of the passage, sitting from 5 in the morning till almost nine at night, plunging in the cold and dirt and dark, and that for two whole days with strange company, and partly because he might have the company otherwise of some of his acquaintance, fellow commoners of our own college, and the carrier to lend them horses [to] go along with them and direct them all the best way, and so be but half the time that he should have been in the coach.[14]

The reference to 'strange company' indicates a public conveyance. However, the times stated (about 29 hours in total)[15] for a 57-mile journey make clear that the vehicle was a coach-waggon rather than a stage-coach, travelling at about two miles per hour.

The same is probably true of the other references to coaches prior to the Civil Wars. In April 1630 the university authorities required of Thomas James of Cambridge, carrier, that he and his servants 'take not into their waggons or coaches any persons comeing or to come from London to Cambridge' unless such persons had certificates of being clear of plague. In September 1636 the Mayor's Court of Norwich forbade Nicholas Sotherton from sending his 'carts waggons or coaches' to London until further notice because of the plague (John Sotherton of Norwich advertised a 'waggon coach' from Norwich in 1657).[16] John Taylor in his *Carriers cosmographie* of 1637 refers to 'the waggons or coaches from Cambridge', 'the waggon, or coach' from Hertford, 'the waggon or coach' from Hatfield and, less equivocally, 'a coach' from St Albans, but this is insufficient evidence on its own for a stage-coach to St Albans or the other places in 1637. No change of horses was needed for St Albans (22 miles), and vehicles more like stage-coaches than coach-waggons might have been used, but services of this sort could have maintained stage-coach speeds only for the distance a single team could cover – at most about 30 miles. The *Brief Director* of about 1643, largely copied from Taylor, converts his 'waggon or coach' entries to coaches and adds a coach from Stamford, a 'coach and waggon' from Newark (which had coach-waggons but not stage-coaches in 1681) and 'a coach and waggon' from Epsom Wells. The 'Alsberry coach' is mentioned in 1652.[17]

It is possible that some of the vehicles used resembled the stage-coaches, and even had horses harnessed in double file, but were in other respects operated like waggons, without changes of horses. Cressett argued that the first stage-coachmen had developed their services in two stages:

These gentlemen, finding the coaches [i.e. coach-waggons] set up, took the advantage of the late troubles, and when mens horses were taken from them, so that they had not to carry them their journeys, set up these coaches that go with horses two a breast, and for many years travell'd with four horses in a coach, and went to York, Exeter, and Chester in a week [30 to 33 miles per day], and but once a week, all this time there were so few, that they did little or no hurt, but now of late, have set up running stage-coaches, change horses twice a day, run these long journyes in four dayes, to the great prejudice of the countrey, and they have three coaches a week at least, sometimes 4, 5, 6 coaches go to every of these towns.[18]

Although there is no evidence of the first sort of service to York, Exeter or Chester, one service elsewhere may have been of this type. In October 1648 John Taylor travelled on 'the Southamton coach' from London, noting that 'we tooke one coach, two coach-men and foure horses', and that the coach carried five people. This sounds like a stage-coach, but it took three days between London and Southampton, stopping overnight at Staines and Alton (hence 20, 31 and 30 miles on the three days).[19] An overall 27 miles a day would have been slow for a stage-coach even in winter, though a 31-mile day in winter was not unusual. Later use of vehicles similar to stage-coaches could explain why Sir William Dugdale in the late 17th century described what was clearly (from its timings) a coach-waggon not only as 'Coventry coach' but even as 'Coventrie stage-coach'.[20]

The first stage-coaches

When did the first genuine stage-coach operate, changing horses *en route* and achieving a reasonably high speed? Cressett, responding in 1672 to the claim that coaches had been set up 30 years earlier, stated that coaches to Norwich had been established for about 30 years (i.e. since 1642), Exeter between 20 and 30 years (1642-52), Chester for about 20 years (1652), York for about 18 years (1654), and 'the others very lately'.[21] Being anxious to show that stage-coaches were an unwelcome novelty, Cressett might have been expected not to exaggerate their antiquity. However, whether he adequately distinguished between different types of 'coaches' is uncertain. Norwich to London was one of the few long-distance routes on which a stage-coach service would have been feasible during the Civil Wars, given that one side was in control of the whole route throughout the wars, but there is no evidence earlier than 1657. Other first references are to York

On the eighteenth of *April* instant the new Coaches wil be ready both at *London* and *York*, to carry paſſengers between the ſaid Cities in four daies, and ſo to continue : that who pleaſe may come forth of *London* from the *Swan* at *Holborn bridge*, at five of clock in the morning each Monday, Wedneſday, and Friday, and arrive at *York* the fourth day after, and the like from *York* to *London*, ſetting forth the ſame daies, and houres. The rates for each paſſenger wil be 2 *d.* per mile, only at each ſtage 4 *d.* to the Coachman, which comes to 28 *s.* for the whole journey, or for 100 miles 19 *s.* or thereabouts. Each Coach con- taines 14 paſſengers, having three diſtinct rooms, that who pleaſe may have a room for themſelves. The ſame day was reſolved alſo for *Cheſter*, but the Coaches wil not be finiſhed theſe five weeks, whereof particular notice wil be given.

46 *The first advertisement for the York stage-coach, 1653. (Perfect Diurnall, 11 April 1653.)*

47 *The* George Inn, *Coney Street, York, used by one of the York coaches in the 1650s.*

in 1653, Exeter in 1655 and Chester probably in 1657 (Appendix 6). That the others came into being 'very lately' is disproved by numerous advertisements of the 1650s. More credence can be placed on a reference in 1681 to 'before these coaches were in use (which hath not been much above twenty years)'.[22] But the best evidence is provided by advertisements and diaries.

The first unequivocal reference to a stage-coach is an advertisement for the York coach in April 1653 (Fig. 46). It has the air of something experimental: the urge to explain and justify it, the reference to 'new coaches', a type of coach very different from that which became standard, and the fact that similar coaches intended for Chester were not yet completed. The fare was low (1.7 pence per mile), clearly reflecting the intention to carry up to 14 passengers, but the timing – four days in summer – was exactly the summer timing of the York coach for the next century. The advertisement undoubtedly records the first York stage-coach, and probably marks the beginning of the stage-coach system. The date is later than those stated for public coach services in France (by 1575) and Germany (1640), but whether these were really comparable with stage-coaches is doubtful (the French ones at least were probably more like coach-waggons); it is earlier than the first stage-coaches in the Netherlands (1660), which already had excellent passenger services by barge.[23]

By 1658 the York route had higher fares (2.4 pence per mile), almost certainly indicating coaches seating only six, but the same four-day schedule in summer.[24] Revenue from a full load was less (£12 instead of nearly £20), but there was presumably more chance of filling the coach and less strain on the horses. The reason for the change was probably not to do with the horses, since the proprietors would already have known what their horses were capable of, but to do with increased knowledge of the market, which had been less foreseeable.

Whether the Chester coaches did begin in 1653 is unknown, but the York coaches evidently prospered, and coaches to Newcastle and Barton upon Humber (for Hull) were added to the service in 1654. From 1654 to 1658 or later there were two competing York services, and a third appeared briefly in November 1654, though by 1665 there was only a single service again.[25] From 1654 the stage-coach network expanded rapidly, and by the end of the 1650s twenty separate destinations had been recorded (Map 11). The network may well have been larger, since some coaches, such as those to Exeter and Worcester, are known only from a single chance reference in a diary. Not only York but also Canterbury and Dover and Bath and Bristol had competing services in the 1650s, and the fact that custom was worth competing for is clear evidence that the stage-coaches had found a market.

Map 11 *The stage-coach network in the 1650s. The dates are those of the first reference, rather than necessarily when a service started. Dates are in brackets where a service appears to have been short-lived. The Windsor service of 1658 is omitted for lack of space. (Source: Appendix 6.)*

The York coaches were described as post-coaches in 1653-4, but in 1654 the ordinance regulating hackney coaches specifically exempted 'the coaches commonly called stage coaches, coming to, or going from London into remote places', and the Cambridge coach was advertised as a stage-coach in the same year. Another term was hackney-coach, applied to the York coaches in 1656 and 1665 and the Salisbury and Southampton coaches in 1657. Cressett in 1672 wished to suppress 'all hackney stage-coaches and caravans', and Sir John Reresby was apparently still using the terms hackney-coach and stage-coach interchangeably in 1679-89,[26] but from the late 1650s stage-coach appears to have been the usual description. Why the word 'stage' was used is unclear, since both stage-coaches and coach-waggons had regular stages.

The pioneers

The York coach proprietors may well have quarrelled in 1654, since an advertisement stating that the coaches had been removed from the *Black Swan*, Holborn, to the *George* without Aldersgate was quickly countered by one denying it, and there continued to be competing services at both inns until at least 1658. One advertisement lists the four partners who remained at the *Black Swan*: they were Robert Gardner, an innkeeper at York by 1666 (and living in York by 1656), Henry Jackson, a London hackney coachman, Richard Thorndike, another Londoner (though with a Lincolnshire background) and Henry Waters, also a Londoner, holder of a hackney licence bought in the name of his servant and still described as a coachman after leaving the York partnership. This looks like an alliance of London hackney coachmen and an innkeeper, except that Gardner was not the coach's innkeeper in York in 1653.[27]

48 *Coach and carrier advertisements in 1657. (Publick Adviser, 26 May 1657.)*

There was even stronger involvement of London hackney coachmen in the Chester coach: two of those who ran the service from 1657 (William Dunstan and Henry Earl) had been overseers of the Fellowship of Hackney Coachmen; the third (William Fowler) was a coachmaker, though he also (later) had a hackney licence.[28] Of the Exeter coachmasters, first named in 1672, one, Benjamin Fleming, had been an overseer of the Fellowship of Hackney Coachmen, and Fulk Biscabe, son and heir of the other partner, had a hackney licence in 1679.[29] Several Bristol and Bath coachmasters were also London hackney coachmen, including Henry Folbig in 1662 and William Drew in 1663.[30] 'Robert Tobey' had been among those petitioning for the incorporation of the hackney coachmen into a company in 1635, and widow Toobey was a coachmaster to Bristol, Bath and Newbury in 1672.[31] Stage-coachmen were alleged to hold 14 London hackney licences in 1663, and 13 of the 28 coachmasters listed in 1672 had such licences, including coachmasters serving Dover, Northampton, Winchester, Henley, Windsor and Guildford.[32] Although licences could apparently be bought and sold, they tended to be kept by those who had them (sometimes being let out) and to pass to heirs,[33] and may therefore indicate the origins of these coachmasters as hackney coachmen, thereby strengthening the case for seeing the hackney coachmen as the founders of the stage-coach network. The fact that they were sometimes hired for journeys extending far from London may have given them the idea.

It follows from the importance of the hackney coachmen that the network was largely of metropolitan origin. For example, three of the four identifiable York coachmasters lived in London, and the metropolitan origin of this service is also indicated by the proprietors' intention in 1653 to establish coaches both to York and Chester. The Chester coach from 1657 and the Exeter coach, when its partners are named in the 1670s,[34] also had exclusively London partners. Presumably all those coachmasters with hackney licences lived or had lived in London.

There were apparently few innkeepers involved at first. The main exception is Robert Gardner at York, but he was a coachmaster before he is recorded as an innkeeper. Even in 1672 only six of the 28 coachmasters named were innkeepers.[35] Carriers also appear to have played only a small part at first. Apart from Thomas Cramphorn, serving Portsmouth in 1657,[36] no other carrier-coachmasters are recorded until 1672, and even in 1681 few carriers were involved in those coach services first recorded in the 1650s.[37] Of the other proprietors in the 1650s, Onesiphorus Tapp, postmaster of Marlborough, may have seen a coach as a way of conveying letters on his own account, as he was doing (illegally) in 1670.[38] Thomas Southgate, brewer at Norwich, and William Done of the York coach, imbroderer or scrivener in London, came from trades unrelated to coaching.[39]

Growth of the network

Thirteen more stage-coach destinations are recorded prior to 1672, in which year the controversy involving Cressett reveals a further six (Appendix 6). Chamberlayne wrote in 1671 that 'there is of late such an admirable commodiousness, both for men and women of better rank to travel from London to almost any great town of England, and to almost all the villages near this great city, that the like hath not been known in the world, and that is by stage coaches'.[40] Of the coach services listed by Delaune extending more than 80 miles, only those to Bridgnorth,[41] King's Lynn, Taunton and Yarmouth in 1681 and Lichfield, Melton Mowbray and Nottingham in 1690 had not already been recorded in 1672 or earlier.

As for the short-distance coaches, Cressett stated in 1672 that when the Act for restricting the number of hackney coaches in London to 400 came into effect (in 1663), 'there were above 1,200 in London, who finding they could not work, then removed and placed themselves 2 or 3 in a town, in almost every little town or village within 10 or 12 miles, and all along the River of Thames, and at each town near the said river'; 'they set up for stagers, and drive every day to London, and in the night-time they drive about the City'; indeed, 'every little town within twenty miles of London sworms with them'. Another story, also from Cressett, was that innkeepers had established coaches to bring custom to their inns, and competing innkeepers had then been forced to do the same, to their mutual disadvantage.[42] Innkeepers were certainly prominent later among the short-stagers, though few can have felt compelled to compete in this way, since few towns had more than two operators of stage-coaches. As regards the timing, the summer-only Epsom service, run by a Lambeth innkeeper and a London hackney coachman in 1665, is the only one recorded within 20 miles of London by 1671, but at least six places 20 to 30 miles from London had their own coaches by then,[43] and significant growth of short-distance services in the 1660s would be consistent with the statements by both Cressett and Chamberlayne.

The stage-coaches faced a concerted attack in 1672, when innkeepers and postmasters of various towns petitioned the Privy Council against them and Cressett (a lawyer) wrote pamphlets on the petitioners' behalf.[44] They wanted the short stages put down and the long stages restricted to one a week and to certain towns only. The sloppy, inconsistent character of Cressett's arguments probably makes the campaign appear less serious than it really was. The City of London's Court of Aldermen was among those supporting the petitioners, and the House of Commons considered suppressing the stage-coaches in 1671, 1675 and 1678. The Norwich coachmasters took the precaution of obtaining their city's backing.[45] However, neither the Privy Council nor the Commons took action, and the network continued to grow. A new service of particular interest is the Nottingham coach, established in about 1681, since its owners developed a series of coaches serving Derby, Leicester and (briefly) Mansfield and Doncaster.

Another important development was the establishment of increasingly ambitious flying coaches, covering more than the York coach's 51 miles per day. Flying coaches (always flying in summer only) were almost as old as stage-coaching itself: the earliest examples served Cambridge in 1654 and Canterbury in 1657, covering 57 and 56 miles respectively in a day, though neither was described as a flying coach. The term 'flying coach' is first recorded for a Norwich service in 1666, taking two days (55 miles per day); this was also the first example of the coach as the bearer of news, in this case of the Great Fire of London. Oxford flying coaches were established in 1669, covering 58 miles in a day (Appendix 8). Chamberlayne stated in 1671 that flying coaches could make journeys such as London to Oxford or Cambridge 'in the space of 12 hours, not counting the time for dining, setting forth not too early and coming in not too late',[46] and this is borne out by other evidence (Appendix 9). Even greater distances were being covered in one day from the late 1670s, starting with Northampton (67 miles) by 1676[47] and Banbury (76 miles) by 1679. The most impressive one-day coach, covering 92 miles to Cirencester, was established in 1696, though there was also a short-lived one-day Norwich service (110 miles) in 1710. There were also some two-day flying coaches from the 1680s.

New long-distance destinations continued to be added until about 1705, and many more places were served by stage-coach in the 17th century than has usually been recognised. However, not all the new services survived; for example one to Monmouth set up in 1700 by Thomas Puxton, 'who lately drove Glocester stage-coach, as a servant',[48] is never heard of again. After 1705 there were hardly any new destinations over 40 miles from London until the 1760s (Appendix 6). The short-distance network, on the other hand, continued to grow both in number of services and number of destinations throughout the 18th century.

A few provincial services began to appear from about 1700, usually in summer only. In addition to the Newcastle and Edinburgh services already noted (which were not much different from genuine provincial services), there were coaches from York to Hull in 1678 (summer only), Oxford to Bath and Bristol by 1701 (summer only), Gloucester to Hereford in 1705 (run by the Gloucester to London coachmasters), North Walsham to Norwich in 1710 (the first known to have been run independently of any London coach), a Holyhead coach in 1715 and Exeter to Bath in 1716.[49] The North Walsham coach was probably a failure: its proprietor described it as 'a very advantagious stage', but was seeking to sell it, 'designing to undertake brewing and malting' instead. However, the Oxford-Bristol, Gloucester-Hereford and Exeter-Bath coaches continued to be recorded.[50] A little later there were services from Bristol to Gloucester (1721, also linking Bath by 1726), Norwich to Yarmouth (1725, apparently in winter only), Norwich to Bury St Edmunds (1727), Bristol to Salisbury (1730), York to Scarborough (1730, summer only), Norwich to King's Lynn (1737, January-September only) and Norwich to Cambridge (1737, by chaise).[51]

Summer and winter

It has often been claimed that the early stage-coaches ran only in summer.[52] This appears to reflect partly the fact that summer schedules tended to be advertised in March or April, sometimes in terms which could equally apply to a new service, and partly a presumption that the roads were too bad to allow coach services in winter. In fact there is overwhelming evidence, from advertisements, diaries and legal proceedings, that most coaches ran throughout the year. For example, numerous advertisements in the months from November to January record thefts or losses from stage-coaches.[53] Travellers recorded their stage-coach journeys in winter, for example in the York, Chester and Yarmouth coaches; Appendix 8 lists 50 coach journeys made by diarists between November and February. Some coachmasters advertised their winter schedule (Appendix 8). The three examples of coachmasters' accounts, for Exeter, Henley and Birmingham coaches, indicate operation in winter.[54] It could hardly have been otherwise, since horses could not be kept idle without ruinous expense, and buying and selling large numbers of coach horses twice a year would have been difficult and costly.[55]

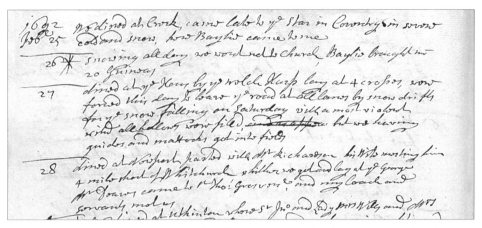

49 *Extract from the diary of Sir Willoughby Aston, recording his journey in the Chester stage-coach (to Whitchurch) in snow in February 1693. (Liverpool RO, 920 MD 174.)*

It might be expected that coach services would have ceased during periods of snow, given that snow can halt traffic on roads and railways even today. However, this was certainly not always the case. Travelling by stage-coach from London to Chester in February 1693, Sir Willoughby Aston came late to Coventry on Saturday 25 February 'in severe cold and snow', and on Sunday it snowed all day (Fig. 49). On the Monday, the coach was

> forced this day to leave ye road at all lanes by snow drifts for ye snow falling on Saturday with a most violent wind all hollows were filld, but we having guides and mattocks got into fields.

By 'all lanes' he presumably meant the narrower parts of the road. Mattocks are tools similar to pickaxes for grubbing up plants, hence their use to gain access to the fields. On the same day the coach reached *Four Crosses* Inn, which was its usual lodging place on that day of its winter journeys from London. Sir Willoughby Aston utterly disposes of the notion that stage-coaches could not operate in winter.

A few services did cease in winter, as discussed below,[56] but they were clearly exceptional. Nevertheless, while winter did not prevent coaches operating, it did have a major impact on services, which has not always been appreciated. Journey times became longer, misleading some writers into seeing trends from year to year where none existed, team sizes were normally increased and frequencies were sometimes reduced, as discussed later.[57]

CHAPTER VIII

PASSENGERS

Stage-coach passengers recorded between 1654 and 1728, mostly in diaries, include the Countess of Ardglass, many gentlemen (11 with knighthoods), several Members of Parliament, a sheriff of Yorkshire, the son of a Cheshire gentleman on his way to Westminster School, the Bishops of Carlisle, Chester and Kildare, the Archdeacon of Stafford and other Anglican and nonconformist clergymen, the wife of the Vicar of Bradford, a Mayor of Yarmouth, an alderman of Worcester (in the custody of a King's Messenger), the son of a York alderman, the Warden of Merton College, several lawyers, merchants, doctors, stewards, scholars and antiquaries, an employee of the Bishop of Durham, several captains or wives of captains, an apothecary selling garden seeds, the children of a goldsmith and a customs officer, an Irish lady with her seven-month-old son and servants, a schoolteacher, a tanner's wife, a cooper, a dry-salter, a bricklayer, a nurse and child, 'an old serving-woman and a young fine mayd' and two prostitutes.[1] Servants sometimes travelled inside the coach with their employer,[2] but sometimes on the box by the driver, in the boot or on horseback.[3]

From this miscellaneous list several conclusions can be drawn. Of course diarists tended to list the more notable passengers, and this may have contributed to the rarity of references to people involved in trade or industry. However, there are enough examples of all the occupants of a coach being listed to make clear that coach passengers came predominantly from the gentry and what may be called 'the middling sort', at least in the long-distance coaches. In April 1687 at Northampton, for example, Colonel Roger Whitley MP 'took place in ye stage-coach, with Sir John Holman, Dr Poole, Lady Shore, her daughter & a gentlewoman from Stafford'. A man travelling from Preston to London in 1663, presumably using the Chester coach, claimed to have come to London with 'persons of greate qualitie, as knightes and ladyes'.[4] In fact stage-coaches appear to have become the main means of long-distance travel to and from London for the gentry, with private coaches as the alternative. Of the six gentlemen who kept the most substantial diaries, from Cheshire, Lancashire and Yorkshire, five normally travelled by stage-coach (though occasionally in their own coach or a hired coach) and one normally by his own coach.[5]

There is no evidence that great nobles used stage-coaches. Nobles would have considered it beneath them to spend several days with the haphazard collection

50 *Hogarth's engraving of a stage-coach in an inn yard, 1747. Note the passengers in a basket at the back and precariously seated on the roof.*

of travellers likely to be found in a stage-coach, and they were expected to make more of a show, so they used their own coaches. For example, in February 1681 the Duke of Newcastle set off from London with three coaches and about 40 attendants on horseback.[6]

Nor were poorer people likely to be found in stage-coaches in any numbers, because of the high fares. Instead they would walk or use waggons or coach-waggons. Pepys and his wife travelled by coach or riding horse, but he thought the waggons good enough for his parents, his sister and servants. In the 1720s and 1730s Sir John Harpur travelled from Derbyshire to London in his own coach with his family, but sent his cook and housekeeper by stage-coach and three or four housemaids by waggon.[7] The two prostitutes travelling from Berkshire to London by stage-coach in 1675 were an exception, but they proved unable to pay when the journey ended. A fellow-passenger

> whisper'd to the coachman to take it out in worke, but the wary fellow reply'd, that was the way to be pay'd indeed, and that he had much rather have the pence then the pox, and so I understood that at last he came to a composition, and tooke the morgage of an under-petticoate.[8]

It is possible, however, that stage-coach passengers were somewhat less well-to-do on the shorter routes, where the fares were less intimidating and where, because there was less advantage from changing horses, the gentry were more likely to use their own carriages. In addition to the two prostitutes, the teacher mentioned above was in the Colchester coach, the tanner's wife and the cooper in the Buckingham coach and the bricklayer in the Cambridge coach.

Women travellers

George Farquhar observed in *The stage-coach* in 1704 that 'Here chance kindly mixes, All sorts and all sexes, More females than men'. That more women than men used stage-coaches cannot be proved, but when Elizabeth Pepys took the stage-coach to Huntingdon in 1663, her company was 'none but women and one parson', much to her husband's satisfaction, and Nicholas Blundell recorded between Newcastle and York in 1706 'myself and five women in the coach'.[9] Stage-coaches certainly increased the opportunities for well-to-do women to travel on their own, such as a young gentlewoman travelling from Exeter to Yorkshire in 1655, 'one lady alone' encountered by Pepys in the Cambridge coach in 1668 and Philip Henry's sister in 1685 – if there were no room in the Chester coach, the journey 'must be defer'd till there is'. Not everyone was relaxed about their womenfolk travelling alone by coach: when Joseph Symson, the Kendal mercer, sent his 22-year-old daughter to London in 1716 she was to stay with a friend in Chester 'until such company as you approve of may be had for her in the stage coach for London, which is a great inducement to let her go that long journey', and she was to be given 'directions what you think proper for she is a stranger to that way of travelling'; for the return journey he considered sending his son to London to accompany her in the coach.[10] Nevertheless, but for the coach, she would probably not have made the journey at all.

Choices: speed and cost

For the gentry and middling sort a range of options other than stage-coaches was available, varying in speed, cost and level of comfort. On a few routes there was the possibility of travel by river, especially the Thames, or by sea, particularly to and from Essex and Kent but also for some longer journeys, such as to and from Newcastle upon Tyne and Edinburgh.[11] A Worcester coachmaster in 1747 advertised connections by wherry from Worcester to Shrewsbury and Glouces-ter.[12] As when sending goods, water transport was cheap, but sometimes slow, especially as boats were usually infrequent, and certainly unreliable (particularly coastal journeys). Between Harwich and London in 1711, the stage-coach cost 16s. and took two days; the passage boat cost 3s. and arrived on the morning of the second day 'if a right wind'.[13] Better-off passengers seem to have made little use of water transport. The only references by diarists to long journeys by water relate to a Scottish gentleman from Leith to London in 1685 (taking 8½ days) and a teacher from Colchester to London and back in 1676 (in each case taking from late afternoon on the first day to early morning on the third).[14] The diaries do on the other hand reveal that even stage-coach passengers to and from Kent commonly travelled by boat between London and Gravesend.[15]

Apart from water transport (and walking), the options all depended on the horse, as riding horse or coach horse, and were therefore subject to many of the same constraints as stage-coaches, especially the limited speed unless fresh horses were provided *en route*. With changes of horses, private coaches could be as fast as stage-coaches. On 9 October 1671 John Evelyn travelled from London to Newmarket (62 miles) in a single day in the Treasurer of the Household's coach, but this was with teams of six and three changes of horses; coming home, on 20 October, the coach took two days. In November 1688, with coaches and horses provided by the Countess of Sunderland and changed at Dunstable, he covered 72 miles from London to Althorp in a day, arriving by 7 p.m.[16]

However, probably few of those who used private coaches for long journeys had the means to arrange changes of horses *en route* (post-horses to draw private coaches were not available for hire until the 1740s),[17] so travellers by private coach usually had to be content with what horses could achieve when used continuously. The same probably applied to most hired coaches. There was also the expense of keeping the horses in London, unless they were hired. Some gentlemen, like Sir Willoughby Aston, had their own coaches for local journeys but tended to use the stage-coaches for longer ones. One who did use his own coach for long journeys was Roger Whitley, of Peele near Chester and Elmhurst near Lichfield. In summer he travelled at the *winter* speeds of the Chester and Lichfield coaches (six and four days respectively) or slightly faster;[18] indeed when he hired horses for the purpose from the coachmaster, William Fowler, in June 1686 he dined and lodged at exactly the places the Lichfield coach did in winter, taking the same four days. One advantage was that he did not feel obliged to halt on Sundays. In summer he covered 30 to 36 miles per day, at an average of 4.0 miles per hour. However, in winter, when the stage-coaches did not change horses either, Whitley's times by his own coach were similar to theirs – usually six or seven days to Chester and four to Lichfield.[19] In 1748-9 Isaac Greene's private coach usually took longer between Warrington and London than the Warrington stage-coach had done 40 years before: six or seven days in winter and five or five-and-a-half days in summer, compared with the stage-coach's six and four days respectively.[20]

Undoubtedly the most common form of travel was riding on horseback. According to Guy Miège in 1691, 'travelling on horseback is so common a thing in England, that the meanest sort of people use it as well as the rest'. It was the main alternative for some regular stage-coach users, such as Dugdale and Bishop Nicholson of Carlisle.[21] Unless horses were changed, 40 miles a day or just over was usual for long journeys,[22] though some riders exceptionally managed nearly sixty. For example, Pepys, with an early start and hard riding, could make Cambridge (57 miles) in a day.[23] Henry Newcome junior on horseback followed the Chester coach's summer stages between Chester and Coventry in March 1694 and June 1698 (41-48 miles per day), but he described 47 miles in

THere is a Stage-Coach goes from the Rain-Deer-Inn in Birmingham, every Monday Morning 6 a Clock, going through Warwick and Banbury, and comes to the Bell-Inn in Weſt-Smithfield every Wedneſday, and ſo returns every Thurſday, to the Rain-Deer Inn in Birmingham every Saturday ; at **18 s.** each Paſſenger, performed by **Nich. Rothwell** of **Warwick.**

51 *Advertisement for the Birmingham coach, 1691. (London Gazette, 11 May 1691.)*

Banbury and Aſtrop-Wells

STAGE-COACH in One Day.

BEgins on *Monday* the 16th of *May,* 1709. and goes all the Summer Seaſon, on *Mondays* and *Fridays,* from the *Three Tuns* in *Banbury* to the *Black Bull-Inn* in *Holbourn* ; and ſets out from thence on *Tueſdays* and *Saturdays,* and ſets out from both Places exactly by Four of the Clock in the Morning : And after the one Days Stage is ended, it will continue in Two Days all the Winter if poſſible.

All Paſſengers are allow'd 14 Pound Weight; and not exceeding that, but what more to pay 1ˢ *per* Pound. You may ſend Veniſon at Reaſonable Rates.

Perform'd, if God permit,   By   {*Charles Stoakes,* *Thomas Dance,* and *William Church.*

At Banbury *you may be furniſh'd with a Coach, Calaſh, Chariot, Hearſe, Mourning Cloaks, Velvet Palls, and all other Things ſuitable upon ſuch an Occaſion.*

A good Chariot and able Horſes may be had at the White-Hart-Inn *in* Ailsbury.

52 *A rare example of a stage-coach handbill, surviving among family papers. (Warwickshire RO, CR 1368/4/P2.)*

March 1675 as an 'unmercifull journey'.[24] On his journeys to Bampton Pepys averaged four miles per hour in summer and somewhat less in winter (less than Thomas Smith's 5⅓ miles per hour between Thatcham and London in September 1720).[25]

Horses might be the traveller's own or hired. If hired, the cost varied according to journey time and the number of changes of horse. Horses could be hired from some carriers, who might then act as a guide and provide a degree of security, although in that case the traveller was restricted to the carrier's speed, without any changes of horse; however, riders were not necessarily required to accompany the carrier.[26] In 1692 Thomas Brockbank was recommended by his parents to hire a horse from the Kendal carrier: 'The price y. usually take for a horse from Kendall to London is 17 or 18£ they maintaining ye horse in ye journey' (clearly a mistake for shillings, hence 0.8 pence per mile). However, he objected, being 'loath to ride ye wooden horse (such are most pack horses)', and bought a horse to ride instead. In the 1670s the same journey was said to cost 'upon a fardel 20 shillings; a horse to themselves 30' (0.9 or 1.4 pence per mile), and in 1719 30s.[27]

Others also hired out horses. In April 1657 the *George* without Aldersgate in London was providing saddle horses on specified days to York for 31s. 3d. (1.9 pence per mile), the hirer 'paying nothing for the horse charges, or for the messenger'; they travelled at four miles per hour and took four days (possibly in summer only). This was the same number of days as the York coach, but was cheaper than the coach's 2.4 pence per mile. The horses were changed once a day. If the same arrangements applied in winter the saddle horses were then both cheaper *and* faster than the coach. Between Oxford and London, Thomas Bew undertook in 1678 to provide horses to complete the journey in one day, 'with a boy to waite on them', again on specified days, for 8s. (1.7 pence per mile), apparently throughout the year, whereas the coach fare is likely to have been 8s. for a two-day journey in winter and 10s. for a one-day journey in summer. The price per mile for horses was similar to that of the York horses for a similar number of miles per day (58 and 51 miles per day for Oxford and York respectively). Horses from Exeter to Dorchester in 1728 to connect with flying coaches were somewhat more expensive: 10s., or 2.3 pence per mile.[28]

Riding by post-horse, changing horse for each stage of 10 to 15 miles or thereabouts, was the dearest form of travel on horseback and the fastest, though it was matched (in terms of days on the road) by a few of the flying coaches. Public use of post-horses had been permitted since 1583-4, though for a long time it was possible on only a few roads. In June 1658 the postmasters on the Chester road advertised what appears to have been a convoy, with horses departing three times a week from London for Chester, Warrington and Manchester, taking four days, at a cost of 3d. per mile 'without the charge of a guide'; it was re-advertised in 1670 at the same price. Threepence per mile had been the maximum charge for posting since 1609, and remained so almost continuously until at least 1749, though the guide's fee, usually 4d. per stage, was extra.[29] Thus posting was dearer than stage-coach travel but, in the Chester case, about as fast in summer and much faster in winter. Other evidence indicates that posting was sometimes even faster: a days' ride could be 70 or so miles, and Pepys sometimes managed seven miles per hour when both horses and roads were good.[30]

Comparisons are difficult for several reasons: miles per hour and per day varied in each case, riding by horse was much cheaper if travellers used their own horses rather than hiring, relative merits varied by season (coaching being more affected by winter conditions than horse-riding), and there were costs other than the direct ones to be taken into account. For example, it was necessary to take more servants when travelling on horseback: Cressett noted that if coach passengers rode instead, 'many of them would without doubt ride with a servant, some with two or three, which now travel either without men, or with a boy only behind the coach'.[31] Costs were also affected by the number of people travelling together and the length of the intended stay in London (and thus the cost of keeping horses there). There could also be extras: according to Cressett, passengers in the York, Chester and Exeter coaches paid not only a fare of 40s. each way, but 1s. to each of eight coachmen at the end of their stages and 3s. more 'for the drink the coachmen have upon the road', adding 14 per cent to the fare, a figure for which there is independent confirmation.[32] Table 5 sets out a hierarchy of speeds and costs, but all the figures are approximate.

Table 5. Costs and speeds of passenger transport in summer in the late 17th and early 18th centuries

Type of transport	Typical miles per day	Miles per hour (approx.)	Cost (pence per mile)
1. Post horses	60-70	Up to 7	3.3
2. Flying stage-coach	55-76	4½	2.3-3.1
3. Stage-coach	41-52	4½	2.3-3.1
4. Hired horses	51-58	4	1.7-2.3
5. Horses	40-47	4	?
6. Private coach	30-36	4	?
7. Horses hired from a carrier	25-33	?	0.8-1.4
8. Coach-waggon	25-33	2	1.2-1.7
9. Waggon	20-25	2	0.7-1.4

Sources: see text and notes below.

Notes: 2. A few flying coaches covered more miles per day, but set off around midnight. 2 & 3. Includes 0.3-0.4 pence per mile for gratuities and drink for coachmen. 2, 3 & 8. See Appendices 8 to 10. 4. Based on the York, Oxford and Dorchester examples, with changes of horses at least in the York case. 6. Without changes of horses; based on Roger Whitley's journeys. 7. Based on the Kendal example and Appendix 4, part B. 9. See Appendices 4 and 10.

Choices: comfort and safety

There were other considerations besides speed and cost. Chamberlayne in 1671 emphasised the coaches' relative comfort, being 'sheltred from foul weather and foul waies, free from endammaging ones health or body by hard jogging or overviolent motion'.[33] In winter, stage-coaches were less attractive in terms of speed but even more attractive in terms of shelter. Not surprisingly, while riding a horse might be agreeable on a fine day or for short journeys, riding day after day whatever the weather on long journeys (apart from posting) was largely abandoned by those who could afford stage-coaches or private coaches as soon as those were available.

Indeed, when stage-coaches began there were some who regarded coach travel as effeminate. When Thoresby's father hired a coach to convey his son from Hull to York in 1678, 'it proved a mortification to us both, that he was as little able to endure the effeminacy of that way of travelling, as I was at present to ride on horseback'. Cressett described stage-coaches as an 'effeminate kind of travelling' (indeed 'ignoble, base and sordid'), which in reply was compared with the criticisms of 'down-pillows and feather-beds, night-caps, close-stool and warming pans'. Both Sir Fulwar Skipwith in 1654 and the Rev. Henry Newcome in 1669, travelling from London to Worcester and Chester respectively, sent their wives in the stage-coach while making their own way on horseback. However, that attitude towards coach travel did not last long; nor could it have done given the importance private coaches acquired as status symbols by the late 17th century.[34] None of the other diarists give any hint of shame at travelling by stage-coach, and many had a coach of their own. Both Newcome and Thoresby later made several stage-coach journeys. Several stage-coach travellers were happy to be accompanied by their servants on horseback, and in 1750 the Chester proprietors hired out saddle horses for that purpose.[35] The defender of stage-coaches against Cressett noted in 1672 that 'of those that would keep servants and horses, the most of them do still, and make them ride by the coach side, notwithstanding they themselves go in the coach'.[36]

The degree of comfort was only relative anyway. Nicholson once complained of being 'crippled in a narrow and nasty coach', and on another occasion, feeling ill, was 'not able to endure the coach', though he soon changed his mind and hired horses to overtake and rejoin it. Thomas Smith after a day and a half in the Bristol coach in June 1718 referred to 'the fatigue of heat and dust', and in the York coach in June 1723 Thoresby 'found the dust and heat troublesome'.[37]

Another benefit of stage-coaches, according to their defender in 1672, was for 'multitudes of ancient persons, women, children, sick and infirm, which cannot travel any other way, besides many more who are indisposed to ride on horseback'; there were also 'many others able enough to travel on horseback, and amongst those divers gentlemen and persons of good quality, who would not willingly be met on the road with a portmantle behind them, and yet have not fortunes so plentiful as to keep horses and men for that service'.[38] As already indicated, stage-coaches created new possibilities of travel for well-to-do women on their own.

Stage-coaches also had disadvantages. The most significant was travelling with strangers. In no other circumstances would a 17th-century gentleman or woman spend days at a time cooped up with people, possibly from quite different backgrounds, whom he or she did not know. Cressett inevitably made much of this: 'What conveniency is it to be stuft up in a coach with strangers, old sickley diseased people crying children … crowded with their bundles and boxes, and almost poysoned sometimes with there nasty sents.'[39]

For once Cressett had a valid point. In February 1683, before what was apparently his first stage-coach journey, Thoresby was 'Up pretty timely preparing for a journey & somewhat concern'd about company, very timerous of being confined to a coach for so many days in unsuitable company & not one person I know of, beg'd earnestly of God to keep me from all snares & temptations.' Sometimes passengers were pleasantly surprised: for example, in 1711 Nicholson in the York coach 'had the agreeable company of Capt. Wilson and his well-bred lady, from Jamaica'. Newcome in the Lichfield coach in 1681 'had the company of a fine gentleman, which was a great comfort to me'. The less fortunate might have had the company of the two prostitutes, and gentlemen probably did not relish close association with a dry-salter or a bricklayer. In George Farquhar's *The stage-coach* of 1704, the disbanded captain lists 'this confounded company' in the stage-coach as 'a big-belly'd farmer's daughter, an Irish wit, a canting Quaker, a City whore, and a country parson', to which his servant adds 'And a disbanded captain, Sir, for want of a strolling lawyer, or a nurse and a child, to make up a clever stage-coach set'. John Verney travelled by stage-coach in 1682 with 'a tanner's wife on top … a cooper in the next degree, and a third person with her suckling child. A reeking scent did frequently reach my too sensible nostrils'. Thomas Smith in the Bristol coach in 1718 had 'but indifferent company, viz sick and unhealthy people', and on the return journey 'five persons unknown to me'. The atmosphere between passengers must often have been frosty. Newcome encountered 'not much talk' in the Lichfield coach in 1681, 'the Countess of Arglass being reserved'.[40]

The remedy was to hire the whole coach. Elizabeth Freke hired the King's Lynn coach in 1699 'that we might travill att ease up to London'. Marmaduke Rawdon did the same from Exeter (with three friends) in December 1655, with the result that a gentlewoman travelling to Yorkshire might have had to wait a week for the next coach had she not been 'a proper hansome yonge woman'. Rawdon said to her,

> Mistress, I am your countryman, and you shall nott only have a place, but you shall have the best place in the coach, and that he would taike itt to his care to make much of hir all the journie; and soe he did, for he sett hir by him selfe att the brood end of the coach, and she dined and supt constantly with them, and would not suffer hir to pay anie thinge.[41]

Sir Willoughby Aston was offered the Lichfield coach in 1686 for '£7 the whole to myself if but 4, if more £7 10.0.'.[42] Such behaviour increased the likelihood of other people being unable to travel when they wanted.

Another disadvantage of stage-coaches was having to follow the coach's itinerary, which often involved starting very early and which prevented visits on the way. When Symson considered sending his son to accompany his daughter back from London in the Chester coach in 1717, he noted that this 'would have been both chargeable and hindered him from doing business in the road which must be neglected if he come in the coach'.[43]

There were coach accidents too. More are recorded for the York coach than for any other: Anne Murray was lucky not to be involved in one when a bridge without parapets was taken carelessly in 1656; Rawdon sprained his arm when the coach overturned near Baldock in 1657; three people were drowned when the coach overturned the ferry boat across the Trent near Newark in 1694; all the passengers were drowned when the coach toppled off a bridge in snow in 1698; the Bishop of Lincoln saw 'the York coach over-turn'd before our eyes' in 1709; and two poles broke on the coach in 1711. James Gordon, reaching London safely by the York coach in March 1709, 'had great reason to bless God, being often in great danger of being overturned the way was so wretchedly bad & the waters were very much out which increas'd the danger'.[44] However, the defender of stage-coaches argued in 1672 that accidents were fewer than on horseback, 'as falls from horses, catching colds, and other distempers in wet and

Thomas Stirrop. I have known the Prisoner eight Years, he always bore a good Character; he has lodged with me three Weeks; since he came from the *Indies* I never locked up any Thing, if he had been a Rogue he might have robbed me——He was a Supernumerary Man at the Wells.

Samuel Barrett. I have known the Prisoner ever since he was born; he was never brought up to any Business; he lived four Years with a Gentleman at *Snaresbrook*, upon the Forest, Guilty, **Death**.

The Prosecutor said he had been informed, and believed the Prisoner was drawn in, that he did not abuse him, and recommended him to the Favour of the Court for his Majesty's Mercy.

Prisoner. I saved his Life *.——

† 13. Joseph Leath, late of the Parish of *Southall*, in the County of *Middlesex*, was indicted for assaulting *William Herne* on the Highway, putting him, in Fear, and taking from him 10s. in Money, *Sept.* 13. his Property.

He was a second Time indicted for assaulting *John Jennings* on the Highway, putting him in Fear, and taking from him 5s. 6d. in Money, *Sept.* 13. his Property.

William Herne. On the 13th of *September*, I was going to *Aylesbury* in the Stage-Coach, between 9 and 10 in the Morning the Prisoner came up to the Coach, and said, there was a Lawyer in the Coach who had 200l. and he would have it, then he produced the Pistol: He put his Hat into the Coach, and held the Pistol in one Hand cross the Wrist of the other; he swore he would shoot my Brains out if I did not tell him which was the Lawyer; I said, there was never an one here, and then he demanded my Money; I gave him 10 or 11s. and a few half Pence——I put it into his Hat; after he had got Money from every one, he wished us a good Journey, and rode off towards *London*: There were three Ladies, Mr. *Jennings*, and myself in the Coach.

Prisoner. What Dress was I in?

Herne. You had on a loose white Duffel Coat, a kind of a Rug Coat, and I believe the same Waistcoat you have now.

Prisoner. What Horse had I?

Herne. A dark bay Horse.

Prisoner. Was there any Marks upon it?

Herne. I could not see any.

John Jennings. The Prisoner is the very Person who came up to the *Aylesbury* Coach, *September* 13, between 9 and 10 in the Morning, about a Quarter of a Mile on this Side *Southall*; he enquired for a

Lawyer, who he said was in the Coach, and had 200l. and he swore he would blow Mr. *Herne*'s Brains out if he did not tell him which was the Lawyer; after he had taken Mr. *Herne*'s Money he came to me, with a Pistol in one Hand, and his Hat in the other. I believe he had 7s. or 8s. of me, then he collected Money of the Ladies; he had Money of one of the Ladies before he took Mr. *Herne*'s Money; after he had robbed the Ladies, he seemed to direct his Discourse to me, and said, that I was the Lawyer, and swore, if I would not deliver him the 200l. he would blow my Brain out; I said, he was under a Mistake, that I was no Lawyer; I shewed him my Hands to convince him that I was not, for I am a Dyer by Trade; then he said, D——n you, give me what Money you have; I said, Sir, I had given you that already.

Prisoner. Take Notice, he says that I had the Ladies Money first.

Jennings. I saw one of the Ladies throw a Purse into his Hat before he took Mr. *Herne*'s Money.

Herne. I did not know that there was any given to him before he had mine.

Prisoner. Was my upper Coat buttoned or unbuttoned?

Jennings. It was loose.

Prisoner. What coloured Horse had I?

Jennings. A large Horse, of a dark bay Colour, I cannot say whether it had any Marks.

Ellis Pugh. On the 13th of *November* last, I was on horseback upon the Road, and about two Miles on this Side *Southall*, the Prisoner passed by me. I observed in him what is not very common in Travellers, he took too much Notice of my Horse, and asked several impertinent Questions. Said he, *is not your Master a Lawyer?* I said, yes; said he, *and you are a Welshman?* Yes, said I; we had a great deal of Discourse, he went a Mile and an half with me, and all on a sudden I lost him. I was making a Toast at *Southall*, and the Coach stopped at the Door, I believe my Master (Mr. *Potter*) came in first; I saw the Ladies crying, and they were complaining of being robbed; said I, *was it by a Man in a great Coat, and a dark cropt Horse?* They said, yes: When I came to *Cheshunt*, a Quaker told me, he heard the Person who had robbed the Coach in the Morning had been pursuing it again, and that he was in the Town; in the mean Time the Prisoner came riding by, said I, There's the Man; he had changed his Dress; at the Time he rode through the Town he was in the Dress he is now,

* This may be probable, for Spinckes the Accomplice says, that Leech told him the Prosecutor knew him.

with

53 *Proceedings in the Old Bailey on 7 December 1743 at the trial of Joseph Leath for robbery of the Aylesbury stage-coach, showing the level of detail often available from this source. The lawyer carrying the £200 which the highwayman was seeking testified that he had been sitting on the coach-box next to the driver and offered the highwayman two guineas, 'which he refused, and said, he never robbed any body upon the coach-box'.*

unseasonable weather; especially of casualties by the rising of waters and fords'.[45] There was no safe form of travel in the 17th and early 18th centuries. Some coach travellers were relatively unlucky: Newcome experienced four mishaps in five journeys between 1669 and 1686 (one coach overturning twice and another breaking its axle-tree twice). On the other hand, Nicholson experienced only one coach accident during 12 journeys, Dugdale none during about 70 journeys and Aston none during 17 journeys.[46] Overall, the diarists record ten accidents in 258 journeys, or 24,700 miles: five overturnings, one lost wheel, two broken axle-trees and one broken pole.[47] None of these prevented the coach reaching its usual lodging place and only one caused injury (Rawdon spraining his arm when a York coach 'overthrew').

Coach travellers may have been more likely than horse-riders to be robbed. There are numerous references in newspapers and the records of Old Bailey proceedings to highwaymen robbing stage-coaches, and the gathering together of well-to-do people in coaches without the means of flight made them a tempting prospect. For example, the Dover coach was robbed by five highwaymen in 1698 and a passenger who resisted was killed.[48] The incidence of highway robbery varied, being least during periods of war.[49] It was probably especially high in 1721, when a gang including Ralph Wilson was in league with the keeper of a London livery stable, who, in return for a cut, provided horses at all hours (hired horses were usually used, because less easily identified). Wilson later wrote that:

> As he kept a livery-stable, we had an opportunity of getting out at all times in the night: so that we harrass'd almost all the morning stage-coaches in England. One morning we robb'd the Cirencester, the Worcester, the Glocester, the Oxford, and Bristol stage-coaches, all together; the next morning the Ipswich and Colchester, and a third morning perhaps the Portsmouth coach. The Bury coach has been our constant customer; I think we have touch'd that coach ten times: For any of these we never went further than the Stones-End.[50]

This gang always robbed coaches within four miles of London, and Wilson believed it could have continued for years had it not made the mistake of robbing the mail.

While passengers were easily frightened by suspicious-looking men on horseback, the actual incidence of robbery appears to have been small. Only one robbery was recorded by a diarist in 258 journeys (it happened to Dugdale near Dunstable in 1673), though Elizabeth Freke travelled in a Canterbury coach which was beset by five highwaymen and escaped.[51] Coaches routinely travelled in the dark, but highwaymen seem to have disliked the night-time, because they more easily aroused suspicion and it was harder to see the prey and whether it was armed.[52] It was also harder for them to hire horses at night. Coaches often travelled in convoy near London, and although this was not always effective it must sometimes have deterred highwaymen.[53] Otherwise coachmasters do not seem to have taken precautions. None of the coachmasters' inventories records firearms, apart from the musket of John Holloway, Chester proprietor, in 1689,[54] and there is no evidence of stage-coaches carrying guards in the 17th or early 18th centuries, except an advertisement that the Cirencester coach would do so 'the whole season of flying' in 1738; not until 1764 does another advertisement refer to guards.[55]

Thus stage-coaches had both advantages and disadvantages, and many of the diarists used different means of travel on different occasions, reflecting for example whether they were travelling alone or with their families and whether they wished to pay visits or sightsee on the way. Whether their horse or horses would be useful or an encumbrance in London was probably also significant.

The experience of stage-coach travel

How did stage-coach passengers amuse themselves during long days cooped up in a coach? Pepys, typically, went through virtually the whole range of possibilities during a day in the Cambridge flying coach in 1668. His fellow passengers included 'one lady alone that is tolerable handsome, but mighty well spoken, whom I took great pleasure in talking to, and did get her to read aloud in a book she was reading in the coach, being the King's Meditations; and then the boy and I to sing'; after dinner ('we dining all together and pretty merry') he slept most of the way. Coach travel was undoubtedly more fun with Pepys than with the Rev. Henry Newcome, who, as discussed earlier, used the Lichfield coach in 1681: 'We have the better journey because we have not much talk (the Countess of Arglass being reserved,) and so not troublesome nor sinful.'[56]

Reading aloud or privately was probably common, at least when the leather flap was open allowing light in. In the Chester coach in 1712 Matthew Henry read King's *History of the Apostle's Creed* 'to redeem if possible a little time'. When Philip Doddridge took the coach to Hinckley in 1722,

> My company was as good as I could have expected. There was indeed one violent Tory;
> but when he knew that I was a dissenter, he had the good manners to drop the discourse.
> We had a volume of Dryden in the coach, and that served to entertain us when the
> conversation began to flag.

In 1710, shortly after the impeachment of Henry Sacheverell for seditious sermons, Matthew Henry had 'very good company' in the Chester coach – 'in all ye way to London we had not once Sachevrools name in ye coach'. Marthae Turner travelled by coach in the 1730s with 'three ladies from York and an old bachelor with whom we did not fail to divert ourselves all the way ... all courted him by turns ... The gentleman had discernment enough to see that all I meant was to pass a few cheerful hours at no other expense than a ridicule of the extravagancies of mankind in love'. John Lauder in the York coach in 1667 'had large discourses of the idleness and vitiousnese of the citizens wifes at London being wery cocknies'.[57]

When Rawdon used the stage-coach to York in August 1658, his Spanish boy rode beside the coach, 'leadinge a spare geldinge for his maister to ride uppon when he thought fitt'. 'A big fatt gentleman' travelling in the York coach in March 1656 'lighted outt to walke a litle', and this was probably common, especially in winter, when the coach's pace was slower; indeed it was probably required when ascending or descending steep hills.[58]

Coaches stopped for dining, generally in the middle of the day's journey, and those with the longest hours usually stopped for breakfast too, and in a few cases for evening refreshments.[59] According to a fictional account of a journey in the Exeter coach written in 1725:

> They most unmercifully set us to dinner at ten a-clock, upon a great leg of mutton. It is
> the custom of these dining stages, to prepare one day beef, and another our present fare;
> it is ready against the coach comes: And tho' you should have a perfect antipathy, there
> is no remedy but fasting: The coachman begs your pardon; he would not stay dressing
> a dinner for the King (God bless him) should he travel in his coach.[60]

Passengers usually shared the cost of dining. When the coach carrying the two prostitutes stopped to dine, they 'would not stir out of the coach, for feare the custome of travellers should be put in practice where all pay alike'. When the coach carrying Roger Whitley stopped for dinner at Barnet in 1687, he noted that 'ye women dined by ym selfes'. Thoresby observed upon leaving Stamford in 1714, 'Had other passengers, which, though females, were more chargeable in wine and brandy than the former part of the journey, wherein we had neither; but the next day ... we gave them leave to treat themselves'.[61]

CHAPTER IX

COACHMASTERS

Whereas in the 1650s most coachmasters were Londoners, by the 1680s it was common for stage-coaches, like carrying firms, to have proprietors only at the provincial destination; indeed, by then many coachmasters *were* carriers. For example, the proprietors of the main Gloucester coach in 1681 were Susanna Bower and Dorothy Cromwell, both of Gloucester and widows of Gloucester carriers. In 1704 there were four shares in this coach, two held by John Wood, carrier, one by William Jordan, gentleman (who had married one of the widows), and one by Thomas Huff, waggoner, all of Gloucester. In that year Wood sold his shares to a Gloucester innkeeper, James Pitts, who by 1715 was sole proprietor.[1]

In contrast, the four partners in the Exeter coach in 1677 were all Londoners: Benjamin Fleming, coachman, William Baker, citizen and leatherseller, Fulk Biscabe, citizen and armourer, and John Booth, citizen and innholder (in fact innkeeper at the coach's London inn).[2] Similarly, the Chester coach continued to have three London partners, who until 1688 were Henry Earl, described in his will as a coachmaster, William Fowler, citizen and coachmaker, and John Holloway, citizen and leatherseller.[3]

A third type, with partners based between the two destinations, is exemplified by the Bristol, Bath and Newbury coaches. In 1672 their proprietors included widow Toobey, almost certainly of Reading (where her son was continuing the business in 1681), Mr Baldwin, an innkeeper at Twyford near Reading, Mr Drew, an innkeeper at Newbury, and Mr Wells, an innkeeper at Bath.[4]

The York coach was different again. In the 1680s, as in the 1650s, it had partners in both York and London, related by marriage, although whether the marriage resulted in the business relationship or vice versa is unknown. The York partners were Francis and Margaret Gardner, the latter being Robert Gardner's widow and owner of the coach's inn, the *Black Swan*, Coney Street. The London partner, Henry Molden, described himself as a coachman.[5]

Thus the longer-distance coaches might have proprietors at the country terminus, in London, at places between or at several of these. Partly this reflected their origins, the earliest coaches tending to have London partners (with exceptions such as Norwich and Salisbury),[6] but the situation could change, as discussed below. Carriers had to live near the source of their trade, so coachmasters who were also carriers almost inevitably lived at or near their country terminus, but the coachmaster was otherwise under no such compulsion. His customers were not concentrated in one area like the carrier's, he had less need (or opportunity) to search for business other than through general advertising, and he had much less work to do at either terminus than the carrier. There was less need for personal contact and trust in coaching, since passengers could largely look after themselves, rather than being lost or stolen; diarists virtually never recorded coachmasters by name.[7] Furthermore, at least in summer, coach teams were changed *en route*, so that whereas a carrier could inspect all his horses at regular intervals from the

The Reasons Humbly offered for continuing the Stage-Coaches upon the grand Roads of this Kingdome

ANSWERED.

First and Second Reason.

THe keepers of the said Coaches apprehending the usefulness of them to the publick, and being by Counsel advised it was lawful to set them up, did about 30. years sithence set them up, have ever sithence continued them, at their very great charge & hazard for the conveniency of the subject & to the general satisfaction of those that have used them; layd out all their stocks upon, and spent all their time in management of them, by means whereof they have rendred themselves unfit for any other course of lively hood for support of themselves and families.

Answer By the Stage-Coaches on the Grand Roads of *England*, is meant *Exeter*, *Salisbury*, *Bristol*, *Southampton*, *Dover* *Norwich*, *Lincoln*, *Northampton* *York* *Westchester*, and *Shrewsbury*, the owners of which Coaches, joyn in opposing the suppressing.

Norwich was set up about 30 years, sithence *York* about 18. *Chester* about 20, *Exeter* between 20 and 30. the others very lately.

The first stage-Coaches were long Coaches in the middle of the Waggons, that travelled with their horses one before another, about 20 or 25 miles a day, were a week or eight dayes going to *York*, *Exeter*, and *Chester*, and so proportionably to the other stages.

These travelled easy, carryed sick and Antient people, journeys suitable to their strength, and went not above once to a place, in one week, so did no great hurt.

And as it was a great conveyency to the Subject, that could not travel any other way, so it was lawful to set them up.

But the persons who now keep Stage Coaches, are not the men that first set them up, nor have they continued them 30 years, or been since they undertook them a conveniance to the Subjects that have used them, any way answerable to the grandure of the mischiefs they have been, and are, to Trade in general, especially to the Manufacturers of Wooll, Leather, Iron, the staple commodities of the Kingdome, who ought to be encouraged; nor have they given that general satisfaction to those that have used them, as will appear in the answer to their Arguments.

But these Gentlemen finding the Coaches aforesaid set up, took the advantage of the late troubles, and when mens horses were taken from them, so that they had not to carry them their journeys, set up these Coaches that go with horses two a breast, and for many years travell'd with four horses in a Coach, and went to *York*, *Exeter*, and *Chester* in a week, and but once a week, all this time there were so few, that they did little or no hurt, but now of late, have set up running Stage-Coaches, change horses twice a day, run these long journeyes in four dayes, to the great prejudice of the Countrey, and they have three Coaches a week at least, sometimes, 4. 5. 6. Coaches go to every of these towns, which is a great destruction to the Countrey as will hereafter appear.

From these Gentlemen example it is, that now all great towns in *England* have set up Stage-Coaches and every little town within twenty miles of *London* swarms with them, to the almost utter destruction of the Countrey.

These Stage Coachmen that have been the principal occasions of this incomparable advantage to the Kingdome, having laid out their stock, their time, and their wit, to contrive this Ruine, and who have no way to live but upon the further destruction of the people, hope therefore that they shall be continued, and allowed. For *York* and Lincoln Stage is kept by Mr. Doin a Scrivener by trade, Mr, Gardner an Innholder in *York*, and a Coach and Hornes-maker, followes the trade, The Widdow Hayhort who is Licensed to keep a Coach in London and keeps an Inn. Exeter Coach is kept by Mr. Fleming a Licensed Coach in London, Mr. Bifcopy and Mr. both rich men and of other imploy. Shrewsbury and Chester Coach kept by Mr. Hathoway Mr. Fowler and Mr. Eatle, all rich men, and Licensed to keep Coaches in London, and the last of them followes the trade of Coach and Harness making. Dover Stage kept by Mr. Jones Licensed in London, Northampton, by Mr. King Licensed in London. Winchester and Henly, by Mr. Hathoway and Mr, Robinson, both Licensed, Windsor, by Mr. Sadler a Licensed man, and Mr. Lee a Rich Barber Chyrurgeon. Glocester, Bedford, Huntington, by Mr. Comwell, Mr, Rash, Mr, York, All three of them great Carryers and keep Waggons. Bristol, Bath, Newberry, by Mr. Baldwin that hath an Inn at Twiford, Mr. Wells Innholder at Bath, Mr. Shute a Baker and Mr. Drew Innkeeper at Newberry. Redding Coaches, the owners Inholders in Redding, Tunbridge, Mr, Forster, and others, all Licensed in London. Gilford, Mr. Kemp Licensed in London. Mr. Smart Innholder in Gilford. Oxford, Mr. Moore, and Mr. Battlet both Waggoners and Carryers. Salisbury, Mr. Minchin a Carryer, the others great Inholders in Salisbury, and so in most towns of England, (except here about London, which are all set up within few years) The owners of Stage-Coaches are Inholders, first, one in a town set up a Coach, brought all Guests to his house, Then a second, third and fourth in a town set them up to bring guests to their houses, and run one against the other, killed multitudes of Horses and almost ruin'd one another, insomuch that excepting these Long Stage-Coaches, (who you see know not how to live, though qualified as aforesaid) they would be glad all over *England* to have them put down, that all might go down, for then trade would be defused, and each expect a Trade according to the reception they had for their Guests.

3. Reason

54 *One of John Cressett's pamphlets arguing against the stage-coaches in 1672, including his analysis of the coachmasters. (SP 29/319, No. 200.)*

provincial terminus or any other point on the route a coachmaster could not, which meant either living somewhere between the coach's termini where teams were changed, having partners at several different places or travelling regularly to see the horses; hence the variety of arrangements just described.

Other occupations

According to Cressett in 1672, the long-distance coachmen 'are all of them either innholders, or coach or harness-makers, following those trades, or carriers, or licensed coachmen in London ... The other stage-coaches are all, or most of them, kept either by inn-holders' or by former hackney coachmen without licences.[8] Cressett provided evidence to support this as regards the longer stages (Fig. 54), and it can be confirmed for the 1680s from other sources.

The importance of carriers by 1681 is obvious in Delaune's lists: carriers were then involved in 20 of the 61 services covering 40 or more miles from London, and in 1690 in 19 of the 55 such services (15 of which were wholly owned by carriers), as well as in a few shorter-distance coaches. Six carrier-coachmasters were recorded in 1672, including Mr Cromwell of Gloucester, Mr Rush of Bedford and Mr Minchin of Salisbury,[9] some of whom had probably been the founders of their coach services. Not only had carriers long been involved in passenger transport (hiring out nags or accommodating passengers in waggons), but they also had the business contacts which facilitated the establishment of a coach. Since coach and waggon horses were probably similar in this period,[10] carriers may also have had an advantage in being able to switch horses between the two businesses and thus make the best possible use of the horses' costly labour. This is supported by the fact that almost all the carrier-coachmasters carried by waggon rather than packhorse.[11] However, the benefits of combining carrying and coaching were not so great that the majority of carriers at places which could support a coach service did so, or that carriers never sold their coaching interests.

Innkeepers had become heavily involved in coaching by the 1680s, sometimes through obtaining shares in existing coaches. Examples in 1672 included Mr Gardner and widow Hayhurst (York coach), Messrs Baldwin, Wells and Drew (Bristol, Bath and Newbury coaches), Mr Smart (Guildford coach) and several proprietors of Salisbury and Reading coaches.[12] The best example is John Booth of the *Saracens Head*, Friday Street, London, who was involved in Exeter, Taunton and Bristol coaches in 1681 (he was also a lace merchant). Booth was the first example of what was later a common type, the London innkeeper with interests in coaches on several different roads. However, he soon sold his share in the Exeter coach and by 1690 apparently retained only his interest in Bristol coaches.[13] The main benefit to innkeepers of owning a coach may have been the opportunity to persuade passengers to stay at their inn, though passengers were under no obligation to do so.[14]

Innkeepers may well have dominated the shorter-distance services from the beginning, as Cressett claimed. Those of the 1680s who can be identified are Peter Blackwell of Chipping Barnet (the *Antelope*), Matthew Freer of Aylesbury, Arthur Palmer and Thomas Robinson of Chelmsford and Anthony Wright of Romford.[15]

Hackney coachmen were much less significant in stage-coaching in the 1680s than the 1650s, but a list of hackney coachmen licensed in 1685 includes at least seven stage-coach owners. For some of these, such as John Holloway and Henry Earl of the Chester coach, the hackney licences must by then have been simply a valuable possession, enabling them to hire out coaches and horses within 12 miles of London, rather than an essential part of their livelihood. Hackney coachmen were most heavily involved in 1681 in services to Windsor, no doubt tempted there by the presence of the court; among them was Elias Gliss, whose stock at his death in 1697 included six hackney coaches, twelve horses and two coach licences.[16] The hackney coachmen had argued in 1663 that all stage-coaches within 30 miles of London should be suppressed, since they could perform this service at the same rates.[17]

Cressett provided only two examples of coach and harness makers among coachmasters (Mr Fowler of the Chester coach[18] and Mr Gardner of the York coach, who was also an innkeeper); no others have been found prior to the 1730s. A few other occupations are recorded. In 1672 Mr Lee of the Windsor coaches was 'a rich barber chyrurgeon' and Mr Shute of the Bath and Bristol coaches was a baker. Henry Robinson, a lace-buyer, had a coach between Buckingham and London in 1683. In contrast to the carriers, few coachmasters were farmers, but examples are Michael Minchin of Salisbury in 1679, Andrew Hart of Cambridge in 1681, and, somewhat later, the Beecrofts of Norwich in 1710 and 1723 and James Blackbourne, Boston coachmaster, in 1742. Among these at least Hart and Blackbourne were also carriers. As already discussed, several major figures combined coaching, carrying and another trade: it was evidently possible for an energetic individual to run a coach as one of a group of businesses.[19]

Where does this leave the owner-drivers sometimes believed to have been the pioneers of stage-coaching? Many coachmasters had other occupations which would have left insufficient time for them to drive their coaches, but not all did so, and some were described as 'coachman' in their wills. However, most of these had too many coaches and teams and too many services per week to drive their coaches themselves, and inventories and legal proceedings often record their employment of drivers. For example, among the Exeter partners, even the one described in 1677 as a coachman employed a driver, who gave evidence in a lawsuit.[20] John Holloway's inventory names the drivers of the coaches used between Chester and the *Welsh Harp*.[21] Except among the short-stagers, only five definite owner-drivers are recorded, all in the 18th century and two of them provincial: in 1710 Samuel Bunn intended 'to leave off driving the stage coach from Northwalsham to Norwich'; up to 1717 Daniel Crosland, with one coach and four horses, drove his coach between Bury St Edmunds and London; in 1720 James Toogood bought the Dorchester coach and 'for the better care and satisfaction of his passengers, drives the whole stage himself'; in 1722 Samuel Bartlett sometimes drove his own Oxford to London coaches, though the Chancellor's Court, having received complaints about his behaviour, ordered him to stop doing so; and in 1728 Joseph Singleton advertised his intention to provide a weekly York to Newcastle coach 'and to drive himself'.[22] Owner-drivers existed but were extremely rare: anyone wealthy enough to own several coaches and teams usually had better ways of using his time than driving a coach.

The short-stagers such as Francis Snow of Uxbridge are at first sight more promising as owner-drivers. Snow began his working life as a husbandman in

55 The Coach and Horses, *Bethel Street, Norwich. In 1736 Thomas Bateman's London waggons and coaches were setting off from the* Coach and Horses. *Bateman had purchased Thomas Southgate's coaches and waggons in 1710, and, since an earlier Thomas Southgate had been of St Giles parish (in which much of the inn is situated) when he advertised the first Norwich stage-coach in 1657, it is possible that the* Coach and Horses *was Norwich's first coaching inn. The building is apparently of 17th-century date. Early stage-coaches were often associated with public houses called the* Coach and Horses, *though of course not every inn now bearing that name was associated with an early stage-coach.*

the Brill area. In about 1669 he became servant to Lady Clarke in Oxfordshire and at Hillingdon, Middlesex, and for the next 20 years 'was part of the said tyme her coachman & the rest of it did look after or manage her parsonag at Hillingdon for her'. In 1689 or 1690, aged about 50, he began to keep the Uxbridge stage-coach, and was described as a stage-coachman in his inventory of 1704.[23] Possibly he did drive the 36 miles a day required for a daily Uxbridge service, and a Bow and Stratford coachman in 1715 and a Chelsea coachman in 1749 certainly drove their own coaches, but the only other example shows that the short-stagers sometimes employed drivers. In 1691 one Thomas Boulton 'who drove the stage-coach for his master Thomas Rapeir of Chiswick' ran away taking some of his master's money.[24] Short-stagers who were innkeepers cannot have been driving their own coaches. Even the London hackney coaches were not always driven by their owners.[25]

A new form of ownership appeared in 1695 which was sometimes adopted later. In that year a new Norwich coach was established, because, it was claimed (somewhat vaguely), the existing coaches had been 'so ill performed, that the passengers travelling therein, have been very much incommoded, and the journeying by the said coaches rendred very irksome and burdensome':

And forasmuch as no single person, or five or six in company would venture to set up a new stage; it was therefore thought reasonable and necessary, that a more considerable number should joyn together, and by a joynt stock set up a new and more convenient stage ... ; which accordingly is done by the subscription of above 200 persons. And it is by the subscribers agreed, that what profit shall be made of the moneys employed in the said stock, above 10l. per cent. per annum [10%] shall be applyed to charitable uses.[26]

This was not only the first subscription coach but also the first named coach – the 'Confatharrat' (presumably *Confederate*).[27] Whether it prospered and provided any benefit to the poor is unknown.

Delaune listed 11 female coach proprietors, all of whom (with one possible exception)[28] were widows. Only three (at most) were listed both in 1681 and 1690 – widow Barnet (Reading and Newbury coach), Margaret Gardner (York coach) and Mrs Elizabeth Twitty (widow Twittey in 1690 – Worcester coach).

Wealth

Cressett described many of the longer-distance coachmasters as 'rich men', and many were indeed men of substance, frequently with not only expensive teams and coaches but also inns, carrying businesses or other interests. The most well-to-do among them included John Holloway of the Chester coach, with ready money amounting to £626 in 1689, Thomas Jaques of the Portsmouth coach, innkeeper at Petersfield's largest inn (the *White Hart*) and three times Mayor, Andrew Hart of Cambridge, who was an alderman and had lands at Caxton, and Onias Phillippo of Norwich, who owned houses in six parishes in 1693 and was the brother of a High Sheriff of Norfolk. Several, such as Henry Earl of the Chester coach, bought property along their coach's route.[29] These were among the 46 coachmasters (nearly a quarter of the total) dignified by Delaune as 'Mr'.[30] Other coachmasters who became or had been mayors included Samuel Lyon of Northampton in 1715 and Henry Robinson of Buckingham. The latter established an assembly room, a bowling green and a London stage-coach in Buckingham and sought political power there; though denounced by his main gentry opponent as 'a mean, rude, debauched fellow unfit for society, much less governance', he briefly became mayor under James II.[31]

In terms of coaching stock there was a wide range from John Holloway of the Chester coach, with 31 horses and ten coaches, to Francis Snow of Uxbridge with nine horses and two coaches and William Hickman of Barnet with five horses and three coaches. In inventories, the proportion of the value of the coachmaster's goods accounted for by the coaching stock varied widely: from Matthew Freer's 15 per cent to John Smead's 93 per cent (Appendix 7). The capital required to establish a coach service was not enormous – typically £50 to £250 (though perhaps twice as much to purchase a going concern) – so the range overlapped that of the start-up costs for some of the lesser trades in London, such as carman (£60 to £100), and some of the middling ones, such as apothecary (£50 to £200), mason, tailor and vintner (all £100 to £500).[32] The majority of coachmasters whose wills have been found were able to sign their name, but there were exceptions, including Benjamin Fleming, Exeter coachman, and Henry Waters and Henry Molden, York coachmen.

Change among the coachmasters

The locations and occupations of coachmasters continued to change after the 1680s, as shown in Table 6. As regards locations, the trends from the 1650s were the declining importance of Londoners, the rise and then fall in the proportion

Table 6. Occupations and residences of coachmasters, 1654-1740

Date	1654-9	1672	1681-90	1715-40
No. of coachmasters' names recorded	16	28	99	110
No. identified	12	28	67	64
Occupations				
Hackney coachmen	6	13	5	0
Coachmen	2	0	13	8
Carriers	1	6	30	8
Innkeepers	1	6	14	27
Others	4	5	4	3
Places of residence				
London	8	15	12	6
Intermediate	1	3	16	33
Provincial destination	2	7	33	23

Sources: for 1654-9, newspapers, and see text; for 1672, SP 29/319, No. 200, with wills etc.; for 1681-90, Delaune 1681 and 1690, with Chancery and Exchequer records, wills, inventories and Corporation of London RO, Misc. MSS. 212.7 (list of hackney licences 1685); for 1715-40, newspapers, especially LEP, with wills etc.

Notes: Only coachmasters covering 40 or more miles and serving London are included; coach-waggons are excluded. 'Identified' means either residence or occupation or both have been identified. Hackney coachmen are those with licences, not necessarily acting as such; all are assumed to be London-based. 'Coachman' are those for whom that is specifically recorded as their occupation. Some coachmen had more than one occupation, so figures may not add up. The proportion of carriers in 1681-90 is inflated because there is a complete list of them. The 14 coachmasters briefly involved in the Warrington coach in 1738-40 are excluded.

NORWICH, June the 1st, 1741.

WHEREAS it was advertised in the last Saturday's News-Papers, that the London Stage-Coach would set out from the Duke's-Palace on Thursday the 11th of June, by which some may think it to be the old Stage kept by Mr. James Nasmith and Mrs. Beecroft ; but that is still kept by them, and goes from Mrs. Beecroft's House near Tombland in Norwich : This new Coach is set up by the Landlord at the Bull-Inn in Bishopsgate-Street, and some Landlords on the Essex Road, to bring Guests to their own Houses : But the Proprietors of the Old STAGE-COACH are determined to send out a Coach on the 11th of June, to go the Essex Road, by Way of Bury, from Mrs. Beecroft's in Norwich, and the Green-Dragon Inn in Bishopsgate-Street in London, every Thursday Morning from each Place ; and also to continue the old Stage, every Monday and Friday Morning, by the Way of Newmarket. N. B. As the Landlords who have set up the new Coach have advertised to carry Passengers at Fifteen Shillings each, the Proprietors of the old Stage will carry at the same Price.

WHEREAS there was an Advertisement put out June 1, 1741, to inform all Persons that the New Stage-Coach from Norwich to London was set up by the Landlord at the Bull-Inn in Bishopsgate-Street, and some other Landlords on the Essex Road, to bring Guests to their Houses ; it is very plain the Design of this is to insinuate to the Passengers, that they are to be imposed on when they come to these Landlords Houses : But to prevent those Insinuations having any Influence on them, they must be very sensible that such Imposition on them must be against the Interest of both their Houses and Coach : All the Advantage these Landlords design is, to support a Coach from Norwich to Lynn to and from London through Bury, which was dropt some little Time since ; and being willing to give up all those Advantages other Stage-Masters used to make, (who are not Landlords) This is to inform the Publick, that the Stage-Coach from Mr. JOHN GODFREY's in Norwich takes up Passengers at Fifteen Shillings each to London, and at the Bull-Inn in Bishopsgate-Street in London to Norwich at the same Price. N. B. And carries Passengers to and from Norwich to Bury at Five Shillings a Passenger, if Room in the Stage.

By Us, {
Thomas Goodchild.
St. George Norman.
Alexander Appleyard.
Benjamin Pottinger.
}

56 & 57 *Advertisements for an established Norwich stage-coach and a new competitor in 1741. (*Norwich Gazette, *20 & 27 June 1741.)*

based at provincial destinations, and the increasing proportion at intermediate places, who were the majority in 1715-40. The changes in occupations were in part related to these trends: the declining importance of hackney coachmen (all Londoners), the rise and then fall in the proportion of carriers (almost all based at provincial destinations) and the inexorable rise in the proportion of innkeepers, who were dominant in 1715-40.

The changing pattern in the earlier period is symbolised by William Drew, coachmaster to Bristol and Bath, who was a London hackney coachman in 1663 but an innkeeper at Newbury by 1672.[33] The Salisbury coach was owned by two Salisbury men in 1664 (one apparently a farmer), then from about 1690 to 1719 by an innkeeper roughly mid-way at Hartfordbridge, and subsequently by an Egham innkeeper, with innkeeper-partners at Salisbury and elsewhere, until at least 1746.[34] Whereas the Exeter coach was owned by four Londoners in 1677, by 1690 an Exeter carrier, resident at Exeter, had two of the four shares; the owner of another share (obtained through marriage) was later recorded living at Dorchester, and the other was a London painter who had inherited a share. In 1705 the carrier's shares were sold to an Exeter tucker. A Salisbury innkeeper was later among the proprietors.[35]

The changing pattern is just what might have been expected. The potential of the long-distance stage-coach was first perceived from London and was exploited predominantly by the hackney coachmen. Others then adopted the innovation, especially carriers, together with others who could see the advantage of setting up a stage-coach from their own town or city. But the business which stage-coaching complemented best was innkeeping, and the best place of residence for the coachmaster was an intermediate one, and these factors gradually asserted themselves. As already indicated, coaching imposed much less work on the innkeeper than carrying, it could be combined advantageously with the hiring out of horses and coaches and it brought custom to the inn. The latter was especially so at intermediate places, since at the two termini passengers were more likely to make their own arrangements. Moreover, since teams were changed at intermediate places, residing at such places made it easier to keep an eye on them. Hence also the increasing tendency to have partners at more than one place; the Gloucester coach, for example, had a partner at Oxford from 1741 – the first who was not a Gloucester resident.[36]

Despite the increasing role of innkeepers there continued to be a variety of partnerships in the 18th century, and patterns established early were sometimes tenacious, such as the dominance of carriers at Norwich, where a challenge from innkeepers of London and intermediate places was beaten off by aggressive fare-cutting in 1741.[37] Other coaches which continued to be run by carriers in the 1730s and 1740s included those of Taunton (John Whitmash of Taunton), Boston (James Blackbourne of Peterborough) and Birmingham (Nicholas Rothwell of Warwick). A postmaster, Thomas Hartcup, was one of the Canterbury coach's owners in 1750.[38] Innkeepers might be at the provincial destination, intermediate places or London, and they were sometimes in partnership with others; for example, the Lincoln coach in 1732-3 was run by John Vinter, innkeeper at the Dolphin, Huntingdon, and Thomas Yonick, coachman of London.[39]

Another change in the 18th century (connected with the dominance of innkeepers and intermediate locations) was an increasing concentration of ownership, foreshadowing the later tendency of innkeepers to be partners in several coaches with different destinations. The greatest coachmaster of the period was Thomas Smith, a London coachmaker, who by 1736 had shares in the Nottingham group of coaches, the Northampton coach and the Chester and Lichfield coaches and full ownership of the Daventry coach. However, in that year he sold them all and became an innkeeper at Whetstone.[40] Less spectacular but more typical examples are Thomas Taylor of Bury St Edmunds, with Bury, Yarmouth and King's Lynn coaches in 1737 and briefly a Norwich one in 1739, and William Haynes of Oxford, with Gloucester, Oxford and Abingdon coaches in 1741. The few provincial services often belonged to London coachmasters; for example, in 1730 John Whitmash of Taunton had coaches both from Taunton to London and Exeter to Bath.[41]

The Warrington coach of 1738-40 deserves mention here as the first owned (albeit briefly) by a large partnership of innkeepers. Its leading partners in 1738 were a stable-keeper and a coachmaker of London, who held three of the eight shares, but by April 1739 the partners included 11 innkeepers along the route. However, the route was not divided into separately operated stages, and expenses were paid by the partnership as a whole. Rather than have his own stage, the innkeeper at Stone received only a guarantee that the coach would call at his inn and six horses be stationed there. Moreover, the innkeepers sold out in 1740, after which the coach had just two proprietors.[42] Teams were not yet changed frequently enough, and not for enough of the year, to justify short, separately operated stages; the age of large partnerships of innkeepers lay in the future.

CHAPTER X

COACHES, HORSES AND TEAMS

Coaches

The advertisement for 'new coaches' to York in 1653 stated that 'Each coach containes 14 passengers, having three distinct rooms, that who please may have a room for themselves'. Such coaches were perhaps a development from the coach-waggon. However, six-seater coaches soon became the norm: they were in use on the Exeter route in 1655 and almost certainly on the York route by 1658.[1] They remained the norm until the 1750s.

The few contemporary drawings of stage-coaches indicate that they were little different from the gentlemen's coaches depicted by Loggan (e.g. Fig. 58), though they may have been more robustly constructed. The rear axle was fixed to the axle bed, but the front axle was capable of swivelling. Coach bodies were made of wood covered by leather, and were suspended on leather straps from poles which rested on the axle at the back and probably on a cross-piece supported by the axle bed at the front (Fig. 59). The York coaches

58   *Engraving of a coach by David Loggan in 1675.*

59 *Engraving of a coach at the head of the stage-coach list in the* Merchants and traders necessary companion *of 1715. The method of suspending the coach-body is clearly shown.*

were advertised in 1654 as 'the post hanging coaches'. Coaches could sway from side to side but not backwards and forwards, which would have increased the horses' labour. Coaches used within London were loosely slung, since they otherwise transmitted all the jolts of cobbled surfaces, but on rutted country roads loosely slung coaches might swing so much that they overturned, and travelling coaches therefore had to be tightly slung, losing some of the benefit of the slinging. Steel springs for coaches were invented in England in about 1670, but were not applied to stage-coaches until 1752. In 1760 stage-coaches were said to last only 2½ to three years.[2]

The coachman sat in a raised position in front, on a bar or box between the two poles from which the body was suspended.[3] There are references to boots (occasionally a 'box') at the back, in which poorer passengers or servants sometimes travelled at reduced fares, though there are not many examples of people travelling in the boot. Edward Parker, who used the Chester coach in 1663, wrote that

> My journey was noe way pleasant, being forced to ride in the boote all the waye. ... This travell hath so indisposed mee, yt I am resolved never to ride up againe in ye coatche. I am extremely hott and feverish.[4]

Anthony Wood stated that the first Oxford flying coach had 'a boot on each side', which must have meant a boot on each side *at the back*, rather than at the sides of the coach, which would have been dangerous and troublesome in narrow roads. This is supported by the fact that passengers in the boot apparently faced sideways – 'carried backe to backe'. However, two of the six York coaches in an inventory of 1672 were described as 'a boote coach', as if only a certain type of coach had boots.[5] The boots were mainly for luggage, which was certainly carried at the back (hence the many advertisements recording the loss of articles from behind stage-coaches).[6]

Inside the coach, the six seats were apparently at the two 'ends', facing backwards and forwards, one being known as 'the brood end'.[7] In 1657 the York coach was to take up a gentlewoman and her maid:

When she lookt into the coach, seeinge booth the ends full, she askt the coachman where she was to sitt; he told hir the ends were full, and that he could nott displace aney of the gentlemen that were thir; 'Well then', saith she, 'my maide shall sitt in a boote; but if I cannott have a place att one end for my selfe, I will nott goe'.[8]

This was resolved by one of the gentlemen giving her his seat. There are several references from 1672 to 1689 to '3 end coaches', on the York, Chester and Tonbridge routes, but it is not clear what these were.[9] The middle seats at each end were probably always unpopular.[10] Until well into the 18th century no-one sat on the roof.

At first all coaches had leather flaps or curtains instead of windows, and must have been extremely gloomy when the flap had to be closed. According to Aubrey the first 'glass coach', with windows, was brought to England by the Duke of York shortly after the Restoration, and coach glass was soon being manufactured. Pepys travelled in a glass hackney coach in 1668, and it is unlikely that the stage-coaches lagged behind the hackneys. One of Thomas Hayhurst's six York coaches in 1672 was a glass coach, and John Holloway had six glass coaches for the Chester and other services in 1689. However, in 1721, prospective customers of the Chester coach were told that they 'may have a chariot, or glass coach, instead of a curtain coach', which indicates that glass coaches were not always used even then. A glass coach was also an optional extra on the Lincoln route in 1733, and, as late as 1752, an Irish gentleman who travelled in summer by stage-coach from Nottingham to London and London to Bath 'very frequently regretted being so confined in these kind of vehicles, which afford no other prospect than what you have inside, as there is no glass in 'em'.[11]

Before the 1750s there is little evidence of technical innovation in stage-coaches. Even when a new term is used for the vehicle, it is not usually clear what was new, as in the case of the 'new large easy machine coach' to Northampton in 1728 (the first application of the word 'machine' to a stage-coach), the 'three-end stage-coach, on Mr Rowe's new principle' to Windsor and Portsmouth in 1734 and Richmond in 1735, and the 'stage-chaises' to Chester in 1750.[12] None of these seem to have been faster or cheaper than ordinary coaches.[13]

60 *Engraving from an undated handbill for the Canterbury coach. (Corporation of London RO, PD/100/18.)*

More significantly, from the 1720s there were a few flying coaches carrying only four passengers. These were presumably smaller and lighter, making possible smaller teams. They were serving Newbury in 1727, Blandford and Dorchester in 1728 and Sherborne in 1734. Such vehicles may explain the very early adoption of summer schedules to Newbury in 1723 (by 23 February). The Newbury and Blandford coaches (but not the Sherborne one) had exceptionally low fares – 1.7 or 1.8d per mile.[14] However, if four-seater coaches were so successful, it is difficult to see why they were not adopted more widely, and none of these services seems to have lasted more than a few years.

Horses and teams

Coach horses were the largest horses in existence in the 17th and early 18th centuries. Advertisements referred to them as if they were a separate type of horse, and of 67 coach horses whose sizes were stated between 1682 and 1745 all but five were from 15 to 16 hands high,[15] whereas horses exceeding 15 hands were otherwise rare. Defoe twice mentioned heavy horses: those bred in the Somerset Levels, sold to London 'for cart horses, and coach horses, the breed being very large', and those reared in Leicestershire, 'the largest in England, being generally the great black coach horses and dray horses'.[16] Although stage-coach horses were not necessarily the same as those used for coaches in general they are unlikely to have been smaller. In 1672 stage-coach horses were said to eat twice as much as saddle horses, and the defender of stage-coaches argued that the existence of coaches resulted in there being more horses of bulk and strength.[17]

Of the 29 advertised coach horses whose colour was given, 22 were black, which indicates the importance of imports in improving the breed (nine large black Dutch coach mares, recently imported, were advertised for sale in 1727).[18] Coachmasters' inventories, when sufficiently precise, list geldings and 'stone horses' (stallions), but not mares.[19]

Of the 16 references (other than in inventories) to the teams used for longer-distance coaches, the seven indicating teams of four horses are from late March to June.[20] The nine indicating teams of six horses are from late October to March, apart from one to the York coach in September 1654 and one to the Chester coach in early October 1723, when the coach was still following its four-day summer schedule.[21] (Possibly six-horse teams were sometimes used at the beginning and end of the period of summer schedules.)[22] The inventories which describe teams separately present a similar picture. For example, Thomas Hayhurst was using six-horse teams for the York coach in November 1672, whereas Henry Molden was using four-horse teams for the same coach in June 1691.[23] Smaller teams were sometimes used, especially for short-distance coaches, such as an Enfield coach drawn by three horses in 1737,[24] and there are a couple of references to teams of eight being used for especially bad stretches of road,[25] but it is clear that teams of four horses in summer and six in winter were the norm, at least for longer-distance coaches.

Unlike waggons and coach-waggons, stage-coaches harnessed their horses two abreast. This was undoubtedly more efficient, as indicated above, but it is necessary to explain why stage-coaches could adopt the practice when waggoners apparently could not. Waggoners could not do so because the roads were generally too narrow both for horses in double file and for the waggon driver riding or walking beside them.[26] If the waggoner instead rode on the vehicle and the horses were two abreast, he could not adequately have controlled more than four horses, and one or more extra men would have been needed. Coaches, on the other hand, normally had only four horses in summer. Moreover, whereas waggon horses, proceeding at what seems to have been a natural speed of about two miles per hour, probably required only intermittent urging on by the waggoner, which could be administered to a team of six or more while walking or riding beside them, coach horses travelled faster and so are likely to have needed more continuous attention from the driver, making a more compact arrangement necessary. Removing the driver from the road to the vehicle enabled the horses to be placed in double file and so resolved this problem. There was the same disadvantage as for waggons of needing an extra man for teams of more than four horses, but the advantages of double file made this more worthwhile for coaches and the extra man was needed only in winter. Also, postilions seem to have been cheap: in 1760 the wages of coachmen and postilions were said to be 15s. and 3s. or 3s. 6d. per week respectively.[27]

All the illustrations of coaches showing teams of six have both a coachman driving from the coach and a postilion sitting on one of the leading horses, whereas none shows teams of four with a postilion.[28] The postilion must have been responsible for steering, and in 1656 Anne Murray blamed one who entered a bridge without parapets carelessly for nearly causing the coach's destruction.[29] The middle horses of a team of six must have been driven by the coachman, since the postilion could not have controlled horses which were behind him. They appear to have been controlled by reins routed through the headgear of the horses nearest the coach (reflecting the fact that the coachman was placed fairly low) (Figs. 45 and 58).

In the 11 inventories where the values of horses and coaches are given separately, horses averaged 70 per cent of the value of the coaching stock and coaches and harness, together with any hearses and chariots, 30 per cent, though the figures varied widely.[30] The values of horses averaged £5 8s. 0d. and those of coaches £12 0s. 0d.[31] Like 19th-century coachmasters, they may have kept the best horses near London: in 1689 John Holloway's London coaches and horses were more valuable than those kept at Whitchurch.

The penultimate column of Appendix 7 indicates the numbers of horses kept per double mile (i.e. the number required per mile of road if the service had been daily each way). There are many uncertainties here, including the extent to which horses were kept for other purposes, such as hiring out. Nevertheless, there is a tolerable consistency about the number of horses per double mile, which was normally from 0.4 to 0.6 in summer and 0.5 to 0.8 in winter. For comparison, in the 1830s, when coach speeds were much greater, 0.8 horses were required per double mile in summer and 0.9 (sometimes nearly 1.0) in winter.[32]

Horses and costs

As in the case of waggons, costs were largely determined by the number of horses kept. The best available breakdown of costs is William Morris's statement of his expenses for a quarter-share in the Exeter coach in 1688-9 (Fig. 61). Disregarding (as capital expenditure) £76 10s. 0d. paid for horses and coaches when taking over the share, the costs were 77.5 per cent for provender and other costs directly related to the number of horses (except new horses), 10.5 per cent for new horses, 7.4 per cent for coaches and 4.6 per cent for staff.[33] The figure for coaches, expressed as a sum per week, probably indicates not a hiring arrangement, since Morris had bought his coaches, but the average cost of maintaining them. The horses accounted for about 88 per cent of expenditure, the bulk of this being for provender.

A similar conclusion can be drawn from the accounts of the Henley coach in 1699, though these do not include any expenditure on new coaches or new horses. Horse costs totalled 94 per cent, and provender alone 82 per cent.[34] Later figures, for Manchester and Leeds coaches in 1760-1 (more complete but possibly affected by turnpiking), indicate horse costs totalling about 78 per cent and provender alone 62 per cent; the other costs were coachmen and postilions 11, coaches about 6 and tolls 5 per cent.[35]

Expenditure on provender depended in the short term less on market prices than on the coachmaster's bargains with innkeepers. Cressett complained that 'the coachmen agree with the innkeeper beforehand to have their hay and oats at so low a rate, that he loseth by them, and is forced to beat down the price of them in the market, yet must let the coachman have them for

61 *Schedule attached to William Morris's answer in the Court of Exchequer in 1689 concerning his share in the Exeter stage-coach. It records his receipts at Exeter and London for almost a whole year, and, at the bottom, his outgoings for coaches, men, horsemeat, shoeing and horses. (E 112/598/541.)*

what he pleaseth, otherwise he carries his passengers to other inns'.[36] In this, the coachmaster's practice followed the carrier's, but the coachmaster probably had a stronger bargaining position because of the well-to-do passengers he brought.

According to Cressett, four coachmen were used on a journey to Exeter, York or Chester, suggesting that each performed a day's journey in summer. This is supported by the existence on the Exeter route in the 1680s of a coachman who drove between Salisbury and Dorchester (45 miles). The Exeter coach therefore needed only four coachmen in summer, each covering 270 miles per week, though at least six, plus six postilions, in winter. Morris's 'two men' for his quarter-share is hard to explain, except perhaps as an average. The coachmen driving Thomas Baldwin's Bristol and Bath coaches in 1724 were organised differently. For the thrice-weekly flying coaches (in two days), two coachmen covered the whole distance from London to Bath, working six days a week, travelling 327 miles and enduring very long hours. A third drove them only between Bath and Bristol, but there were perhaps more coaches between those places than just the London ones. Each of the three-day coaches, one a week to Bath and the same to Bristol, had its own coachman who drove the whole distance, again working six days a week and covering 218 and 244 miles per week respectively.[37]

Few other employees were needed. Postilions were required in winter. It was probably usual to employ a horsekeeper at the home base, but otherwise horsekeepers were employed by inns rather than coachmasters. The York coach had a 'clark for the stage coaches' at York, and Thomas Jaques of Petersfield employed a man at his London inn in the late 1660s and 1670s to look after his coaches and their passengers, paid half as much as the man who looked after his waggons there.[38]

The cost structure of coach businesses, especially the dominance of horse costs, provides the basis for examining individual coach businesses in the next chapter.

CHAPTER XI

COACH BUSINESSES

The Exeter coach

This chapter examines the best-documented stage-coach businesses. The Exeter coach falls into that category because of an Exchequer lawsuit in 1687-90 in which John Morgan, the heir to a quarter-share, successfully defended his right to it against the other partners.[1]

The business was almost certainly the one first mentioned in 1655. From 1677 it had four partners, each with a quarter-share.[2] In 1689 William Morris had 12 horses for carrying on his quarter-share, and there were also four horses held in common between the partners, indicating a total stock of 52, probably forming 13 teams of four in summer and eight or nine teams of six in winter. Morris's two coaches indicate a total stock of eight.[3]

The manner of operation was set out in an indenture of March 1677 (quoted in the Exchequer proceedings):

> for the carrying on and continueing a stage together and driveing and manageing the same with four coaches and able horses for conveying passengers from London to Exeter and from Exeter to London which said stage was and is to be performed by the said agreements and covenants in four dayes in summer and each copartner is to maintaine one dayes stage with good and able coach and horses at his owne charge and in the winter in six dayes and each coach is to goe thro the said journey from London to Exeter at his own charge.[4]

Both the Chester and York coaches, covering similar distances, also lengthened their journeys from four days to six in winter. The winter arrangement was the system of alternate journeys long practised by carriers, in which each proprietor carried out a whole journey in his turn, paying all the costs incurred.[5] The summer arrangement, on the other hand, was the later stage-coach system: division of a route into stages or districts in which each proprietor horsed the coaches and provided drivers at his own expense, with receipts allocated between the partners in proportion to the work done by their horses. In this period each coach proprietor also provided his own vehicles, so there were virtually no joint costs. Receipts were divided equally between the Exeter partners once a month.

The route was not the post road through Andover, Salisbury and Sherborne, with its many steep hills.[6] Horses drawing vehicles were more demanding than post-boys, packhorses and riding horses, and good surfaces and, above all, easy gradients could make it worthwhile to follow a longer route. The coach route was through Sutton, Salisbury and Dorchester, with the advantage of long stretches on chalk, which provided a relatively hard and well-drained surface.[7] In summer, in 1658 and the late 1680s, the coach lodged on the second and third nights from London at Salisbury and Bridport, and in a fictional account written in 1725 the overnight stops were at Hartley Row, Salisbury and Bridport, giving days (from London) of 39, 44, 60 and 38 miles.[8] Thus there was one longer than usual day, of 60 miles, and the purpose of the four horses held in common may have been to draw the coaches the extra miles on that day, so that no partner was disadvantaged.[9] With three services a week, each team covered only 84 miles per week, much less than the typical waggon team and drawing smaller loads but at greater speed.

The winter frequency is uncertain. According to the defender of stage-coaches in 1672, whereas Cressett had assumed six coaches to or from York, Chester and Exeter every week (three each way), in fact 'never above four coaches travel the winter half-year', and 'sometimes the coaches go but once a week'. Exeter services were certainly reduced to weekly in winter 1655, but William Morris's receipts in 1688-9 indicate three services per week and in October 1699 one of the proprietors stated that the coaches usually ran three times a week.[10] With three services a week in winter and almost the same number of horses (in nine teams), each team would have covered about 121 miles per week – much more than in summer, and on poorer roads, but in larger teams and at lower speeds.

The Chester coach

The Chester coach is the best recorded of all the early stage-coaches. In April 1657 there were three services a week, passing through Stone rather than along the later route further west, but with what was until at least 1750 the standard summer time of four days. The service became weekly in October 1657, returning to thrice weekly the following spring. In March 1659, in what looks like a transitional arrangement between winter and summer (five days and twice weekly), services alternated between two routes: one via Coventry, Lichfield and Stone (this, truncated, later formed the Lichfield service), and the other said to be via Birmingham, Wolverhampton, Shrewsbury, Newport,

to Chester where we Lodged at the Coach & Horses,[1] we found Cozen Thomas Gillibrond & his Doughter Jane there.[2]

27 My Wife & her Maid Ellen Howerd, Cozen Jane Gillibrond, Lieftenant Barker, Lieftenant Sole & I began our Journey towards London in the Stage Coach from Chester, we din'd at the Georg in Whit-Church; then to New-port where we lodg'd at the Whit Swan.

28 From Newport we came to the Welsh-Harp where we dined thence to Coventry where we Lodg'd at the Coach and Horses.

29 From Coventry we came to Northhampton a very pritty Town, the Market place large, the Streets broad and a very handsom Church, we din'd there at the Black Bull, thence to the Swan in Newport-pannell where we took a Refreshment, 'tis Famous for Bone-Lace weaving, thence to Woobourn where we Lodged at the George.

30 From Woobourn we came to St Albans where we dined at the Black Bull, thence to the George in Alders Gate London where Mr Parks met us & brought us to Mr Hattons Wax Chandlor at the Golden Ball in Great Duke-Street where we Lodged whilst we stay'd in Town.

31 I Payed Mr Magen £3 from Mrs Leconby. We dined at Mr Parks with Pat: Clark & Mr Medcalf. I went to the four Swans at the Miles End in Stepney

62 *Extract from the diary of Nicholas Blundell, published by the Record Society of Lancashire and Cheshire, for 27-30 May 1723, recording a journey in the Chester stage-coach. Many diaries of this period have been published, though (unlike this one) not all are complete transcripts.*

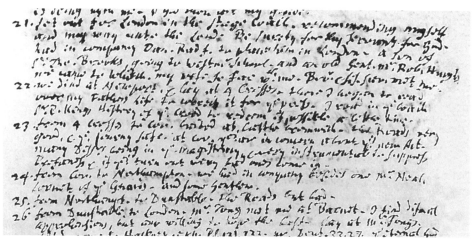

63 *Extract from the diary of Matthew Henry for January 1712, recording a journey in the Chester stage-coach in winter. (Bodleian Library, MS Eng Misc e.330, f. 109v.)*

Whitchurch and Holywell, though Shrewsbury was probably always a separate service or branch and there was probably only a branch coach to Holywell (west of Chester).[11]

This apparent experimentation gave way in the 1660s to long-term stability and a single route via Northampton, Coventry and Whitchurch. Twenty-one journeys in the Chester coach are recorded by diarists, of which nine were in winter, from 1669 to 1740, and 12 were in summer, from 1690 to 1723, together with one summer journey just from Coventry to London in 1677 (Appendix 8). Journey times were invariably the same – four days in summer, six in winter – and so were lodging places (Map 12). The only differences relate to two of the dining places in winter and two in summer.[12]

More detailed information is provided by the inventory of John Holloway, one of the three proprietors, dating from September 1689 (Figs. 64 and 65). Holloway's household goods were all in London, but he had horses and coaches both in London and at Whitchurch. The horses must have been organised for summer services. In London there were eight coaches and 17 horses, apparently in four teams.[13]

The information about the Whitchurch horses provides the key to understanding the Chester coach. At Whitchurch there were three teams, each of four horses, plus 'Old Ranter' (presumably a horse) and one nag. One team was '4 Chester horses'; the two others were known by the names of their drivers. Coaches are recorded only for the latter two, probably indicating that the same coaches went through to Chester. The debts owed by Holloway related only to services from Chester as far as the *Welsh Harp*, Stonnall. There were debts to the ostler and two separate men for horsemeat at Chester and the same at Whitchurch and Newport; £6 was owed to Mr Smith 'at the Welchharp Stonell'. Evidently the service on that part of the route was performed exclusively by Holloway in summer, and teams and coaches were changed at the *Welsh Harp*, where Holloway's exclusive territory ended.

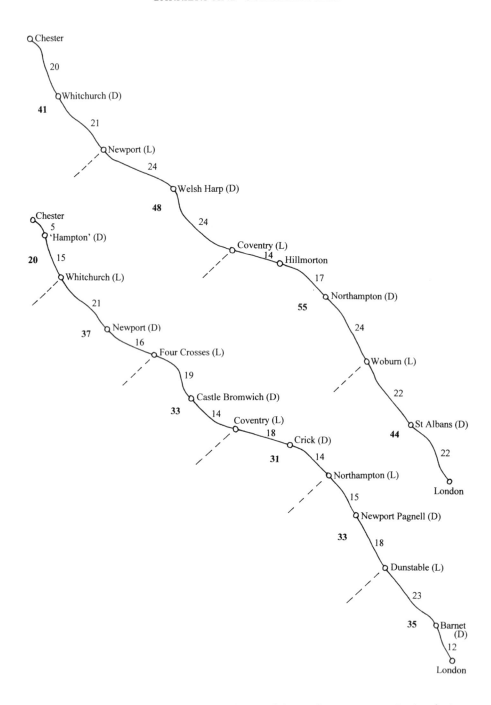

Map 12 *The Chester stage-coach and its lodging and dining places in summer (top) and winter (bottom), 1669-1740. Here and on subsequent maps, 'L' indicates a lodging place and 'D' a dining place; figures in bold indicate the miles covered in a whole day. The map is based on 21 descriptions of journeys by diarists. Lodging places never varied, but several of the dining places did vary. (Sources: diaries used in Appendix 8.)*

The Whitchurch horses and coaches were therefore used for the first day and a half out of Chester. The existence of '4 Chester horses' indicates that one team was used for the first half day, travelling to and fro between Chester and Whitchurch. The other two teams presumably dealt with two successive half-days between Whitchurch and the *Welsh Harp*, lodging overnight at Newport (see Map 12). For two coaches a week,[14] these were all the teams needed, and each team would have covered four stages each week (a total of 81 to 85 miles). This was the pattern for almost the whole route in summer: teams covering stages of 20 to 24 miles, and one change of team each day, with the exception of the second day out of London, where 55 miles was too much for two teams. The arrangement was the same as the 'fresh horses once a day' of April 1657.[15] Teams were undoubtedly changed at the coach's dining places, and three of the four were equidistant between the lodging places, thereby equalising the work of the teams.

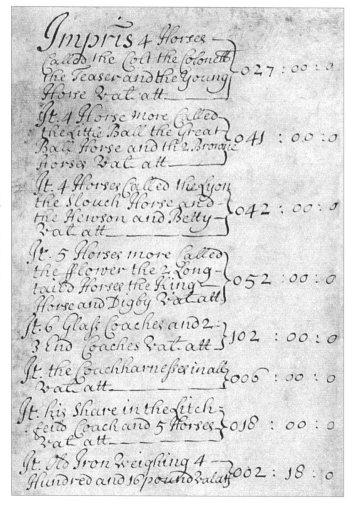

64 *Extract from the exceptionally detailed inventory of John Holloway, one of the Chester coachmasters, of September 1689. This records his London teams and coaches. (Corporation of London RO, Orphans Inventories 2170.)*

Goods at the Intestates House at Whitchurch in the County of Salop. Appraised by Thomas Yonde and William Robinson as ffolloweth (vizt)

Item 4 Chester Horses by their Names Lutwich Blackbird Betty and Lyon vat att ____ 023 : 00 : 0

Item Rich: ffoxes 4 Horses Little Ball Snip sorrell and Prettyman vat att ____ 034 : 00 : 0

Item Robert Davies 4 Horses Great Ball the Gelding Lyon and Watt vat att ____ 028 : 00 : 0

It Old Ranter vat att 001 : 10 : 0

It Rich: ffoxes Coach vatat 011 : 00 : 0

It Rich: ffoxes Harnesses Old Coate and Capp vatat 002 : 00 : 0

It Robt Davies Coach Lyned with redd Coath vat att ____ 009 : 00 : 0

It Robert Davies Harnesses old Coate and Capp Harnesses pretty ffresh vat att ____ 006 : 00 : 0

It 4 old Harnesses for the Chester Horses vat att ____ 001 : 00 : 0

It 13 Horse Cloths 12 Suringcles 10 Halters vat att ____ 000 : 12 : 2

It One Bay Saddle Nag at Willm Robinson vatat 003 : 00 : 0

65 *Another extract from the inventory of John Holloway, recording his teams and coaches at Whitchurch. (Corporation of London RO, Orphans Inventories 2170.)*

Blundell normally recorded in his diary halts only for dining or lodging, but on 1 October 1723, on the day when the coach covered 55 miles, he stated in addition that at Hillmorton, between Northampton and Coventry, 'we had 6 fresh horses'.[16] As on the Exeter route, having one long day's journey with an extra change of horses was clearly more economical than equalising the length of each day's journey. Matthew Henry twice described this day's journey as 'tedious'.

In winter, lengthening the journey to six days meant fewer miles per day – 30 to 37 miles except on the first day out of Chester (20 miles), where the short journey would have provided time for passengers to reach the coach from their homes (or vice versa). Diary entries suggest that the service remained twice weekly in winter, and this was certainly the case in 1715 and 1716.[17] Whereas in summer dining places tended to be equidistant between lodging places, this was less so in winter, suggesting that (as on the Exeter route) the same team drew the coach for the whole day rather than teams being changed at the dining places.

Holloway's debts indicate two separate sources of provender at Chester, Whitchurch and Newport, and use of more than one inn in a town may have been common, perhaps one for up and one for down journeys, as Pepys encountered during his stage-coach journey to and from Cambridge.[18]

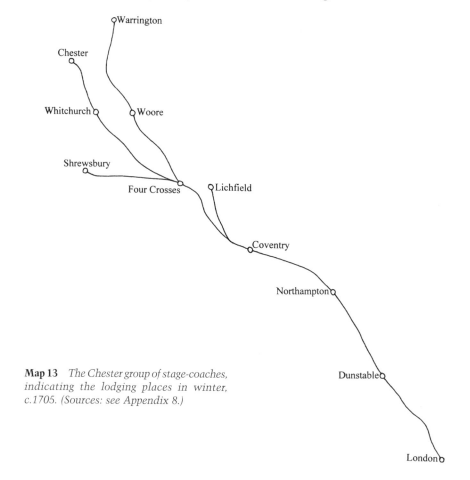

Map 13 *The Chester group of stage-coaches, indicating the lodging places in winter, c.1705. (Sources: see Appendix 8.)*

The Chester coach was one of a group of services in the same ownership (Map 13). In 1690 Delaune listed departures on Monday and Thursday to Chester, Monday to Shrewsbury and Tuesday to Lichfield,[19] thereby indicating that the Lichfield coach was a separate service rather than a branch. The Shrewsbury coach was also a separate service, since when Dugdale travelled in it in summer its stages differed from those of the Chester coach.[20] Neither Lichfield nor Shrewsbury coaches needed a day's journey of 55 miles, since both routes (126 and 162 miles respectively) divided conveniently into days of about 40 miles. Their first nights out of London in summer were spent at Woburn (44 miles) and Hillmorton (a further 40 miles), though the Lichfield coach once lodged the first night at Brickhill (on a parallel road) and twice on the second night at Crick (three miles short of Hillmorton).[21] In winter, lodging places were the same as for the Chester coach where the routes coincided.

Holloway's inventory includes £18 for 'his share in the Litchfield coach and 5 horses'. An appraiser would not have included the value of a share in a stage-coach as such, and what this probably represents is the value of the stock associated with that share, namely five horses held in common. The reason for such a joint stock may have been the same as that suggested in the Exeter case, to cover the extra miles on the long day, though only if 'the Litchfield coach' signified the whole group of coaches, including the Chester one.

The partners did not necessarily keep horses only for the stage-coaches. Holloway seems not to have let out horses, but William Fowler loaned horses to draw Roger Whitley's coach in 1686-9 (on one occasion with a coachman and postilion) and Henry Earl was letting out horses in 1709; his charge at Chester was 'about 4 coach horses to London vidt 24s a day when they travail, 10s when they rest' (slightly above the London hackney rate of 20s. and 10s. respectively in the 1650s).[22]

One innovation, probably under the same management, was a service from London to Warrington in 1703 (twice weekly in summer and weekly in winter), diverging from the Chester route at the *Four Crosses*. It had the same schedule of four days in summer and six in winter as the Chester coach, though the journey was about eight miles longer. It is not clear whether the Warrington coach continued after 1710, but by 1737 there was a Warrington coach following a different route, via Towcester, Coventry and Stone (then largely turnpiked).[23]

Another important aspect of the Chester coach is that, like the Exeter coach, it did not follow the post road. The post road to Chester via Towcester, Coventry and Stone was described by Ogilby in 1675 as 'one of the most frequented roads of the kingdom', but he also noted alternative routes, including that used by the Chester coach. The Chester coach used both routes in 1659 but subsequently only the Whitchurch one, which tended to follow watersheds and avoid river crossings. It was already in 1623 much frequented by wheeled traffic, and, judging by the amount of stabling available along it, was about as busy in the 1680s as the post road. Roger Whitley also followed the Whitchurch route even when in his private coach, whereas the horse-hiring service between London and Chester in 1663 used the post road through Stone. As late as 1750 the road via Stone was described (by a horse-rider) as 'mighty good though in some places stony and rough for a coach and worse for post chaises'.[24]

66 *The* Four Crosses *near Cannock. The right-hand part is dated 1636; the left-hand part dates from about 1700, and was presumably built with money generated by the Chester and other coaches. The Chester coach lodged at the* Four Crosses *in winter at least from 1669 to 1740. So did the Warrington coach and almost certainly the Shrewsbury coach. Passengers had no choice of inn at such an isolated place; the Bishop of Chester in 1687 considered the* Four Crosses *'a deare inne', and Thomas Wilson in 1731 described it as 'a base extravagant inn'.*

As well as the Chester and Exeter coaches, the Gloucester, Shrewsbury and Yarmouth coaches also avoided Ogilby's roads. The Bristol coaches followed his route only between Beckhampton and London, and the York coaches did so only north of Huntingdon. Some stage-coaches did follow his routes, for example to Norwich, Worcester, Southampton and Stratford upon Avon, but it is clear that Ogilby's roads were not always as dominant as is usually assumed.[25]

The York coach

The York coach had the same timings as the Exeter and Chester ones – four days in summer and six in winter – but had to cover more miles – 51 per day in summer, compared with 46 and 47 respectively. There was a connecting service from York to Newcastle and Edinburgh and (at least in 1658 and from 1695) a linked service from London to Wakefield. The London to Lincoln coach, which diverged from the York route at Grantham, had also been founded by the York partners, but apparently passed into separate hands between 1672 and 1681.[26]

The stages are indicated by diaries from 1667 to 1711, together with advertisements of 1653 and 1658 (Map 14).[27] In summer the dining places were not equidistant between the lodging places, suggesting that at least on the two longest days there were two changes of horses rather than one. Lodging places remained

67 *The* Bell, *Stilton, dating from the 17th century. Little information is available about the inns used by the York coach, but the coach normally dined at Stilton in winter, and it is likely that the* Bell *was used at least in some periods.*

the same from 1658 to 1709, except that at first Bawtry may have been used rather than Barnby Moor.[28] The Wakefield coach had the same lodging places and diverged north of Doncaster.[29]

In winter, distances per day ranged from 29 to 37 miles, the shorter distances nearer London perhaps reflecting the difficulties on roads passing over clay. The one change in lodging places was that by 1702 Buckden had apparently been superseded by nearby Huntingdon.[30] The Wakefield coach again had the same stages in 1712-23, but lodged at Buckden rather than Huntingdon.[31]

Further information is provided by the inventory of Henry Molden, the coach's London partner, of June 1691.[32] Molden had 25 horses (including one saddle horse) and two coaches, as well as a half-share in a coach and horses part-owned by Francis Gardner, the York partner. By analogy with the stock used for the Exeter coach, Molden's 25 horses suggest a half-share, which his stake in the shared coach and horses confirms. The latter's value indicates four or five shared horses, and therefore a total stock for the York coach of about 54 horses. The shared horses and coach may have had a similar purpose to the Exeter coach's shared horses. In summer, the 13 or so York teams would each have covered about 93 miles per week, somewhat more than the Exeter or Chester teams. At least some of Molden's horses were apparently based at Biggleswade, where one of the appraisers lived,[33] and were therefore approximately mid-way between London and Stamford. Molden's two coaches were the absolute minimum needed for the thrice-weekly service.

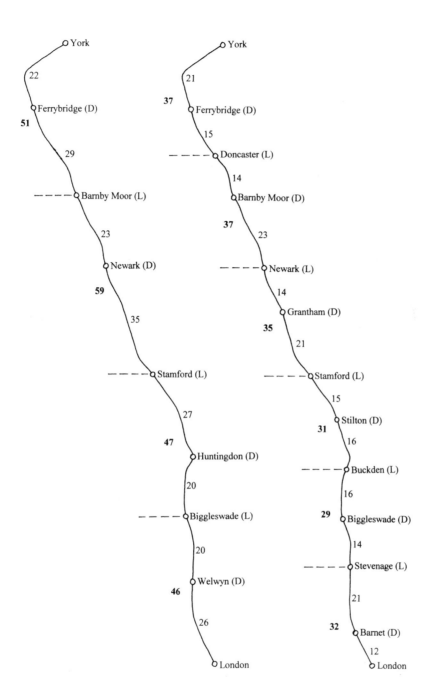

Map 14 *The York stage-coach and its lodging and dining places in summer (left) and winter (right). The map is based on Thoresby's journeys in 1683, but with some of the dining places in winter taken from Nicholson's journeys in 1702-11. The two disagree only in respect of Nicholson lodging at Huntingdon instead of Buckden. (Sources: Thoresby; Nicholson.)*

The Yarmouth coach

Onias Philippo's Yarmouth coach, first mentioned in 1681, was a particularly fast one, which until at least the 1740s took two days in summer (66 miles per day) and three days in winter (44 miles per day). The best evidence for it is provided by the Rev. Rowland Davies's diary, which records three winter journeys and one summer journey in 1689-90 (Map 15).[34] The coach's route swung round via Newmarket and Bury St Edmunds to avoid as far as possible the clays of Essex and Suffolk. The short journey times probably reflected unusually level and good roads, but also, in summer, the very early start at 3.30 a.m. on the first day out of London, when the coach covered 76 miles. This was in July, when the roads

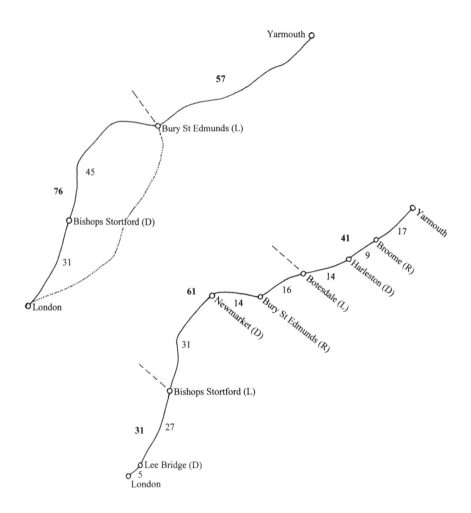

Map 15   *The Yarmouth stage-coach and its lodging places in summer (top) and winter (bottom), based on the Rev. Rowland Davies' down and up journeys in July and October 1689 respectively. 'R' indicates refreshments or breakfast. On his down journey in November 1689, Davies dined at Bungay instead of Harleston. The dotted line on the upper map marks the new route adopted by 1735. (Source: Davies, pp. 29-30, 56-7, 64-5.)*

68 *The* White Hart, *Scole, a substantial roadside inn, built in 1655. The Yarmouth coach stopped there for breakfast during the Rev. Rowland Davies's journey towards Yarmouth in November 1689.*

were at their best, but the speed in the morning was nevertheless an unimpressive 3.9 or so miles per hour.

The days' journeys were even more uneven in winter (31, 61 and 40 miles), and the shortness of the journey as a whole was made possible by the great distance covered on the second day, for the larger part of which a remarkable speed of 5.6 miles per hour was recorded in October 1689. Whereas the first day was typical for a winter coach, the miles covered on the second indicate that (unusually for winter) the teams were changed, each then covering about 30 miles. In winter 1743 the coach was setting off from Yarmouth at 4 a.m., the earliest winter departure time recorded.[35]

The Yarmouth coach was recorded as twice weekly in 1681, 1690 and winter 1717, but otherwise all advertisements from 1717 to 1750 indicate a weekly service. This created difficulties in organising teams so as to take over from each other while still covering a reasonable number of miles per week.

Consequently ownership was always combined with that of another coach – at first Norwich (with shared routes probably as far as Scole) and subsequently Bury St Edmunds. In 1717 the three proprietors were Charles Hoy of Bishop's Stortford, Robert Cooke of Bury, carrier, and Edmund Talbott of Bury, coachman, and all three were also coachmasters between Bury and London. In 1737, by which time the route was via Braintree and Sudbury instead of Newmarket, one of William Allen's and Thomas Taylor's three services per week between Bury and London formed part of the Yarmouth service and another formed part of the King's Lynn service; places on these were available for Bury passengers only if not needed by Yarmouth and King's Lynn passengers. This still left the problem of organising teams for a weekly service between Bury and Yarmouth. In summer 1741 an advertisement indicated that two teams were kept for this stretch, each of which would have covered a mere 57 miles per week, but in relatively long stages of 28-9 miles.[36]

The Southampton and Cirencester coaches

The Southampton and Cirencester coaches were also flying coaches covering exceptional distances in summer, 80 and 92 miles per day respectively. The evidence for the Southampton coach concerns where its two owners, each with a half-share, lived in 1738-9 and the stock they advertised for sale. Their locations at Egham and New Alresford, and the assumed stop at Farnham between them, divided the route almost exactly into 20-mile stages (Map 16). The business was divided into a 'lower part' and an upper one. In June 1738 Elizabeth Skinner at the *King's Arms*, Egham, owner of the upper part, had two coaches and 12 horses, indicating three teams. As the coach was thrice-weekly, each team would have covered four stages, or 80 miles, per week. The journey is likely to have taken about 18 hours, and the coach in fact set out at 11 p.m. and travelled overnight.[37]

In winter, the coach remained thrice-weekly, but set out at 6 a.m., probably taking two days. In October 1739 William Freeman at the *George*, New Alresford, owner of the lower part, had two coaches and two sets of horses, which was probably the winter arrangement, with teams of six, each covering 120 miles per week.

Cirencester Flying Stage Coach in one day, goes out from the King's Head Inn in Cirencester, every Monday, Wednesday and Friday, at 3 in the Morning, and comes to the Bell-Savage Inn on Ludgatehill, and Returns from thence every Tuesday, Thursday and Saturday, at the same time, through Henley, Abingdon, Farrington &c. to the King's Head in Cirencester.

69 *The first advertisement for the one-day Cirencester coach, in 1696. (London Gazette, 14 May 1696.)*

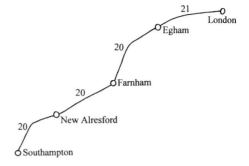

Map 16 *The Southampton stage-coach, 1738. (Sources: LEP, 11 April, 27 June 1738, 2 October 1739.)*

The Cirencester coach appears to have been organised similarly, though operated from a central point by a single owner. In 1730 its owner, Richard Bartholomew, was based at the *Red Lion*, Benson (Fig. 70), which divided the route into 49 and 42 mile stretches, indicating stages of 21 to 25 miles in summer. Like the Southampton coach it was setting off at 11 p.m. in summer 1738. In winter it took two days.[38]

70 *The former* Red Lion, *Benson, Oxfordshire, re-faced in the 1680s or 1690s. The Cirencester coach was operated from here by Richard Bartholomew up to 1730. From the 1730s one of the coach's proprietors was James Kemp, who was still innkeeper at the* Red Lion *and Cirencester coachmaster in 1764.*

Oxford and Worcester coaches

Information is provided about Oxford coaches by Aston's diary in 1686-91 and other diaries from 1703 to 1733.[39] The coaches took one day in summer and two days in winter. In 1686-91 the lodging place in winter and dining place in summer were in the middle of the route, at High Wycombe or nearby Beaconsfield or Loudwater; thereafter only High Wycombe is recorded. Not surprisingly at least one coachmaster, Stonell of Oxford in the 1720s, kept his horses and horsekeeper at High Wycombe.[40] The journey was thus split fairly evenly into two sections of 26 to 32 miles. This was reasonably easy work for the teams in winter, but longer than the typical stage in summer, and did not necessarily indicate where teams were changed.[41]

The Worcester coaches covered almost exactly twice the distance, half of it on the same road (Map 17), but the annual pattern was different. There were two coaches (at least until 1717), one via Islip and Moreton-in-Marsh (but later Oxford instead of Islip) and one via Oxford and Stow-on-the-Wold. Almost all the information available relates to the former. It was run from at least 1681 to 1744 by members of the Winslow family: up to 1710 by two innkeepers at places where the coach lodged in winter and (probably) dined in summer – Thomas Winslow of the *Red Lion*, High Wycombe, and John Winslow of the *White Hart*, Moreton-in-Marsh. At the latter, John Winslow ran the stables and the Worcester coach and his wife, Anne, ran the house itself. In summer the coach took two days, lodging at Islip. The one mid-winter journey recorded took four days. However, there was also a three-day schedule, advertised or otherwise recorded only in February and March, and this appears to have been a transitional timing between summer and winter.[42] The road west of Oxford

71 *The* Swan, *Tetsworth, an early 17th-century inn remodelled and re-fronted in about 1700. The Oxford coaches dined here in winter in the 1680s and subsequently.*

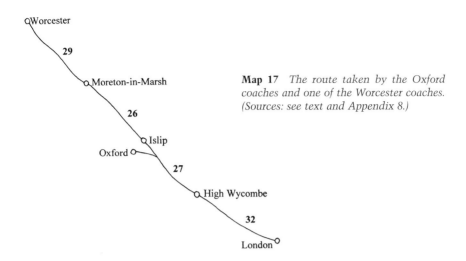

Map 17 *The route taken by the Oxford coaches and one of the Worcester coaches. (Sources: see text and Appendix 8.)*

may have been more challenging than that shared with the Oxford coaches, since even in the 1740s and early 1750s the two-day schedule began only in late April or early May, long after the Oxford coaches had begun their one-day schedule.

Henley and Windsor coaches

Accounts survive for the Henley and Wallingford coach in 1699 because an innkeeper took over the stock as security for debt, continuing the coach service, and the former coachmaster sued him in an attempt to recover it.[43] John Hatheway had been operating a Henley coach by 1672; it is listed in 1681 as thrice-weekly, but is wrongly omitted in 1690. In 1694 Hatheway, 'being antient', retired, and William Hall purchased the two coaches and nine horses for £125, outbidding an innkeeper.[44] Hall extended the service to Wallingford, running at least one coach a week to Henley and one to Wallingford. He baited his Wallingford horses at the *Bear* in Maidenhead, where he 'generally putt in ffresh horses to runn the rest of the stage', and his Henley horses at the *George* in Colnbrook. The Henley route divided neatly into 20 and 18 mile stages either side of Colnbrook, but extending the route to Wallingford with stables at Maidenhead meant 29 and 19 mile stages.

In September 1699 Stephen Fisher, innkeeper at both those inns, had the horses seized for debt and ran the service himself. By then there were only six horses. At first Fisher served Wallingford twice a week, and then from late October to the end of December Henley twice a week. Teams were probably of four horses only,[45] and, perhaps to compensate, they covered relatively few miles per week – 65 and 51 miles in the two periods. Neither Hall nor Fisher, nor Hatheway before them, were owner-drivers: all employed a coachman. Later, in 1717, the Henley coach was operated in a more typical way, with six-horse teams in winter.[46]

At Windsor, 26 miles from London, the number of services rose and fell in response to the monarch's use of Windsor Castle. In 1681 there were 45 scheduled coaches per week (about 7 per cent of total stage-coach mileage), several London hackney coachmen having been tempted to provide regular services, whereas in 1690 there were only 18 per week. In March 1682 Thomas Adams and Richard Alsop of Westminster and William Russell of Windsor, all coachmen, agreed jointly to rent a stable at the *White Hart*, Windsor 'for the then summer season'. Adams had two coaches and the others one each, 'and each of them were to keepe horses proporconably'. Anyone keeping an extra horse not needed for the stage-coaches was to pay 6d. per night per horse for hay. Bookkeepers and porters were employed in London and Windsor, paid for proportionately, as was the rent of the stable. Alsop described himself as 'one that dealt in stage coaches and hiring of horses & other concerns', and Adams had a hackney licence.

Soon Adams was coming to Windsor with three sets of horses and Alsop with two. There was also private hiring: Adams once provided Queen Catherine with 'a sett of horses' from Windsor to London. However, in late June or early July Charles II removed his court to London, and the partnership was dissolved in August, leaving behind a tangled set of accounts and a lawsuit.[47]

Short stages

The short stages look to modern eyes like commuter coaches, with Delaune's 'in and out every day' referring to coaches entering London in the morning and leaving in the evening. However, this was not always (and perhaps not usually) the case. In April 1699 Robert Daniel's Highgate stage-coach was advertised as leaving London at 7 a.m. and returning from Highgate at 6 p.m. daily during the summer. In October 1738 John Andrews' Harrow coach left London at 8 a.m. and returned to London the same day. Between Epsom and London, despite Defoe's reference in the 1720s to 'men of business, who are at London upon business all the day, and thronging to their lodgings [at Epsom] at night', four separate coaches advertised in May or June between 1665 and 1725 left London in the morning (at 7 or 8 a.m.) and Epsom in the afternoon (at 3 p.m.), though there were also coaches in 1718 and 1721 which did the reverse. The Highgate and Harrow arrangement was consistent with Cressett's observation that the short-stagers 'drive every day to London, and in the night-time they drive about the City'.[48] It may have been better suited to gentlemen and merchants who visited their suburban properties for a few days or weeks at a time than coaches which entered London in the morning and left in the afternoon. However, preferences were perhaps changing by the 1720s, since, unlike the Harrow coach, the Croydon, Stockwell and Richmond coaches in 1726-35 all set off to London in the morning and returned in late afternoon. Another change was that some of the short stages became more frequent: there was an hourly service to Bow and Stratford by 1705 and the same to Hampstead in 1728.[49]

The two best-recorded short stages are Francis Snow's at Uxbridge in 1704, for which he had nine horses and two coaches, and Joseph Ironmonger's at the *Queen's Head*, Stanmore in 1728, operated with four horses and two coaches (Appendix 7). Snow had a typical number of horses per mile covered, but Ironmonger had remarkably few, which suggests that, where teams could conveniently be organised to cover fewer miles per stage (such as the 13½ miles between Stanmore and London) they could cover more miles per week.

Fares and profits

The information available on coach fares is set out in Appendix 10. Four general statements of the level of fares from 1673 to 1720 all indicate 2.4 pence per mile (in 1720 2.4 pence for ordinary coaches and 3.0 pence for flying coaches). The fares actually paid or advertised bear out these general statements, except that 3.0 pence was too high for flying coaches: almost all fares between 1654 and 1750 were from 1.8 to 2.7 pence per mile (2.4 to 2.7 pence for the York, Chester and Exeter coaches).

The level of fares did not vary significantly over time between 1654 and 1750, reflecting the fact that there was no long-term trend in provender costs or coachmasters' costs in general.[50] In the short term, high-cost periods sometimes coincided with fare increases[51] and low-cost periods with fare reductions,[52] but sometimes there were reductions in high-cost periods;[53] in fact Appendix 10 shows no clear relationship between costs and fares.[54] Coachmasters were to some extent shielded from changes in costs by their agreements with innkeepers, at least in the short term, and there was often considerable stability in fares, or only slight variation, as for the Chester, York, Bristol and Bath, Yarmouth, Oxford and Salisbury coaches. Where fares were low this sometimes resulted from competition:[55] the uniquely low Norwich fare in winter 1741 (0.8 pence per mile) was a furious response to a new competitor, which succeeded in forcing it off the road.[56]

There is some evidence in Appendix 10 that the shorter-distance coaches were relatively cheap, despite the high price of oats and hay close to London.[57] Possible reasons for this might be greater competition, greater ability to vary the level of service in response to demand, and (over very short distances such as Stanmore to London) ability to use teams in very short stages.

There is little sign of higher fares for flying coaches, despite the figure stated in 1720. Indeed sometimes their fares were unusually low, as to Salisbury, Newbury, Banbury, Oxford, Cambridge and all East Anglian destinations. Fares seem to have been the same in winter as for a flying coach in summer, for example to Yarmouth and Oxford.[58] Of course, on the very few routes where both flying and ordinary coaches were offered in summer, higher fares could be charged for the former as the premium service. In 1728 the fare from Salisbury to London was 20 per cent dearer when the coach was flying,[59] and at Bath in 1748-9 the two-day flying coach was 25 per cent dearer than the three-day coach. Otherwise, fares for flying coaches were no different from those for ordinary coaches.

There is virtually no evidence either of the other possible variation by season – higher fares in winter.[60] Whereas the carrier provided the same or a similar service in winter but may sometimes have raised his charges, the coachmaster kept the same fare but provided a poorer service. There is some evidence of regional variation, since fares in East Anglia were almost uniformly low, though not outside the range recorded elsewhere; this probably resulted from its relatively level roads. As for fares at intermediate places, these rarely seem to have been dearer per mile than those for the full journey, despite the disadvantage of having the coach occupied only part of the way. However, passengers could usually join the coach at intermediate places only if it was not already full. For example, in 1736 Farnham passengers were not allowed to take places in the Winchester coach until two days before departure.[61]

The coachmaster received some income other than ordinary fares, including fares from any passengers conveyed in the boot. If 'riding behind the coach' meant travelling in the boot (rather than riding a horse behind the coach), the boot fare was half the normal one.[62] Packages were also carried, such as oysters from Colchester to London, venison from the Peterborough and Stamford area to London (nine does on one occasion in 1707), a trunk containing the Duke of Ormonde's clothes in the Rochester coach, pieces of lace in the Taunton coach for a milliner in Piccadilly, and a large truss of stockings directed to Halesworth. A spaniel 'supposed to follow Rygat coach' was lost in 1693, as was a bitch from the Colchester coach in 1744.[63] A Cambridge coach in 1657 advertised carriage at 3s. 6d. per cwt (16 pence per ton-mile), slightly less than carriers' charges for gentlemen's goods, but charges for passengers' luggage above the free allowance (generally from 12 to 20 lb) were usually much higher – from 29 to 36 pence per ton-mile in the five examples from 1667 to 1712.[64] In the Henley case, packets and parcels brought in at least 12s. per week, about 12 per cent of total receipts for this somewhat low-earning coach.[65] Another possibility, albeit illegal, was to carry letters. Coachmasters of Reading, Marlborough and Southampton and their drivers were summoned before the Privy Council for this offence in 1670, and the involvement of coaches from Bedford and nearby towns in conveying letters to London in 1680 has been noted already.[66] Some coachmasters, such as Fowler and Earl, hired out horses, though this obviously involved extra expenditure on horses or interruptions to the coach service. Advertisements frequently offered hearses, and several inventories record them. For example, in 1698 the Nottingham coachmasters pointed out that 'any person may have a coach or chariot at Nottingham to Mansfield, or any part of England, or a mourning coach or hearse, or hackney horses'.[67]

Information on overall costs, receipts and profits is available only for the Exeter and Henley coaches, and, since it emanates from lawsuits and also relates to fairly short periods, must be treated with caution. The two sets of figures for the Exeter coach cover the firm as a whole for three months in 1688 and one of the partners (William Morris) for almost the whole of the following year (Fig. 60).[68] The former was said to have been compiled from the accounts kept at the coach's inns. They agree reasonably well in terms of costs per mile, but not for receipts per mile. Morris's account for the longer period suggests that the coach barely broke even: receipts 9.4 pence per mile, costs 9.4, profit 0.01. The figures for the whole partnership for three months indicate a healthier balance: receipts 11.6 pence per mile, costs 9.9, profit 1.6 (£94), suggesting (if maintained through the year) a profit of nearly £100 per quarter-share per year. The partners had an interest in minimising their profits, but must have been aware that they might have to provide documentary evidence. Receipts are likely to have been recorded systematically, since they had to be divided between the partners, and omissions from them were probably marginal, whereas costs provided more scope for falsification. However, even if the figures were accurate, the receipts and profits might simply reflect an untypical year for the Exeter coach.[69]

The value of the Exeter figures lies chiefly in showing how precarious a trade stage-coaching was, and particularly how dependent on filling a good proportion of the seats. According to the defender of stage-coaches in 1672, the York, Chester and Exeter coaches 'go sometimes empty, sometimes but with one or two in them', and the average was four in the six places.[70] The Exeter figures are broadly consistent with this: the average number of passengers in 1688-9 was 3.6, as was the break-even point. In the shorter period average loads were 4.4 passengers and the break-even point was 3.8.[71]

That the Exeter coach was usually profitable is indicated not only by the fact that it continued to operate but by the sums paid for two shares in the 1680s – £250 and £237.[72] For both sales, the sum per horse was between £18 and £19. For comparison, a half-share in the Gloucester coach, requiring about nine horses, was sold in 1704 for £120 (£13 per horse), and the Henley coach was sold in 1694 and 1708, with nine and eight horses respectively, for £125 and £100 (£14 and £13 per horse).[73]

The Henley coach's costs in 1699 substantially exceeded its income: in the two periods, receipts were 7.0 and 6.3 pence per mile and costs were 9.4 and 12.9.[74] The numbers of passengers per coach (3.5 and 3.3 in the two periods) were well below the numbers required to break even (4.8 and 6.4). Fisher claimed the losses resulted from 'the great price of corne and hay ... by the losse of horses and weare and tare of coaches wheeles and harnesse and the small number of passengers'. However, he may have inflated his costs, since he had an advantage in showing the coach to be loss-making, and much of the expenditure remained in his hands anyway as one of the coach's innkeepers. In fact he even had a motive for *making* the coach loss-making in the short term, in order to discourage the previous owner from reclaiming it. The small number of passengers was a genuine problem, and so was the high price of provender in 1699, but Fisher also charged relatively low fares – 2.0 pence per mile to Wallingford and then 1.9 pence per mile to Henley.[75] With the latter fare, the number of passengers required to break even exceeded the coach's capacity. If the Henley coach had been irretrievably loss-making, Fisher would presumably not still have been operating it at his death in 1706, and nor would the coach and eight horses have been sold in 1708 for £100.[76] Nevertheless, both the Henley and Exeter accounts indicate that stage-coaching was a high-risk venture, in which control of costs (especially provender costs), careful setting of fares and above all success in filling seats were crucial.

Coach-waggons and caravans

Coach-waggons co-existed with stage-coaches from the 1650s, providing a slower but cheaper service.[77] However, there were not many of them: Delaune records a few coach-waggons, waggon-coaches and caravans (ten in 1681, six in 1690), almost all from Hertfordshire, Warwickshire, Northamptonshire or Lincolnshire, though he probably did not consistently distinguish them from waggons.[78] In one case (Ongar in 1690) the operator had both coach-waggons and coaches to the same place.

The three examples of speeds suggest that coach-waggons varied in character: the Newcastle-under-Lyme coach-waggon covered 25 miles per day regardless of season in 1677-98, making it comparable to waggons; the Warwick coach-waggon was covering about 33 miles per day in April 1678, but whether this was the summer or winter timing is unknown; the Coventry coach-waggon in 1659-82 was somewhat faster than ordinary waggons in summer (31 miles per day), but

> The Gosport Carravan near Portsmouth which lay at the Swan Inn at Holborn-Bridge, is Remov'd to the Talbot-Inn near the Maypole in the Strand, and goes from thence with 6 able Horses every Monday Morning by 6 at farthest, and is at the 3 Tuns the Post-house in Gosport Tuesday Evening; and returns from thence every Friday Morning and is at the Talbot-Inn Saturday Evening, for 9 s. each Passenger. And a Waggon for carrying Goods and Passengers in 3 Days from the 3 Tuns in Gosport to the Greyhound Inn in Southwark, will begin and set out from Gosport on Monday the 6th of February, and will return from the Greyhound Inn every Thursday and be at Gosport every Saturday.

72 *Advertisement for the Gosport caravan in 1710. (Daily Courant, 27 January 1710.)*

comparable in winter (23 miles per day) (Appendix 8). Dugdale in the 1670s and 1680s used sometimes the Chester or Lichfield stage-coaches (two days to Coventry in summer, three in winter) and sometimes the Coventry coach-waggon (a day longer in each case). Coach-waggons were probably a declining breed, and no references to them have been found later than 1698, or possibly 1707.[79] A few unusually large coaches (sometimes called 'long coaches') continued to be recorded throughout the 18th century, but usually at greater than coach-waggon speeds.[80]

Caravans lasted longer. Cressett used the terms 'long coach' and 'caravan' interchangeably in 1672, and caravans too seem to have been intended largely for passengers (at similar fares to coach-waggons), as well as for the more urgent goods.[81] However, 18th-century caravans were usually faster than coach-waggons had been. Miles per day of the three examples from 1710 to 1749 (Gosport, Bury St Edmunds and Devizes) ranged from 36 to 46 miles – not much less than the stage-coaches. The latter two ran in summer only, but the Gosport caravan was covering 41 miles per day in January (Fig. 72); possibly it ran all night, like the later flying waggons, whereas the Bury St Edmunds and Devizes caravans certainly stopped overnight. The Bath caravan in April 1706 and the Gosport one in January 1710 had teams of six. Delaune lists caravans only to High Wycombe and Rugby, and although they became more common in the 18th century (13 services in 1765, all in south-east England or East Anglia), they never became a significant part of road transport.[82]

CHAPTER XII

COACH OPERATION

The coachmaster's most important decisions, apart from those concerning route and fares, related to how he organised and worked his horses. There are three important measures here, each with its own particular significance – miles per day, miles per hour and (as regards the teams) miles per week.

Miles per day

Miles per day was the most important measure to passengers, since it determined the length of their journeys, and it is therefore the best recorded. Doubt has sometimes been expressed, especially by historians who have failed to distinguish between summer and winter timings, as to whether the times stated in advertisements were actually kept to, but the diarists prove that they almost invariably were. Appendix 8 provides numerous examples of diaries confirming the timings given in advertisements. The only diary reference to a journey not completed in the usual or advertised time is Sir Justinian Isham's relating to the Northampton flying coach in June 1725:

THE TAUNTON STAGE-COACH, in three Days to London, and from London to Taunton in the like Time, begins Tuesday the 22d of this Instant May, from the Saracen's Head in Friday-street, at Five o' Clock in the Morning; and out of Taunton on Thursday following, at Three o' Clock in the Morning; and so continue every Tuesday and Thursday the whole Summer. Dines at the Angel Inn in Yeovil, or the White Hart Inn at Sherborn every Thursday, upwards and downwards, lodge every Wednesday Night at Shaston downwards, and every Thursday Night upwards, sets out from thence at Three o' Clock in the Morning, and at Five the next Morning for London. The Price of Passengers and Luggage as usual. Places may be regularly enter'd, with timely Notice, to and from Yeovil, Sherborn, and Shaston. The Coaches are remov'd from the New Inn to the White Hart in Castle-Town, Sherborn.

Perform'd (if God permit) by JOHN WHITMASH of Taunton, (with three fresh Sets of Horses on the Road) who keeps Coaches, Chariots, Hearse; and a handsome Mourning Coach, with able Horses, to lett to any Part of England.

73 *Advertisement for the Taunton coach in 1733. The reference to 'three fresh sets of horses on the road' indicates a new team in the middle of each of the three days (like the Chester coach), and therefore a total of six stages, averaging 25 miles each. (LEP, 17 May 1733.)*

> The great rains had made ye waters so much out at Newport, that we were oblig'd to leave ye coach at Lathbury, and go over in a boat, swimming the horses, and when there cou'd get no farther, it being equally impassable at ye other bridge. So great a flood had not been known for many years.

The next day he 'rid from Newport to Dunstable, and from thence in ye coach to London'.[1] Another problem with the Northampton coach led to a writ of 1673 complaining that the horses had tired and a passenger had been left many hours alone at night until fresh horses were procured, but the complaint is consistent with a team reaching the end of its normal stage and the next team not being ready.[2]

There are no examples of the well-recorded York, Wakefield, Chester, Lichfield, Oxford and Cambridge coaches not achieving their usual times, although bad roads occasionally meant winter schedules continuing into May. The Chester coach stuck to its winter timing even during a period of snow, though snow, like floods and like plague in 1665, probably did sometimes halt services.[3] Rothwell's Birmingham coach followed an absolutely regular pattern of days in London, admittedly in summer only, from July 1743 to July 1745, apart from two Wednesdays instead of Thursdays almost at the start of operation in April 1744 and one Friday in June 1744.[4] Seventeenth- and early 18th-century coachmasters only occasionally added 'if God permit' when advertising timings.[5] The very name indicated that coaches kept to stages, and they did so even if it meant the York coach 'travelling near two hours by ye light of a lanthorn' to reach Stamford at nearly 11 p.m. in April 1709, or continuing until between 1 and 2 a.m. to reach Barnby Moor in April 1712. Cressett probably exaggerated only slightly when he stated that even if passengers had to wait half a day for repairs to the coach, they would then 'travel all night to make good their stage'.[6] There seems to have been a little flexibility over places of dining, and to some extent over route (hence the diversion of the Oundle coach via Higham Ferrers in 1699 to pick up relatives of the Treshams), but not over places of lodging.[7]

The evidence of timings can therefore be examined with some confidence. Appendix 8 includes 525 examples, taken from advertisements (61 per cent), diaries (33 per cent) and other sources (6 per cent), of which 71 per cent relate to summer and 29 per cent to winter. If the York, Chester and Exeter coaches are taken as the standard – 46 to 51 miles per day in summer – the exceptions can be identified. (Sundays, on which coach travel was illegal, are disregarded in all cases.)[8] There were obviously some journeys which did not neatly fill whole days, and this accounts for some of the low figures, for example between York and Newcastle (48 and 33 miles on the two days).

The clearest exceptions are the flying coaches, such as those to Yarmouth, Southampton and Cirencester discussed in the previous chapter. Some of these flew only in high summer, when the roads were at their best. All the diary references to journeys of 60 or more miles a day are from May to August, as are most of the advertisements prior to the 1720s, other than several in April for Banbury (1690 and 1705), Bristol and Bath (1709 onwards) and Yarmouth (1717). The one-day Cirencester coach advertised on 14 May 1696, covering an impressive 92 miles, was re-advertised on 20 August 1696 as a two-day coach. The most remarkable schedule of all, Norwich to London in one day (110 miles) in 1710,

74 *A coaching hamlet: Sandy Lane, between Bath and Marlborough, consisting of two inns. The further building was the* Bear Inn, *apparently of the late 17th century;* Bell Farm *on the right probably incorporates much of the former* Bell Inn. *The two-day Bristol coach dined here until at least 1752.*

was specifically stated as for June and July only, and was apparently not repeated in subsequent years. From the 1720s flying coaches became more numerous, and most then operated throughout the summer, though a small and declining number of high-summer schedules continued.[9] However, in some cases (Salisbury, Winchester, Southampton, Cirencester and Harwich) the one-day coach actually set off at 11 p.m. or midnight.

There were some two-day flying coaches, for example to Yarmouth and Nottingham, but three days of long hours and jolting was probably considered too much for passengers; the only example (Exeter in three days in 1738, 61 miles per day) appears to have been short-lived. The York, Chester and Exeter coaches therefore remained relatively slow in terms of miles per day.

The organisation of the York, Chester and Exeter teams suggests that, at typical coach speeds, stages of about 20 to 24 miles four times a week, as in the Chester example, was the arrangement which enabled the horses to do most work while still making it possible for the teams to take over a twice- or thrice-weekly coach from each other; shorter stages might have been more efficient, but would have needed more frequent services to be feasible. If a day's journey longer than about 50 miles was needed it was achieved by an additional change of team, as on the Chester route between Coventry and Woburn. This was also the basis of flying coach operation. For example, the Northampton flying coach (67 miles) was advertised in 1717-31 as using three sets of horses (about 22 miles per stage), and the Southampton and Cirencester coaches in the 1730s evidently used four sets of horses (20 and 21-5 miles per stage respectively).[10] Nevertheless, evidence from the Yarmouth and Wallingford coaches suggests that for weekly services there were occasionally longer stages of 28-9 miles, which were compensated for (at least in the Yarmouth case) by fewer miles per week.[11]

In winter, typical journeys were 29 to 36 miles per day, performed without changes of teams. J. Batchelor, looking back in 1762 over the 60 or so years during which his family had run the Lewes coach, taking two days in winter (29 miles a day), stated that 'many aged and infirm persons, who did not chuse to rise early in the morning, were very desirous to be two days on the road for their own ease and conveniency'.[12] However, there were several significantly faster coaches

Map 18 *Stage-coach journey times in summer, c.1735. All the one-day and two-day coaches shown are flying coaches; many slower coaches are ignored. The reason why the two-day and four-day lines are so close is that the four-day destinations did not have flying coaches. Some earlier evidence is included, notably for Warrington and Banbury. Flying coaches setting off around midnight are included as one-day coaches. (Source: Appendix 8.)*

covering 42 to 46 miles per day, or 57 miles in the case of Sudbury (Appendix 8). The Yarmouth coach certainly changed teams *en route* in winter, and probably most of these others did too.[13]

Summer timings most often began in April, but occasionally earlier or later (Appendix 8).[14] Coaches sometimes began their summer schedule at significantly different dates in different years, as in the York, Oxford and Salisbury cases, suggesting that the date was determined by the state of the road in each year.[15] When Matthew Henry took the Chester or Lichfield coach from Coventry to London on 10-12 May 1711, taking three days and stopping at its winter lodging places, he noted 'the roads exceeding deep, never known so at this time of the year'.[16] Winter timings nearly always began in October. There was usually a sharp break between summer and winter schedules,[17] but two flying coaches had a transitional timing: one of the Worcester coaches in February-March and the Nottingham coach in February to April or May and late September to late October or early November (Appendix 8).

There was one possibly distinctive group of coaches in summer other than the flying ones: those providing only a weekly or fortnightly service. Such a frequency must have made it uneconomic to organise changes of teams *en route*, unless the horses could also be used for other purposes. Delaune lists 24 such services covering 40 or more miles from London.[18] In four of these cases, part of the route was shared with another coach in the same ownership: Beccles with Ipswich, Taunton with Exeter, and Shrewsbury and Lichfield with Chester.[19] In 11 cases (46 per cent of the weekly or fortnightly services, compared with 29-31 per cent of all coaches covering 40 or more miles) the coachmaster was also a waggon proprietor, and may have been able to transfer horses between the two types of vehicle. That leaves nine cases, several of which, like the Melton Mowbray coach, appear to have been short-lived, and one of which, the Bridgnorth coach, was probably the extension of a Worcester coach (with the same London inn and days). Weekly and fortnightly coaches might be expected to have been slower (in terms both of miles per day and miles per hour) than stage-coaches proper in summer, when the latter changed their teams. Many of the coaches covering less than 40 miles per day in summer were indeed only weekly, such as the Taunton one, no longer linked to the Exeter coach, in 1730 (38 miles per day), whereas by 1733 the Taunton coach was twice weekly and covering 50 miles per day. The difficulty of organising changes of teams for infrequent services helps explain why, unlike carriers by waggon, coachmasters preferred to provide a frequent service rather than sending several vehicles at a time once a week,[20] though a more frequent service also gave passengers greater choice.

Map 19 *Stage-coach journey times in winter, c.1735. In contrast to the summer map (where the situation had been changed by the spread of flying coaches), this map would be little different if drawn for the 1650s. This map, unlike the summer one, includes some intermediate stops. (Source: Appendix 8.)*

Miles per hour

Diarists and others only occasionally gave both departure *and* arrival times for coaches. Twenty-seven examples are available – 19 summer timings and eight winter ones (Appendix 9). The miles per hour derived from these are mostly approximate because assumptions have to be made about the length of stops for passengers to eat or for feeding the horses.[21] The longer these stops were, the shorter the time spent travelling and therefore the greater the speed. Travellers generally mentioned stops only for dining, except on the longer days' journeys. In summer, horses were normally changed where the passengers dined, but in winter the horses were fed at the dining places rather than changed, and this may have taken longer. Even on some of the longer days' journeys in the more detailed diaries, no stops other than for dining are recorded, for example during Pepys's journeys to and from Cambridge. However, some diarists did record extra stops, especially for breakfast (probably in some cases reflecting an additional change of horses). For example, William Schellinks, in a one-day coach from Canterbury to London in August 1661, had new oysters and a cup of sack at 9 a.m. at Sittingbourne, 15½ miles from Canterbury.[22] Somewhat later, in 1752, a traveller in the two-day Nottingham and Bath coaches had both breakfast and dinner on each day, and on one day a further stop at St Albans, during which there was just time to view the church, and in 1753 a new one-day Dover coach allowed one hour for dining and half an hour each for breakfast and evening refreshment.[23] There were sometimes stops for breakfast or refreshments in winter too.[24] In Appendix 9 one hour is allowed for dining,[25] half an hour for other stops actually recorded and half an hour for breakfast in a few other cases where the starting time was very early.

The summer speeds ranged from 3.0 to 5.5 miles per hour, but 14 of the 19 examples were between 4.0 and 4.9 miles per hour. The average is 4.3 miles per hour. Speed clearly varied, reflecting the quality of different stretches of road, the tiredness or otherwise of the horses and the attentiveness of coachman and postilion. The lowest recorded speed (3.0 miles per hour from Stamford to Barnby Moor in April 1712) occurred at the beginning of the period of summer schedules; on the following day the diarist wrote 'To Doncaster (12 miles) in little more than two hours' – actually 14 miles and therefore just under seven miles per hour. (According to Defoe, the Bawtry to Doncaster road, comprising two-thirds of that 14 miles, 'never wants any repair', and it was not felt necessary to turnpike it until 1776.)[26] During Schellinks' journey in the Canterbury coach in August 1661, speed ranged from about 3.5 miles per hour between Sittingbourne and Chatham to perhaps 5.6 miles per hour between Chatham and Gravesend. It must always have been uncertain at what hour passengers would reach that night's lodging, and advertisements virtually never gave arrival times, though a prospective traveller in the Nottingham coach in 1724 was willing to forecast his arrival at Nottingham the following day 'about 6 or 8 o'clock in the evening'.[27] Nevertheless, most summer speeds were from 4.0 to 4.9 miles per hour.

Summer coach speeds were thus little faster than walking speed. When Anne Murray travelled south by the York coach in September 1654, a footman being sent to her sister followed the same route, and she gave him money for his food and lodging after she joined the coach, 'because I thought itt not reasonable to expect hee could keepe up with itt'. However:

> Affter wee had gone halfe the first day's journy, and the coachman driving att a great rate, I heard the coachman and postillian saying, 'Itt cannott bee a man, itt is a devill, for hee letts us come within sight of him, and then runs faster then the six horses'. So hee stops the coach, and inquires if any of us had a footman. I told him I had. 'Then (said he,) pray make much of him, for I will bee answearable hee is the best in England'. When I found hee could hold outt (as hee did all the way), I made him run by the coach; and hee was very usefull to all in itt.[28]

The speeds in Appendix 9 demonstrate that flying coaches were no faster on the road than other stage-coaches. The Colchester coach (only 52 miles) had one of the higher speeds (4.8 miles per hour), whereas the Yarmouth flying coach in July 1689 had over part of its route one of the lowest (3.9 miles per hour). Evidently the flying coaches normally flew only by means of longer hours on the road; hence the very early starts – in some cases at or around midnight. (An advertisement for a two-day Norwich coach in 1739 stated that 'moons will be carried before the coach (when dark) in mornings and evenings, for the safety of the coach in travelling'.)[29] The one-day Cirencester coach which departed at 3 a.m. in mid-summer 1696 needed to travel only at 4.7 miles per hour to arrive at midnight;[30] by 1738 it was setting off at 11 p.m. The one-day Norwich coach of 1710, despite setting off at 2 a.m. 'exactly', did require greater speed (about 5.2 miles per hour to arrive by midnight), but this was not implausible on a good road; the Norwich fare (2.7 pence per mile) was only a little higher than other East Anglian fares. The similarity in travelling speeds is reflected in the similarity in fares per mile between flying and other coaches, as discussed earlier; significantly higher speeds would have required much higher fares.

Speeds were lower in winter than summer, though the range of examples overlaps that of summer speeds. Setting aside the exceptional Yarmouth example and the example which included a breakdown, the remaining six ranged from 3.2 to 3.7 miles per hour and averaged 3.4 miles per hour. One of the Yarmouth speeds is the highest recorded in any season (5.6 miles per hour), but on one of the least hilly roads in the country and in October, well before the worst of the winter. As in summer, speeds might vary – in Schellinks' case in November 1661 from 2.6 miles per hour between Canterbury and Sittingbourne to 4.8 miles per hour between Rochester and Gravesend.

The longer journey times in winter reflected not only lower speeds but also fewer hours on the road. Whereas in summer a day's journey might consist of two periods on the road each of five or six hours (longer in a flying coach), in winter those two periods might be only 4½ or five hours each; hence the slightly later departure times common in winter. The more relaxed atmosphere of coach travel in winter is indicated by Thoresby's diary. On 20 February 1683, in the York coach between Doncaster and Newark, he recorded 'Morning visiting the church', and the coach reached Newark 'very timely', which was followed by 'transcribing some monumental inscriptions in the church. Evening, with our company'. In contrast, on 4 April 1683, on the down journey (with summer schedules), at Baldock, 'As we passed I espied a pretty hospital, but could not be permitted to stay for inquiry'. Even the Archbishop of Canterbury could not be humoured in summer: Archbishop Wake (at Buckden) wrote in April 1709 that 'In the morning the Bishop Carlisle just called upon me: but being in the York coach could not make him stay with me.'[31]

Why four to five miles per hour?

Why did stage-coaches travel at four to five miles per hour in summer, rather than faster or slower? The consistency of summer speeds suggests that the main reason was the capabilities of the horse as a draught animal rather than what customers wanted, which would have resulted in a greater range of speeds and fares. What coachmasters were seeking to do was to travel as much as possible above the waggon speed of about two miles per hour (the speed at which carriage by horse-drawn vehicle was cheapest)[32] without killing the horses and without significantly (or perhaps at all) exceeding the cheapest cost for a stage-coach load. More miles per hour generally meant greater cost, for horses were working fewer hours per day or week, drawing smaller loads, consuming more provender or wearing out more quickly. Coach horses certainly drew lighter loads than waggon or coach-waggon horses. Waggon horses in the 17th century could generally draw about 6 cwt of loading each,[33] and dividing the weight of the waggon itself (perhaps 18 cwt)[34] between a team of six raises this figure to about 9 cwt. A full coach-load of six passengers plus coachman, allowing 1½ cwt per person (including luggage) was perhaps 10½ cwt. Coaches, though sturdy, must have weighed less than waggons, being smaller in area and not having to withstand such a great weight; a reasonable guess is half the putative waggon weight – about 9 cwt.[35] The total load may therefore have been about 19½ cwt – almost 5 cwt per horse in teams of four, or just over half the load of a waggon horse. The lighter loads per horse are probably the key to stage-coach speeds and to the transition from coach-waggon to stage-coach, though in summer coach horses also usually benefited from fewer hours' work per day and fewer miles per week, and perhaps also from the rudimentary springing of the coach.

The first systematic analysis of the work of horses dates from the 19th century, particularly Brunel's treatise, *On draught,* of 1831.[36] According to Brunel, increasing speed from two to 4½ miles per hour reduced the force of traction of which the animal was capable by about 62 per cent.[37] However, this was for horses working in both cases six hours per day, whereas the stage-coach horse in the calculation above worked only about half the hours of a waggon horse on its working days in summer and about five-sixths as many miles per week, so the reduction in force was less. Brunel's figures suggest that, taking the load to be drawn by stage-coach horses in summer in the 17th and early 18th centuries as a given, four to five miles per hour was the speed at which conveying coaches was cheapest. By implication, coachmasters had decided that there was insufficient demand for greater speeds at significantly greater prices.

Miles per week and seasonal variation

For the coachmaster, one of the most important measures was the miles per week his teams could cover. Miles per week per team in summer derived from inventories were most often from 80 to 93 (Appendix 7).

In winter the poorer roads did not alter the optimum speed, at which carriage was cheapest, though they did make carriage at *all* speeds more expensive by increasing the draught required. However, if loads remained constant throughout the year, as in the case of stage-coaches, the optimum speed for those particular loads will have been lower in winter. If coachmasters had attempted to continue with both the same loads and the same speeds in winter, the extra strain on the horses would have necessitated shorter stages, larger teams, fewer miles per week per team, larger provender rations[38] or several of these, resulting in considerably greater expense.

Instead, coachmasters generally opted in winter for larger teams combined with lower speeds and longer journey times. The reduced speed increased each horse's draught power, and the increase in team sizes further increased the draught available, thereby providing the power to cope with winter roads. At first sight this strategy meant that many more horses were needed. However, having to buy and then sell substantial numbers of horses every year would have been difficult and expensive,[39] especially if all coachmasters were trying to do so at the same time, and it would be surprising if that was what happened.

The missing factor here is miles per week. Since miles *per hour* were reduced, and teams of six meant smaller loads per horse, the teams could work longer hours with fewer rest days, covering more miles per week, despite the poorer road conditions. On Brunel's figures, reducing speed from 4.3 to 3.5 miles per hour meant the horses could work about 50 per cent more hours per day. William Morris's account for the Exeter coach indicates that he had 12 horses throughout the period from May 1688 to April 1689, and the teams' miles per week apparently increased from 84 to about 121 in winter. Thus the Exeter coach could continue through the winter without substantial extra expense (or increased fares), at the cost of lengthening journey times from four days to six. The Southampton coachmasters acted similarly.[40]

However, the Exeter and Southampton coaches' way of adapting to winter was not necessarily the only one. The first comprehensive view of how stage-coach services changed in winter is provided by *The intelligencer: or, merchants assistant* of 1738, which is far more thorough than Delaune in specifying winter frequencies and also gives departure times. Most longer-distance coaches adapted in some way, almost invariably with later departure times in winter, but the majority kept the same frequency all year. The majority of shorter-distance coaches (travelling 11 to 40 miles from London) changed neither frequency nor departure times in winter. For the one-third of longer-distance coaches which did reduce their frequency in winter, the most common pattern, adopted by the York and Chester coaches among others, was three services a week in summer and two in winter.[41] Thus the seasonal adjustment in these cases was made by changing the frequency, not by working the teams more miles per week. This is reflected in the inventory evidence, which indicates that the number of horses per mile covered was often higher in winter (sometimes about 0.7 horses per double mile compared with about 0.5 in summer).[42]

Evidently there were several different ways of adjusting to winter, perhaps none of them wholly satisfactory, involving different trade-offs between miles per hour, per day and per week, team sizes and provender rations. The extent to

> **Boston, Spalding, and Peterborough Stage-Coach, in Three Days,**
>
> SETS out from the Horse-Shoe Inn in Goswell-street, near Alderfgate-Bars, London, every Thurfday at Four o'Clock in the Morning, and will be at Bofton on Saturday. Returns from the Red Lion Inn in Bargate in Bofton, every Monday Morning at Six o'Clock; takes up Paffengers the fame Day at the Poft-Houfe in Spalding; goes from the Poft-Houfe in Peterborough on Tuefday Morning, and will be at London on Wednefday.
>
> The Rates are as follow,
>
> | From London to | Bofton | 1 | 3 | 6 |
> |---|---|---|---|---|
> | | Spalding | 1 | 1 | 0 |
> | | Peterborough | 0 | 16 | 0 |
>
> Perform'd by
>
> JAMES BLACKBORN.
>
> N. B. The Mafter of the Stage-Coach, Waggon, and Pack-Horfes, will not be anfwerable for any Plate, Jewels, Writings, or any other Goods, unlefs the fame fhall be enter'd in his Books, at their Value, and paid for according y.
>
> Note, The Peterborough Waggon comes to the above Inn every Saturday Morning, and returns every Monday Morning at Seven o'Clock; alfo the Kettering and Whitney Waggons come in every Wednefday in the Afternoon, and return the next Morning at Six o'Clock. The St. Neots and Baldock Waggons come in every Saturday Morning early, and return the fame Day at One o'Clock.

75 *Advertisement for the Boston coach, 1738. (LEP, 2 May 1738.)*

which custom varied seasonally may also have been significant. In 1688-9 the Exeter coach averaged 4.0 passengers in April to September and 3.2 in October to March, whereas the London receipts of Rothwell's Birmingham coach in 1734-6 were only about a third as much in November to February as in May to July.[43]

Such variation could make worthwhile the most extreme response to winter – the stopping of services altogether – but only if the coachmaster had other work for his horses, such as waggon haulage. For example, Lord Fitzwilliam observed on 8 November 1705 that the cessation of Fearey's Peterborough coach for the winter might result in the days of Fearey's waggons being altered, and stated a week later that he would be sending many things by the waggons now that they were twice a week. James Blackbourne of Peterborough, whose Boston to London coach (probably the successor to Fearey's) was also summer only, was transferring at least some of his horses between coaches and waggons according to season and possibly alternating them between coach and waggon journeys in 1742.[44] Coachmasters who were also innkeepers with large horse-hiring businesses could also transfer horses from one business to another, and this may account for the Banbury coach being summer only in 1716.[45] Rothwell's Birmingham coach was summer only from autumn 1736 until 1745, but Rothwell also ran waggons and packhorses. Summer-only coaches remained very unusual (only ten were listed in 1738), and a rival Birmingham coach which continued to operate in winter scorned Rothwell's in 1738 for 'not having a due attendance in the winter', boasting that 'we have hitherto gone through without any difficulty'.[46]

CHAPTER XIII

STAGE-COACHES, TURNPIKES
AND STEEL SPRINGS

The development of stage-coaching

The development of stage-coaching faltered in the early 18th century. Of the new destinations first listed in 1705, many were only extensions of existing coaches and several are not recorded again. Hardly any new destinations were added between 1705 and 1760 (Appendix 6). Some established services ceased: the Kettering coach is not recorded after 1705, the Wakefield coach not after 1723 and the Banbury and Oundle coaches not after 1726. The total number of services extending 40 or more miles from London grew little if at all in the first half of the 18th century (Table 7), at a time of rising population both in London and in England as a whole.[1] Most of the long-distance services were apparently still being provided in the 1740s by the firms established in the 17th century,[2] unchallenged by competitors, indicating that entry to the trade on roads already served was difficult. Some middle-distance counties saw no change at all: destinations, days and inns in Bedfordshire were identical in 1690 and 1738. In so far as there was growth, it was in the shorter-distance services (40 or fewer miles from London), and also, from the 1720s, on a small scale in provincial stage-coaching.[3]

Even more significant was the inability of coachmasters to improve the quality of service. Journey times established in the 17th century, often as far back as the 1650s, usually continued until the 1750s or 1760s (Table 8); no doubt many coaches, like the Chester one, continued to use the same dining and lodging places. Such reductions in journey times as there were usually resulted from the introduction of flying coaches, and, since there was little or no increase in miles per hour, involved extra hours on the road.

The evidence gathered in this book indicates why stage-coaching developed so little in the first half of the 18th century. Travel by stage-coach was dearer and often slower than on horseback; indeed it was not much cheaper than using post-horses (Table 5). Though faster than private coaches without changes of teams, stage-coaches had the disadvantages of having to share the vehicle with strangers and lack of flexibility. Faster stage-coaches on 17th- and early 18th-century roads would have required a considerable increase in the number of horses, making stage-coach travel even more expensive, and coachmasters evidently doubted that there would be sufficient customers at much higher fares. Moreover, from the 1740s stage-coaches faced new competition: postmasters and innkeepers began to

Table 7. Numbers of stage-coach services and miles per week, 1681-1765

Distance covered from London (miles)	Services per week							Miles per week (thousands)		
	1681	1690	1705	1726	1738	1755	1765	1681	1755	1765
Up to 10	108	135	202	243	583	415	531	1.5	4.2	5.8
11-40	191	170	184	213	228	241	289	8.6	9.9	13.1
41-80	77	97	110	99	74	104	159	8.6	12.3	18.8
81-120	20	16½	35	32	27	41	72	4.3	8.6	14.5
Over 120	25	28	26½	33	25	26	68	7.4	8.2	23.8
Total	421	446½	557½	620	937	827	1119	31.2	43.2	76.0
Total over 40	122	141½	171½	164	126	171	299	21.1	29.1	57.1

Sources: Delaune 1681, 1690; *The traveller's and chapman's daily instructor* (1705); Charles Pickman, *The tradesman's guide; or the chapman's and traveller's best companion* (1727); *The intelligencer: or, merchants assistant* (1738); *A complete guide to all persons who have any trade or concern with the City of London* (1755, 1765).

Note: Frequencies are the summer ones. Figures for 1681 and 1690 have been adjusted as explained in Appendix 1, but probably still omit some services; other years have been adjusted similarly. Coach-waggons are excluded. Compilation of these figures involves numerous assumptions (especially for services of 10 miles and under), and there may be undetected under-recording in some years, so, while the figures indicate the general development of stage-coaching, they should not be relied on for detailed trends from year to year.

hire out post-chaises (the first apparently being those between London and Bath in 1742), and also horses to draw gentlemen's own carriages (Fig. 76), thereby remedying the difficulty of providing changes of team for private coaches.[4]

Turnpikes and stage-coaching

How could stage-coaches begin to provide a better service? Vehicles could be improved, but the aim was to make them lighter, more durable and more comfortable, a combination which depended partly on technical developments but also on better roads. Horses could also be improved and horses more suited to greater speeds could be used, but this is likely to have depended on change in the nature of their task: sheer strength was the main requirement for coach-horses on 17th-century roads. Economies of scale were potentially very large in road transport, through larger firms with more frequent services rather than larger vehicles,[5] but (unlike in carrying) there were few longer-distance routes with sufficient custom for competing services and therefore there was little scope to combine firms, though this does seem to have happened where possible (on the Bristol, Worcester and Canterbury routes).[6] In general, economies of scale depended on an increase in coach traffic.

Consequently there could be little improvement in coach services without better roads, which were especially important for vehicles travelling at relatively high speeds.[7] Better roads meant roads which were better surfaced, better drained and wider, with fewer steep hills. They were eventually provided through turnpiking, though the innovation was slow to spread following its introduction in 1663; the second turnpike was not established until 1695. By 1714 there were numerous scattered lengths of turnpike road, mostly short. Though scattered, they formed a coherent response to road conditions. On the better roads only short sections with the worst conditions were turnpiked. For example, the four turnpiked stretches of the Chester coach's road, none longer than seven miles, included the Hockliffe area, which was notoriously bad in winter. The first part of the Norwich road turnpiked (in 1696 and 1708) corresponded almost exactly to the part across boulder clay. Only three stretches of turnpike road were longer than 21 miles, and none were roads favoured by the stage-coaches: the Great North Road via Ware to Wansford, which included the original turnpike of 1663 and the part of the Great North Road which the York coaches avoided and where Thoresby recorded a higgler drowning; part of the Chester post-road from Dunstable to Dunchurch, again avoided by the stage-coaches; and the London to Harwich road via Colchester, shunned by the Norwich and Yarmouth stage-coaches in favour of the Newmarket route.[8]

76 *Advertisement for post-chaises and for horses to draw gentlemen's own post-chaises between London and Portsmouth, 1744. (LEP, 22 September 1744.)*

General Post-Office, London, Sept. 22, 1744.

POST-CHAISES,

Between LONDON *and* PORTSMOUTH, *by the Way of* HARTFORD-BRIDGE.

THIS is to acquaint the Publick, That the several Post-Masters on the Road between London and Portsmouth, are ready to furnish Gentlemen, or others, with Post-Chaises, safe, easy, and well secur'd from the Weather, upon as short a Warning as for Post-Horses, at any Hour, either of the Day or Night. Gentlemen who have Occasion to go Post on the above Roads, are desired to apply to Mr. William Miller, Post-Master, at the White Bear in Piccadilly.

A Post-Chaise may be had at any of the Stages on the Portsmouth Road, to go part or all the Way, for one or more Stages, for those who do not chuse to travel in the Night.

N. B. All Gentlemen that travel in Post-Chaises of their own, upon the Roads where Post-Chaises are already set up by the Authority of this Office, may be supply'd with Horses at the several Stages on those Roads at the Rate of Nine-pence per Mile.

By Command of the Post-Master-General,
GEORGE SHELVOCKE, Secretary.

By 1719 the Oxford route was largely turnpiked, and by 1730 the coach routes to Birmingham, Bristol, Canterbury, Cirencester, Ipswich, Northampton, Nottingham, Worcester and York were all more than 50 per cent turnpiked. The overall percentage of 18 of the main coach routes turnpiked rose from 12 per cent in 1714 to 30 per cent in 1720, 55 per cent in 1730, 63 per cent in 1740, 71 per cent in 1750 and 89 per cent in 1760.[9] Tolls were extremely low in relation to coach fares.[10] The Yarmouth coach and probably the King's Lynn one transferred from the Newmarket road to the turnpiked Essex road by 1735 and the Warrington coach to the largely turnpiked Daventry and Stone road by 1737,[11] and there was a Birmingham coach on the Daventry road from 1730 and a Lichfield coach there from 1738. However, the Ware and Daventry/Stone roads failed to attract the York and Chester coaches respectively. Moreover, there is hardly any evidence of shorter journey times, and none for shorter summer timings (other than through flying coaches), until the 1750s and 1760s.[12] It is not surprising that journey times remained unchanged for the Chester coach, whose route was still only 42 per cent turnpiked in 1750 (although it might have transferred to turnpiked roads had there been advantage in doing so), but it *is* surprising that summer timings did not accelerate for coaches such as those to York (route 89 per cent turnpiked by 1750) and to Yarmouth and Beccles (using the Essex road).

Many more flying coaches were established, but there had been flying coaches long before any turnpikes existed, and new ones continued to appear on unturnpiked or largely unturnpiked roads, for example to Dorchester, Sherborne and Salisbury in the 1720s and 1730s. They probably reflected increased willingness among passengers to endure longer days in order to arrive sooner, though it is possible that in some cases smoother roads created by turnpiking made longer days more endurable and safer.

One change by the 1730s was that summer schedules started earlier on some routes (Appendix 8). At Oxford, whereas in 1669-72 one-day coaches started in late April or May, by about 1700 they did so in late March and by the late 1730s between mid-February and early March. The one-day Cirencester coach which started in mid-May in 1696 was starting in mid-March to early April by the 1730s. A Newbury coach in 1723 was covering a remarkable 59 miles a day at a speed of 4.1 miles per hour as early as 23 February (on a route 48 per cent turnpiked). However, again there is no clear relationship with turnpiking. Oxford coaches started flying earlier before any of their route was turnpiked, and what seems to have made this possible was not better roads but earlier departure times – 4 a.m. instead of 6 a.m. for Oxford coaches and 11 p.m. instead of 3 a.m. for the Cirencester coach.[13]

Winter journey times do seem in some cases to have been falling by the 1730s and 1740s, notably on the York, Oxford, Lichfield, Worcester and Sudbury routes (Table 8 and Appendix 8). In the York case (in 1733) this was achieved at first by reducing the Stamford to London section, largely turnpiked, from three days to two. However, the new daily mileages were not usually impressive: York 45 between London and Stamford, Oxford 39, Lichfield 42, Worcester 38. Similar mileages had been achieved by other coaches long before turnpiking. Even for Sudbury (57 miles), the one-day journey in 1738-40 could have been arranged by changing the teams once, as the Yarmouth coach did on its middle day, and the coach anyway reverted to two-day operation in winter 1741-2. That turnpikes were not necessarily the cause of reduced winter journey times is supported by the fact that the Exeter coach had cut its winter journey from six days to 4½ (40 miles per day) by 1752, when hardly any of its road was turnpiked. To some extent the coachmaster had a choice of journey time regardless of turnpiking: he could cut the number of days by organising changes of teams and increasing the hours on the road. As in summer, shorter journey times in winter may reflect nothing more than increased willingness by passengers to endure long days.

Could there have been benefits from turnpiking other than greater speed? The coachmaster might have responded to better roads not with reduced journey times but with smaller teams, horses covering more miles per week or larger loads, all of which should have been reflected in lower fares. There is some evidence of larger loads, as a few coaches (the first of them on the Essex road) began to advertise that they carried outside passengers. The earliest examples are Ipswich and Beccles in 1734, Yarmouth in 1741, Norwich to King's Lynn in 1743, Worcester in 1747, Harwich in 1750 and Blandford in 1753.[14] However, there is no evidence of smaller teams,[15] horses covering more miles per week, and above all of lower fares. Fare reductions should have taken place if anywhere on the Essex road, which Defoe in 1724-5 regarded as the best in England and which had caused at least one coach to change its route. However, not only did the Yarmouth coach continue until at least 1764 to take two days in summer, as in 1689, but its fare seems to have remained at 20s. for almost the entire period from 1689 to 1764. Also, although the Yarmouth coach changed its route, Bury St Edmunds coaches continued to follow both the Newmarket and Essex roads, and an attempt to establish Norwich coaches using the Essex road in 1739-41 was beaten off by the existing operator on the Newmarket road.[16] There must have been some benefit from turnpiking to cause the Yarmouth coach to change its route, but, even on what had become the best road in England, it was clearly very limited prior to the 1760s, and insufficient to bring about reduced journey times or lower fares.

Thus the stage-coaches confirm the impression gained in respect of carriers that turnpikes at first had little impact. There were several reasons for this. First, even the better trusts implemented existing repair methods more effectively rather than developing improved methods or creating better routes. Some stretches of road appear to have been turnpiked precisely because they included steep hills,[17] and these began to be superseded only in the 1750s. Repair methods sometimes consisted of little more than spreading gravel on the road.[18] Some trusts lacked easy access to stone for road-mending. For example, Defoe noted that the turnpiked parts of the Great North Road, 'which were before intolerable, are now much mended', but had not reached the 'perfection' of the London to Colchester road because of the difficulty and cost of obtaining suitable stone.[19] The trusts' ambitions may have been limited to bringing poor stretches of road up to the quality of the better ones, and road quality in winter closer to that of summer; this is supported by the fact that at first usually only the worst stretches were turnpiked, that gaps between turnpiked sections of major roads were only very gradually filled by new trusts, and that at least some of the early trusts were expected to be extinguished once the road had been put into repair.[20] Secondly, the trusts' ability to raise money was limited in this period, and they therefore took time to have an impact. Even in the 1760s the initial act of 'putting the road in repair' sometimes took most of a decade.[21] Thirdly, a number of the early trusts appear to have been completely ineffective, notably on parts of the main Bristol road, some of which was superseded by alternative routes from the 1750s.[22] Fourthly, given the short lengths of road controlled by many trusts, even a successful trust might, on its own, have little impact on a long-distance service. The very limited impact of the early turnpike trusts helps to explain the deep hostility some of them encountered.[23]

Stage-coaches in the 1750s and 1760s

When and how did turnpikes begin to have a greater impact on coach services? Table 8 shows that winter journey times began to be significantly reduced on many routes in the 1750s. No winter timings except (briefly) that to Sudbury

Table 8. Shortening of stage-coaches' journey times

WINTER

Places and miles	Old timings	mpd	New timings	mpd
York 202	1654-1733: 6 days	34	1733: 5 days (1764: 3 days)	40, 67
Chester 188	1669-1740: 6 days	31	1761: 3 days	63
Exeter 182	1655-77: 6 days	30	1752: 4½ days (1757: 4 days; 1760: 3 days)	40, 46, 61
Taunton 151			1764: 3 days (1765: 2 days)	50, 76
Nottingham/ Derby 126/7	1699-1700: 3½ days	36	1761: 3 days (1767: 2 days)	42, 64
Worcester 115	1705: 4 days	29	1742-50: 3 days (1753: 2 days)	38, 58
Norwich 110	1739-41: 3 days	37	1755: 2 days (1761: 1½ days)	55, 73
Gloucester 108	1731-49: 3 days	36	1752: 2 days	54
Salisbury 84	1753: 2 days	42	1762: 1 day	84
Ipswich 70	1733: 2 days	35	1764: 1 day	70
Northampton 67	1712-59: 1½ or 2 days	34-45	1767: 1 day	67
Oxford 58	1670-1733: 2 days	29	1735: 1½ days (1754: 1 day)	39, 58

SUMMER

Places and miles	Old timings	mpd	New timings	mpd
York 202	1653-1756: 4 days	51	1763: 3 days (1764: 2 days, dep 10 p.m.)	67, 101
Chester 188	1657-1750: 4 days	47	1761: 2 days, dep 1 or 2 a.m.	94
Exeter 182	1658-1756: 4 days (but 3 days 1738)	46	1757: 3 days (1761: 2 days)	61, 91
Taunton 151	1733-61: 3 days	50	1763: 2½ days (1765: 2 days)	60, 76
Nottingham/ Derby 126/7	1698-1763: 2 days	64	1764: 1 day	127
Bristol 122	1709-57: 2 days	61	1763: 1 day, dep 10 p.m.	122
Worcester 115	1675-1766: 2 days (1738-53, 3-4 a.m.; 1763-6, 7-8 a.m.)	58	1774: 1 day, dep 8 or 9 p.m.	115
Norwich 110	1666-1761: 2 days (but 1 day 1708-10)	55	1762: 1 day, dep 12 midnight	110
Gloucester 108	1731-56: 2 days (but 1½ days 1715)	54	1761: 1 day, dep 10 p.m.	108
Salisbury 84	1724-59: 1 day, dep 11 p.m.-1 a.m.	84	1762: 1 day, dep 4 a.m.	84
Dover 71	1658-1751: 1 day plus		1753: 1 day	71

Notes: 'mpd' is miles per day. Summer timings are for the fastest coaches (e.g. ignoring the 3-day Bristol coaches); they ignore transitional timings (e.g. to Worcester) and are occasionally for a high-summer schedule.

Sources: Up to 1750: Appendix 8. York: LEP, 12 Apr 1753; *York Courant*, 6 Apr 1756, 15 Mar 1763, 28 Feb, 30 Oct 1764. Chester: *Adams's Weekly Courant*, 17 & 31 Mar, 6 Oct, 3 Nov 1761. Exeter/Taunton: *Sherborne Mercury*: 3 Feb 1752, 29 Mar 1756, 30 May 1757, 28 Nov 1757, 3 Nov 1760; *Sherborne Mercury*, 6 May 1754, 20 Apr 1761, 27 June 1763, 2 Jan 1764, 12 Nov 1764, 18 Feb, 21 Oct 1765. Nottingham: *Derby Mercury*, 3 Apr, 23 Oct 1761, 1 Apr, 19 Aug 1763, 18 May 1764; *Northampton Mercury*, 9 Nov 1767. Worcester: *Berrow's Worcester Journal*, 12 Apr, 20 Dec 1753, 24 July, 20 Nov 1755, 17 Mar 1763, 2 Jan, 10 Apr, 14 Aug, 6 Nov 1766, 7 Apr 1774. Norwich: *Norwich Mercury*, 15 Feb, 25 Oct 1755, 7 Feb, 20 Nov 1756, 17 Jan, 17 Oct 1761, 27 Mar 1762. Gloucester: *Gloucester Journal*, 14 Nov 1752, 2 Apr 1754, 6 Apr 1756, 24 Mar 1761. Salisbury: *Salisbury Journal*, 5 Nov 1753, 31 Mar 1755, 5 Mar 1759, 1 Mar, 12 Apr, 1 Nov 1762. Ipswich: *Ipswich Journal*, 10 Mar 1764. Northampton: *Northampton Mercury*, 29 Oct 1759, 9 Nov 1767. Oxford: *Jackson's Oxford Journal*, 7 Sept 1754, 7 Mar 1767. Bristol: *Felix Farley's Bristol Journal*, 9 Feb 1754, 10 Apr 1756, 9 Apr 1763. Dover: LEP, 30 Mar 1751, 3 Feb 1753.

exceeded 46 miles per day until 1752;[24] then between 1752 and 1755 the Gloucester, Worcester, Oxford and Norwich coaches are all recorded covering 54 to 58 miles per day. In the Gloucester and Oxford cases, the departure and arrival times indicate speeds of 4.0 and 4.8 miles per hour respectively, and therefore that the increased miles per day were not achieved merely through longer hours on the road (Appendix 9). On the Gloucester, Worcester and Norwich routes the winter timings caught up with the summer ones, albeit temporarily. Sixty miles a day was exceeded in 1761-2 by the Chester, Norwich and Salisbury coaches and in 1764-5 by the Ipswich, York and Taunton coaches (all 63 to 84 miles per day).

Summer journey times were not usually reduced until the 1760s, though there were a few exceptions, such as the Trowbridge 'flying vehicle' of 1753 (a remarkable 101 miles in a day, but departure at 10 p.m.).[25] But between 1761 and 1764 the Exeter, Chester, Gloucester, Norwich, Bristol, Nottingham and Derby, York, Frome and Leicester coaches are all recorded covering from 91 to 127 miles per day, though some of these were in fact setting off the previous evening.[26] By 1764 the majority of coach journeys were taking only half as many days in summer as they had done ten years earlier.

Reduction in journey times was accompanied by improved vehicles, especially, from 1752, by vehicles with steel springs. These were first used on stage-coaches between Maidenhead and London in May 1752, and were adopted in the same year by Reading and Newbury services (with speeds of 6.0 and 5.4 miles per hour respectively; Fig. 78) and in the following year by some services on other roads.[27] In 1752-3 such vehicles were called stage-chaises, probably reflecting

READING *Stage Chaise,*
Made with Steel Springs, and as easy as any Post-Chaise; to carry Four Passengers, at Six Shillings each Passenger, either going to, or coming from London; Children on Lap, Half Price;
SETS out on Friday the 17th Instant from Mrs. Sarah Clowes's, known by the Name or Sign of the Black Horse Inn in Reading aforesaid, in the County of Berks, every Day in the Week at Five o'Clock in the Morning, and returns the same Day by Eight o'Clock in the Evening to the said Black Horse Inn in Reading, and so continues Changes Horses at Mr. Green's, at the Sun Inn in Maidenhead, every Morning by Seven o'Clock, and at Mr. Atkins's at the Sun Inn in Hounslow by Ten, to get to the Black Bear Inn in Piccadilly by Twelve o'Clock: Sets out from the said Black Bear Inn at One o'Clock, and returns to Reading by Eight o'Clock the said Evening.
Books kept, and Places taken, at the said Mrs. Clowes's; at Mr. Green's, at the Sun at Maidenhead, and at the Black Bear in Piccadilly, at 3 s. Entrance, and the remaining 3 s. to be paid before setting out. Each Passenger to be allow'd eight Pounds Weight. Small Parcels taken in at the abovesaid Houses, and carefully deliver'd with Speed.
Note; No Money, Plate, Jewels, nor Writings, if lost, to be made good, unless enter'd and paid for as such.
Perform'd by
WM. GREEN, *and Co.*

77 *Advertisement for Reading stage-chaises on steel springs, 1752. This is one of the earliest advertisements to give both departure and arrival times. (LEP, 11 July 1752.)*

BATH, BRISTOL and LONDON,
FLYING MACHINE, in One Day,

BEGINS Flying To-morrow, from the Bell Savage on Ludgate-hill, London, and continues going every Sunday, Tuefday, and Thurfday Night, at Eleven o'Clock, to Bath ; and from Gerard's-Hall Inn, in Basing-Lane, near Bread-Street, every Monday, Wednefday, and Friday Night, at Ten o'Clock, for Briftol, and carries Paffengers and Parcels as ufual. To Briftol 30 s. to Bath 28 s.

The two Days Machine as ufual, from the Saracen's Head in Friday-Street, the Bell-Savage on Ludgate-Hill, and the One Bell in the Strand; at Six o'Clock. The Fare as ufual, to Bath 25 s. to Briftol 27 s. Half to be paid at taking the Places, and the other Half at going into the Machine.

All the above Machines call at the White Bear, Black Bear, and the Old White-horfe Cellar, Piccadilly. Performed by

T. BANNISTER, London,
W. CLARKE, Reading,
R. HOLLIWELL, Newbury,
T. HANCOCK, Marlborough, and
J. GEASIER, Bath.

78 *The first advertisement for a one-day Bristol coach, albeit with departures at 10 or 11 p.m. The two-day coach continued, at a lower fare, but there was no further mention of the former three-day coach. (LEP, 14 April 1763.)*

earlier use of steel springs on post-chaises. From 1754 they were usually called 'machines', but it is clear that not all machines had steel springs. All the steel-sprung vehicles prior to 1764 held only four inside passengers, though most carried outside passengers too.[28] In 1753 the Dover machine, holding four passengers, was on 'four French steel springs, after the model of the new fashion'd post-chaises' (indicating that the new springs were a foreign import), and the 'Bristol flying machine' in 1754 was '(instead of the stage-coach) intirely new, and hangs on steel springs'.[29]

Another innovation, though possibly reflecting earlier practice, was to combine small teams with frequent changes of team: the 'Northampton new berlin stage' in 1752 held four passengers and had teams of two horses, changed four times on the road (every 13 miles). It combined a high advertised speed (6.1 miles per hour) with a low fare (2.1 pence per mile), but the low fare was evidently unsustainable; between 1753 and 1755 it varied from 2.7 to 3.2 pence per mile for the same service.[30] Teams sizes were rarely specified in this period, so it is unclear how common such an arrangement was.

Some reduction in journey times could have been achieved through longer hours on the road, and this was certainly a factor in some cases, but the increasingly numerous advertisements and a few diaries stating both arrival and

Ipswich, August 17, 1764.

The LONDON and IPSWICH POST-COACHES,

SET out on MONDAY the 27th Instant, at Seven o'Clock
in the Morning, from the BLACK BULL INN in BISHOPS-
GATE-STREET, London, and at the same time from the GREAT
WHITE HORSE INN in IPSWICH, and continue every Day (Sundays excepted) to be at the above Places the same Evening at Five
o'Clock. Each Passenger to pay Three-pence per Mile, and be
allowed *Eighteen* Pounds Luggage ; all above to pay one Penny
per Pound, and so in proportion. The Coaches hang upon Steel-
Springs, are very easy, large, and commodious, carry six Inside-
passengers, and no Outside-passengers whatsoever ; but have great
Conveniences for Parcels or Game, (to keep them from the Weather) which will be delivered at London & Ipswich the same Night.

As these Coaches are set out for the Ease and Expedition of Gentlemen and Ladies travelling, the Proprietors humbly hope for
their Encouragement, and are determined to spare no pains to ren-
der it as agreeable as they can. Performed, if God permit, by

Peter Sheldon, at the Bull in Bishopsgate-Street, London,
Thomas Archer, at the White Hart, Brentwood,
Charles Kirby, at the Black Boy, Chelmsford,
George Reynolds, at the Three Cups, Colchester, and
Charles Harris, at the Great White Horse, Ipswich.

N. B. The Proprietors will not be answerable for any Money,
Plate, Jewels, or Writing, unless enter'd and paid for as such.

IPSWICH MACHINE, (On Steel Springs)
To carry four Inside Passengers,

SETS out from the Coach-Houses in Ipswich on MONDAYS,
WEDNESDAYS, and FRIDAYS, to the CROSS-KEYS Inn in
Gracechurch-Street, London ; and returns for Ipswich on TUES-
DAYS, THURSDAYS, and SATURDAYS. Sets out from each Place
at Six o'Clock in the Morning.

Each Inside Fifteen Shillings, allow'd 24lb. Weight of Luggage,
all above to pay 1d. per Pound : Outsides Eight Shillings. Small
Parcels, and Game, qualified, will be taken due Care of, and deliver'd with Dispatch.

The Ease, Safety, and Convenience of this Machine has been
long experienced. We return our sincere Thanks for the Encouragement already given to it, and hope to merit a Continuance of
the Favour of the Publick. Proper Time is allowed to breakfast
and dine on the Road. If a Family take the four Inside-Places,
and chuse to set out at Seven o'Clock in the Morning, it shall be
comply'd with, provided they signify the same at the Time of taking the Places.---Perform'd (if God permit) in Eleven Hours, by
RICHARD DAVE and WM. BLAKELY.

IPSWICH STAGE-COACH, sets out from the Cross Keys
Inn in Gracechurch-Street, London, on MONDAYS, WEDNES-
DAYS, and FRIDAYS ; and returns from Ipswich, on TUESDAYS,
THURSDAYS, and SATURDAYS. Sets out from each Place at
Four o'Clock in the Morning. Each Inside Twelve Shillings ; al-
lowed 30 lb. of Luggage, all above that Weight to pay one Shil-
ling for every 20 lb. Outsides, and Children in Lap, Half-price.
Parcels, Game qualified, &c. will be taken due Care of, and deli-
ver'd with Dispatch. Perform'd (if God permit) in 14 Hours, by
R. DAVE and WM. BLAKELY.

BECCLES STAGE-COACH to London, in two Days, sets
out from the King's Head Inn in Beccles on MONDAYS & WED-
NESDAYS ; and sets out from the Cross Keys Inn in Gracechurch-
Street, London, on MONDAYS and FRIDYAS, for Beccles. Sets
out from London at Four o'Clock in the Morning, from Beccles
at Five o'Clock. Each Inside Twenty Shillings ; allowed 30 lb.
Weight, all above to pay 1 d. per Pound. Outsides and Children
in Lap, Half-price. Parcels, Game qualified, &c. will be taken
due Care of, and deliver'd with Dispatch. Perform'd (if God permit) by R. DAVE and W. BLAKELY.

⁂ Money, Plate, Watches, Jewels, or Writing, the Masters
will not be accountable for, if not enter'd in their Book and paid
for as such.---We return our sincere Thanks for the Encouragement already given to these Coaches, and will endeavour to merit
a Continuance of the Favour of the Publick.

79 *Advertisements for Ipswich coaches in 1764. The upper one has the fastest schedule recorded, indicating a speed of just over eight miles per hour. The lower one provides an example of a coachmaster providing two types of service, one taking 11 hours and the other 14 hours. Peter Sheldon, who had a stake in both Ipswich and York coaches (Fig. 80), was an early example of a London innkeeper with coaches on several roads. (Ipswich Journal, 8 September 1764.)*

departure times indicate that miles per hour also tended to increase (Appendix 9). Despite this, the level of fares changed little. The average for 226 fares found in advertisements between 1752 and 1768 was 2.5 pence per mile (2.3 in East Anglia).[31] 136 were within the range 2.0-2.7 pence per mile, only 17 were below that range[32] and virtually all the 73 above that range were for coaches covering an unusually large number of miles per day. In fact there was a reasonably clear relationship between speeds and fares in the 1760s. A fare of 2.2 to 2.6 pence per mile, which had formerly paid for services averaging about 4.3 miles per hour, now paid for 5.4 to 5.8 miles per hour; in East Anglia, 1.6 to 2.1 pence per mile was now sufficient for 5.6 to 6.1 miles per hour. Evidently, in these cases, higher speed than previously was not incurring extra cost, though income from outside passengers may have covered some rise in costs. An unusually detailed diary description of two journeys in one of the two-day Chester coaches in 1761 (at speeds ranging from 4.8 to 5.8 miles per hour in early October) suggests that the horses continued to be changed at intervals of about 20 to 25 miles.[33]

Even faster services were being provided in the 1760s at a higher price: from 3.0 to 3.4 pence per mile for speeds of 6.3 to 7.5 miles per hour, or, in East Anglia, 2.3 to 3.0 pence per mile for 6.5 to 8.2 miles per hour. The higher fares indicate that these speeds *did* incur extra cost, and were presumably achieved by using more horses and working shorter stages, with the teams covering fewer miles per week. This is supported by five examples of coaches in the mid-1760s with proprietors spaced about ten miles apart, indicating stages of about that length instead of the usual 20 to 25 miles in summer; all five had high fares of 3.0 pence per mile. For example, the times for the Southampton coach advertised in September 1764 indicate 7.3 miles per hour, and it had eight proprietors, each eight to 13 miles away from the next.[34] Thus by the 1760s there was the beginning of that differentiation of services by speed and cost which was such a feature of the industry later, whereas previously costs had increased too fast as speed rose to make such variation feasible. Many coachmasters now had two services with different speeds and fares; for example, an Ipswich coachmaster in September 1764 offered a choice between a machine taking 11 hours (at 2.6 pence per mile) and a stage-coach taking 14 hours (at 2.0 pence per mile) (Fig. 79).[35] Another change, brought about by shorter stages and larger partnerships, was the increased involvement of London innkeepers, who would later become dominant in stage-coaching.

Higher speeds without increased cost, and the smallness of the extra cost incurred by the fastest coaches, indicate that the draught required was being reduced. This was brought about in two ways: by improved roads and by steel-sprung vehicles.

The turnpike trusts' ability to raise funds quickly increased considerably from about 1750 as a result of the use of subscriptions – promises of money by large numbers of people in advance of a trust's formation, instead of a few large individual loans as previously. Some new stretches of road were constructed[36] (though not on the scale achieved later) and, probably of greater importance, some stretches with steep hills were superseded by other routes. For example, on the Bristol route the Chippenham road replaced the Sandy Lane one in the

1750s, attracting at least one of the Bath stage-coaches to it in 1754.[37] From the 1760s turnpike trusts (and others) began to build bridges on new sites and replace earlier bridges; they were increasingly able to obtain good road-mending material, sometimes assisted by canals; and they increasingly employed professional surveyors.[38] Clearly the trusts were becoming more ambitious about the quality of their roads.

However, the reduction in winter and summer timings occurred on so many different roads within such short periods in each case as to suggest that a technical innovation was the direct cause, rather than improvement in the state of the roads, which must have varied greatly from one road to another. That innovation was clearly the use of steel springs. In the 1750s, all or virtually all the higher speeds recorded (from 5.3 to 6.8 miles per hour) were for vehicles with steel springs.[39] In some cases, the first mention of steel springs coincided with the reduction in journey times, as at Oxford in winter 1754, Boston in 1759, Chester in 1761, Salisbury in 1762, and Ipswich in winter 1764, although elsewhere steel springs are mentioned earlier.[40] In the case of the one-day Salisbury coach in 1762, the 'very neat machine' on steel springs 'to make travelling more agreeable than it ever was' (and which was to make 4 a.m. instead of 11 p.m. departures possible in summer) was still being built when the new service was advertised, and the new timing depended on the vehicles being completed.[41]

The effect of steel springs will have been to cut the draught power required, both directly, by reducing the impact of shocks, and indirectly, by enabling coaches to be less stoutly constructed. However, they were at first used mainly on some of the short and middle-distance routes near London and on provincial services, and only in the 1760s adopted widely for long-distance coaches.[42] John Whitmash, for example, had steel springs on his Exeter to Bath coaches in 1754, but not on his Taunton to London coaches until 1764. The problem was almost certainly breakages, especially on poor roads which gave sudden shocks to the coach.[43] The springs were apparently suitable at first only for smaller, lighter vehicles – hence the usual complement of four inside passengers; no coaches with steel springs are recorded as having room for six inside passengers until 1764.

Steel springs were clearly being developed further around 1760. A series of patents for improved coach springs were granted from 1757 to 1766, all but one of them to Richard Tredwell, a London blacksmith, who obtained four between 1759 and 1766. Tredwell stressed that his patent springs were lighter and less liable to break than the ones previously used. Those made under the 1759 patent he claimed could carry double the weight of other springs of the same size. However, in 1759-60 many of them were in fact breaking, causing 'greatly decreased' demand for them, and he was liable to the coachmakers if they broke within six months. In Chancery proceedings shortly afterwards, Tredwell blamed poor-quality steel supplied by his Walsall ironmonger, which is perhaps why he was living in Rotherham when his next patent was taken out in 1763.[44] It was probably when Tredwell solved the problem of breakages that steel springs were applied to larger coaches and widely adopted and coach speeds significantly increased. The long-forgotten Tredwell is almost certainly one of the key figures in 18th-century road transport, influencing private carriages as well as stage-coaches.

The Proprietors of the Original York, Doncaster, Stamford, *and* London

Flying Post Coaches on Steel Springs, with Postillions,

BEG Leave to return Thanks to Gentlemen, Ladies, and others for the Countenance already given to the said Carriage, and hope that the Care and Attention already shewn to oblige the Public, will merit their future Favours and Encouragement; and as they find it more agreeable to the Public in general to take three Days during the Winter Season, they propose next Monday, the 5th of November, to set out from Mr. Howard's in Lendal, or the George in Coney-street, York, at Six in the Morning, breakfast at Tadcaster, dine at Doncaster, and lie at Tuxford; the second Day breakfast at Newark, dine at Colesworth, and lie at Stilton; and the third Day breakfast at Bugden, dine at Stevenage, and from thence to London. These Coaches are made roomy to carry six inside Passengers, each to pay Threepence per Mile, and allowed 14 lb. of Luggage; all above to pay Threepence per Pound, or in Proportion to the Miles they go. They carry no outside Passengers, but have very good Conveniences for carrying of Luggage, Parcels, and Game, which will be the greatest Care taken of, and deliver'd in London and York the same Nights they arrive. *Perform'd by*

P. Sheldon, at the Bull in Bishopsgate street, London.	W. Crabtree, Grantham.
	J. Ridgill, Newark.
T. Topham, Barnet.	J. Harris, Tuxford.
H. Howard, Hatfield.	F. Bingley, Barnby-Moor.
T. Whittington, Stevenage.	R. Shaw, Doncaster.
G. Fletcher, Biggleswade.	— Denton, Ferrybridge.
W. South, Bugden.	M. Todd, Tadcaster.
A. Clarke, Stilton.	H. Howard, } York.
M. Skurray, Stamford.	W. Baldock, }
T. Tinkler, Colesworth.	

☞ They set out every Day from York for London, and from London for York, Sundays excepted.

The Proprietors of York, Darlington, *and* Newcastle Flying Post-Coaches on Steel Springs, with Postillions, (From York to Newcastle in One Day)

TAKE this Method of returning Thanks to Gentlemen and Ladies for the great Encouragement they have met with; and, in order further to oblige the Public, they propose to set out from York three Times each Week, instead of two as formerly, viz. Monday, Thursday, and Saturday, and to set out from Newcastle for York on the same Days. They begin to set out from the George in Coney-street, or Mr. Howard's in Lendal, York, on Monday next, the 5th of November, at Four in the Morning, breakfast at Boroughbridge, dine at Darlington, and from thence to Newcastle. The Coaches are made roomy to carry six inside Passengers, each to pay Threepence per Mile, and allowed 14 lb. of Luggage; all above to pay Three Halfpence per Pound, or in Proportion to the Miles they go. They carry no outside Passengers, but have very good Conveniences for carrying of Luggage, Parcels, and Game, of which the greatest Care will be taken, and delivered in York the same Night the Coaches arrive, and forwarded for London the next Morning by the Post-Coach. *Perform'd by*

W. Parker, Newcastle.	H. Abbot, Boroughbridge.
T. Baumbrough, Durham.	H. Howard, } York.
J. Carter, Northallerton and Darlington.	W. Baldock, }

☞ The Masters will not be accountable for Money, Plate, Jewels, Watches, Rings, or Writings, unless deliver'd as such, and paid for accordingly.

80 *Advertisement for York and Newcastle coaches, taking three days between London and York in winter, 1764. The 17 proprietors between London and York indicate relatively short stages, and there was a correspondingly high fare of three pence per mile. (York Courant, 30 October 1764.)*

The development of steel coach springs and better roads were almost certainly linked, given that steel springs were likely to snap on bad roads. It was probably the gradual improvement of the roads which made it worthwhile to develop steel springs suitable for stage-coaches, though the *timing* of the increase in coach speeds was determined not directly by the improvement in the roads but by the availability of more durable steel springs. In contrast, for carriers there was a more direct link between better roads and greater loads per horse, which is probably why rates of carriage were affected by turnpikes slightly earlier than stage-coach speeds.

As stage-coaches speeded up, the number of services (especially long-distance services) began to increase, despite growing competition from post-chaises, which could travel at nine or ten miles per hour by 1761.[45] The number of stage-coach services per week from London covering over 80 miles rose from about 52 in 1738 to 67 in 1755 and 140 in 1765 (Table 7), through a combination of more frequent services by existing firms, new competitors (for example to York, Chester and Exeter) and new destinations. The latter included Manchester and Leeds in 1760, Kendal and Frome in 1762 and Poole by 1764.[46] There were also new provincial services, such as from Birmingham to Worcester in 1753 and Manchester to Liverpool in 1760, though very few until 1764.[47] Increasing competition put pressure on fares,[48] but the stage-coaches' cost structure limited the scope for fare reductions, and the main result of greater competition was probably to increase the quality of service, especially speed.

One aspect remained unchanged until surprisingly late: although there was less difference between summer and winter as regarded timings, stage-coaches continued to use teams of six and postilions in winter. The Norwich coaches were still doing so in 1771, when their owners were advised to follow the example of the Windsor coaches by making the front wheels of their coaches five feet high and doing without the two extra horses and postilion.[49] If the Norwich coaches with their relatively flat roads required six horses, most others must have needed them too. This changed later in the 1770s.

After the 1760s change appears to have been incremental, bringing rising speed without significantly increasing the numbers of horses required. In the 1830s the number of horses per double mile even at ten miles per hour was only about 0.9, compared with 0.4 to 0.8 in 1650-1750.[50] Increased speed without substantial extra cost made possible the great increase in the number of services and in competition, thereby providing both economies of scale and the spur to greater efficiency. However, speeds rose only gradually: the average for mail-coaches was 7.3 miles per hour in 1792 and 9.4 in 1836, and in 1831 the fastest stage-coaches were said to travel at 11 miles per hour – 'very near to the utmost limits which nature has prescribed for animal exertion'.[51] There were significant reductions in journey times,[52] but there was no further step change such as occurred in the 1750s and 1760s, when speeds rose from a typical 4 to 5 miles per hour in summer to 5½ to 7½ miles per hour. The 1750s and 1760s, especially the latter, were the crucial decades in setting the stage-coach industry on its trend of rising efficiency and growth.

CHAPTER XIV

CONCLUSION

Stage-coaches, carriers and roads

Road transport before turnpiking has attracted more than its fair share of myths, so it is worth emphasising here some of the main conclusions of this study. First, long before turnpiking, there was a large network of London carriers, much valued by the communities they served. There was also a substantial network of stage-coaches.

Secondly, a large part (probably the greater part) of the goods transported by road went by wheeled vehicle, and this had been the case since the 14th century or earlier.[1] The role of packhorses in the pre-turnpike era has been exaggerated by most writers. Where packhorses were used, it was usually because they had particular advantages, such as greater speed, not because the use of vehicles was physically impossible.

Thirdly, the regularity of stage-coach, waggon and packhorse services to and from London in the 17th and early 18th centuries is thoroughly documented. Indeed the organisation of services, including agreements with innkeepers to use the same inns for each night of each journey, depended on this regularity. Where water transport was also available it was above all the regularity and reliability of road services which persuaded customers to pay their relatively high prices. Symson expected the Kendal packhorse carriers to be punctual to the hour,[2] and although this cannot be confirmed for carriers in general, or even for the Kendal carriers, it is significant that one of their regular users believed it.

Fourthly, road services – even stage-coaches – operated regularly both in summer and winter. Stage-coach services did not cease in winter as so often asserted. The evidence for their operation in winter, sometimes even during heavy snow, is as varied and plentiful as could be wished. The main roads to and from London were not impassable in winter, either for packhorses or vehicles.

Fifthly, a substantial proportion of goods transport, and probably by far the greater part if measured by value rather than volume, was by road rather than by water. Road transport was not too expensive for higher-value or perishable goods, including the produce of the country's main industry (textiles), even for journeys as long as Kendal to London.

At the start of this book it was indicated that roads were good or bad in terms of what they allowed or did not allow road users to do, and we can conclude, therefore, that the condition of the main roads to and from London was not such as to prevent regular services by packhorses or vehicles even in winter, nor services which were affordable for many users. The main roads evidently varied in quality, but it was sometimes possible to avoid the poorer ones such as the Ware road, Thoresby's description of which during flooding has so coloured popular views of the roads before turnpiking. Lesser roads were occasionally said to be impassable in winter, but such references are few, and even in these cases it is not always clear that they were physically impassable, as opposed to being impassable at reasonable cost for low-value goods such as coal and timber.[3]

All this has consequences for the notion, popular among local historians, that many communities were isolated. Moving people or heavy goods over long distances (other than by water) was expensive, but lighter goods could easily reach areas distant from London, as is indicated by the consumer luxuries obtained by Symson at Kendal in 1711-20. This was less easy where there was no direct London carrier, but local carriers and other forms of local carriage greatly extended the area served by the London carriers.[4]

However, it is important not to go the opposite extreme and exaggerate the quality of roads and road transport, and the extent to which they met the needs of those wishing to travel or send goods. While the state of the roads did not prevent reliable and, for many purposes, affordable road transport, this means that providers of road services were able to deal with the problems caused by bad roads, rather than that the roads were necessarily good. In fact there are several clear indications that road transport was hampered by the state of the roads. First, while packhorses were economic, it was the poor quality of the roads which allowed them to be so: on good roads they would soon have become uneconomic and been replaced by waggons, as eventually happened in the 18th century. Secondly, the large difference between stage-coaches' summer and winter timings indicates how severely bad conditions in winter affected services. Thirdly, the major increase in the productivity of both carrying and coaching services from the mid-18th century, though not solely attributable to better roads, does indicate how poor-quality roads had kept carriers' and coachmasters' costs high. Fourthly, there do appear to have been parts of northern England where wheeled vehicles could not be used, or at least not used economically, and a few towns, such as Leeds, which appear to have been inaccessible by wheeled vehicle at reasonable cost.[5]

Bad roads particularly raised the cost of greater speed, and it was therefore the stage-coaches which were most affected by them. Faster coaches could not be viable without improved roads. Whereas there could be a large network of London carriers, growing in capacity as the economy developed, the stage-coach industry reached a plateau in the early 18th century, and it needed improved roads, combined with technical innovation, to resume its growth. Until the 1750s the turnpikes provided little help.

The importance of the London carriers

Assessing the importance of the London carriers is complicated by the fact that, unlike the stage-coaches, they were not providing a new form of transport in the century after 1650. The main developments occurred before and after that period: the growth of the network probably from the late 14th to 16th centuries,

81 *The* White Lion *(left) and* White Hart *(right) in Broad Street were Bristol's two main coaching inns in the first half of the 18th century. Both were timber-framed, but the* White Lion *had been re-faced in baroque style in the late 17th century. The* White Lion *was a rare example (outside London) of a major coaching inn from before 1750 which remained so until the end of stage-coaching.*

the shift from carts to waggons (especially in the 1610s), and the major growth in productivity from the 1740s or 1750s. Speed did not increase in the period covered here (except at the very end of it where flying waggons were established) and rates of carriage did not decline (except possibly in some places where waggons replaced packhorses). The carriers' impact cannot be assessed by comparing towns with and without them, or examining towns newly acquiring them, as can often be done for navigable rivers and canals. Everywhere had roads and, potentially, London carriers; if new needs arose, road transport could respond easily with additional services.

In fact the ubiquity of London carrying services is the key to understanding their importance. Their contribution was to enable other economic influences to operate more freely, less constrained by distance than would otherwise have been the case. Whereas canals promoted regionally-integrated economies,[6] London carriers promoted an integrated national economy. Thus, for the lighter, higher-value items, road transport, by providing a reliable and affordable means of obtaining raw materials and distributing finished goods, enabled production to take place wherever factors such as low labour costs made it most profitable. For example, a type of cloth, or light metal goods, could be produced in one area and supplied throughout the country and overseas, and seeds could be grown in the Chelmsford and Colchester area and supplied throughout the country.[7] Only one intermediary – the London carrier – was required between a mercer in distant Kendal and his customers in London, or between shopkeepers anywhere served directly by London carriers and their London suppliers. Road transport could assist even where only a small proportion of the product was sent by road, since it meant urgent orders could be attended to and reduced the need to keep large stocks. Even towns with no water transport at all could flourish, such as Frome, noted by Defoe as 'being, not only no sea-port, but not near any sea-port, having no manner of communication by water, no navigable river at it, or near it. Its trade is wholly clothing, and the cloths they make, are, generally speaking, all conveyed to London'.[8] Much of the wool used in Frome was also conveyed long distances by road, sometimes from London.

In ways such as this the carriers contributed to a more efficient economy, and above all to the specialisation by town or area which was such a feature of industry, and to a lesser extent agriculture, in England, giving rise to further major consequences such as economies of scale and the development of ancillary trades. An example of such specialisation in the period covered here is the rapid growth of Yorkshire's worsted industry, heavily dependent on road transport, from the late 17th century.[9]

While England's main transport advantage over most nearby countries may have been its excellent water transport (especially coastal transport), it also had a more effective road haulage trade than France and a far better one than Spain (though the Netherlands, with its well-organised river transport, probably had a better goods transport system overall). French carriers were prevented by law from having regular departure days and from carrying the smaller parcels, and there was probably a much less dense network of services.[10] England also had the advantage of being relatively small, the significance of which is highlighted by the falling off in the number of carrying services over about 80 miles from

London (Map 1). For these reasons the impact of carriers on industrialisation and urban growth is likely to have been greater in England than elsewhere. Certainly there was a strong contrast between England and France in the extent to which industries were concentrated regionally, with major concentrations of production in France even in the cloth industry only beginning to emerge by about the beginning of the 18th century.[11]

London of course had by far the largest network of carriers in England (and probably in Europe), and the most efficient services. Economies of scale in carrying, particularly as a result of larger firms, mainly belong to a later period than that covered here, but busier routes are always likely to have had a more even flow of loading and thus greater ability to match capacity to demand. There was also much more chance of a direct service being available to or from London than to or from anywhere else. Something of the overlapping provincial networks recorded in the late 18th century[12] evidently existed much earlier, but transfers between carriers meant risk of delay and loss, and therefore direct services were preferred, which favoured London.

In some respects in London, as elsewhere, carriers simply facilitated the operation of other economic influences. As regards manufacturing, for example, the carriers assisted many London industries, bringing them raw materials and distributing their produce, but they also helped some industries to relocate to places with cheaper labour, land and coal while maintaining access to London's market and its distribution network. Complete relocation was not common in the period covered here (being largely confined to shoemaking and framework knitting), but in some cases London became only one of several manufacturing centres, and sometimes *parts* of industries moved elsewhere. For example, in the late 17th century Lancashire began to make watches, including parts to be used by London watchmakers, which would certainly have been conveyed by road. In silk manufacture, not only did Macclesfield start to become a serious rival to London, but the London manufacturers themselves began to put out the twisting of raw silk to low-wage areas, using road transport to do so. By 1750, 70 per cent of hosiery output, previously focused in London, was accounted for by Nottinghamshire, Derbyshire and Leicestershire.[13] Thus carriers, like other forms of transport, assisted the process whereby industries were relocated on the principle of comparative advantage, and promoted London's increasing specialisation in the finishing and assembly trades and also the inter-dependence of London and provincial towns.

Carriers had a clearer positive impact on London's long-established but increasing roles as a centre of distribution and as a port. Cause and effect cannot be disentangled, but by the 17th century London had both the best carrying network and the only one which extended throughout England. These roles contributed to London's rapid growth and the failure of regional capitals (other than those which were themselves ports or manufacturing centres) to match it. Between 1650 and 1750 London's population grew by 80 per cent, compared with 56 per cent for the 14 provincial towns which were largest in 1650, or 39 per cent if the two most populous (the strongly industrial Norwich and Bristol) are excluded.[14] Carriers were of course only one of many interlocking factors; for example, London's carrying network and its port each contributed to the

82 *A toll gate near Bristol: St Michael's Hill Gate, showing the gate, the toll collector's cottage and the board listing the tolls.*

development of the other. Also, the quality of London's carrying network could not prevent other ports expanding faster than London's in the 18th century.

In other respects too the carriers assisted London's growth, for example by acting as the main conduit for cash being transferred to the city by country landowners. Even as regards industry, the carriers promoted London's growth by enabling it to concentrate on what it did best and to strengthen its role as part of an 'urban system'[15] of inter-dependent towns and cities.

The importance of the early stage-coaches

What conclusions can be drawn about the importance of stage-coaches in their first century? The total numbers of stage-coach passengers were small. For example, given that a stage-coach carried an average of four persons per journey, the York, Chester and Exeter coaches in a year each conveyed about 620 passengers each way – a tiny number moving between the metropolis and some of England's major provincial cities. However, that is not a fair assessment. The stage-coaches carried people of economic and political importance, travelling to and from London for business, political or social reasons. Moreover, for almost everyone, long journeys by *any* means were only occasional, and a mere two journeys a year were enough to participate in the London season, with all its vast economic, political and social ramifications. And the county elites were small: perhaps 70 or 80 families in a typical county.[16] Allowing an average of two persons per family inside the coach, a thrice-weekly stage-coach could transfer an entire county elite to London in nine weeks. The stage-coaches also helped to remedy some of the deficiencies in the postal system, improving the circulation of business and other information. The shorter- and middle-distance coaches may have made a small contribution to internal trade, as in the case of the man who travelled by coach to Oxford to sell garden seeds in 1667.[17]

Stage-coaches were of course only an addition to existing means of travel. Nevertheless, they enabled some to travel who could not otherwise have done so, especially well-to-do women on their own, as discussed earlier. More generally, the widespread use of stage-coaches revealed by diaries suggests that the stage-coach made travelling more agreeable, or at least less alarming. They are likely therefore to have increased the willingness to travel, especially to and from London. Cressett and his opponent agreed in 1672 that the stage-coach encouraged people to travel, and the latter estimated that at least half of those who used the stage-coaches would not otherwise have travelled at all.[18]

The early stage-coaches were therefore important in two ways. First, they encouraged people to travel, especially to and from London. Secondly, they gave rise to an established group of firms which were able to expand once conditions were right, as they were in the second half of the 18th century, and also provided the example of regular coach services for would-be new entrants.

The road services of 1650-1750 in perspective

One of the findings of this book is that there was a sharp increase in road transport's effectiveness in the 1750s and 1760s following a period of relatively little change. That sharp increase was especially marked in passenger transport, where the combination of turnpike roads and steel springs permitted greater speeds without increased cost. This resulted in rapid growth in the number of coach services and other forms of passenger transport, and a great increase in the willingness to travel. This in turn had immense economic and social consequences, resulting for example from the ability of merchants and tradesmen to travel more easily, the faster and freer flow of information and the growth of tourism and travel for social reasons.[19]

The 1750s and 1760s also saw a major increase in the efficiency of London carrying, reflected mainly in falling rates of carriage, though where flying waggons were adopted there were also faster deliveries.[20] However, the impact on customers or potential customers is less clear than in the case of stage-coaches. Some new traffic was attracted, and the trend towards regional specialisation certainly intensified in the second half of the 18th century, but for most of the carriers' customers the cost of carriage to or from London was already only a tiny proportion of the value of the items conveyed. Since, even from Kendal to London by packhorse, carriage accounted for only about 6 to 8 per cent of the value of the cloth conveyed, and for West Country cloth from Exeter only about 2 to 4 per cent of its value,[21] caution is needed in assessing the effect of reduced charges for long-distance carriage. On the other hand, the replacement of packhorses by flying waggons was clearly beneficial, in Exeter's case reducing journey times from 5½ to 4½ days, and the output of the London carrying trade certainly grew in the 18th century.[22] More significant than changes in London carrying may have been increased efficiency and professionalism in local carrying, which must often have had a greater impact because rates of carriage could be high in relation to the value of heavy items conveyed for short distances. This perhaps contributed to more efficient methods of distributing industrial products.[23] However, while local carriers too could benefit from better roads and better waggon horses, the extent to which local carrying services became more numerous, regular and efficient in the mid-18th century needs more research.

In the carriers' case it is as instructive to look backward in time as forward. In particular, to what extent can the regularity and efficiency of the carrying services of 1650-1750 be read back into previous centuries? As regards the roads themselves, England may well have participated in the 'road revolution' of western Europe in the 13th century, though the evidence of its bridges and causeways suggests that the process of improvement began earlier: at most places where there was a bridge in 1750 there had been one in 1250, and often since before 1100; almost all of these bridges were wide enough for wheeled traffic.[24] Whereas most haulage was by oxen in the 12th century, horses were dominant in haulage by the end of the 13th; their greater speed contributed to a large increase in trade. Most carriage in the 14th century was by cart.[25] In the 14th century the speeds of vehicles carrying goods appear to have been similar to those in 1650-1750. Rates of carriage, taking into account changes in provender costs, were apparently no higher than in 1650-1750, and were possibly lower, despite an increase in the capacity of draught horses between the 14th and 17th centuries.[26]

However, there is no evidence of public carrying services by road until the last decade of the 14th century. Until such services were established, while there was no difficulty sending relatively large consignments which formed a full load for a cart or gang of packhorses, there was no easy way of sending small consignments at reasonable cost. The London carrying network appears to have developed significantly in the 15th century, alongside the cloth industry, though nearly all the London carriers recorded then served large towns or cities, and the widespread network depicted in Taylor's *Carriers cosmographie* may not have come into existence until the 16th century.[27] Nevertheless, many towns did acquire London carriers in the 15th century, and new services could be established wherever there was sufficient loading. (The main subsequent change was the replacement of two-wheeled carts by four-wheeled waggons, which did not result in increased loads per horse and was therefore probably of marginal benefit, through the smaller likelihood of vehicles overturning and the reduced number of drivers per ton carried).[28] As for regularity, those carriers who could also use their horses for farming might in some cases have provided irregular services, but there is virtually no evidence of this at any period,[29] and it would have been hard for an irregular service to survive anywhere where there was competition. In general the requirement for regularity was inherent in the economics of carrying firms, because of the need to feed horses even if they were not working, so the likelihood is that the regularity observable in 1650-1750 also existed in the 15th century. Therefore, for all the intervening period London carriers were promoting regional specialisation and metropolitan growth, helping to support new industries and to turn the whole of England into London's hinterland and London into the centre of an urban system. That long-sustained influence was undoubtedly a crucial part of the background to the Industrial Revolution. Linked by the London carriers, as well as other forms of transport, the metropolis and regional or local concentrations of industry grew together.

In this and other respects the London carriers were continuing in 1650-1750 to do what they had already done for several centuries. But the importance of a form of transport in a particular period does not depend on it doing something new. Nor does it depend on that form of transport becoming significantly more effective: innovation in transport may give rise directly to new economic activity, but, equally, its impact may not be felt (or not felt in full) until much later when new transport requirements develop for other reasons.

The latter was the case with carriers. The significance of the London carriers of 1650-1750 is that, while they continued to perform similar roles and to facilitate other economic forces, those roles became more and more important as the economy grew and the country progressed towards the first Industrial Revolution, in a process which has been summed up as 'enhanced regional specialisation and intensified commercial integration within an emergent national economy which was increasingly influenced by participation in a nascent world economy'.[30] In that century London's population grew rapidly – by at least 50 per cent; its port became the leading European port by about 1700 and the centre of a worldwide empire and a developing world economy; new products such as tea, tobacco and calicoes poured into London from overseas and were distributed throughout the country; manufactured imports were to a large extent replaced by domestic production, sometimes drawing raw materials through London, and often sending produce to London for consumption, domestic distribution or export; and new consumer goods appeared and existing ones became affordable as the 'consumer revolution' intensified.[31] By linking communities throughout the country to London and, through London, to the increasingly integrated world economy, the London carriers and their horses had a role in all these profound economic changes; therein lies their fundamental and increasing importance in the century after 1650.

APPENDICES

APPENDIX I

PLACES SERVED BY DELAUNE'S CARRIERS AND COACHMASTERS, 1681 AND 1690

The figure given after 'Carriers', 'Waggons' or 'Coaches' is the number of services per week. Figures after place-names indicate the number of firms there. 'Carrier' normally meant carrier by packhorse. Where a service is not stated as carrier, waggon or coach, it is placed where it is most likely to belong, on the basis of direct evidence, comparison with other entries in 1681 and 1690 or inference from destination, inn or frequency; where none of these help, it is listed as 'Unspecified'. Place-names have been modernised. Clear errors by Delaune have been corrected, and assumptions occasionally made, but known omissions have not been inserted here. The frequencies given are the summer ones in the few cases where Delaune recorded seasonal variation. Note that carriers often served a wide area around the town listed, sometimes straddling county boundaries, and a few services are listed under different towns at different dates.

Bedfordshire
1681   Carriers 9: Bedford, Cople, Dunstable, Harrold, Luton, Potton. Waggons 3: Bedford, Cranfield, Lidlington. Coaches 4: Bedford, Luton.
1690   Carriers 13: Ampthill, Bedford 3, Biggleswade, Cople, Cranfield, Harlington, Kempston, Leighton Buzzard, Toddington, Woburn 2. Waggons 6: Ampthill, Bedford, Biggleswade, Dunstable, Leighton Buzzard. Unspecified 1: Shefford. Coaches 6: Dunstable, Luton.

Berkshire
1681   Carriers 2: Pusey, Wallingford. Waggons 10: Abingdon 2, Berkshire (sic), Bradfield, Binfield, Hurst, Newbury, Reading, Swallowfield, Wallingford. Coaches 59: Abingdon, Maidenhead, Reading 2, Windsor 8.
1690   Waggons 11: Abingdon 2, Lambourn, Newbury, Reading/Newbury 2, Swallowfield, Wallingford, Wantage, Wokingham 2. Coaches 49: Abingdon, Maidenhead, Reading/Newbury 3, Windsor 3, Wokingham.

Buckinghamshire
1681   Carriers 7: Brill, Buckingham, 'Dreyton', Leckhampstead (?), Long Crendon, Marsh, Stoke Hammond. Waggons 16: Amersham 2, Aylesbury, Beaconsfield, Chesham 2, Haddenham, Newport Pagnell 2, Olney, Stony Stratford, Wycombe, Wing. Unspecified 1: Wycombe. Caravan 1: Wycombe. Coaches 9: Amersham, Aylesbury 2.
1690   Carriers 6: Brickhill, Buckingham, Long Crendon, Marsh Gibbon, Sherington, Stony Stratford. Waggons 15: Amersham, Aylesbury 3, Buckingham, Chesham,

177

Great Marlow, Haddenham, Newport Pagnell, Olney, Wendover, Wycombe 2. Unspecified 1: Wycombe. Caravan 1: High Wycombe. Coaches 7: Aylesbury 2, Newport Pagnell.

Cambridgeshire
1681   Carriers 7: Cambridge 4, Wisbech. Waggons 6: Cambridge 4, Ely. Coaches 6: Cambridge 2.

1690   Carriers 12: Cambridge 6, Caxton, Wisbech. Waggons 6: Cambridge 3, Linton. Unspecified 1: Ely. Coaches 3: Cambridge.

Cheshire
1681:   Carriers $1^2/_3$: Chester/Nantwich, Chester/Denbigh etc. Waggons 1: Chester/Wrexham/Oswestry.

1690   Carriers 4: Macclesfield, Knutsford/Middlewich/Northwich, Chester 2. Waggons $^1/_3$: Chester. Coaches 3: Chester 2.

Derbyshire
1681   Carriers $2^1/_3$: Ashbourne, Bakewell, Chesterfield. Waggons 1: Ashbourne.

1690   Carriers $1^1/_3$: Bakewell, Chesterfield. Waggons 1: Derby.

Devon
1681   Carriers $1^1/_2$: Barnstaple, Exeter. Waggons 2: Exeter 2. Coaches 3: Exeter.

1690   Carriers $2^1/_2$: Barnstaple/Bideford, Exeter 2. Waggons 2: Exeter 2. Coaches 3: Exeter.

Dorset
1681   Waggons 1: Poole. Unspecified 2: Dorset/Salisbury/Blandford. Coaches 2: Dorchester.

1690   Carriers 1: Shaftesbury. Waggons 1: Poole. Unspecified 2: Dorset/Salisbury/Blandford. Coaches 2: Dorchester.

Essex
1681   Carriers 13: Brentwood, Coggeshall, Dunmow/High Roding, High Roding, Ongar, Saffron Walden, Stambourne, Stanstead Mountfitchet, Witham. Waggons 22: Great Bardfield, Billericay, Braintree, Chelmsford 3, Colchester, Dunmow/High Roding, Hornchurch, Ingatestone, Maldon, Newport, Ongar, Saffron Walden, Woodford. Unspecified 2: Harwich. Coaches 92: Billericay, Braintree/Chelmsford 2, Brentwood, Colchester, East Ham 2, Epping 2, Harwich, Hornchurch, Low Layton, Maldon, Ongar, Romford, Saffron Walden 2, Waltham Abbey, Walthamstow, Wanstead, Woodford.

1690   Carriers 8: Brentwood, Coggeshall, Saffron Walden, 'Sanford', Stambourne, Thaxted, Witham. Waggons 11: Billericay, Braintree, Chelmsford, Colchester 2, Dunmow/High Roding, Hornchurch, Ingatestone, Maldon. Waggon-coach 2: Ongar. Coaches 73: Barking/Wall End, Billericay, Braintree, Brentwood, Chelmsford, Colchester, Epping, Harwich, Hornchurch, Ilford, Low Layton, Maldon, Ongar, Romford, Saffron Walden, Waltham Abbey, Walthamstow, Woodford.

Gloucestershire
1681   Carriers $6^1/_2$: Bristol, Cheltenham, Stroud 4. Waggons $4^1/_2$: Bristol, Cirencester, Dursley, Gloucester 2. Unspecified 3: Gloucester, Wotton-under-Edge/Dursley/Nibley 2. Coaches 13: Bath/Bristol $c.4$, Gloucester 2.

1690   Carriers 6: Bath/Bristol, Bristol, Cheltenham, Stroud 2. Waggons 6½: Bristol 2, Chipping Campden, Cirencester, Gloucester, Northleach, Stow-on-the-Wold. Unspecified 1: Gloucester. Coaches 12: Bath/Bristol *c.*4, Gloucester.

Hampshire

1681   Carrier 1: Portsmouth. Waggons 12: 'Agham', Andover, Basingstoke, Petersfield, Portsmouth 2, Southampton, Wickham, Winchester. Unspecified 3: Gloucester, Coaches 5: Portsmouth 2, Southampton.

1690   Waggons 12: Andover, Basingstoke 3, Fordingbridge/Christchurch, Kingsclere, Portsmouth, Southampton, Winchester. Coaches 10: Basingstoke, Portsmouth 2, Southampton.

Herefordshire

1681   Carriers 2½: Hereford, Ledbury, Leominster.

1690   Carriers 2: Hereford, Leominster.

Hertfordshire

1681   Carriers 5: Hertford, Hitchin, Rickmansworth. Waggons 39: Baldock 2, Bishop's Stortford, Bushey 3, Elstree, Hemel Hempstead, Hertford 2, Hoddesdon, Kimpton, St Albans 5, Sawbridgeworth, Tring, Watford. Unspecified 1: Royston. Waggon-coach 1: Much Hadham. Coaches 37: Barnet, Berkhamsted, Buntingford, Codicote, Hatfield, Hertford 2, Hoddesdon, St Albans 2, Ware, Watford.

1690   Carriers 9: Buntingford, Eastwick, Hertford, Hitchin, Puckeridge, Sandon. Waggons 33: Aldenham, Baldock 2, Bishop's Stortford 2, 'Harding', Hatfield, Hemel Hempstead, Hitchin 2, Hoddesdon, Kings Langley, Park Street, St Albans, Watford 2, Wheathampstead. Unspecified 3: Hemel Hempstead, Royston. Coach-waggons 3: Much Hadham, Hertford. Coaches 61: Barnet 2, Berkhamsted, Bishop's Stortford, Buntingford, Cheshunt 2, Codicote, Hatfield, Hertford 2, Hitchin, Hoddesdon 2, Northaw, St Albans, Ware.

Huntingdonshire

1681   Carriers 5: Abbotsley, Huntingdon, Kimbolton 2, St Ives. Waggon 1: Huntingdon. Coach 1: Huntingdon.

1690   Carriers 4: Huntingdon 2, St Ives, St Neots. Waggons 2: Fenstanton, St Neots.

Kent

1681   Carriers 10: Ashford, Chiddingstone, Cranbrook, Dover, Edenbridge, Queenborough, Tenterden, Tonbridge 2. Waggons 10: Bromley 2, Dover, Sevenoaks. Unspecified 2: Canterbury. Coaches 11: Canterbury, Maidstone, Sydenham.

1690   Carriers 10: Ashford, Canterbury, Chiddingstone, Cranbrook, Edenbridge, Maidstone, Tonbridge, Westerham. Waggons 6: Dover, Sevenoaks, Tonbridge. Unspecified 4: Canterbury, Plaxtol. Coaches 17: Canterbury, Canterbury/Dover, Maidstone, Tonbridge.

Lancashire

1681   Carriers 9⅓: Blackburn etc., Lancaster/Liverpool etc. 2, Manchester 3, Manchester/Stockport, Manchester etc. 2, Oldham/Ashton-under-Lyne, Rochdale etc., Warrington.

1690   Carriers 7⅓: Blackburn etc. 2, Lancaster/Liverpool etc., Manchester 2, Manchester etc., Preston, Warrington.

Leicestershire (including Rutland)

1681   Carriers 3½: Ashby-de-la-Zouch, Bagworth, Kibworth, Loughborough, Wymondham. Waggons 4: Leicester, Lutterworth, Melton Mowbray, Uppingham/Oakham.

1690   Carriers 1: Ashby-de-la-Zouch. Waggons 4½: Great Bowden, Leicester, Loughborough, Lutterworth, Melton Mowbray. Coach 1: Melton Mowbray.

Lincolnshire

1681   Carriers 3: Gainsborough, Lincoln etc., Louth. Waggon 2: Peterborough/Spalding/Horncastle. Coach-waggons 1½: Folkingham, Grantham/Newark. Coach 1: Lincoln etc.

1690   Carriers 2: Gainsborough/Hull, Louth. Waggon 1: Stamford/Grantham. Unspecified 1⅓: Lincoln/Stamford/Grantham, Louth. Coach-waggon 1: Grantham/Newark.

Middlesex

1681   Carrier 1: Staines. Coaches 63: Edmonton 2, Enfield, Fulham, Hampstead 3, Harrow 2, Stanmore, Uxbridge.

1690   Waggon 3: Harrow. Coaches 84: Acton, Brentford, Edmonton 2, Enfield 2, Finchley, Hampstead 3, Harrow, Hendon, Southgate, Uxbridge, Whetstone.

Norfolk

1681   Waggons 5: Norwich 5. Coaches 9: King's Lynn, Norwich 2, Yarmouth/Norwich.

1690   Carrier 1: Norwich. Waggons 3: Burnham, Norwich 2. Coaches 7: King's Lynn, Norwich 2, Yarmouth/Norwich.

Northamptonshire

1681   Carriers 11: Brackley, Castle Ashby, Daventry, Grendon, Northampton, Oundle, Stoke Bruerne, Thrapston/Brigstock, Towcester, Watford, Weston/Weedon/Towcester. Waggons 6: Chipping Warden, Daventry, Kettering, Northampton 2, Weedon, Wellingborough. Coach-waggons 2: Northampton, Towcester.

1690   Carriers 6: 'Bradford', Cottingham/Middleton, Daventry, Kettering, Peterborough, Stoke Bruerne. Waggons 16½: Brackley, Castle Ashby, Daventry 2, 'Fulworth', Grendon, Harringworth, Kettering 2, Northampton 2, Oundle, Towcester 2, Weedon, Wellingborough. Coach 1: Daventry.

Nottinghamshire

1681   Carrier 1: Mansfield. Coach-waggon 1: Nottingham.

1690   Carrier 1: Mansfield. Waggons 2: Nottingham 2. Coaches 2: Nottingham 2.

Oxfordshire

1681   Carriers 5: Barton, Chipping Norton, 'Leachsteed', Mollington, Oxford. Waggons 11: Banbury, Bicester, Burford, Charlbury, Cokethorpe, Hook Norton, Oxford 2, Thame, Witney 2. Unspecified 1: Chinnor. Coaches 7: Henley-on-Thames, Oxford 2.

1690   Carriers 6: Banbury, Burford, Chipping Norton, Milton etc., South Stoke, Thame. Waggons 13: Banbury, Bicester, Burford, Charlbury, Faringdon/Bampton, Hook Norton, Oxford 2, Thame, Witney, Woodstock. Coaches 13: Oxford 5.

Shropshire

1681   Carriers 6½: Bridgnorth/Wenlock, Bridgnorth, Ludlow, Newport/Whitchurch etc., Shrewsbury etc. 2, Whitchurch. Waggon ⅓: Wem. Coach 0: (Bridgnorth).

1690   Carriers 3: Ludlow, Shrewsbury 2. Waggon ⅓: Newport. Coaches 1: (Bridgnorth), Shrewsbury.

Somerset

1681   Carriers 3: Bath, Crewkerne/Yeovil, Wells etc. Waggons 2: Taunton 2. Coach 1: Taunton.

1690   Carriers 3: Crewkerne/Yeovil/Sherborne, Taunton, Wells. Waggons 2: Frome/Warminster, Taunton.

Staffordshire

1681   Carriers 3⅓: Burton upon Trent/Uttoxeter, Lichfield, Newcastle-under-Lyme etc., Tamworth, Wolverhampton. Waggons 2: Tamworth, Wolverhampton.

1690   Carriers 3: Birmingham/Wolverhampton, Newcastle-under-Lyme, Tamworth, Wolverhampton. Waggons 1½: Stafford, Wolverhampton. Coaches 2: Lichfield, Tamworth.

Suffolk

1681   Carriers 5: Clare, Haverhill 3, Lavenham. Waggons 6: Bury St Edmunds, Helmingham, Ipswich, Newmarket, Stowmarket, Sudbury. Coaches 12: Beccles, Bury St Edmunds 3, Ipswich, Newmarket, Sudbury.

1690   Carriers 2: Clare, Lavenham. Waggons 3: Bury St Edmunds, Ipswich, Sudbury. Coaches 7: Beccles, Bury St Edmunds 2, Ipswich, Sudbury.

Surrey

1681   Carriers 4: Bletchingley, Godalming, Lingfield, Shere. Waggons 8: Dorking, Guildford, Reigate. Coaches 56: Clapham, Croydon 2, Dulwich, Egham, Epsom 3, Godalming, Guildford 3.

1690   Carriers 2: Godalming 2. Waggons 3: Guildford, Leatherhead. Coaches 42: Clapham 2, Croydon, Egham, Epsom 2, Guildford 3, Leatherhead.

Sussex

1681   Carriers 12: Battle, Billingshurst/Pulborough, Brighton, Burwash, Chichester 2, East Grinstead, Lewes, Mayfield, Petworth, Shoreham, Wadhurst. Waggons 3: Horsham, Lewes, Petworth. Unspecified 1: Arundel. Coach 2: East Grinstead.

1690   Carriers 21: Battle, Brighton, Burwash, Chichester 2, East Grinstead, Fletching, Horsham, Herstmonceux, Lewes 2, Mayfield, Midhurst, Petworth 2, Rye, Shoreham, Steyning, Waldron. Waggon 1: Lewes. Unspecified 1: Arundel.

Warwickshire

1681   Carriers 4: Dunchurch, Stratford-upon-Avon (?), Warwick 2. Waggons 5: Coventry 2, Kineton, Lawford/Rugby/Dunchurch, 'Texel'. Coach-waggons 3: Coventry, Stratford-upon-Avon, Warwick.

1690   Carriers 2½: Atherstone, Dunchurch, Rugby. Waggons 9: Coventry 3, Kineton, Rugby, Southam, Stratford-upon-Avon, Warwick 2. Caravan 1: Rugby.

Westmorland

1681   Carrier 1: Kendal.

1690   Carrier 1: Kendal.

Wiltshire

1681   Carriers 1⅓: Malmesbury, Marlborough. Waggons 4: Highworth, Marlborough, Salisbury. Coaches 4: Marlborough, Salisbury.

1690   Carrier 1: Marlborough. Waggons 9: Chippenham, Devizes, Highworth 2, Marlborough 2, Salisbury, Trowbridge. Coaches 4: Marlborough, Salisbury.

Worcestershire

1681   Carriers 3: Bewdley, Kidderminster/Stourbridge, Stourbridge/Bromsgrove. Waggons 3: Evesham, Worcester 2. Unspecified 1: Worcester. Coaches 4: Worcester 2.

1690   Carriers 2: Bewdley, Worcester. Waggons 4: Evesham, Kidderminster, Shipston on Stour, Worcester. Coaches 2½: Worcester 2.

Yorkshire

1681   Carriers 6⅓: Halifax 3, Leeds, Richmond, Sheffield, Sheffield/Rotherham/Mansfield. Coach 3: York.

1690   Carriers 7⅔: Halifax 2, Keighley, Leeds/Wakefield 2, Richmond, York 2. Coach 3: York.

Wales

1681   Carriers 1⅓: Denbigh/Wrexham/Ruthin, Monmouth.

1690   Carrier 1: Monmouth. Waggon ½: Bettisfield.

Note on Delaune's reliability: As this book indicates, there is a wealth of material confirming the information given by Delaune. However, Delaune himself acknowledged that the 1681 list was not perfect, and some errors and omissions can be identified. Comparison of Delaune's 1690 list and the list of 29 carrying services using seven London inns in 1692 (Fig. 2) provides an extremely good match, but the 1690 list omits the four services from the *Kings Arms*, Leadenhall Street, combines two separate Shrewsbury partnerships, and has what appears to be a transcription error making the Trowbridge service fortnightly instead of weekly. Two innkeepers were denounced in 1690 for lack of co-operation, and there appear to have been problems at several other inns: between 1681 and 1690, carrying services recorded at the *Saracens Head*, Snow Hill, rose from 0 to 14½ and at the *One Swan*, Bishopsgate, from 0 to 10, while those from the *Bear and Ragged Staff* fell from 11 to one. The *One Swan* chiefly served Hertfordshire, where the number of services listed rose from 30 to 41. Essex services fell from 35 to 19.

A few clear omissions can be demonstrated, such as Gilbert Stoughton of Kettering in 1681 (C 5/548/60; C 5/371/39), Mr Warren of Stamford in 1681 (CJ, vol. 11, 1693-97, p. 512) and Richard Hales of Frome in 1681 (C 7/579/80; C 10/414/16). Comparison of the total numbers of services for each county in 1681 and 1690 and taking the higher figure in each case suggests that about fifty services a week at each date, or about 13 per cent of all services, were omitted. Carrying services within 20 miles of London were probably also significantly under-recorded at both dates.

Demonstrable omissions of coaches include Chester, Lichfield and Shrewsbury in 1681 (Appendix 8), Henley, Banbury and Lincoln in 1690 (above, p. 135; *London Gazette*, 24 Apr, 5 May 1690, 26 Sept 1692), and Northampton and Kettering in both 1681 and 1690 (Appendix 8; C 5/371/39). Post-1690 evidence suggests that some services listed in 1681 also existed in 1690, and some services recorded both before 1681 and in 1690 appear to have been omitted in 1681. The figures in the tables and maps in this book assume that the following coach services (per week) were wrongly omitted: in 1681, Banbury 3, Chester 2, Kettering 1, Lichfield 1, Northampton 3, Shrewsbury 1, Tamworth 1, Tonbridge 2, Winchester 3, total 17; in 1690, Banbury 3, Dulwich 6, Henley 3, Huntingdon 1, Kettering 1, Lincoln 1, Northampton 3, Sydenham 6, Taunton 1, Watford 3, Winchester 3, total 31. Probably others were omitted too, and total omissions of about 10 per cent of all services are assumed in chapter 7. The Bridgnorth coach listed is assumed to have been an extension of one of the Worcester coaches and is omitted from the figures.

APPENDIX II

INVENTORIES OF LONDON CARRIERS, 1663-1749

Section (a) contains carriers listed by Delaune whose inventories indicate carriage by packhorses, but also several whose type of carriage is uncertain (i.e. Nos 2, 5, 6, 9), one who operated both packhorses and waggons (No. 29), and three who may also have been operating stage-coaches or coach-waggons (Nos 9, 17, 26). (Note that packhorse carriers might have waggons and gears for farming.) Section (b) contains carriers listed by Delaune whose inventories indicate carriage by waggons. Two also operated stage-coaches or coach-waggons (Nos 31, 32). Section (c) contains carriers running firms listed under other ownership by Delaune (though inventories from the 1680s are instead in sections (a) or (b). Section (d) is London carriers 1728-49.

Year Carrier	Service	Stock
(a) Carriers by packhorse		
1. 1680 Edward Miles	Ludlow 146 W(2p)	12 packhorses, 1 hackney horse (£33)
2. 1680 William Claroe	Worcester 115 W(2p)	23 horses, gears & packsaddles (£116)*
3. 1682 Richard Greenwood	Kendal 263 W(4p)	1 gate of packhorses (£30)*
4. 1682 Richard Hatton	Chester 182 3rd W	20 packhorses (£150)*
5. 1683 George Gulstone	Wymondham (Leics) 103 W	6 horses, 2 waggons (£39)
6. 1684 Thomas Edwards	Grendon 64 W	15 horses (£60) (+ 2 waggons)*
7. 1685 Thomas Bass	Abbotsley 54 W	4 horses, packsaddles (£12)
8. 1686 George Holder	Stroudwater 105 Fort	5 horses, packsaddles (£8)
9. 1686 Griffin Faulkner	Oundle 78 W	19 horses, 2 waggons, 2 coaches, packsaddles (£180)
10. 1686 John Yeats	Kendal 263 W(4p)	13 horses (£81)*
11. 1687 Elizabeth Yeats	Kendal 263 W(4p)	12 horses (£61)*
12. 1687 Thomas Rawlinson	Lewes 49 W(3p)	8 horses, packsaddles (£61)
13. 1689 Nicholas Jarratt	Burwash 48 W	6 horses, saddles etc. (£47)
14. 1690 Matthew Bakewell	Burton 125,Uttoxeter 140 W(2p)	7 horses, 1 coach (£32)
15. 1693 Margaret Mussell	Horsham 36 W	4 horses, packsaddles & harness (£16)*
16. 1694 Robert Long	Monmouth 133 W(2p)	9 horses, packsaddles (£40)
17. 1694 Thomas Baddeley	Newcastle-u-l 151 W(2p)	19 horses, 1 coach (£66)*
18. 1695 Benjamin Bromhead	Lincoln 130 W(3p)	7 horses, saddles (£30)
19. 1695 Abraham Pillin	York 196 3rd W(2p)	16 packhorses (£105)
20. 1696 John Harrison	Chiddingstone 30 W	4 horses (£6)*
21. 1697 George Elliotts	Chesterfield 152 W(2p)	16 horses (£82)
22. 1698 John Hilton	Warrington 186 W(4p)	2 gangs of horses, pack cloths (£150)*
23. c.1700 4 Kendal carriers	Kendal 263 W(4p)	60 horses
24. 1703 Francis Furnes	Louth 145 W	7 horses (£32)
25. 1705 George Glover	Lancaster etc. 240 W(4p)	17 horses, packsaddles (£85)*

26. 1707 John Baddeley	Newcastle-u-l 151 W(2p)	14 horses, 1 coach (£70)
27. 1713 John Frost	Halifax 197 W(3p)	25 horses (£150)*
28. 1713 Edward Lee	Macclesfield 169 W(3p)	Gang of carrying horses
29. 1714 Samuel Whibben	Bristol 122 twice W(3p)	Tuesday's drift of 11 horses, Friday's drift of 12 horses, 14 waggon horses, 3 waggons (1 old) (£250)*
30. 1718 Joseph Naylor	Leeds 192 W(3p)	101 horses (£242)

(b) Carriers by waggon

31. 1681 Andrew Hart	Norwich 110 twice W (+ coach)	34 horses, 5 waggons, 3 coaches (£288)*
32. 1681 Henry Warren	Stamford 87 etc.	21 waggon horses, 13 other horses, 2 coach-waggons, 2 long waggons (£382)*
33. 1682 Michael Whiteing	Cokethorpe 69 W	3 horses, 1 waggon (£10)
34. 1684 George Weedon	Hemel Hempstead 26 W	10 horses, harness (£49)
35. 1684 John Swift	Leicester 98 W(4p)	7 horses, 2 waggons (£35+)*
36. 1685 Silvester Keene	Bristol 122 W(4p)	10 working horses & 1 waggon; 3 running horses (£36) (+ 1 old waggon)*
37. 1685 Richard Mills	Burford 76 W	10 horses, 2 waggons (£51)
38. 1686 Francis Bacherler	Gloucester 105 W(3p)	7 horses, 1 waggon (£36)
39. 1687 Humphrey Swanwick	Whitchurch 162 W	13 horses, 2 waggons (£46)*
40. 1689 Lawrence Standish	Warwick 95 W	21 horses in 3 teams, 5 waggons (2 old) (£71)*
41. 1689 Henry Harwood	Aylesbury 42 W	6 horses, 1 waggon (£18)
42. 1690 James Swan	Saffron Walden 44 W	6 horses, 1 waggon (£110)
43. 1690 John Jordan	Banbury 76 W	12 horses, 1 waggon (£40)
44. 1690 John Roberts	Evesham 97 W(2p)	13 horses, 2 waggons (£62)
45. 1690 Matthew Glover	Hitchin 35 twice W	7 horses, 2 waggons (£32)
46. 1692 Robert Barnes	Lincoln 130 W(3p)	10 horses, 1 waggon (£100)
47. 1692 Jacob Hewett	Wokingham 36 W	6 horses, 2 waggons (£34)*
48. 1693 John Mason	Bushey 17 twice W	6 horses, 2 nags, 3 waggons (£33)
49. 1693 Thomas Bass	Leicester 98 W(2p)	10 horses, 2 waggons, 1 coach (£75)*
50. 1693 Daniel Want	Devizes 91 W	10 horses, 3 waggons (£80)
51. 1695 Robert Ridgwell	Cambridge 52 thrice W	20 horses, 4 nags, 4 waggons (£178)
52. 1696 Elias Buckmaster	Kings Langley 23 twice W	5 horses, 1 waggon
53. 1703 George Elmes	Melton Mowbray 105 W(2p)	8 horses, 1 waggon (£15)
54. 1705 Lawrence Standish	Warwick 95 W(2p)	2 teams, 2 waggons (£100)*
55. 1710 Richard Hales	Frome 108 W	30 waggon horses, 4 hackneys, 4 packhorses, 1 other horse, 6 waggons (1 old) (£243/£600)
56. 1715 John Wood sen	Gloucester 105 W(2p)	2 waggons and horses belonging to them
57. 1715 Humphrey Cooper	St Albans 22 thrice W	8 horses, 1 waggon (£23)*
58. 1723 John Whitmash	Taunton 148 W	28-30 horses, 2 hackneys, 3 waggons
59. 1726 John Dell	Hemel Hempstead 26 twice W	7 horses, 1 waggon (£25)

(c) Delaune's carrying firms recorded under other ownership

60. 1663 Henry Girle sen	Newbury 59 W	15 horses, 1 riding mare, 3 waggons (£108)*
61. 1663 Robert Beecroft	Norwich 110 W	28 horses, 5 waggons (£223)*
62. 1665 Richard Fairebrothers sen	Chipping Warden 82 W	4 horses with packsaddles, 5 horses with gears, 2 waggons (£50)*
63. 1666 Stephen Cooke	Norwich 110 W	12 horses, 3 waggons (£63+)*
64. 1666 Robert Bird	Andover 67 W	9 horses, 1 waggon (£69)*
65. 1667 Leonard Mills	Burford 76 W	5 waggon horses, 2 waggons, 8 cart horses and packhorses (£55)*
66. 1699 Francis Carter	Cambridge 52 thrice W	15 horses, 3 waggons (£23)
67. 1705 Thomas Fieldhouse	Shrewsbury 156 W(5p)	15 horses, saddles & gears (£38)*
68. 1707 Richard Hales jun	Trowbridge 101	45 horses, 6 waggons (£500)

69. 1714 –	Evesham 99 W(2p)	7 horses, 1 waggon
70. 1717 John Goldring	Portsmouth 73	22 horses, 1 nag, 4 waggons (2 old) (£125/£250)
71. 1718 George Whitehead	Melton Mowbray 105 W(2p)	18 horses, 3 waggons (£87)*
72. 1722 William Weedon	?Hemel Hempstead 26	14 horses, 2 nags, 3 waggons (1 old) (£57)*

(d) London carriers 1728-49

73. 1728 Thomas Varley	York 196, Leeds 192	18 packhorses
74. 1742 James Blackbourne	Peterborough 79	20 horses, 2 waggons, 1 stage-cart, 1 coach (£124)*
75. 1743 John Hacker sen	Leicester 98	14 horses, 2 waggons
76. 1747 –	Reading 41	6 horses [+ waggon(s)]
77. 1747 William Iliff	Exeter 182	128 horses in 15 teams, 14 waggons
78. 1747 Thomas Knowles jun	Lancaster 240 monthly	22 packhorses
79. 1749 –	Liverpool 207, Manchester 187	14 horses, 2 waggons
80. 1749 John Clowes	Manchester 187	20 packhorses

Notes

All the entries in the table are from probate inventories (sometimes recited in Chancery suits), with the exception of Nos. 28, 52, 56 and 58, which are descriptions from wills, Nos. 42, 50, 51, 55, 68, 70 and 77, which are lists of stock recorded in Chancery suits, No. 23, which is from a list of carriers at Kendal, and Nos. 69, 73, 75-6 and 78-80, which are from newspaper advertisements. Frequency is taken from Delaune 1681 or 1690 and relates to the service as a whole ('2p' or '3p' indicates the number of partners recorded by Delaune); 'W' is weekly; 'Fort' is fortnightly. Carts in inventories are ignored. Carrying and farming stock cannot always be distinguished or separated, so the values (rounded to the nearest pound) are approximate; the value is underlined if it was payment for the business (including goodwill) rather than a valuation of stock. An asterisk indicates ploughs or substantial farming stock.

1. Mr Miles is listed in 1681 (probably Edward Miles's son, also Edward). **2.** Also four waggons. Mary Clare is listed in 1681. **4.** Also four other horses and two colts. Described as two gangs of packhorses by Delaune in 1681. **6.** Edwards's son Edward was a waggon-user by 1689 (PROB 11/375, q. 15; London Metropolitan Archives, MJ/SP 1689 Aug 8), and Delaune records him as such in 1690. **9.** Faulkner's coach may have been the Oundle stage-coach. **10.** Also four other horses and a mare. **11.** Also 'foure worke horses'. **17.** The coach was probably the Newcastle coach-waggon, mentioned from 1677 to 1698 (Appendix 8, part C). **18.** One of Bromhead's partners was Robert Barnes, a waggon-user (No. 46 below). **26.** See note for No. 17. **28.** Also had three cart or drawing horses and a colt. **29.** Also 'five ordinary horses at grass'. **31.** The horses included Hart's coach horses. The £288 included £50 for 'iron & materialls in ye smiths shopp'. **32.** Delaune in 1681 ignores the Stamford waggon, but lists Warren's Newark coach-waggon. **34.** Described as a waggoner, but no waggon listed. **37.** Leonard Mills, his brother (PROB 11/325, q. 118), is listed in 1681. **40.** Two partners (his sons) are listed in 1690. **41.** Widow Harwood's waggon is listed in 1690. **46.** See note for No. 18. **51.** Also 'three over worn horses' and two lame horses. **58.** Also four plough horses. Wrongly listed as a packhorse service in 1690. **66.** Carter had purchased Ridgwell's business (C 8/651/1; No. 51 above). **67.** John Fieldhouse was a Shrewsbury carrier in 1690, and two of the three inventory compilers were London carriers at Shrewsbury in 1690. The 'gears' and 'a payre of wheeles' suggest use of waggons by 1705. **68.** Hales had married Elizabeth Turner, probably the widow of the John Turner listed in 1690 (C 5/355/1). **73.** Described as 'one of the ancient gangs that has gone with goods from York, Leeds and Wakefield to London'. **74.** Blackbourne also ran the Boston coach in summer.

References

1. Herefordshire RO, Episcopal Consistory Court. **2.** PROB 4/7440. **3.** Lancashire RO, WRW.K. **4.** Cheshire RO. **5.** PROB 4/19021. **6.** PROB 4/9995. **7.** Huntingdonshire RO. **8.** C 6/258/53. **9.** PROB 4/15212. **10.** Lancashire RO, WRW.K. **11.** Lancashire RO, WRW.K. **12.** PROB 4/12556; PROB 11/387, q. 67. **13.** PROB 4/19418. **14.** Lichfield Joint RO. **15.** West Sussex RO, Ep I/29/106/252. **16.** C 5/126/4. **17.** PROB 4/7099. **18.** Lincolnshire RO, INV 192/211. **19.** Borthwick Institute (Doncaster). **20.** Kent Archives Office, PRS/I/8/28. **21.** Lichfield Joint RO. **22.** Lancashire RO, WCW. **23.** Fig. 13. **24.** Lincolnshire RO, Louth wills, 1703 W50. **25.** Lancashire RO, WCW. **26.** PROB 4/22269. **27.** Borthwick Institute (Pontefract). **28.** Cheshire RO. **29.** PROB 3/18/131. **30.** Borthwick Institute (Pontefract). **31.** PROB 4/9544. **32.** PROB 4/12579. **33.** Oxfordshire RO, 88/3/23. **34.** Hertfordshire RO, H23/2548. **35.** Leicestershire RO, PR/I/86/102. **36.** PROB 4/335. **37.** C 6/258/47; PROB 11/383, q. 48. **38.** Gloucestershire RO, Inventories 1686 (281). **39.** PROB 4/15765. **40.** PROB 4/20267; PROB 11/396, q. 104. **41.** PROB 4/13094. **42.** C 8/434/92. **43.** Oxfordshire RO, MS Wills Oxon Peculiar 44/1/9. **44.** Worcestershire RO, Consistory Court 1690, No. 123. **45.** PROB 5/4898. (Also Hertfordshire RO, H22/499; and C 6/419/50.) **46.** Lincolnshire RO, LCC wills, 1692/i/31. **47.** Berkshire RO, D/A1/197/136B. **48.** Hertfordshire RO, A25/4344. **49.** Leicestershire RO, PR/I/98/22 and PR/I/99/20. **50.** C 8/556/74. **51.** C 8/651/1. **52.** Hertfordshire RO, 7HR186r. **53.** Leicestershire RO, PR/I/110/14. **54.** Worcestershire RO, Consistory Court 1705. **55.** C 24/1325, No. 16. **56.** PROB 11/549, q. 230. **57.** Hertfordshire RO, A25/4664. **58.** PROB 11/600, q.238. **59.** Hertfordshire RO, H22/1456. **60.** Berkshire RO, W.Inv. 73/17. **61.** PROB 4/1528. **62.** Northamptonshire RO, Invs 1660s-99, No. 53. **63.** PROB 4/12806. **64.** Hampshire RO, 1666ADO14. **65.** PROB 4/21526. **66.** PROB 4/5343. **67.** Barrie Trinder and Jeff Cox (eds.), *Yeomen and colliers in Telford* (1980), p. 32. **68.** C 7/656/27. **69.** *Worcester Post-Man*, 3 Sept 1714. **70.** C 11/1983/24; C11/2750/14. **71.** PROB 3/17/30. **72.** Hertfordshire RO, H23/2595. **73.** *Leeds Mercury*, 19 June 1728. **74.** PROB 3/41/127. **75.** *Stamford Mercury*, 28 Apr 1743. **76.** LEP, 21 Apr 1747. **77.** C 11/587/9, Iliff's third schedule. **78.** *Manchester Magazine*, 7 Apr 1747. **79.** *Ibid.*, 25 Apr 1749. **80.** *Cheshire Sheaf*, 3rd ser., vol. 10 (1913), p. 90.

CARRIERS' CHARGES, 1655-1751

(A) Actual or advertised charges

Date; journey & miles	Sh.	pptm	Ref
Trade goods – waggon			
May 1657: Norwich 110 (by coach-waggon)	6	13	1
W 1669: Birmingham 111 (stated by an MP as the winter charge)	3	6	2
1674-9: Kettering up 75 (woad; by agreement with a carrier anxious to obtain up loading)	2-2.5	6-8	3
1684-9: Oundle 78 (shopkeepers' goods; probably waggon)	4	12	4
Nov 1689: Mitcheldean (Glos) down 120 (brass wire; possibly to Gloucester only, hence 9-11 pptm.)	4-5	8-10	5
1689-90: Exeter up & down 182 (special agreement for 6s.; normal rate allegedly 8s. during St Nicholas Fair)	6-8	8-11	6
Sept 1690: Exeter down 182 (hats; 15d. for c.21 lb)	6.7	9	7
1693: Derby up 127 (malt; sometimes 3s. 4d. – 6 pptm – if back carriage available)	5.3	10	8
1697: Norwich up 110	6	13	9
1697: Norwich down 110 (but 5s. for silk – 11 pptm)	4	9	9
Feb 1704: Exeter 182 (10s. up; 8s. down; statement by 6 carriers that they wouldnot carry for less)	8-10	11-13	10
1706: Colchester down 52 (wool; 4s. 6d. per pack; probably waggon)	2.1	10	11
1708-9: Norwich 110 (said to be both up & down)	6	13	12
1712: Frome down 108 (wool; reduction from 10s. to 9s. per pack due to competition)	4.7, 4.2	10, 9	13
1720: general 100	4-5	10-12	14
Apr 1725: Exeter down 182	9.3	12	15
Pre-1729: Birmingham 120 (30s. per ton)	3	6	16
Feb 1743: Stamford 93 (probably flying waggon)	4	10	17
Feb 1743: Barton upon Humber 165 (probably flying waggon)	8	12	17
Apr 1743: Spalding 98 (Peterborough 4s. – 12 pptm)	5	12	17
1744: Newcastle upon Tyne 278 (2d. per lb)	18.7	16	18
July 1745: Derby down 127 (5s. summer, 6s. winter)	5-6	9-11	19
1749: Norwich 110	5.2	11	20
Trade goods – packhorse			
1692: Exeter 182 (1½d. per lb all year, but 8s. per cwt for serges)	8, 14	11, 18	21
1692: Leeds 192 & Wakefield 183 down (shopkeepers' goods; 18d. per stone)	12	15-16	21
1692: York down 196 (shopkeepers' goods; 21d. per stone)	14	17	21
c.1700: Kendal up 263 (21s. to 26s. per pack of 256 lb)	9.2-11.4	8-10	22
c.1700: Kendal down 263 (26s. to 28s. per pack of 256 lb)	11.4 -12.3	10-11	22
1706: Wakefield 183 & Leeds 192 down (wool; 15s. or under per pack)	7	9	11

	Sh.	pptm	Ref
Dec 1706: Halifax up 197 (20s. per pack, but request for 22s., i.e. 12.5 pptm)	9.3	11	23
Oct 1711, Aug 1713: Kendal up 263 (cloth; 22s. per pack of 256 lb)	9.6	9	24
Dec 1718, June 1719: Kendal up 263 (cloth; 23s. per pack of 256 lb summer, 25s. winter)	10.1 -10.9	9-10	24
1720: general 100	5-6	12-14	14
1738: Bolton 198 (23s. per pack, but 21s. by 'the month men'; probably packhorse)	9.8-10.7	12-13	25

Trade goods – unspecified

	Sh.	pptm	Ref
W 1655: Bristol 122	4	8	20
Jan 1662: St Ives up 61 (cloves; 1d. per lb)	9.3	37	26
1706: Exeter down 182 (wool; not more than 13s. per pack)	6.1	8	11
1717: Coventry 93 (c.2s. 6d. per cwt summer, c.3s. 6d. winter)	2.5-3.5	6-9	27

Gents' goods – waggon

	Sh.	pptm	Ref
Sept 1674: Cambridge up 52 (milliner's goods; probably gents' price)	4	18	28
1697-1701: Peterborough 79 (6s. per cwt summer, 7s. winter)	6-7	18-21	29
1716: general (3s. 6d. to 4s., 5s. and 8s. for 50, 70 and 150 miles respectively; muddled;probably gents' price)		13-19	30
May 1720: Northampton 67 (½d. per lb by flying waggon; probably gents' price)	4.7	17	31
1744: Newcastle upon Tyne 278 (3d. per lb)	28	24	18

Gents' goods – packhorse

	Sh.	pptm	Ref
May 1657: Newhaven 60 (probably gents' price by packhorse)	5	20	1
May 1657: Rye 63 (probably gents' price by packhorse; also Tenterden 5s. per cwt – 21 pptm)	6	23	1
1661-87: Kendal 263 (generally 2d. per lb)	18.7	17	32
1662, Dec 1663: Monmouth up 134 (large pies; 10s. for 80 lb; 8s. for 65 lb)	13.8-14	25	33
1670s: Kendal 263 (2d. per lb summer, 3d. winter; probably gents' price)	18.7-28	17-26	34
1689-90: Harold (Beds) 60	5	20	35
1692: York down 196	16	20	21
1697-1701: Peterborough 79 (possibly not gents' price)	5	15	29
May 1713: Kendal 263 (picture; 2s. 10d. for 17 lb)	18.7	17	24
1716: general 70 (probably gents' price)	5	17	30

Gents' goods – unspecified

	Sh.	pptm	Ref
July 1678: Ampthill 46	3.5	18	36
1727: Bath up 109 (probably gents' price)	9.3	21	37
Ditto down	7	15	37
Jan 1729: Deene (Northants) 87	6	17	38
1729: Ledbury 124 (agreement for carriage, including a local carrier Tewkesbury-Ledbury)	7	14	39

Uncertain

	Sh.	pptm	Ref
Mar 1705: York up 196 (21s. for 12 stone; packhorse)	14	17	40
Apr 1740, Mar 1750: Stowmarket up & down 74 (price reduction in 1740; waggon)	4	13	41
1743: York up 196 (39s. for 26 stone)	12	15	40

(B) JPs' rates etc. (in alphabetical order of county or town)

Date	Journey, miles and mode	Sh.	pptm	Ref
1707/50	Bristol 122 **wg** (heavier goods 3s. summer, 4s. winter; lighter goods 5s. summer, 6s. winter)	3-6	6-12	42-3

Date	Description			
"	Do **pk** (5s. summer, 6s. winter; lighter goods 1d. per lb – 18 pptm)	5-6	10-12	42-3
1692-1710	Buckinghamshire (winter 12d.; summer 7d. per 10 miles within Chilterns and towards London, 10d. elsewhere)		14-24	44
1693	Cheshire 182 **wg** ((summer 5s. up, 4s. down; winter 7s. up, 6s. down)	4-7	5-9	44
"	Do **pk** (1d. per lb)	9.3	12	44
1694-9	Do (5s. summer, 7s. winter)	5-7	7-9	44
1717/21	Derbyshire 127-52 (rates to 4 places; 10-11 pptm summer, 12-14 pptm winter)	6-7.8	10-14	45
1750	Do (ditto; 10-11 pptm; 13-14 pptm)	6-8	10-14	43
1694-1730	Devon 169 **wg** (6s. summer, 7s. winter; from 1702 summer rate only)	6-7	9-10	46
"	Do **pk** (8s. summer, 9s. winter; from 1702 winter rate only)	8-9	11-13	46
1727-51	Dorset 129 (years often unclear, but 6s. in 1727-8 and 1750-1; in 1750-1, rates to 7 places, all 11-12 pptm)	6-7.5	11-14	47, 43
1716/20/49-51	Essex (3d. per 5 miles)		12	48, 43
1732	Exeter 182 **wg**	8	11	49
"	Do **pk**	10	13	49
1693	Hampshire [**wg**] (1s. 2d. per 20 miles)		14	50
1695-7	Do [**wg**] (1s. per 20 miles)		12	50
1699	Do [**wg**] (1s. 1d. per 20 miles)		13	50
1716/49-51	Herefordshire 138 [**pk**] (¾d. per lb summer, 1d. winter)	7-9.3	12-16	51, 43
1692-1708	Hertfordshire (6d. per 10 miles)		12	44
1749-51	Hull 235 (1s. 9d. per stone)	14	14	43
1692	Kendal 263 [**pk**] (25s. per pack of 256 lb)	10.9	10	24
1750-1	Leicestershire 84-116 (rates to 9 places; 11-12 pptm summer, 12-13 pptm winter)	4-6.5	11-13	43
1696	Lincolnshire/Holland 87-114 (rates to 8 places; generally 15 pptm)	5.5-7	13-16	52
1749-51	Do 98, 114 (Spalding 8s. (20 pptm); Boston 8s. summer, 10s. winter)	8-10	17-21	43
1751	Lincolnshire/Lindsey 136, 145 (Louth 15d. per stone, Horncastle 14d. per stone)	9.3-10	16-17	43
1744	Newcastle upon Tyne 278 [**wg**] (2d. per lb)	18.7	16	18
1710	Northamptonshire 67	4	14	37
1743/9-51	Do	3.5	13	37
1696	Norwich 110 [**wg**]	4	9	53
1674-1703	Oxford 58 [**wg**] (3s. 6d. summer, 4s. winter. Vice-Chancellor's rates)	3.5-4	14-17	22, 54
1749-51	Portsmouth [**wg**] (1s. 4d. per 20 miles summer, 1s. 8d. winter)		16-20	43
1750-1	Shrewsbury 156	6.5	10	43
1692-3	Shropshire 156 **wg** ('carts': 3s. summer, 5s. winter)	3-5	5-8	55
"	Do **pk**	5	8	55
1694-1721	Do **wg** (5s. summer, 6s. winter)	5-6	8-9	44, 55
"	Do **pk** (6s. summer, 7s. winter)	6-7	9-11	44, 55
1722-51	Do	7	11	43-4
1692-1708	Somerset 148	6	10	44
1749-50	Do (6s. per cwt to first stage town (13 pptm if Wincanton), then 12d. per cwt per 20 miles)	6+	12-13	43
1695	Surrey 10-43 (rates to 14 places; 9-15 pptm summer, 11-17 pptm winter, but Kingston 24 & 28)	0.5-2.2	9-17	56
1751	Do (rates to 20 places; 11-13 pptm except Chertsey 10 and Kingston 14)	0.5-2.3	10-14	43
1749-51	Warwickshire (3s. 6d. per 60 miles, then 6d. per 10 miles)		12-14	43

Date	Description			
1736	Wiltshire (12d. per 20 miles)		12	44
1751	York 196 (15d. per stone)	10	12	43
1692	Yorkshire – N. Riding 234 [**pk**] (2d. per lb)	18.7	19	44
1726-46/51	Do (2s. per stone)	16	16	43-4
1692	Yorkshire – W. Riding 192 [**pk**] (1d. per lb; beyond Leeds, 2d. per stone per 20 miles – 16 pptm)	9.3	12	57
1693-1702	Do [**pk**] (15d. per stone summer, 18d. winter; beyond Leeds, 2½d. per stone per 20 miles – 20 pptm)	10-12	12-15	57
1703-43	Do [**pk**] (14d. per stone summer, 18d. winter; beyond Leeds 20 pptm)	9.3-12	12-15	57
1744/8	Do (14d. per stone summer, 15d. winter)	9.3-10	12	57-8
1745-7/9	Do (14d. per stone)	9.3	12	57-8
1750-1	Do (12d. per stone; beyond Leeds 16 pptm)	8	10	43

Notes

All rates here are to or from London. In Part A assignment to categories is sometimes an assumption, but cases of real doubt are indicated. In Part B all rates before 1748 are down ones except those for Oxford and for Cheshire in 1693.

Date: Italicised if the charge was an advertised one. 'W' indicates winter.

Journey etc: 'Up' is towards London; 'down' is away from London. In Part B, 'wg' indicates waggon and 'pk' packhorse.

'Sh.' (shillings per cwt): Packs are assumed to have weighed 240 lb unless indicated otherwise.

'pptm' is pence per ton-mile.

References

1. *Publick Adviser*, 26 May 1657. **2.** Anchitell Grey, *Debates of the House of Commons from the year 1667 to the year 1694* (1769), vol. 1, p. 233. **3.** C 22/946/32. **4.** C 24/1127, Nos. 4 and 15. **5.** C 7/600/27. **6.** C 5/69/82. **7.** C 5/93/65. **8.** John Houghton, *A collection for improvement of husbandry and trade* (1692-1703), 12 May 1693. **9.** C 22/182/32. **10.** West Country Studies Library, photocopy of handbill. **11.** John Haynes, *A view of the present state of the clothing trade in England* (1706), pp. 65-6. **12.** C 6/393/27. **13.** C 24/1325, No. 16, p. 1. **14.** G.J. Gent, *Great Britain's Vade Mecum* (1720), p. 351. **15.** C 11/677/35, Barry's schedule 3. **16.** CJ, vol. 21, 1727-32, p. 486. **17.** *Stamford Mercury*, 17 Feb, 7 Apr 1743. **18.** *Newcastle Courant*, 1 Sept 1744. **19.** *Derby Mercury*, 5 July 1745. **20.** Jackman, pp. 206-7, 717. **21.** Corporation of London RO, Misc. MSS. 31. 6. **22.** Pawson, pp. 38, 42. **23.** Frank Atkinson (ed.), *Some aspects of the eighteenth century woollen and worsted trade in Halifax* (1956), p. 54. **24.** Symson, p. xlix & Nos. 148, 224, 726, 836, 1943, 2000. **25.** A.P. Wadsworth and J. de L. Mann, *The cotton trade and industrial Lancashire 1600-1780* (1965), p. 264. **26.** C 6/63/41. **27.** C 11/974/6. **28.** C 6/53/96. **29.** Fitzwilliam, pp. 11, 80, 83, 87, 89. **30.** London Metropolitan Archives, MSP 1716 Ap/73. **31.** *Northampton Mercury*, 9 May 1720. **32.** McGrath, vol. 44, p. 407. **33.** Stephen K. Roberts (ed.), *The letter-book of John Byrd – customs collector in south-east Wales 1648-80*, South Wales Record Society, No. 14 (1999), pp. 123-4, 148-9. **34.** Hainsworth, p. 78n. **35.** Bedfordshire RO, OR 2071/69. **36.** Earl of Cardigan, 'Domestic expenses of a nobleman's household', *Bedfordshire Historical Record Society*, vol. 32 (1952), pp. 115, 118, 119. **37.** Albert, pp. 172, 260-1. **38.** Eaton, p. 133. **39.** British Library, Add MS 28276, f. 33. **40.** James E. Thorold Rogers, *A history of agriculture and prices in England*, vol. 7 (1902), p. 533. **41.** *Ipswich Journal*, 5 Apr 1740, 3 Oct 1741, 6 Jan, 10 Mar 1750. **42.** Bristol RO, JQS/D/3. **43.** London Metropolitan Archives, MR/WC 1-69. **44.** T.S. Willan, 'The Justices of the Peace and the rates of land carriage, 1692-1827', *JTH*, 1st ser., vol. 5 (1962), pp. 198-202. **45.** J.C. Cox, *Three centuries of Derbyshire annals* (1890), vol. 2, p. 236. **46.** Devon RO, Q/SPc. A5/166/49. **47.** Dorset RO, QS Misc 13. **48** K.H. Burley, *The economic development of Essex in the later seventeenth and early eighteenth centuries*, London DPhil 1957, p. 219; Essex RO, Order Book 1720. **49.** Devon RO, Exeter City records, Bye-laws 1581-1906, box 1, No. 10. **50.** Hampshire RO, Q1/7 and Q1/8. **51.** J.A. Chartres and G.L. Turnbull, *A pilot study of source materials for an economic history of British inland transport and communications 1600-1850*, Social Science Research Council, HR 2674 (1975), p. 32. **52.** VCH, *Lincolnshire*, vol. 2 (1906), p. 340. **53.** C 8/587/35. **54.** *The Oxford almanack* (1692, 1703). **55.** R. Lloyd Kenyon (ed.), *Shropshire county records: orders of the Shropshire Quarter Sessions*, vol. 1, 1638-1708 (n.d.), pp. 140-233. **56.** D.L. Powell and Hilary Jenkinson (eds.), *County of Surrey: Quarter Sessions records*, vol. 5 (1931), p. 82. **57.** West Yorkshire RO, QS 10/9 to 19. **58.** G.L. Turnbull, 'State regulation in the eighteenth-century English economy: another look at carriers' rates', *JTH*, 3rd ser., vol. 6 (1985), p. 110.

CARRIERS' TIMINGS, 1599-1759

(A) Waggons

Date	Destination	Miles	Days	mpd	Notes	Ref.
1599	Ipswich	70	3	23		1
1609-40, *Mar 1729*	Norwich	110	4	28	n1	2
1611-14, 1706	Colchester	52	2	26	n2	3
1612-14	Dunmow	39	2	(20)	n3	4
1613, *Oct 1735*	Bury St Edmunds	72-6	3	24-5	n4	5, 6
Apr 1620	Leicester	99	5½	18		7
1625	Chelmsford	30	2	(15)	n5	4
Nov 1675, May 1750	Coventry	93	3	(31)	n6	8, 6
Aug-Nov 1690, *Mar 1748*	Devizes	91	3	30		9, 6
Sept 1691	Bishop's Stortford	31	1	31		10
Apr 1705	Burnham (Norfolk)	125	5	25		11
Apr 1705	Lichfield	120	6	20		12
1706-9	Staines	20	1	20	n7	13
Jan 1710	Gosport	82	3	27		12
1712	Hartley Row	39	2	20		14
Apr 1715	Ludlow	146	5u, 4½d	29-32		15
1719	Manchester	187	9+	21		16
Feb 1719	Nottingham	126	5-5½	23-5	n8	17
May 1720	Northampton	67	2	(34)	n9	18
Jan/July 1722	Exeter	182	8u, 6d	23-30	n10	19
Mar-Oct 1724	Dorchester	129	4½	29		20
Mar-Oct 1724	Dorchester-Exeter	53	2	27		20
Apr 1727	Bristol	122	5	24	n11	21
Mar/Nov 1728, Jan 1733	Stamford	87	3	(29)	n12	22, 6
Apr 1728, May 1744	Southampton	80	3	27		23
Nov 1728	Northampton	67	2u	34		18
Apr 1729, Apr 1755	Gloucester	105	4	26	n13	24
May 1731	Birmingham	111	5u, 4d	22-8		25
Jan 1733	Stamford	87	4	22	n14	22
1733-4	Derby	127	5s, 6w	21-5	n15	26
May 1734	Newark	122	5½u, 4½d	22-7		22
May/June/Dec 1734	York	196	6-8	25-33	n16	22, 6
Mar 1735	Northampton	67	3u, 2½d	22-7		18
June 1735	Thrapston	76	3	25	n17	18

Date	Destination	Miles	Days	mpd	Notes	Ref.
Oct 1735	Norwich	110	3½	31	n18	2
Oct 1735	Bury St Edmunds	72	2½u, 3d	24-9	n18	6
1737	Shrewsbury	156	7-9	17-22		27
May/Oct 1739	Stowmarket	74	3	25		28
June 1740, Feb 1753	Dorchester	129	6	22		6, 29
Nov 1742	Banstead	15	6 hours	(2.5 mph)		6
May 1744	Sheffield	162	6	27		23
July 1745	Derby	127	6	21		30
July 1747	Exeter	182	6u, 7d	26-30		31
Oct 1747	Bristol	122	6	20		32
Mar 1748	Trowbridge	101	4	25		6
Mar 1748	Chippenham	96	3	32		6
Dec 1750	Tetbury	102	4u, 4½d	23-6		24
Nov 1751	Northampton	67	2½	27		18
1753	Liverpool	207	9-11	19-23	n19	33
May 1754-8, Apr 1759	Taunton	148	6	25		31
Mar 1755, July 1759	Yeovil	125	4½	28		31
Apr 1755	Chard	143	5½u, 5d	26-9	n20	31
May 1759	Salisbury	84	3u, 3½d	24-8		29
May 1759	Salisbury	84	4u	21		29
June 1759	Manchester	187	9u, 8d	21-3		34

(B) Packhorses

Date	Destination	Miles	Days	mpd	Notes	Ref.
1620s	Shrewsbury	156	c.7	22	n21	35
1680s	Kendal	263	10-10½	25-6		36
1706-9	Egham	42	1	42	n22	37
Sept 1714	Bristol	122	4	31	n23	38
Dec 1720	Hereford	138	5	28		21
Dec 1720	Monmouth	133	5	27		21
Jan/July 1722	Exeter	182	5½	33		19
July 1725	Halifax	197	7	28		39
June 1728	Stamford	87	29 hrs	3.0 mph	n24	22
Aug 1729	Leeds	192	7	27		40
Nov 1745	Birmingham	120	3	40		41
1753	Liverpool	207	9	23		33

(C) **Carts.** Oundle-London (for venison), from 26 June, 25 hours, 78 miles, hence 3.1 mph (*Stamford Mercury*, 8 June 1738).

Notes
All services are London ones. After 1734 flying waggons and waggons which probably travelled during part of the night are excluded.
Date: Italicised if the source is an advertisement.
Days: 'u' is up, 'd' is down, 'w' is winter, 's' is summer.
Miles: Determined on the basis of the actual route if known.
mpd, i.e. miles per day: in brackets if clearly an exceptional type of service (e.g. a flying waggon) or possibly not full days.

1. Via Thetford and Ware in the 17th century (NA, STAC 8/90/19). **2.** Two-day duration deduced from the overnight stop at Ingatestone (24 miles from London) (1611-14). **3.** Overnight (up) at Epping; possibly not two full days. **4.** Via Duxford and thus Newmarket (NA, REQ 2/396/21) (1613); probably via Sudbury (1735). **5.** Overnight (down) at Brentwood (19 miles); probably not two full days. **6.** Probably a coach-waggon in 1675 (same timing as for Dugdale's journeys from Coventry). **7.** Exeter and Trowbridge carriers. **8.** Six days including Nottingham to Mansfield by horse. **9.** Flying waggon. **10.** Down timing recorded only in July. **11.** Overnight at Maidenhead, Theale, Marlborough, Pickwick. **12.** For venison and other perishable goods (1728). **13.** Began 1 Apr (1729). **14.** Via Oundle (three days thence – 26 mpd). **15.** Sometimes five days down in winter. Summer began 14 May 1734. **16.** Summer 6-6½ down, 7½ up; winter 7 down, 8 up. Another York waggon about a day faster in each case (28-36 mpd). **17.** Overnight at St Albans and Bedford. Also a venison service in 24 hours (3.2 mph). **18.** Up from Bury, departing at night and arriving early in the morning; from Norwich, reaching London at night or very early the following morning and leaving at night. **19.** Summer 9 days up, 10 days down; winter 11 days. Via Stone, Lichfield, Daventry. **20.** Waggons from Chard in 1746/51/9 taking five days each way are described as flying waggons, but also as 'lodging' on the way (*Sherborne Mercury*, 17 Feb 1746, 22 Apr 1751, 12 Feb 1759). **21.** Complaints they sometimes took longer. **22.** Exeter carrier. **23.** Assumes 'Tuesdays drift' and 'Fridays drift' in the inventory refers to departure days from Bristol. **24.** Packhorses or carts. Began 11 June. No rest periods assumed here.

References

1. W.H. Richardson (ed.), *The annalls of Ipswiche ... by Nath. Bacon ... 1654* (1884), pp. 402-3. **2.** Norfolk RO, Norwich City records, Assembly Books 1585-1613, f. 390, 1613-42, ff. 10, 278, 364; *Norwich Mercury*, 29 Mar 1729, 18 Oct 1735. **3.** NA, REQ 2/310/68; John Haynes, *A view of the present state of the clothing trade in England* (1706), p. 91. **4.** Essex RO, Quarter Sessions transcript, 206/43, 250/16. **5.** Historic Manuscripts Commission, 14th report, vol. VIII (1895), p. 141. **6.** LEP, 16 Nov 1728, 21 Dec 1734, 23 Oct 1735, 21 June 1740, 11 Nov 1742, 5 Mar 1748, 26 May 1750. **7.** William Lilly, *The life of William Lilly* (1774), p. 11. **8.** *City Mercury*, 4 Nov 1675. **9.** C 8/556/7. **10.** *London Gazette*, 17 Sept 1691. **11.** *Post-Man*, 10 Apr 1705. **12.** *Daily Courant*, 18 Apr 1705, 27 Jan 1710. **13.** C 6/381/3; C 5/244/9. **14.** C 22/533/15, Edmund White. **15.** *Worcester Post-Man*, 8 Apr 1715. **16.** House of Lords Record Office, Lords Main Papers, 2 Feb 1718/19. **17.** *Yorkshire diaries and autobiographies*, Surtees Society, vol. 65 (1877), p. 197. **18.** *Northampton Mercury*, 9 May 1720, 4 Nov 1728, 3 Mar, 23 June 1735, 4 Nov 1751. **19.** *Exeter Mercury*, 23 Jan, 20 July 1722. **20.** C 11/1189/64. **21.** *Evening Post*, 15 Dec 1720, 25 Apr 1727. **22.** *Stamford Mercury*, 14 Mar, 30 May 1728, 25 Jan 1733, 16 & 23 May, 6 June 1734. **23.** *Daily Journal*, 20 Apr 1728; *Daily Advertiser*, 23 & 28 May 1744. **24.** Herbert, pp. 70-1, 73-4, 81-2. **25.** John Lewis, *Printed ephemera* (1969), p. 43. **26.** H.S. Twells, 'Mr Drewry and the Derby waggons', *Journal of the Derbyshire Archaeological and Natural History Society*, new ser., vol. 16 (1942), p. 62-3. **27.** Harper, vol. 1, p. 109. **28.** *Ipswich Journal*, 12 & 19 May, 6 Oct 1739. **29.** *Salisbury Journal*, 5 Feb 1753, 20 May 1754. **30.** *Derby Mercury*, 5 July 1745. **31.** *Sherborne Mercury*, 13 July 1747, 6 May 1754, 31 Mar, 5 May 1755, 17 May 1756, 8 May 1758, 16 Apr, 9 July 1759. **32.** J. Latimer, *The annals of Bristol in the eighteenth century* (1893), p. 268. **33.** *The Liverpool memorandum-book ... for the year MDCCLIII* (1753). **34.** G.L. Turnbull, *Traffic and transport: an economic history of Pickfords* (1979), p. 17. **35.** T.C. Mendenhall, *The Shrewsbury drapers and the Welsh wool trade in the XVI and XVII centuries* (1953), p. 35. **36.** M.L. Armitt, *Rydal* (1916), pp. 451, 453; with Delaune 1681 and 1690. **37.** C 6/381/3. **38.** PROB 3/18/131; with *London Gazette*, 4 Sept 1693; *The traveller's and chapman's daily instructor* (1705); Richard Burridge, *A new review of London* (1722). **39.** *Leeds Mercury*, 6 July 1725; with Burridge, *New Review of London* (1722, 1728); Charles Pickman, *The tradesman's guide; or the chapman's and traveller's best companion* (1727). **40.** *Leeds Mercury*, 5 Aug 1729. **41.** *Aris's Birmingham Gazette*, 11 Nov 1745.

APPENDIX V

PROVENDER FOR CARRIERS' AND COACHMASTERS' HORSES, 1687-1745

The small number of accounts between carriers and coachmasters and their inn-keepers provide valuable information about the amounts of provender consumed (set out in the table below), and by implication about the types of horses used. In each case the rations were for one day, as indicated by cases where a team stayed for more than one day or a horse was left behind. In Hales's case hay for carriers' horses in the Staines area was 'by the night four pence and six pence for each horse if he stay or is sett up a whole day and night together' (C 22/533/15, Edmund White), and Hales's payments were always 6d. per horse. Only in Want's case is there doubt about this, since the journeys were unusually fast and the rations unusually low, but the lower figures are plausible if Want was providing a caravan service with relatively light loads.

In 1712, on the London-Basingstoke road, 'itt hath been usuall and customary for the innkeepers on the said road to allow common carryers that usually sett up their wagon horses with them hay gratis for each drivers horse for each teeme ... att all such times as hay is sold att reasonable rates' (C 22/533/15, Edmund White). Since the number of horses is normally stated only in respect of the hay provided, omission of drivers' horses affects the calculations of the oats and beans consumed, since there would be more horses consuming them than were recorded. Want's account indicates that the custom also existed at Maidenhead. It is assumed below that the custom did not apply at Dorchester or London. Also, some carriers, such as Hales and Rothwell, did not provide their waggoners with ponies. A saddle horse required half as much provender as a draught horse (London Metropolitan Archives, X88/1, p. 200).

In and around London it is probably safe to assume that something close to the Winchester bushel of eight gallons was used, although even here there were variations. At Dorchester in 1693 a bushel of ten gallons was used for oats and malt, but the Winchester bushel for other produce (Peter J. Bowden (ed.), *Economic change: wages, profits and rents 1500-1750* (1990), pp. 309, 311). If this applied in Weare's case, one would expect oat consumption to appear unusually low and the ratio of beans to oats to be unusually high, whereas the opposite was the case, so it is unlikely that Weare's account is affected by the ten-gallon bushel. The same perhaps applies to Morris at Bridport in 1687-8, especially as his packhorses received more oats and beans than Barry's at Staines.

Type of horse	Carrier/ coachmaster and place	Dates	Hay per horse per night	Oats per horse per week (pecks)	Beans per horse per week (pecks)
Waggon horses	Want at Maidenhead	Aug-Nov 1693	6d.	11.0	3.6
"	Barry at Staines	Sept 1707-Nov 1709	6d.	13.4	3.9
"	Hales at Staines	Apr-Oct 1709	6d.	15.6	3.9
"	Weare at Dorchester (London horses)	Mar-Oct 1724	6d.	19.4	5.1
"	Weare at Dorchester (Exeter horses)	Mar-Oct 1724	6d.	17.9	4.1
"	Rothwell in London	July 1743-July 1745	12d.	9.3	4.7
Pack-horses	Morris at Bridport	Aug 1687-Jan 1688	3d.	10.5	3.5
"	Barry at Staines	Oct 1706-July 1707	6d.	9.7	2.4
"	Rothwell in London	July 1743-July 1745	12d.	11.2	5.6
Coach horses	Fisher at Maidenhead and Colnbrook	Sept-Dec 1699	6d.	17.5	3.5
"	Rothwell in London (3-day schedule)	July 1743-July 1745	10d.	10.5	3.5
"	Ditto (2-day schedule)	July 1743-July 1745	10d.	11.8	3.9

Sources: C 8/556/7; C 6/381/3; C 5/244/9; C 11/1189/64; C 104/218, Cremer *v.* Rothwell; C 7/237/28; E 112/726/106.

Notes: For Morris and Rothwell, the amounts provided were unvarying or almost unvarying; in the others amounts varied (usually substantially) and are averaged here, except that for Fisher the rate for four horses (the usual number) is used and for Weare the rates for the usual team sizes are used.

Want: Rations are assumed to be for a whole day. Ponies are assumed to consume at half the rate of waggon horses.

Barry's waggon horses: Ponies not allowed for; uncertain whether they should be.

Weare's London horses: Also 3.2 pecks bran. Teams usually of seven horses, but same total amounts once given to a team of six and once to a team of eight. Reduced from 6 Aug to 18.0 pecks oats, 4.8 pecks beans, 3.2 pecks bran.

Weare's Dorchester horses: Also 1.4 pecks bran. Same total amounts for teams of six (10 times), seven (11 times, from 12 May to 5 Sept) and eight (once); calculated here as if for teams of 6½.

Rothwell's packhorses: Hay 10d. per night for the pony; pony assumed here to have half the ration of oats and beans; same amounts of oats and beans when three packhorses, and usually the same beans if four.

Fisher: In the 1690s, according to a former driver of the Henley coach, 'the customary way of feeding stage coach horses then was to give amongst 4 horses between their comeing in one night and goeing out the next morning two bushells of oates and halfe a bushell of beanes' (E 133/62/37), i.e. 14 pecks oats, 3.5 pecks beans. Rations rose in late November to 17.5 pecks oats, 4.4 pecks beans.

Rothwell's 2-day coach horses: Oats increased to 12.3 pecks in June 1745.

EARLIEST REFERENCES TO STAGE-COACHES, 1653-1762

Only London services are listed here, together with connecting services when in the same ownership as the London one. From 1681, only services extending 40 miles from London are included. Brackets around the date indicate that the service was apparently short-lived; an asterisk indicates that it was clearly indicated as new or recently established. References to 1681, 1690, 1705, 1726 and 1738 are to the carrier and coach lists used in Table 7.

Services listed here were sometimes to places already served by coaches to somewhere else. Also, apparently new services were sometimes the extension of an existing coach to a new destination, and therefore were not wholly new; such extensions could also be ephemeral.

Destination	Date	Source
York	1653*	*Perfect Diurnall*, 11 Apr 1653.
Newcastle upon Tyne	1654	*Severall Proceedings of State Affaires*, 23 Mar 1654. [Associated with the York coach; probably always a connecting service from York.]
Chipping Norton	(1654)	*Ibid.*, 22 June 1654. [Also a service in 1726.]
Cambridge	1654	*Perfect Diurnall*, 28 Aug 1654.
Lincoln/Barton upon Humber	1654	*Severall Proceedings in Parliament*, 28 Dec 1654. [Associated with the York coach until between 1672 and 1681 (SP 29/319, No. 200).]
Worcester	1654	Diary of Sir Fulwar Skipwith, Warwickshire RO, MI 213, 21 Dec 1654.
Southampton	1655	F.P. and M.M. Verney (eds.), *Memoirs of the Verney family during the seventeenth century* (1907), vol. 2, p. 9.
Winchester	1655*	*Ibid.* [Winchester coaches are also recorded in 1672 (SP 29/319, No. 200) and 1705, but not in 1681 and 1690.]
Exeter	1655	Rawdon, pp. 70-1.
Salisbury	1656	Sir William Dugdale's diary, *Athenaeum*, 3 Nov 1888.

Stafford	(1656)	*Ibid.* [Possibly a coach-waggon.]
Chester	1657	*Mercurius Politicus*, 9 Apr 1657. [There is no evidence that the Chester coaches expected to start in May 1653 actually did so (*Perfect Diurnall*, 11 Apr 1653).]
Norwich	1657	*Ibid.*, 23 Apr 1657.
Bath & Bristol	1657	*Publick Adviser*, 26 May, 22 June 1657. [Two separate services, one readvertised in 1658 as a Marlborough service.]
Portsmouth	1657	*Ibid.*, 26 May 1657. [Possibly a coach-waggon in 1657, but see C 8/216/59 for c.1660.]
Chelmsford	1657	*Ibid.*, 2 June 1657.
Luton	1657	*Ibid.*
Aylesbury	1657	*Ibid.*, 16 June 1657. [But an Aylesbury coach was mentioned in 1652 (Historic Manuscripts Commission, appendix to 7th report (1879), p. 458a).]
Canterbury & Dover	1657	*Ibid.*, 22 June 1657. [Two services in 1658 (*Mercurius Politicus*, 13 May, 17 June 1658).]
Wakefield	(1658)	*Mercurius Politicus*, 8 Apr 1658. [Associated with the York coach. Not listed in 1681 or 1690, but mentioned in diaries from 1695 to 1723 (Appendix 8).]
Edinburgh	1658	*Ibid.* [Associated with the York coach; probably always a connecting service from York or Newcastle.]
Plymouth	(1658)	*Ibid.* [Probably a connecting service from Exeter.]
Windsor	1658	*Ibid.*, 22 Apr 1658.
Marlborough	1658	*Ibid.*, 30 Sept 1658. [Advertised the previous year as serving Bristol (*Publick Adviser*, 22 June 1657). Recorded until 1726.]
Berkhamsted	1660	Dugdale (2), July 1660.
Oxford	1661	Wood, vol. 19, p. 385.
St Albans	1663	Dugdale, p. 112.
Tonbridge	1663	*A list of the 400 hackney-coaches licensed in July and August, 1662* (1664), p. 12.
Rochester	1663	*The Newes*, 10 Dec 1663.
Huntingdon	1663	Pepys, vol. 4, 14-15 June 1663.
Guildford	1664	Diary of Samuel Woodforde, Bodleian Library, MS. Eng. misc. f.381, f. 77r.
Ware & Wadesmill	1664	*The Intelligencer*, 18 Apr 1664. [A 'passage coach'.]
Epsom	1665	*The Newes*, 1 June 1665; *The Intelligencer*, 12 June 1665.
Ipswich	1667	SP 29/193, f. 73. [The reference is to 'Ipswich coachman' taking mail-bags to London.]
Reading	1670	NA, PC 2/62, p. 188.
Tamworth	1671	Dugdale, p. 134. [Not recorded after 1690.]

Beccles	1671	Suffolk RO (Lowestoft), ref 1227, S.W. Rix Beccles Collections, Division IV, No. IV, f. 337. [Probably always an extension of the Ipswich coach.]
Northampton	1672	SP 29/319, No. 200.
Shrewsbury	?1672	*Ibid.* [Possibly existed by 1659 as part of the Chester group of coaches – *Mercurius Politicus*, 24 Mar 1659.]
Henley	1672	*Ibid.*
Gloucester	1672	*Ibid.*
Bedford	1672	*Ibid.*
Newbury	1672	*Ibid.*
Dorchester (Dorset) & Blandford	1672	*Ibid.*, No. 202.
Kettering	c.1674	C 5/371/39. [Recorded until 1705, and from 1753 (*Northampton Mercury*, 19 Feb 1753).]
Barnet	1675	*London Gazette*, 2 Aug 1675.
Colchester	1675	Bodleian Library, MS Rawl, D1114, 19 Aug 1675.
Harwich	1675	Jackman, p. 125.
Taunton	1677	*The Mercury: or Advertisements concerning Trade*, 7 Mar 1677.
Lichfield	1677	Dugdale, p. 139. [Probably originated in the 1650s or 1660s as part of the Chester group of coaches.]
Birmingham	(1679)	Dugdale, p. 141. [Probably based at Banbury. The next Birmingham coach, mentioned in 1691, was based at Warwick (*London Gazette*, 11 May 1691), and probably had a continuous history thereafter.]
Nottingham	1681*	Andrew Browning (ed.), *Memoirs of Sir John Reresby* (1991), p. 219. [Described as 'lately sett up' in Jan 1684 (C 9/397/39).]
Abingdon	1681	Delaune 1681.
Braintree & Bocking	1681	*Ibid.* [Two separate services to Braintree, in the same ownership as Chelmsford coaches.]
Bridgnorth	1681	*Ibid.* [Probably an extension of a Worcester coach.]
Bury St Edmunds	1681	*Ibid.* [Two or three separate services.]
King's Lynn	1681	*Ibid.*
Newmarket	1681	*Ibid.*
Saffron Walden	1681	*Ibid.*
Sudbury	1681	*Ibid.*
Yarmouth	1681	*Ibid.*
Astrop Wells	(1683)	*London Gazette*, 21 June 1683. [Probably the Banbury coach.]
Buckingham	(1683)	Bedfordshire Historical Record Society, vol. 57 (1978), p. 36. [For 1737, see G. Eland (ed.), *Purefoy letters 1735-1753* (1931), vol. 2, p. 244.]

Basingstoke	(1690)	Delaune 1690. [Also a service in 1726.]
Daventry	1690	*Ibid.*
Melton Mowbray	(1690)	*Ibid.* [But John Merrill of Melton Mowbray, carrier, had 'a coach, waggon, & an old coach' in 1667 (Leicestershire RO, PR/I/66/31).]
Newport Pagnell	(1690)	*Ibid.* [Also a service in 1738 (LEP, 15 Apr 1738.]
Banbury	1690	*London Gazette*, 24 Apr, 5 May 1690. [Two separate services; one may have originated in 1679 or earlier (Dugdale, p. 141). Recorded until 1726.]
Warwick	1694	*Ibid.*, 19 Apr 1694. [The proprietor had advertised a Birmingham coach via Warwick in 1691 (*London Gazette*, 11 May 1691).]
Mansfield	(1694)	*Yorkshire diaries and autobiographies in the seventeenth and eighteenth centuries*, Surtees Society, vol. 77 (1886), p. 64. [Not recorded after 1700 – *Flying Post*, 2 May 1700. Part of the Nottingham group of coaches.]
Doncaster	(1695)	*London Gazette*, 9 May 1695. [An extension of the Nottingham coach.]
Oundle	1695	Edmond Malone (ed.), *The critical and miscellaneous prose works of John Dryden* (1800), vol. 1, part 2, pp. 41-2. [Probably dated back at least to 1686; see PROB 4/15212. Recorded until 1726.]
Cirencester	1696	*London Gazette*, 14 May 1696.
Wallingford	(1696)	E 133/62/37. [An extension of the Henley coach.]
Farnham	(1697)	*Post-Man*, 15 July 1697.
Peterborough	1697	Fitzwilliam, pp. 16, 18, 40. [Possibly the Boston coach.]
Derby	1698	*Post-Man*, 23 June 1698. [Part of the Nottingham group of coaches.]
Monmouth	(1700)*	*Post-Boy*, 25 May 1700.
Rye	(1700)	*Post-Man*, 10 Aug 1700. [Also a service in 1726.]
Leicester	1700	*Flying Post*, 22 Oct 1700. [Part of the Nottingham group of coaches; probably not a separate destination for long.]
Wolverhampton	1702	*Ibid.*, 14 Mar 1702. [Recorded until 1726.]
Warrington	1703*	*Post-Man*, 18 Mar 1703. [Probably part of the Chester group of coaches. Not recorded between 1710 (Henry, 2 Aug 1710) and 1726.]
Hereford	1703	C 7/270/74. [An extension of the Gloucester coach.]
Stratford upon Avon	(1705)	Warwickshire RO, CR 1368/4, Nos. 1-2. [Associated with the Banbury coach. Also a service in 1726.]

Andover	1705	*The traveller's and chapman's daily instructor* (1705).
Boston & Louth	1705	*Ibid.* [Only Boston in 1734-7 (LEP, 29 Oct 1734, 26 Apr 1737).]
Chichester	1705	*Ibid.* [Probably an extension of the Guildford coach.]
Coventry	1705	*Ibid.* [Possibly the coach-waggon. Also a service in 1726.]
Gosport	1705	*Ibid.*
Lewes & Brighton	1705	*Ibid.* [Only Lewes in 1725 (*Daily Courant*, 24 Apr 1725).]
Market Harborough	1705	*Ibid.* [Probably part of the Nottingham group of coaches. Also a service in 1726.]
Rugby	1705	*Ibid.* [Probably an extension of the Daventry coach. Also a service in 1726.]
Stow	(1705)	*Ibid.* [Probably an extension of an Oxford coach.]
Towcester	(1705)	*Ibid.*
Stony Stratford	(1720)	*Evening Post*, 4 June 1720.
Ross	(1722)	*Gloucester Journal*, 11 June 1722. [Probably the Hereford coach.]
Leighton Buzzard	1726	*Daily Post*, 28 Apr 1726.
Ely	1726	*The tradesman's guide; or the chapman's and traveller's best companion* (1727). [Probably an extension of the Cambridge coach.]
Witney	(1726)	*Ibid.*
Sherborne	(1733)	LEP, 15 Feb 1733. [Also LEP, 4 June 1734.]
Wisbech	1738	*The intelligencer: or, merchants assistant* (1738). [Probably an extension of the Cambridge coach.]
Trowbridge	1753	*Salisbury Journal*, 28 May 1753. ['Flying vehicle'.]
Chard	(1755)	*Sherborne Mercury*, 24 Mar 1755.
Leeds	1760	E 134/8 Geo III Easter 10.
Manchester	1760	*Ibid.*; *Manchester Mercury*, 15 Jan, 18 Mar 1760. [Two services, one an extension of the Warrington coach.]
Frome	1762	*Sherborne Mercury*, 29 Mar 1762.
Kendal	1762	LEP, 4 Mar 1762. [Probably an extension of the Warrington/Manchester coach.]

INVENTORIES OF COACHMASTERS, 1666-1738

Coachmaster	Date	Destination, miles and frequency	Stock	(1)	(2)	(3)
1. Stephen Pricklove of St Albans, coachman	Feb 1666	[St Albans 22], 3pw (1681)	ii gray stoned horses & 1 black one (£15); i old black ston'd horse 1 bro[?] bald horse & a lame geldinge (£9); ii bay geldings 1 moone eyed and one lame; viii p of harness halters and other matterialls; ii old coaches & iii old wheeles & other lumber; pair of old fore coach wheels	–/104	0.73 (w)	
2. Thomas Hayhurst of London, innkeeper	Nov 1672	York 202, 3pw (1681) (probably ½ share)	[24 horses in 4 teams, 6 coaches]	248/405		
3. William Waterson of Cambridge	Dec 1681	Cambridge 57, 3pw	One coach 4 horses harness & all materialls to them belonging (£30); one chariot (£16); one herse (£2); 1 other coach with harness (£15); 6 horses more (£28); 1 other coach with 4 horses (£30); one horse (£1.5)	122/177	0.53 (w)	114
4. Matthew Freer of Aylesbury, innholder	1683	Aylesbury 42, 3pw (1681)	Fourteene horses and a colt (£40); two coaches and harnesse (£10)	50/337	0.67	84
5. William Hickman of Chipping Barnet	Aug 1685	Barnet 12, daily (1690)	Five geldings with coach harnesse & three old coaches & a shed to put them into (£21.10.8)	22/42	0.42	

Name	Date	Service	Description			
6. Thomas Coates of Reading, Esq	July 1686	Reading 42, daily (2 partners) (1681)	15 coach horses at £2.10s a peice (£37.10); two coaches with harnesses & wheeles vallence (£12)	50/c.391	0.71	84
7. William Morris	1688-9	Exeter 182, 3pw (1690) (¼ share)	[12 horses, 2 coaches]	–	0.57	84
8. John Holloway, citizen & leatherseller of London	Sept 1689	Chester 188, Lichfield 126, etc. (3 partners)	[31 horses (£251.10), 10 coaches (£122), harnesses (£15)]	410/1127	0.65	87
9. Henry Molden of London, coachman	June 1691	York 202, 3pw (1690) (½ share)	[25 horses (£157.10), 2 coaches (c£20), harness etc. for 20 horses (c£23)]	201/269	0.53	93
10. Robert Tooby of Reading, coachman	Aug 1694	Bristol 122 & Bath 109	[29 horses (c£170), 5 coaches and 7 sets of harness (c£48)]	c218/c259		
11. John Hathaway of Henley, stage-coachman	1694/5	Henley 38, 3pw (1681)	Two coaches and nine horses with their harness spring trees and all other furniture and tackle thereto belonging (£125)	125/–	0.47	
12. Humphrey Richards of Oxford, coachmaster	1696	Oxford 58, 3pw (2 partners) (1690)	Fourteen horses (£83.10); four coaches, one calash, one hearse, & all things belonging to ye hearse (£52.5); four sets of harness, two postillion harness horse cloths, bridles, & saddles (£5.15)	142/294	0.48	88-116
13. William Hall of Henley, yeoman	Sept 1699	Wallingford 48 & Henley 38, each weekly	Two coaches 5 stone horses one gelding harnesse & bridles for eight horses halters for 4 horses with two paire of spring trees & other necessaryes belonging to the said coaches	–	0.42	

Name	Date	Route	Inventory description			
14. John Smead of Dorchester	Feb 1700	Exeter 182 & Taunton 148	Twenty two horses (£176); the twelve harnesses upon the Exeter stage (£4.10); the six harnesses upon the Taunton stage (£3.10); the old and spare harnes (£5); the Taunton coach (£15); the old coach (£6); the coach at Salisbury (£15); three coaches on the road (£40)	265/285		
15. Thomas Dye, groom of Magdalen College, Oxford	1703	Oxford 58, 3pw (1690)	Edward Allens coach carriage & harness (£14); the foure geldings he drives to London (£24); [7 horses (£16)]; [old wheels, an old carriage, harness, 4 old brasses (£2.15)]; Fosters stage coach carriage and wheeles (£5); the foure stone horses Foster drives (£23); a chariott and carriage and foure harnesses (£9)	94/180	0.52	
16. Francis Snow of Uxbridge, coachman	July 1704	Uxbridge 18, daily (1690 & 1705)	Three stone horses and six geldings (£39); two old coaches and wheeles and eight paire of old harnesse (£12)	51/76	0.50	
17. Anne Fisher of Maidenhead, innholder	June 1708	Henley 38, 3pw (1705)	The Henley stage coach & eight horses (£100)	100/–	0.42	
18. Thomas Beecroft of Norwich, carrier/coachman	Nov 1710	Norwich 110, 3pw (1705 & 1710) (2 partners)	One & twenty horses (£80); three coaches, one hearse, one chaise with the harnes (£50)	130/383	0.76 (w)	110
19. Robert Feary of Peterborough, yeoman [carrier]	May 1712	Lincoln 139, [weekly?]	[10 horses and 10 pairs of harness (£200)]	–	0.43	139
20. 4 partners	Oct 1712	Edinburgh 406, fortnightly (etc.)	Eighty able horses	–	0.64 (w)	
21. Daniel Crosland of Bury St Edmunds	1717	Bury St Edmunds 72	Coach [£25] & four old horses [£15] with harness for six horses	40/–		

22. John Towse of Hartfordbridge, innholder	Apr 1719	Salisbury 84	[3 stage-coaches and 30 horses]	–		
23. John Beecroft of Norwich, coachman	Feb 1723	Norwich 110	A coach a charett a chase and harse a pair of old weels (£26); 3 setts of harnesses (£2.10); 10 old horses (£35); 2 coaches and harness for 8 horses (£24); 6 horses (£54); 4 horses (£10)	152/270		
24. Joseph Ironmonger of Stanmore [innholder]	Aug 1728	Stanmore 13½, daily	Two coaches, one chariot, and four good able horses, with harness, &c.	–	0.30	81
25. –	Aug 1730	Abingdon 59, 3pw (1733)	Two good coaches, 12 good horses, and three sets of good harness	–	0.41	118
26. George Hutton, Robert Birch & Thomas Hunt of London	Nov 1733	York 202, twice weekly	Nine sets of able horses	–	0.80 (w)	90
27. Robert Yorke and John Nightingall	Jan 1735	York 202 and Wakefield 185, each weekly	50 able horses	–	0.78 (w)	
28. Mrs Elizabeth Skinner of Egham [innholder]	June 1738	Southampton 80, 3pw (½ share)	Two good coaches, twelve able horses and harness	–	0.60	80
29. 7 partners	Dec 1738	Warrington 196, weekly	[4 coaches, 24 horses]	–	0.73 (w)	98
30. William Freeman of New Alresford [innholder]	Oct 1739	Southampton 80, 3pw (½ share) (1738)	[2 sets of horses, 2 coaches]	–	0.60 (w)	120

Notes

The sources are probate inventories, except Nos 7, 11, 13, 17, 19, 21 and 29, which are listings of stock in lawsuits, and Nos 20, 22, 24 to 28 and 30, which are from advertisements either of services or of stock for sale. Destinations and frequencies are from Delaune, from *The traveller's and chapman's daily instructor* (1705) or from the same source as the listing of stock, except as indicated in the notes below; frequencies are from the same year as the stock listing unless indicated otherwise. '3pw' indicates thrice weekly. Listings of stock are verbatim (but with capitalisation modernised) unless in square brackets. '(1)' is value of coaching stock and total value of inventory (£); it excludes debts and leases, but includes cash in hand (£626 in No. 8); underlining indicates that the sum was for the business rather than just the stock. '(2)' is number of horses per 'double mile' (i.e. for a daily service, except Sunday, each way; six miles covered each way by a weekly service equals one double mile); 'w' indicates winter. '(3)' is miles covered per team per week (the number of teams being an assumption in most cases).

1. No direct evidence Pricklove was a London coachman, but a St Albans coach is unlikely to have been serving anywhere else. **2.** 'Widow Hayhunt' was a York coach proprietor (and London innkeeper) in 1672; Thomas Hayhurst was a licensed hackney coachman at the *Black Swan*, Holborn (the York coach's inn) in 1662 (*A list of the 400 hackney-coaches licensed in July and August, 1662* (1664)). The coach's winter frequency is uncertain. **5.** Presumably related to the William Hickman of Chipping Barnet listed in 1690. **7.** The last two columns take account of the four horses held in common by the four partners, and relate to the Exeter service as a whole. **8.** Holloway's 14 horses at Whitchurch apparently provided a twice-weekly service over the 65 miles between Chester and Stonnall, and the last two columns are based on these alone. **9.** Assets included a half-share of another coach and four or five horses, worth £22.15.0. The last two columns assume 54 horses in 13 teams for the York service as a whole. **10.** Toobey's services in 1690 were twice weekly to Bath and Bristol and twice weekly to Bristol (one of three partners), and twice weekly to Bath and Bristol and daily to Reading and Newbury (sole ownership). **12.** The last two columns assume that Richards was sole proprietor by 1696. **13.** Valuations varied widely: from £16 to £60 for the horses and from £8 to £36 for the coaches and harness. **14.** Recorded only as an Exeter coachmaster in 1690, with a quarter share (E 112/598/541). **15.** The inventory was made between June and September. With only two teams, each would have covered 174 miles per week, so the relatively low-value horses individually listed were probably used for coaching. **18.** The 1710 frequency is from *Norwich Gazette*, 20 May 1710. The value of the farming stock was £35, apart from £145 for 'the corne & hay in the barnes'. **20.** The horses clearly included those kept for the weekly Newcastle to York coaches and the thrice-weekly York to London coaches, and this is reflected in the penultimate column. **21.** Crosland sold his stock in 1717 to Edmund Talbott of Bury, whose inventory, of May 1725, lists horses (£42), two stage-coaches (£10 and £8), seven carriages of various sorts (£26.15.0) and ten pairs of harness (£15), together with goods totalling £15.5.0 (Suffolk RO, IC 500/3/45/14). **22.** Towse is identified as the Salisbury coachmaster in C 11/372/49. **23.** The farming stock totalled £33. **24.** Two-horse teams assumed in final column. **25.** Frequency from LEP, 21 Apr 1733. **26.** The penultimate column assumes the nine teams were each of six horses. **28.** Frequency from LEP, 11 Apr 1738. **30.** Frequency from *The intelligencer: or, merchants assistant* (1738).

The following may also have been London coachmen: Andrew Clarke of London, innkeeper, 1666 (11 horses, 3 coaches; possibly Rochester coachman, but possibly the coachman's father; Corporation of London RO, Orphans Inventories 294(B)); Roger Hare of Uxbridge, coachman, 1673 (5 horses, 1 coach; London Metropolitan Archives, AM/PI 1673/19); John Clark of Cheshunt, 'stage coach master', 1728 (12 coach horses, 5 coaches and chaise; PROB 3/27/13); Thomas Hassall of Chester, coachman, 1730 (13 horses, 2 coaches, new coach unfinished, hearse and mourning coach; Cheshire RO).

References

1. PROB 4/22069. **2.** PROB 4/14082. **3.** PROB 4/420. **4.** PROB 4/17190. **5.** Hertfordshire RO, A25/4182. **6.** PROB 4/5360. **7.** E 112/598/541. **8.** Corporation of London RO, Orphans Inventories 2170. **9.** PROB 4/5871. **10.** PROB 4/9736. **11.** E 133/62/37, p. 8; *London Gazette*, 21 May 1694. **12.** PROB 5/4196. **13.** E 133/62/37, p. 3. **14.** PROB 4/17640. **15.** Bodleian Library, University Archives, Chancellor's Court inventories, vol. D-F, Hyp B/12. **16.** London Metropolitan Archives, AM/PI 1705/7. **17.** E 112/777/62. **18.** C 11/1166/39. **19.** C 11/2/7, Savage's answer and John Firby's deposition. **20.** *Newcastle Courant*, 13 Oct 1712. **21.** C 11/2287/35. **22.** *Evening Post*, 14 Apr 1719. **23.** Norfolk and Norwich RO, Norwich Archdeaconry inventories, 1723 & 1723/4 f. 9. **24.** LEP, 6 Aug 1728. **25.** LEP, 1 Aug 1730. **26.** LEP, 27 Nov 1733. **27.** *Leeds Mercury*, 7 Jan 1735. **28.** LEP, 27 June 1738. **29.** C 11/2086/35. **30.** LEP, 2 Oct 1739.

APPENDIX VIII

Coach and Coach-Waggon Timings, 1648-1750

Entries for each season are arranged as follows: (a) the Chester, York and Exeter coaches and related services (b) other services covering 107 or more miles (with related services grouped) (c) the Canterbury, Cambridge and Oxford coaches (all covering a similar distance) (d) other London services of over 40 miles, and (e) provincial services.

(1) Summer

Date	Destination and miles	Days	mpd	Comments	References
(a)					
Mar-May 1657 (S 1673, July 1679), May 1690, Apr 1700/1, July 1701/10/11, May 1712, July & Aug 1713 (July 1716, Apr 8 May 1717), Sept 1717, May 1718, Apr 1721, May & Sept 1723, *Mar or Apr 1744/5/7, June 1750*	Chester 188	4	47	Coventry 2 days; Stone 3 days; fresh horses daily (1657). Diarists sometimes joined or alighted south of Chester, usually at Whitchurch. Began 26 Mar, 8 Apr, 30 Mar (1744/5/7). Dep 5 a.m. (1745/7). 'Stage-chaises'; began 18 June; dep 6 a.m. (1750).	1-13
24 Mar 1659, 7-12 Oct 1687	Chester 188	5	(38)	With 4 horses, apparently a transitional timing (1659). Switched from summer to winter schedule at Coventry (1687).	2, 14
Apr 1677	Coventry 98	2	49	Chester coach.	15
July 1677/8, Oct 1678/81, Aug 1683, Apr 1701, *Apr 1721* (June 1725), *July 1738, Apr 1742*	Lichfield 126	3	42*	Via Northampton; diarists sometimes Coleshill-London only (1677-1701). Via Birmingham (1738-42); began 17 July, 12 Apr (1738/42); dep Lichfield 8 a.m. (1742).	15-18, 11, 5, 19-20

Date	Place			Notes	Ref
Mar 1703	Warrington 196	4	49	Began 29 Mar; dep 5 a.m.	21
July 1710	Eccleshall 149	3	50	Presumably Warrington coach.	7
June 1742, July 1743, Apr 1744	Lichfield 126	2	63	Began 25 June (1742); via Birmingham.	20
Apr & May 1653, Mar/Aug 1654, Apr 1657/8 (S 1673), Mar 1678, Apr 1683, June & July 1693, June 1694, Apr 1698, Apr 1706, Apr & June 1709, Sept 1715, Apr 1738/49	York 202	4	51	Began 1, 26 Apr, 18 Mar, 12, 21, 24 Apr (1657/8/78/1706/38/49). Dep 5 a.m. (1653), London <c.6.30 a.m. (1683>; 5 a.m. (1706), 4 a.m., York 5 a.m. (1749). 2 firms; Stamford 2 days, Bawtry 3 days (1658). Diarist Ferrybridge-London only (1693-8).	22, 3, 2, 4, 23-31
Mar, May & Aug 1654, July 1706	York-Newcastle 81	2	41	Overnight at Darlington, hence 48 and 33 miles; diarist York-Durham only (1706).	22, 8
Apr 1658, Apr or May 1702/4/5/8 (2)/12/14, June 1723	Wakefield 185	4	46		2, 25, 24, 28
Aug 1733	York 202	5	(40)	Began 27 Aug; Stamford-York 3 days, Stamford-London 2 days; apparently the winter timing (see Nov 1733 below).	12
May 1734	Edinburgh 406	9	45	Via Berwick; claimed to be 3 days sooner than any other coach.	27
Apr 1658 (S 1673), 7 Mar 1677 (S 1677, June 1725), Apr 1750	Exeter 182	4	46	Began 26 Apr; Salisbury 2 days, Bridport 3 days (1658). 1725 source is fictional account of journey. Began 16 Apr (1750).	2, 4, 32-3
Apr 1738	Exeter 182	3	61*	Began 24 Apr; overnight at Sutton and Dorchester.	12
(b)					
Apr 1671, Sept 1733, Mar 1734/9/40/3/50	Beccles 110	2	55*	Dep Beccles and Ipswich 5 a.m. (1750). Overnight at Ipswich (1733-50), hence 70 and 40 miles; see Ipswich below.	34-5

May 1691, Mar 1730/44/5, Apr 1746, Mar 1747/9	Birmingham 120-3, 111	3	40-1, 37	Began 6 Apr, 26 Mar, 1 Apr, 23, 6 Mar (1730/44/5/7/9). Dep Birmingham 6 a.m. (1691). Dep 4 a.m. (1730/45-7). Via Banbury (1691), Daventry (1730), Islip and Warwick (1744), Aylesbury (1747).	36-7, 20, 12
May 1731	Birmingham 120	2½	48	Began 24 May; dep London 5 a.m., Birmingham 6 a.m.; via Banbury.	38
June 1744, May 1745/6, S 1747/9, Apr & June 1750	Birmingham 122-3	2	61-2*	Began 12 June, 28, 20 May, 17 Apr (1744-6/50). Dep 4 a.m. (1744), 3 a.m. (1745/6/50). Via Islip and Warwick (1744-6), Oxford and Stratford UA (1750).	20, 12
May 1728, Apr 1745	Blandford 113	2	57*	Dep London 5 a.m., Blandford 4 a.m.; overnight at Basingstoke; 4 passengers (1728). Began 20 May, 17 Apr.	12, 33
Apr 1737, May 1738	Boston 114	3	38	Began 28 Apr; dep London 4 a.m., Boston 6 a.m.; overnight at Peterborough.	12
1667, Apr 1718, Mar-Sept 1719, Mar 1720, Sept 1721, May 1724, Apr 1730, Mar 1733/48/9	Bristol 122 and Bath	3	41	Dep 5 a.m.; summer assumed (1667). Dep London 6 a.m., Bristol 3 a.m. (1733). Bath-London only in 1667/1721/48/9.	39-42, 12, 43
Apr 1709, May 1711, Apr 1718, June 1718 (2), Mar 1719/20, May 1721 (2), Apr 1723, May 1724, Apr 1726/8/30/3/48/9	Bristol 122 and Bath	2	61*	Began 28 Apr (1718), 30 Mar to Bath (until Sept), c.9 Apr to Bristol (until late Aug) (1719), 28 Mar to Bath (1720), 1, 4, 1, 6, 2, 4, 3 Apr (1723/6/8/30/3/48/9). Dep Bristol 1 a.m. (1730/3), London 4 a.m. (1733). Arr after 9 p.m. at Newbury, near 8 at London (1718). Only Sandy Lane-London (1718/21), Bath-London 1748/9.	21, 40, 44, 42, 12, 43
Apr 1695	Doncaster 169	4	42	Began 23 Apr; via Nottingham.	36
June 1720	Dorchester 129	3	43		40
May 1728/50	Dorchester 129	2	65*	Salisbury in 1 day, hence 84 and 39 miles; 4 passengers; dep 6 a.m. (1728). Overnight at Andover; dep 11 p.m. (1750). Began 27, 21 May.	45, 33

Date	Destination			Notes	Refs
(S 1713), Mar or Apr 1731/38-42, May 1745, Mar or Apr 1746-50	Gloucester 108	2	54*	Began 15 Mar, 3, 9, 7 Apr, 30, 29 Mar, 7 Apr, 30, 30 Mar, 11 Apr, 20 Mar, 20 Mar, 9 Apr (1731/8-42/6-50), 3 a.m. (1739), 3 a.m. (1746-8).	46-8
Aug 1715	Gloucester 108	1½	72		40
June 1722	Ross 124	2½	50*	Dep Ross 1 p.m.; overnight at Gloucester and Oxford.	48
S 1736	King's Lynn 112	2	61	Via Essex road and Bury St Edmunds.	12
June 1714, Mar 1732, Aug 1733, Apr 1734	Lincoln 139	3	46	Began 27 Mar, 8 Apr (1732/4). Via Huntingdon and Grantham (1714).	9, 31, 49
May 1732/4, Apr 1743	Lincoln 139	2	70	Dep 3 a.m.; overnight at Huntingdon (1743); Began 8, 13 May, 11 Apr.	31, 49
Sept 1666, Apr & Sept 1739, Mar 1740, June 1741	Norwich 110, 113	2	55*, 57	Via Essex road; began 18, 2 Apr, 11 June (1739-41). 4 sets of horses between Bury and London (1741).	50-2
(1708-10), May 1710	Norwich 110	1	110	Began 29 May, for June and July only; dep 2 a.m. (1710).	53, 52
June 1698/1705, July 1717, 13 May 1724 [June 1724, c.9 May 1726], Apr 1738/42	Nottingham/Derby (separate services) 126/7	2	63/4*	Dep 4 a.m.; Derby stage began 5 July (1698). Expected to arrive at 6 or 8 p.m. (June 1724). Began 8 May, 26 Apr (1738/42). June 1724 & 1726 examples are Nottingham only and Derby only.	21, 54, 40, 37, 5, 55, 12
July 1698	Mansfield 140	2⅓	60*	An extension of the Nottingham coach (14 miles); dep London 4 a.m.; arr Mansfield 8 a.m., dep 3 p.m.; began 5 July.	54
May & 26 Sept 1699, 23 Mar 1700	Mansfield 140	3	47*	Advertised as until 23 Oct or later (Sept 1699).	54
Mar & Aug 1733	Sherborne 120	3	40	Began 5 Mar; dep Sherborne 5 a.m.; overnight at Salisbury; 'two fresh sets of horses'.	12

June 1734	Sherborne 120	2	60	Began 24 June; dep 2 a.m.; overnight at Andover; 4 passengers; 'three fresh sets of horses'.	12
July 1672	Tamworth 118	3	39	Diarist alighted at Atherstone. Overnight at Dunstable and Watford Gap.	17
15 Mar 1730	Taunton 151	4	38		36
May 1733/4	Taunton 151	3	50	Began 22, 14 May. Dep London 5 a.m., Taunton 3 a.m. Overnight at Shaftesbury. 'Three fresh sets of horses on the road'.	12
Mar 1702	Wolverhampton 134	3	45*	Began 30 Mar; dep 6 a.m.	54
(S 1675), Apr 1706 (Mar 1717), May 1738, Apr 1742, May 1744/7/9/50	Worcester 115	2	58	Began 11 Mar, 8 May, 5 Apr, 28, 18, 2, 1 May (1717/38/42/47/9/50). Dep 4 a.m. (1738/47), 3 a.m. (1742-4/9-50). Overnight at Islip (1675, 1706), Oxford (1738); via Oxford (1742/4). London to Moreton or Stow in 1½ days (1717).	56, 18, 57-8
July 1689, 6 Apr 1717, Mar 1741/50	Yarmouth 131, 127	2	64-6*	<Dep London 3.30 a.m.>(1689). Began 23, 19 Mar (1741/50). Dep 2 a.m. (1750).	59, 40, 51, 35
(c)					
June 1657, Aug 1661 (2), June 1688, Apr 1690, July 1692, May 1720, Apr 1737, Mar 1738/50	Canterbury 56	1	56*	Began 14, 4 Apr, 27, 19 Mar (1690, 1737/8/50). Dep London 5-6 a.m.(1657); <Canterbury 6 a.m. (1661)>; 5 a.m. (1690). Diarist Gravesend-Canterbury only (1661). Dined at Rochester (1720).	3, 60, 36, 61-3
June 1658	Canterbury 56	2	28	Dep Canterbury 9 a.m., London 10 a.m.; overnight at Rochester.	2
Aug 1654, May 1667/8 (2), June 1699, July 1702, Oct 1713, July 1714 (2), June 1723 (2), May 1737	Cambridge 57	1	57	<Dep c.6 a.m. (1668); 5 a.m. (1702).> Via Bishops Stortford (1668).	64, 15, 65-8, 24, 69, 51

					70-1
June & Sept 1667	Oxford 58	2	29	Overnight at Beaconsfield.	70, 6, 36, 18, 72, 46, 40, 73, 69, 37, 74, 12
Apr & Aug 1669, Apr 1671/2, Apr & May 1687, S 1692/1703, 30 Mar & May 1693, 20 Mar, Apr & June 1703, May 1704 (2) [S 1713], 14 Mar 1719, Aug 1719, May 1720, May 1723 (2), Mar 1728/9, June 1733, Feb or Mar 1734-9, June 1741, Mar 1747	Oxford 58	1	58*	Dep 6 a.m. (1669-72), 5-6 a.m. (1693), 4 a.m. (1738-9). Began 26 Apr, 15 May, 29 Apr, 11 Mar, 24 Feb, 6 Mar, 14, 20 Feb (1669/71/2/1734-8).	
(d)					
June 1654	Chipping Norton 77	2	39		22
May 1658	Dover 71	2	36		2
24 Mar 1664	Salisbury 84	2	42		75
(1671-1702)	General	1	40-50*	But mentions Oxford and Cambridge as one-day destinations; corrected to 50-60 miles in 1704 edition.	53
Aug 1675	Colchester 52	1	52	Via Ingatestone; <dep 5.30 a.m.>	76
June 1676, July 1682, 29 May 1710, Aug 1713, May 1717, Apr 1722/3, 28 May 1723, Apr 1728-30, May 1731, Mar or Apr 1735-8/44/7-50	Northampton 67	1	67*	Began 8, 1, 7, 20, 21, 19, 18, 10 Apr, 19, 30 Mar, 4 Apr, 20, 19 Mar (1723/8/9/30/5-8/44/7-50). Dep 4 a.m. (1717-23/31), 3 a.m. (1728-30). With 3 sets of horses (1717-36).	15, 77, 49, 78, 12
July 1679	Banbury 76	1	76	Birmingham coach (via Solihull).	15
May 1680, Apr 1738	Newport Pagnell 52	1	52	Horses changed at Barnet and Dunstable (1680). Dep Newport 4 a.m., London 5 a.m.; fresh horses at St Albans (1738).	79, 12

Date	Place			Notes	Ref
June 1680	Ampthill 46	1	46	Bedford coach.	15
June 1683	Astrop Wells 73	1	73		36
Apr 1690/1705, May 1709	Banbury 76	1	76	2 firms; one began 21 Apr (1690). Began 16 May; dep 4 a.m. (1709).	36, 80
Apr 1694	Warwick 99	2	50	Dep Warwick 5 a.m.; London 6 a.m.; via Aylesbury.	36
14 May 1696 (1708-10), Mar 1731/8 (S 1739), Mar or Apr 1739-43/6-50	Cirencester 92	1	92*	Dep 3 a.m. (1696). Via Henley and Abingdon (1696, 1738). Began 25, 27, 26, 31, 16, 15, 21 Mar, 14 Apr, 23 Mar, 4, 3 Apr, 19 Mar (1731/8-43/6-50).	36, 53, 12, 48, 47
20 Aug 1696	Cirencester 92	2	46		36
Sept 1699	Oundle 78	2	39	Via Bedford; overnight at Silsoe.	81
21 May 1700	Melton Mowbray 105	1½	70*	Dep London 5 a.m., Melton 12 noon.	54
July 1703, 6 Mar 1708	Leicester 99	2½	40	Overnight at Woburn and Market Harborough (1703).	18, 21
Apr 1705	Stratford upon Avon 99	2	50	Began 3 Apr; dep London 4 a.m.; via Aylesbury and Banbury.	80
(1708-10), Apr 1738	Southampton 80	1	80	Began 17 Apr (1738).	53, 12
(1708-10), Mar 1737/9/50	Bury St Edmunds 76, 72	1	72-6	Began 21, 5, 19 Mar (1737/9/50). Dep London 3 a.m. (1737); dep 2 a.m. (1750). Via Sudbury (1737-9).	53, 82, 35
(May 1711)	Harwich 73	2	37	Overnight at Witham.	83

Date	Destination			Notes	Ref
May 1711 (c.1723), Sept 1733, Mar 1734-6/9/40/3/50	Ipswich 70	1	70*	Began 25, 17, 22, 26, 24, 21, 19 Mar (1734-6/9/40/3/50). Dep London 3 a.m. <1711> (1734/9-43), 2 a.m. (1750), Ipswich 3 a.m. (1739-43), 1 a.m. (1750).	83-4, 35
Sept 1718	Reading 42	1	42	Dined at Slough.	85
June 1720	Stony Stratford 54	1	54	Began 13 June.	40
May & June 1722, Mar, June & 9 Oct 1727, Sept 1734	Bury St Edmunds 72, 76	2	36-8	2 firms (1722/7). Began 28 May, 27 Mar (1722/7). Dep London 4 a.m. (1722), Bury 6 a.m., 7 a.m. (1722/7). Overnight at Bishop's Stortford (via Newmarket) and at Braintree.	82
23 Feb 1723, Apr 1727	Newbury 59	1	59*	Via Windsor and Reading; dep London <3 a.m.> (1723), 4 a.m., 4 passengers (1727).	44, 37
Apr 1723/43	Huntingdon 66	1	66	Dep 3 a.m. (1723). Began 2, 11 Apr.	37, 49
May 1724, June 1726, Apr 1734, Mar 1738, Apr 1746/8	Salisbury 84	1	84*	Began 25 May, 29 Apr, 27 Mar, 20, 11 Apr (1724/34/8/46/8). Dep 1 a.m., 11 p.m. (1724/48). Diarist Salisbury-Brentford only (1726).	40, 86, 12
May 1725	Lewes 49	1	49	Began 5 May; dep 5 a.m.	11
June 1725	Northampton 67	2	(34)	One-day coach delayed by flooding.	77
May 1726, Mar 1737	Leighton Buzzard 42	1	42	Dep 6 a.m.; via Hemel Hempstead (1737). Began 7 May, 26 Mar.	37, 78
Apr 1727/36/8/9	Winchester 66	1	66*	Began 3, 17, 9 Apr (1727/38/9). Dep 12 midnight (1727), 11, via Farnham (1736).	37, 12
Apr 1727, Mar 1737/9, Apr 1750	Sudbury 57	1	57	Began 21, 5 Mar, 23 Apr (1737/9/50). Dep London 4 a.m. (1727).	82, 35

Apr 1733, June 1741	Abingdon 59	1	59*		12
Mar 1750	Harwich 73	1	73*	Began 21 Mar; dep London 11 p.m.	35
(e)					
Mar 1730	Bristol-Salisbury 52	1	52	Began 25 Mar.	42
Mar 1730	Bath-Exeter 84	2½	34	Began 24 Mar; overnight at Taunton.	36

(2) Winter

Date	Destination and miles	Days	mpd	Comments	References
(a)					
Feb 1669 (W 1673), Jan 1686, Feb 1689/90/3/1702, Jan & Feb 1712, 25-30 Oct 1731, Mar 1740	Chester 188	6	31	Diarists sometimes joined or alighted at Whitchurch 1686-1712.	16, 4, 6, 87-8, 7, 74, 89
Jan 1679/80, Feb & Dec 1681, Nov 1682, Dec 1683, 10-12 May 1711	Coventry 98	3	33	By Chester or Lichfield coaches.	15, 17, 7
6-9 May 1679, 16-19 Oct 1683, Mar 1684, Feb 1686, Dec 1700	Lichfield 126	4	32	Diarists sometimes between Coleshill and London only.	15, 17, 6, 18
Mar 1707	Warrington 196	6	33		9

W 1742-3, Dec 1743, Feb & Nov 1744/5	Lichfield 126	3	42	Began 12 Dec (1743). Via Birmingham.	20
Dec 1654, Oct 1667 (W 1673), Feb 1679, Oct 1686, Mar 1692, Nov 1702, Feb 1703/5, Mar 1709, 5-11 Apr 1711, 13-18 Oct 1712, Jan 1734	York 202	6	34	Diarist joined or alighted at Ferrybridge in the 1692/1703/5/12 examples (alighting on the 6th day).	90, 71, 4, 24, 14, 26, 28, 25, 29, 49
Dec 1654	Barton upon Humber 174	5	35		90
Oct 1656	Doncaster 165	5	33		91
Feb 1683	York 202	5	(40)	By 'hackney coach'; not certain this was the stage-coach.	92
Nov 1695, Feb 1698, 6-11 Apr 1713, 14-19 Oct 1717, Mar 1723	Wakefield 185	6	31		26, 25, 24
Dec 1707	Stamford 93	3	31	York coach.	28
Oct 1712	Edinburgh 406	13	31	Began 13 Oct.	93
Jan 1729	York-Newcastle 81	3	27	Dep 5 a.m.	94
Nov 1733	York 202	5	40		12
Dec 1655 (W 1673/7)	Exeter 182	6	30		91, 4, 32
(b)					
(Dec 1699)	Dorchester 129	3	43		95

Oct 1731, Nov 1738/47/9	Gloucester 108	3	36	Began 9 Oct, 9, 6 Nov (1731/47/9). Dep 6 a.m. (1747/9).	47, 96, 48
Dec 1736, 3 Oct 1741	King's Lynn 112	3	37	Dep 7 a.m.; 5 sets of horses (1741). Via Essex road and Bury.	12, 52
28-30 Mar 1664	Norwich 110	2½	44	Overnight at Barton Mills and Bishop's Stortford; arr London 2 p.m. on 3rd day; possibly transitional timing.	97
20 Oct & Nov 1739, Sept 1740, 3 Oct 1741	Norwich 110, 113	3	37-8	2 firms, via both Newmarket and Essex roads. Overnight at Bury (1739). Began 30 Sept; dep London 7 a.m. (1740). Began 5 Oct; dep 7 a.m.; 5 sets of horses (1741).	51-2
Mar 1681	Nottingham 126	4	32	Assumes 1 further day for c.35 miles between diarist's home and Nottingham.	92
26 Sept 1699, 8 Oct 1700, 17 Feb 1702, 6 Mar 1708, Feb 1725, Feb & Apr 1735, Feb 1737	Nottingham/ Derby (separate services) 126/7	3	(42)	Advertised as until 23 Oct or later (1699). Dep London 6 a.m.; 2 days to Market Harborough (1700). Began 8, 24 Feb (Derby 3 Apr), 28 Feb (1725/35/7). Evidently a transitional timing at first. Nottingham only in 1700/2.	54, 21, 37, 98, 78, 12
2 Nov 1699, 22 Oct 1700	Nottingham 126	3½	36		54
Nov 1699	Mansfield 140	4	35		54
25 Apr 1683, Feb 1685	Tamworth 118	4	30	Via Northampton and Dunstable.	15
Dec 1654	Broom (Warks) (115)	3	38	i.e. Worcester coach in 3 days. Broom is off the route, in SW Warwickshire.	99
29 Mar 1697, 21-3 Mar 1700, 18-20 Feb 1703 (Mar 1717), Oct 1742/8/9/50	Worcester 115	3	38	Dep London 6 a.m. (1697). London to Moreton or Stow in 2½ days (1717). Began 3, 2, 22 Oct (1748-50).	36, 18, 57-8
Jan 1705	Evesham (115)	3½	29	i.e. Worcester coach in 4 days. Overnight at High Wycombe, Islip and Moreton.	72

Mar 1687, 21-3 Oct & Nov 1689, Feb 1690, Oct 1717/43	Yarmouth 131, 127	3	42-4	Began 4 Oct (1743). Dep <Yarmouth c.5 a.m. (Oct 1689)>, London 8 a.m. (1717), 6 a.m., Yarmouth 4 a.m. (1743).	100, 59, 40, 52
(c)					
28 Oct & Nov 1661	Canterbury to Gravesend 37	1	37	<Dep Canterbury 7 a.m.>	60
Jan 1721, Dec 1722, Nov 1723, Sept 1737/8, Oct 1750	Canterbury 56	2	28	Began 26, 25 Sept, 1 Oct (1737/8/50). Dep 7 a.m. (1750). Overnight at Rochester (1721-3).	101, 69, 66, 63
28-9 Oct 1717	Cambridge 57	2	29		102
Jan 1670, Dec 1686, Jan & Nov 1687 Mar 1688, Nov 1691, W 1692/1703, Mar 1703, Nov 1704/5, Mar 1713, Dec 1721, W 1727-8, Dec 1731, Feb 1733	Oxford 58	2	29	Overnight at Loudwater (1686), Beaconsfield (1687/8), Wycombe (1691, 1704/5/13/28/31/3).	88, 6, 70, 18, 72, 28, 37, 73-4
Oct 1735	Oxford 58	1½	39	Began 27 Oct, dep Oxford 6 a.m., arr London 11 a.m.; dep London 5 a.m., arr Oxford 11 a.m.	12
(d)					
19-20 Apr 1677	Bedford 54	2	27	Overnight at St Albans; winter assumed.	16
Nov 1679	Marlborough 77	2	39		103
Feb 1687, Jan 1706 (2), Feb 1723	Reading 42	1	42	Via Colnbrook (1687). Dined Slough (1723).	6, 18, 44
Feb 1702, Sept 1731	Northampton 67	1½	(45)	Possibly the Nottingham coach (1702). Arr noon 2nd day; began 20 Sept (1731).	54, 12
W 1709-10	Banbury 76	2	38	'If possible'.	80

Date	Destination and miles	Days	mpd	Comments	References
16-17 Oct 1712, 20-1 Apr 1713, Nov 1715, 17 Oct 1717, Dec 1732, Sept 1735	Northampton 67	2	34	Began 4 Dec, 15 Sept (1732/5).	77, 40, 49, 12, 78
21 Oct 1725	Oundle 78	2	39	Overnight at Biggleswade; dep London 5 a.m., Oundle 6 a.m.; winter assumed.	49
Sept 1733	Ipswich 70	2	35	Began 15 Sept.	35
Nov 1734	Portsmouth 73	2	37	Dep 6 a.m.	12
2 Oct 1735 (W 1739), W 1740	Cirencester 92	2	46		12
30 Oct 1738, W 1739-40	Sudbury 57	1	57	Dep London 4 a.m. (1738)	82
3 Oct 1741	Bury St Edmunds 72	2	36	Dep 7 a.m.; 4 sets of horses.	52
3 Oct 1741	Sudbury 57	2	28	Dep 7 a.m.; 3 sets of horses.	52
3 Oct 1741	Braintree 41	1	41	Dep 7 a.m.; 2 sets of horses.	52

(3) Coach-waggons and caravans

Apart from the Warwick example, the coach-waggons here are identified from the speed (and in 1657 also the fare) rather than being specified as such.

Date	Destination and miles	Days	mpd	Comments	References
19 Oct 1648	Southampton 80	3	27	Overnight at Staines and Alton (hence 20, 31 and 30 miles).	104

May 1657	Coventry 93	*2½-3*	*31-37*		3
May & June 1659, Sept 1660/79, May & Sept 1682	Coventry 93	3	31	Overnight at Towcester and Redbourn (hence 26, 36 and 31 miles) (1679/82).	15
Oct 1660, Nov & Dec 1682	Coventry 93	4	23	Presumably the winter timing.	15
8-13 Oct 1677, May 1686, June 1698	Newcastle-under-Lyme 151	6	25	First 2 nights at Bruerton and Allesley (hence 24 and 31 miles) (1677). Lodged at Coventry Tues (58 miles), Weedon Wed (23 miles), Fenny Stratford Thurs (23 miles), leaving 47 miles (1698).	16, 88
1-3 Apr 1678	Warwick 99	3	33	'Coatch-wagon'; arr by 3 on 3rd day.	105
Jan 1710	Gosport 82	2	41	Caravan; dep London 6 a.m.; 6 horses.	11
May 1718	Reading 42	1	42	'Berlin coach'; began 19 May; dep 5 a.m.	40
Apr 1722/3	Bury St Edmunds 72	2	36	Caravan; began 9, 23 Apr; dep Bury 7 a.m., London 6 a.m.; overnight at Braintree.	82
May & June 1740, *Mar 1749*	Devizes 91	2	46	Caravan; <dep 3 a.m.>; overnight at Reading; arr London 6 p.m. (May 1740). Overnight at Theale; arr Devizes 5.15 p.m. (June 1740). Began 27 Mar; dep Devizes 1 a.m., London 2 a.m. (1749).	106, 12
Nov 1743	Northampton 67	1½-2	34-45	'Ge-hoe coach', carrying 8; 6 horses; began 24 Oct.	78

Notes

Several entries are included where the journey time is not directly stated but the coach is described as flying and it is clear what flying meant; this applies to Canterbury in 1688-92, Oxford in 1693, 1719/29/47, and Bristol and Bath in 1709/11/Apr 1718/19/20/3/4/6; also the non-flying Birmingham coach which was contrasted with the two-day coach in 1747/9.

Seasons: Until the 1730s references from May to Sept are assumed to be summer timings (except in two cases where winter schedules clearly continued into May, and the Nottingham example in Sept 1699); from Nov to Feb they are assumed to be winter timings, except the Newbury example in 1723; in Mar, Apr and Oct they are placed in the season which seems most appropriate, the few doubtful cases being indicated as such. The same is largely true in the 1730s, though with summer timings at Oxford in Feb and winter timings at Northampton, Ipswich, Canterbury and Norwich in Sept.

Dates: Dates are in normal type for diary or other references to a journey already completed, italics for advertisements and brackets for other references. '&' indicates more than one journey or advertisement; '(2)' indicates more than one actual journey. 'W' and 'S' indicate winter and summer. Dates set out as, e.g. March 1740/3 or March 1740-2, indicate an advertisement in that month in each of those years.

Days: Sundays are not counted.

Miles: See p. 239 below.

mpd (miles per day): The figure is in brackets when the timing is clearly not a normal summer or winter one. An asterisk indicates that the coach was described as a flying coach, even if in only some of the references.

Comments: Departure times are in diagonal brackets < > if from diaries rather than advertisements.

References

1. *Publick Intelligencer,* 16 Mar 1657. **2.** *Mercurius Politicus,* 9 Apr 1657, 8 Apr, 13 May, 17 June 1658, 24 Mar 1659. **3.** *Publick Adviser,* 26 May, 2 & 22 June 1657. **4.** *Harleian miscellany,* vol. 8 (1746), p. 544. **5.** National Library of Wales, MS 1600E, No. 390 (1679), Ottley/Pitchford 2615 (1724), ditto 2617 (1725). **6.** Aston, 920 MD 173, 7-13 Jan, 9-12 Feb, 6-7 Dec 1686, 28-9 Jan, 21 Feb, 19 Apr, 17 May, 8-9 Nov 1687, 5-6 Mar 1688, 7-13 Feb 1689, 16-20 May 1690; 920 MD 174, 9-10 Nov 1691, 23-8 Feb 1693, 12-16 Apr 1700, 16-20 Apr 1701; 920 MD 175, 11-15 July 1701. **7.** Henry, 12-15 July, 31 July-3 Aug 1710, 10-12 May, 30 July-2 Aug 1711, 21-6 Jan, 18-23 Feb, 12-15 May 1712, 20-3 July, 12-15 Aug 1713. **8.** Blundell, vol. 110, p. 114; vol. 112, pp. 208-9; vol. 114, pp. 105, 116. **9.** Nicholson, 24-9 Mar 1707, 14-16 June 1714, 23-7 May 1718. **10.** Symson, Nos. 1324, 1554, 1591. **11.** *Daily Courant,* 27 Jan 1710, 3 Apr 1721, 24 Apr 1725. **12.** LEP, 9 May 1728, 18 Mar 1729, 25 Mar, 1 May, 21 Sept 1731, 2 Dec 1732, 15 Feb, 27 Mar, 21 Apr, 17 May, 21 & 30 Aug, 27 Nov 1733, 7 Mar, 23 Apr, 9 May, 4 June, 26 Nov 1734, 18 Feb, 2 & 30 Oct 1735, 6 Mar, 20 Apr, 4 Dec 1736, 8 & 12 Feb, 26 Apr 1737, 16 Feb, 14 Mar, 6, 11, 15, 18 & 22 Apr, 2 May 1738, 6 Mar, 5 & 12 Apr 1739 (latter in advert for house at Poulton), 25 Mar 1740, 4 June 1741, 10 Apr 1742, 21 June 1744, 4 Apr 1745, 17 Apr 1746, 10 & 12 Mar 1747, 29 Mar 1748, 25 Feb, 18 Mar 1749, 14 Apr, 2 & 21 June 1750. **13.** *Adams's Weekly Courant,* 24 Mar 1747, 19 June 1750. **14.** Diary of Thomas Cartwright, British Library, Add MS 24357, 28 Oct-3 Nov 1686, 7-12 Oct 1687. **15.** Dugdale, pp. 102-47. **16.** Newcome, vol. 1, p. 179, vol. 2, pp. 220, 222-3, 239. **17.** Dugdale (2), 11-13 July 1672, 5-7 Jan 1680, 8-10 Feb, 25-7 Oct, 28-30 Dec 1681, 28-30 Nov 1682, 15-17 Aug, 16-19 Oct, 18-21 Dec 1683. **18.** David Robertson (ed.), *Diary of Francis Evans, Secretary to Bishop Lloyd, 1699-1706,* Worcestershire Historical Society (1903), pp. 14-15, 42-3, 78, 81-2, 108, 120, 124, 126. **19.** *Warwickshire and Staffordshire Journal,* 20 July 1738. **20.** *Aris's Birmingham Gazette,* 12 Apr, 21 & 28 June 1742, 11 July, 5 Dec 1743, 6 Feb, 12 Mar, 23 Apr, 4 June, 5 Nov 1744, 11 Feb, 11 Mar, 13 May, 18 Nov 1745, 14 Apr, 12 May 1746. **21.** *Post-Man,* 23 June 1698, 18 Mar, 6 Apr 1703, 6 Mar 1708, 18 Apr 1709, 12 May 1711. **22.** *Perfect Diurnall,* 11 Apr 1653; *Severall Proceedings of State Affaires,* 5 May 1653, 23 Mar, 22 June, 24 Aug 1654; *A Perfect Diurnall: or, Occurrences,* 29 May, 21 Aug 1654. **23.** Lambeth Palace Library, MS 1834, f. 24. **24.** Thoresby, vol. 1, pp. 154-6, 161-4; vol. 2, pp. 207, 229-30, 233, 355, 382. **25.** Diary of Sir Walter Calverley, British Library, Add MS 27418, 5-8 June 1693, 6-9 May 1702, 22-5 May 1704, 19-24 Feb, 23-6 Apr 1705, 3-6 May 1708, 13-18 Oct 1712, 6-11 Apr 1713, 14-19 Oct 1717. **26.** Diary of Sir Walter Calverley, in *Yorkshire diaries and autobiographies in the seventeenth and eighteenth centuries,* Surtees Society, vol. 77 (1886), pp. 49, 55, 63, 68, 74. **27.** Charles G. Harper, *The Great North Road* (1922), vol. 1, pp. 34, 35. **28.** Nicholson (2), vol. 2, pp. 185-6, 193; vol. 4, pp. 16, 51-2, 57, 63; vol. 35, pp. 94-5. **29.** G.D. Henderson and H.H. Porter (eds.), *James Gordon's diary 1692-1710,* Third Spalding Club (1949), pp. 176, 179. **30.** Clyve Jones and Geoffrey Holmes (eds.), *The London diaries of William Nicholson Bishop of Carlisle 1702-1718* (1985), p. 634. **31.** *York Courant,* 11 Apr 1732, 25 Apr 1738, 18 Apr 1749. **32.** *The Mercury: or Advertisements concerning Trade,* 7 Mar 1677; E 112/598/541; Mrs Manley, *A stage-coach journey to Exeter* (1725). **33.** *Salisbury Journal,* 17 Mar 1745, 23 Apr, 28 May 1750. **34.** Suffolk RO (Lowestoft), ref 1227, S.W. Rix Beccles Collections, Division IV, No. IV, f. 337 (reference kindly supplied by Peter Edwards). **35.** *Ipswich Gazette,* 8 Sept 1733, 16 Mar 1734, 15 Mar 1735, 20 Mar 1736; *Ipswich Journal,* 10 Mar 1739, 15 Mar 1740, 19 Mar 1743, 10 Mar, 21 Apr 1750. **36.** *London Gazette,* 21 June 1683, 14 June 1688, 24 Apr, 5 & 12 May 1690, 11 May 1691, 30 Mar, 15 May 1693, 19 Apr 1694, 9 May 1695, 14 May, 20 Aug 1696, 29 Mar 1697, 15 Mar 1730. I owe the 1730 reference to Robin Bush. **37.** *Daily Post,* 25 Mar 1723, 13 May 1724, 3 Feb 1725, 28 Apr 1726, 29 Mar, 25 Apr 1727, 28 Mar

1728, 2 Apr 1729, 28 Mar 1730. **38.** John Lewis, *Printed ephemera* (1969), p. 43. **39.** R.C. Tombs, *The King's post* (1905), p. 24. **40.** *Evening Post*, 4 Aug, 24 Nov 1715, 6 Apr, 2 July, 5 Oct 1717, 19 Apr, 27 May 1718, 14 & 26 Mar, 9 & 29 Apr, 29 Aug, 10 Sept 1719, 29 Mar, 4 & 28 June 1720, 19 Mar 1723, 21 May 1724, 29 Mar 1726. **41.** Alan Savile (ed.), *Secret comment: the diaries of Gertrude Savile 1721-1757*, Thoroton Society Record Series, vol. 41 (1997), pp. 5-6, 10. **42.** *Farley's Bristol News-Paper*, 30 Mar 1728, 4 Apr 1730. **43.** *Bath Journal*, 21 Mar 1748, 27 Mar 1749. **44.** Diary of Thomas Smith, Wiltshire RO, 161/170, 23-4, 27-8 June 1718, 1-2, 8-9 May 1721, 15-16, 23 Feb 1723. **45.** *Brice's Weekly Journal*, 21 June 1728. **46.** Bodleian Library, University Archives, Chancellor's Court, 134/1/1, 1713 articles. **47.** Herbert, pp. 45-9. **48.** *Gloucester Journal*, 11 June 1722, 28 Mar 1738, 20 Mar, 3 Apr 1739, 18 Mar 1740, 10 & 24 Mar 1741, 9 & 30 Mar 1742, 14 May 1745, 1 & 8 Apr 1746, 17 & 24 Mar, 10 Nov 1747, 29 Mar, 5 Apr 1748, 14 & 28 Mar, 7 Nov 1749, 13 Mar, 10 Apr 1750. **49.** *Stamford Mercury*, 23 May, 17 Oct 1717, 21 Oct 1725, 23 Aug 1733, 3 Jan, 28 Mar, 2 May 1734, 7 Apr 1743. **50.** Robert H. Hill (ed.), *The correspondence of Thomas Corie, Town Clerk of Norwich, 1664-1687*, Norfolk Record Society, vol. 27 (1956), p. 20. **51.** *Norwich Mercury*, 14 May 1737, 7 & 14 Apr, 22 Sept, 20 Oct, 10 Nov 1739, 22 Mar, 20 Sept 1740, 14 Mar 1741. **52.** *Norwich Gazette*, 17 Dec 1709, 20 May 1710, 30 May, 3 & 24 Oct 1741, 24 Sept 1743. **53.** Edward Chamberlayne, *Angliae notitia: or, the present state of England* (became John Chamberlayne, *Magna Britanniae notitia*), part 2 (1671-1710 editions), section on the post. **54.** *Flying Post*, 12 July 1698, 13 May, 26 Sept, 2 Nov 1699, 23 Mar, 21 May, 8 & 22 Oct 1700, 19 Feb, 14 Mar, 2 Apr 1702, 11 June 1705. **55.** John Daniel Leader, *The records of the Burgery of Sheffield* (1897), p. lvii. **56.** John Ogilby, *Britannia* (1675), p. 3. **57.** Gloucestershire RO, D153/19. **58.** *Weekly Worcester Journal*, 5 May 1738, 26 Mar, 17 Sept 1742, 25 May 1744, 1 May 1747; *Worcester Journal*, 22 Sept 1748, 13 Apr, 21 Sept 1749, 29 Mar, 11 Oct 1750. **59.** Davies, pp. 28-30, 55-7, 64-5, 81-2. **60.** Schellinks, pp. 45, 63, 65, 69. Dates corrected from new style. **61.** *City Mercury*, 4 July 1692. **62.** Anonymous diary, British Library, Stowe MS 790, 7 May 1720. **63.** *Kentish Post*, 23 Mar, 17 Sept 1737, 15 Mar, 16 Sept 1738, 17 Mar, 22 Sept 1750. **64.** *Perfect Diurnall*, 28 Aug 1654. **65.** Pepys, vol. 9, 23 and 26 May 1668. **66.** Diary of Edward Southwell, British Library, Eg MS 1628, 13 June 1699; *ibid.*, Add MS 34753, p. 30. **67.** Diary of Francis Burman, in J.E.B. Mayor, *Cambridge under Queen Anne* (1911), p. 115. **68.** *A pattern for young students in the university, set forth in the life of Mr Ambrose Bonwicke* (1729), pp. 96-7. **69.** E. Edwards Beardsley (ed.), *Life and correspondence of Samuel Johnson, D.D.* (1874), pp. 26, 45, 48-50. **70.** Wood, vol. 21, pp. 109, 153, 155, 167, 220-3, 245; *Oxford almanack* (1692, 1703). **71.** Donald Crawford (ed.), *Journals of Sir John Lauder, Lord Fountainhall*, Scottish History Society, vol. 36 (1900), pp. 168, 175-6, 180. **72.** Diary of Francis Evans, Worcestershire RO, 3943, 8 and 17 May, 13-14 Nov 1704, 8-12 Jan 1705. **73.** Diary of Erasmus Philips, in Douglas Macleane (ed.), *A history of Pembroke College, Oxford*, Oxford Historical Society, vol. 33 (1897), pp. 323, 327. **74.** C.L.S. Linnell (ed.), *The diaries of Thomas Wilson, D.D. 1731-37 and 1750* (1964), pp. 39, 44, 93-4, 102. **75.** *The Newes*, 24 Mar 1664. **76.** Anonymous diary, Bodleian Library, MS Rawl D1114, 19 Aug 1675. **77.** Diary of Sir Justinian Isham, Northamptonshire RO, I.L. 2686, 29 May 1710, 17 Oct 1712, 20-1 Apr, 27 Aug 1713, 28 May 1723, 7-8 June 1725. **78.** *Northampton Mercury*, 16 Apr 1722, 8 Apr 1723, 18 Mar 1728, 31 Mar 1729, 13 Apr 1730, 10 Feb, 28 Apr, 8 Sept 1735, 19 Apr 1736, 7 Mar, 11 Apr 1737, 27 Mar 1738, 28 Nov 1743, 19 Mar 1744, 23 Mar 1747, 28 Mar 1748, 13 Mar 1749, 12 Mar 1750. **79.** H.W. Robinson and W. Adams (eds.), *The diary of Robert Hooke … 1672-1680* (1968), p. 445. **80.** Warwickshire RO, CR 1368/4, Nos. 1-2. **81.** Edmond Malone (ed.), *The critical and miscellaneous prose works of John Dryden* (1800), vol. 1, part 2, pp. 87-8. **82.** *Suffolk Mercury*, 1 Apr, 21 May, 25 June 1722, 22 Apr 1723, 20 Mar, 24 Apr, 5 June, 9 Oct 1727, 23 Sept 1734, 28 Feb 1737, 30 Oct 1738, 12 Feb, 9 & 16 Apr 1739. **83.** Diary of James Thornhill, British Library, Add MS 34788, pp. 3, 21. **84.** Defoe, p. 72. **85.** Louis B. Wright and Marion Tinling (eds.), *William Byrd of Virginia: the London diary (1717-1721) and other writings* (1958), pp. 180, 300. **86.** Doreen Slatter (ed.), *The diary of Thomas Naish*, Wiltshire Archaeological and Natural History Society, Records Branch, vol. 20 (1965), p. 79. **87.** Diary of Roger Whitley, Bodleian Library, MS Eng. Hist. *c.*711, 6-12 Feb 1690. **88.** Diary of Henry Newcome junior, Manchester Local Studies Unit, microfilm 136, 22-3 Jan 1670, 3-7 May 1686, 14-16 June 1698, 18-25 Feb 1702. **89.** Thomas Pennant, *The journey from Chester to London* (1782), p. 137. **90.** *Severall Proceedings in Parliament*, 28 Dec 1654. **91.** Rawdon, pp. 70-1, 81. **92.** Andrew Browning (ed.), *Memoirs of Sir John Reresby* (1991), pp. 169, 219, 288. **93.** *Newcastle Courant*, 13 Oct 1712. **94.** *York Mercury*, 24 Dec 1728. **95.** Somerset RO, DD/X/WH1 1a. **96.** Jackman, p. 137n. **97.** Diary of Dr Edward Browne, British Library, Sloane MS 1906, ff. 62-3. **98.** *Derby Mercury*, 27 Mar 1735. **99.** Diary of Sir Fulwar Skipwith, Warwickshire RO, MI 213, 21 Dec 1654. **100.** Richard F.E. Ferrier and John A.H. Ferrier (eds.), *The journal of Major Richard Ferrier, M.P.*, Camden Soc., new ser., vol. 53 (1895), p. 15. **101.** Anonymous diary, British Library, Add MS 60522, f. 65. **102.** Anthony Hammond's pocket-book, British Library, Add MS 22584, 28-9 Oct 1717. **103.** *English Reports*, vol. 89, pp. 836-7. **104.** John Chandler (ed.), *Travels through Stuart Britain: the adventures of John Taylor, the water poet* (1999), p. 209. **105.** *The diary of Henry Teonge … 1675 to 1679* (1825), pp. 229-30. **106.** Marjorie Reeves and Jean Morrison (eds.), *The diaries of Jeffery Whitaker, schoolmaster of Bratton, 1739-41*, Wiltshire Record Society, vol. 44 (1989), pp. 36, 38.

Stage-Coach Speeds, 1661-1768

(1) 1661-1742

Date	Journey and miles	Times	Hours	Comments	mph	Refs
	SUMMER					
Aug 1661	Canterbury-Gravesend 34	6 a.m. to 2 p.m.	7	Refreshments at Sittingbourne; delayed almost an hour by Chatham market; 1 hour allowed for these.	4.9	60
May 1668	London-Cambridge 57	6 a.m. to 9 p.m.	14	Dined.	4.1	65
May 1668	Cambridge-London 57	6 a.m. to c.7.45 p.m.	12¾	Dined. Arr 'before 8 a-clock'.	4.5	65
Apr 1669	Oxford-London 58	6 a.m. to 7 p.m.	12		4.8	70
1671-1702	London-Oxford or Cambridge 57-8		12	'Flying coaches make 40 or 50 miles in a day, as from London to Oxford or Cambridge, and that in the space of 12 hours, not counting the time for dining'.	4.8	53
Aug 1675	London-Colchester 52	5.30 a.m. to c.6.15 p.m.	10¾	Dining and 2 other stops. Arr 'a little after 6'.	4.8	76

Date	Route	Times	Hours	Notes	m.p.h.	Ref.
May 1680	London-Newport Pagnell 52	4 a.m. to 5 p.m.	11½	Changed horses at Barnet and Dunstable; dined at latter.	4.5	79
June 1683	Oxford-Astrop Wells 22		4	Advertised time.	5.5	36
July 1689	London-Bishop's Stortford 31	3.30 a.m. to 12 noon	8	Yarmouth coach. ½ hour breakfast stop assumed.	3.9	59
July 1702	London-Cambridge 57	5 a.m. to c.8 p.m.	14		4.1	67
May 1709	Stamford-Barnby Moor 59	c. 3.15 a.m. to 8.30 p.m.	15¾	York coach. Dep a little after 3; ½ hour breakfast stop assumed.	3.7	28
May 1711	London-Ipswich 70	3 a.m. to 10 p.m.	17½	½ hour breakfast stop assumed.	4.0	83
Apr 1712	Stamford-Barnby Moor 59	5 a.m. to c.1.30 a.m.	19½	Wakefield coach.	3.0	28
Oct 1713	Cambridge-London 57	c.4 a.m. to c.7.15 p.m.	14¼	From a biography. 'He got up by three o'th'clock, and was not in London till past seven'.	4.0	68
Aug 1719	London-Tunbridge Wells 36	c.8 a.m. to c.7 p.m.	8½	Bread and butter at Bromley (½ hour assumed) and 2 hours stated for lunch at Sevenoaks.	4.2	85
23 Feb 1723	London-Newbury 59	c.3 a.m. to 7 p.m.	14½	Baited at Windsor; dined at Reading.	4.1	44
June 1725	Hartley Row-Salisbury 44	3 a.m. to 2 p.m.	10	Exeter coach. Source is a fictional account of a journey.	4.4	32

Date	Route	Time	Hours	Notes	mph	Ref
March 1733	Bristol-Bath 13	1 a.m. to 4 a.m.	2¾	Source is advertised departure times at Bristol and Bath; ¼ hour deducted to allow for loading at Bath.	4.7	12
Apr 1739	Norwich-Bury St Edmunds 41	6 a.m. to 6 p.m.	11	Advertised time.	3.7	51
WINTER						
Nov 1661	Canterbury-Gravesend 34	7 a.m. to 6.30 p.m.	10½	Dined.	3.2	60
Jan 1686	Whitchurch-Four Crosses 37	c.6.30 a.m. to c.5.30 p.m.	10	Dined at Newport at noon; hence speeds of 3.8 and 3.6 mph for the 2 parts of the day.	3.7	6
Oct 1689	Yarmouth-Botesdale 40	c.5.15 a.m. to 6 p.m.	11¼	Dep after 5 a.m. Dined; also drank sherry at Broome.	3.6	59
Oct 1689	Bury St Edmunds-Bishop's Stortford 45	c.11 a.m. to 8 p.m.	8	Dined.	5.6	59
Oct 1689	Bishop's Stortford-London 31	c.8 a.m. to 7 p.m.	9	Dined. Had to walk 2 miles after breakdown in Epping Forest (1 hour allowed for this).	3.4	59
6 Apr 1711	Stevenage-Huntingdon 33	6 a.m. to 7.15 p.m.	(12¼)	York coach. 2 poles broken, and set fast near Hinchinbrook. Arr 'a little after seven'.	(2.7)	28
Dec 1725	Bristol-Bath 13	2 a.m. to c.6 a.m.	3¾	(See note to March 1733 above.)	3.5	A
Winter 1742	London-Oxford 58	7 a.m. to 5 p.m. twice	18	Source is a statement made long after 1742.	3.2	B

'mph' is miles per hour. All the sources are diary entries unless the contrary is indicated in the Comments column. References relate to the list in Appendix 8, except A, which is *Farley's Bristol News-Paper*, 24 Dec 1725, and B, which is British Library, Add MS 27828, p. 16. For assumptions about the time occupied by dining etc., see text. Where the source gives only a time of getting up, an hour is allowed here before departure (i.e. Cambridge 1713 and Newbury 1722).

(2) 1752-68

Date	Journey and miles	Times	Hours	mph	ppm	Comments
May 1752	Marlborough-Bath 31	c.9.30 a.m. to c.7 p.m.	8½	3.6		Traveller's description. ½ hour assumed for 9 a.m. breakfast. Arr Sandy Lane c.1 p.m. (hence 4.3 and 3.2 mph).
June 1752	Northampton-London 67	12 hours stated	11	6.1	2.1	Berlin coach, 4 passengers, 2 horses, 4 changes of team. (Fare rose to 2.7 ppm 1753, 3.2 ppm 1754, 2.9 ppm 1755.)
July 1752, Apr 1754	Reading-London 42	5 a.m. to 12 noon; back 1 p.m. to 8 p.m.	7	6.0	1.7, 2.0	Stage-chaise, steel springs, 4 passengers, 2 changes of team. 2 services 1754; one returns 10 a.m.-5 p.m.
Aug & Sept 1752	Newbury-London 59	6 a.m. to by 6 p.m.	11	5.4	2.0	2 services. Stage-chaises, steel springs, 4 passengers, 2 changes of team.
Feb 1753	Buntingford-London 32	6 a.m. to 1	7	4.6		Summer. (Similar times Apr 1755; dep between 6 & 7, May 1757, so 4.9 mph.)
Mar 1753	Cambridge-London 57	12 hours stated	11	5.2		Dep 6 a.m. Summer.

Date	Route	Times				Notes
May & Nov 1753, Aug 1754, Apr & May 1755	Do	8 a.m. to by 6 p.m. down; 7 a.m. to by 5 (but 4 p.m. May 1753)	9	6.3	2.5	1753: 'Flying stage close chaise', steel springs, 4 passengers, 4 horses (in Nov); dined. 1754-5: landau, steel springs, 6 horses, 'coach-price' (but flying machine Apr 1755; 4 fresh horses every 16-20 miles June 1755).
Oct 1753	Gloucester-London 108	3 a.m. to by 6 p.m. next day.	27	4.0	2.6	Winter. Assumes same times on both days.
Aug 1754	London-Chelmsford 30	7 a.m. to 12 noon; 2 p.m. to 7 p.m.	5	6.0		Machine, steel springs, 2 changes of horses; no stops but to change horses.
Sept 1754	Oxford-London 58	6 a.m. to by 6 p.m.	11	5.3	2.6	Machine, steel springs, 4 passengers. Summer.
Winter 1754-5	Do	5 a.m. to by 6 p.m.	12	4.8	2.6	Ditto. Winter.
Mar 1755	Norwich-Newmarket 48	6 a.m. to c.6.30 p.m.	11½	4.2	2.7	Light machine, 4 passengers.
Mar 1755	Bath-London 109	5 a.m. to 7 p.m. on each day	26	4.2	2.0	Machine.
May 1755	Maldon-London 38	5 a.m. to between 1 and 2	8½	4.5		Stage fly. Via Danbury.
Aug & Sept 1755	St Ives-London 61	5 a.m. to by 7 p.m.	13	4.7	2.4	Light machine coach; fresh horses every 16-20 miles.
Apr 1756	Cambridge-London 57	7 a.m. to c.4.30 p.m.	8½	6.7		'Fly'.

Date	Route	Times	Hours	Speed	Speed	Notes
Apr 1759	Coventry-London 98	3 a.m. to 7 p.m.	14½	6.8	3.1	Flying machine, steel springs, 4 passengers.
June 1759	Do	7 a.m. to c.5 p.m.	8½	6.7		Diary. 'Fly'. Breakfast and dinner.
Feb 1761	Norwich-London 110	6 a.m.to next day between 6 and 7 p.m.	23	4.8	2.7	Summer. Machine, 4 passengers. Assumes same times on both days.
Mar 1761	Coventry-London, Coventry-Chester 98/89	2 a.m. to by 7 p.m. next day.	15½	6.3/5.7	3.2	Machine, steel springs. Assumes same times on both days between Chester and London.
Apr 1761	Coventry-London 98	3 a.m. to 6 p.m.	13½	7.3	3.1	Flying machine, steel springs, 4 passengers.
Oct 1761	London-Fosters Booth 66	c.12.30 a.m. to c.12.15 p.m.	11¼	5.9		Diary. Breakfast; 2 changes of horses. Chester coach.
Oct 1761	Meriden-Chester 86	1 a.m. to c.8 p.m.	17½	4.9		Diary. Summer. Breakfast and dinner. 5.3 & 4.8 mph up & down from Lichfield.
Apr 1764	Norwich-Diss, London-Diss 20/92	12 midnight to c.3.30 a.m.; 12 midnight to c.4 p.m.	3½; 14½	5.7/6.3		Flying machine.
Aug 1764, Apr 1765	London-Birmingham 111	Midnight to 6 [p.m.]	16½	6.7	3.4	Flying machine, steel springs, 4 passengers. Via Coventry.
Sept 1764, Mar 1765	Ipswich-London 70	7 a.m. to 5 p.m.	8½	8.2	3.0	Post-coach, steel springs, 6 passengers, no outsiders. Breakfast and dinner mentioned 1765.

Date	Route	Timing	Hours			Notes
Sept 1764	Do	11 hours stated	9½	7.4	2.6	Machine, steel springs, 4 passengers. Breakfast and dinner mentioned.
Sept 1764	Do	14 hours stated	12½	5.6	2.1	Stage-coach.
Sept 1764	London-Southampton 80	6 a.m. to 6 p.m.	11	7.3	3.0	Post-coach, steel springs, 4 horses, 2 postilions, 6 passengers, no outsiders.
Mar 1765	London-King's Lynn 104	6 a.m. to 1 p.m.	18	5.8	2.1	Machine.
Apr 1765	Gloucester-London 108	10 p.m. to 7 p.m.	19½	5.5	2.6	Double post-coach, steel springs, 8 passengers.
Apr 1765	London-Highworth 81	4 a.m. to 7 p.m.	14	5.8	2.2	Machine. Via Wantage.
May 1765	Oxford-Bath 69	4 a.m. to c.7 p.m.	13½	5.1	3.1	Diary. Machine. Breakfast and dinner; 1 hour between getting up and departing assumed.
June 1765	Kettering-London 75	2 a.m. to 5 p.m.	13½	5.6	2.4	Flying stage-coach.
Jan-Aug 1766	Worcester-Oxford 57	7 a.m. to c.6 p.m.	10	5.7		Machine. Same timings all year.
1767	Colchester-London 52	9 a.m. to by 4 p.m. up; 7 a.m. to by 3 p.m. down	7-8	6.5-7.4	2.3	Fly, 4 passengers.
1767	Do	5 to by 2	9	5.8	1.8	Stage-coach, 6 passengers.

Year	Route	Times				Notes
1767	Do	9.30 to 6 p.m.	7½	6.9	3.0	Ipswich post-coach, steel springs, 4 horses, 2 postilions, no outsiders.
1767	Do	9 to by 6 p.m. up; 7 to c.2.30 down	7½-8	6.5-6.9	2.3	Ipswich machine. Dines at Colchester on down journey.
1767	Do	8 to 6 p.m. up; 5 to 1.30 down	8½-9	5.8-6.1	1.8	Ipswich coach. Dines at Colchester on down journey.
1767	Do	5 a.m. to 2 p.m.	9	5.8	1.6	Harwich stage-coach, 6 passengers.
1767	Colchester-Norwich 61	5 a.m. to c.5 p.m.	11	5.5		Norwich machine.
1767	Harwich-Colchester, London-Colchester 21/52	3 a.m. to c.7; 1 a.m. to 10	4; 8½	5.3/6.1	2.6	Fly, 4 passengers.
Mar 1767	Salisbury-London 84	11 p.m. to c.4 p.m.	15½	5.4	2.6	Fly, 6 insiders. Distinguished from the same operator's flying machine.
1768	Southampton-Farnham 39	5.45 a.m. to 12.30 p.m.	6¾	5.8	2.4	Machine, 6 passengers.
Sept 1768	Tunbridge Wells-London 36	7.30 a.m. to c.4 p.m.	7	5.1		Diary. Fly. Breakfast; presumably dinner too.
Dec 1768	Copdock-Norwich 46	6 a.m. to c.4 p.m.	8½	5.4	2.9	Diary. Winter timing. Breakfast and dinner.

The sources are advertisements or directory entries except as indicated. All relate to London coaches, except Oxford to Bath in 1765. For departures at 3 a.m. or earlier, one hour is allowed for dinner and half an hour for breakfast; otherwise only one hour for dining (unless additional information is available). Return timings, where given, were the same as those in the table. All timings are summer timings except as indicated. Pence per mile ('ppm') is sometimes for a longer journey than that covered by the timings. Numbers of passengers refer to inside passengers only.

References:
Narrative of the journey of an Irish gentleman through England in the year 1752 (1869), pp. 135-9; LEP, 27 June, 11 July, 18 Aug, 16 Sept 1752, 14 Mar, 16 Apr 1754; *Northampton Mercury*, 5 Mar 1753, 31 Mar 1755; *Cambridge Journal*, 24 Feb, 26 May, 3 Nov 1753, 31 Aug 1754, 5 Apr, 17 May, 21 June 1755, 14 May 1757; *Gloucester Journal*, 2 Oct 1753; *Ipswich Journal*, 24 Aug 1754; *Jackson's Oxford Journal*, 7 Sept 1754; *Norwich Mercury*, 15 Feb 1755; *Bath Journal*, 31 Mar 1755; *Ipswich Journal*, 31 May 1755; *Cambridge Journal*, 16 Aug, 27 Sept 1755, 17 Apr 1756; *Coventry Mercury*, 9 Apr 1759; Susan and David Neave (eds.), *The diary of a Yorkshire gentleman: John Courtney of Beverley, 1759-1768* (2001), pp. 15-16; *Norwich Mercury*, 17 Jan 1761; *Adams's Weekly Courant*, 31 Mar, 28 Apr 1761; British Library, Add MS 27971; *Ipswich Journal*, 24 Mar 1764; *Aris's Birmingham Gazette*, 20 Aug 1764, 1 Apr 1765; *Ipswich Journal*, 8 Sept 1764, 16 Mar 1765; *Salisbury Journal*, 10 Sept 1764; *Ipswich Journal*, 9 Mar 1765; *Jackson's Oxford Journal*, 13 Apr 1765; John Beresford (ed.), *The diary of a country parson: the Reverend James Woodforde*, vol. 1 (1924), pp. 46-7; *Northampton Mercury*, 3 June 1765; *Berrow's Worcester Journal*, 2 Jan, 14 Aug 1766; *Keymer's memorandum-book for ... 1767* (Essex RO, D/DU 459/1); *Sherborne Mercury*, 30 Mar 1767; *The Southampton guide* (1768), pp.57-8; Basil Cozens-Hardy (ed.), *The diary of Sylas Neville 1767-1788* (1950), pp. 45, 53, 56.

STAGE-COACH AND WAGGON FARES, 1650-1750

Entries for coaches are arranged in the same way as in Appendix 8.

Date	Destination/miles	Sh.	ppm	Note	Reference
Coaches					
(a)					
1657	Chester 188	35	2.2		A2, A3
1658/62/72ws/1712w/15/16	Chester 188	40	2.6	n1	A2, 1-3
1731w/50	Chester 188	42	2.7		A74, A12
1738/43w/4ws/5w	Lichfield 126	27	2.6*	n2	A19-20
1742	Lichfield 126	25	2.4*		A20
1653	York 202	28	1.7	n3	A22
1658/72ws/1712/33ws	York 202	40	2.4	n1	A2, 2, 5, A12
1667w	York 202	45	2.7		A71
1658	Edinburgh 406	80	2.4		A2
1658/1712w	Edinburgh 406	90	2.7		A2, A93
1706/29w	York-Newcastle 81	20	3.0	n4	3, A94
1735w	York 202	45; 40	2.7; 2.4	n5	6
1655w/8/72ws	Exeter 182	40	2.6	n1	A91, A2, 2
1728	Exeter 182	45	3.0	n6	A45
(b)					
1734/9/40/3/50	Beccles 110	20	2.2*	n7	A35
1658	Bristol 122	20	2.0		A2
1663/72ws	Bristol 122	25	2.5		8, 2
1667/1748/9	Bath 109	25	2.8*		A39, A43
1672ws/1719/48/9	Bath 109	20	2.2*		2, A40, A43
1719	Bristol 122	23	2.3*		A40
1691	Birmingham 120	18	1.8		A36
1730	Birmingham 111	25	2.7		A37
1731	Birmingham 120	21	2.1		A38
1744/5/9/50	Birmingham 123	25	2.4*	n8	A20, A12
1728	Blandford 113	16	1.7	n9	A12
1737/8	Boston 114	23½	2.5		A12
1750	Dorchester 129	24	2.2*		A33
1713w/15	Gloucester 108	20	2.2*	n10	11, A40
1722	Ross 124	27	2.6		A48
1750	Gloucester 108	23	2.6		A48
1710	Norwich 110	25	2.7*	n11	A52
1741	Norwich 110, 113	15	1.6*	n5	12
1741w	Norwich 110	7½	0.8	n12	A52

1699	Nottingham/Derby 126/7	25	2.4*	n13	13
1724	Nottingham/Derby 126/7	26	2.5*		A37
1733/4	Sherborne 120	25	2.5*	n9	A12
1730	Taunton 151	30	2.4		A36
1702	Wolverhampton 134	25	2.2		A54
1738/42/4/7	Worcester 115	25	2.6*	n7	A58
1689ws/1717ws/43w/50	Yarmouth 131, 127	20	1.8-1.9*		A59, A40, A52, A35
1741	Yarmouth 127	22	2.1*	n7	A51

(c)

1658	Canterbury 56	12	2.6		A2
1654/7	Cambridge 57	10	2.1*		A64, A3
1669/71	Oxford 58	12	2.5*	n10	A70
1667/72/82/4/9ws/92ws/					
1703ws/03/21w/31w/33w/41	Oxford 58	10	2.1*	n10	A71, A70, 11, 15, 3, A73-4, A12
1682w/4w	Oxford 58	8	1.7	n10	11

(d)

1654	Chipping Norton 77	12	1.9		A22
1657/84/1728	Salisbury 84	15	2.1*		A3, 19, A45
1657	Southampton 80	15	2.3		A3
1657	Luton 32	5	1.9		A3
1658	Dover 71	15	2.5		A2
1662	Aylesbury 42	8	2.3		20
1663	Huntingdon 60	17½	3.5		21
1671-1710ws	Per 5 miles from London	1	2.4		A53, 22
1672ws	Northampton 67	16	2.9		2
1672ws	Reading 42	7	2.0		2
1672ws	Salisbury 84	20-25	2.9-3.6	n14	2
1673ws	Within 20 m. of London	4	2.4		23
1673/6w	Northampton 67	15	2.7		24
1690	Banbury 76	14; 10	2.2; 1.6*	n5	A36
1691ws/1701ws	Per 5 miles	1	2.4	n15	25
1697	Tunbridge Wells 36	8	2.7		26
1699	Wallingford 48	9; 8	2.3; 2.0	n5	27
1699-1703ws	Henley 38	6	1.9		27
1700	Melton Mowbray 105	20	2.3*		A54
1707w	Windsor 26	2½	1.2		28
1707	Windsor 26	3½	1.6		28
1711	Harwich 73	16	2.6		A83
1714-17ws	Brentwood 19	3	1.9		29
1720ws	Per 100 miles	20	2.4		30
1720ws	Do (flying coach)	25	3.0*		30
1720	Stony Stratford 54	9	2.0		A40
1722/37/50	Bury St Edmunds 72	12	2.0*		A82, A35
1722	Bury St Edmunds 76	15	2.4		A82
1725w	East Grinstead 29	5	2.1		9
1725	Reigate 22	4	2.2		9
1725	Lewes 49	12	2.9	n16	A11
1725w	Oundle 78	15	2.3		A49
1727	Newbury 59	9	1.8*	n9	A37
1728	Horsham 37	8	2.6		9
1734/9/40/3	Ipswich 70	13	2.2*	n7	A35
1734w	Portsmouth 73	18	3.0		A12
1735/6	Northampton 67	14	2.5*		A78
1735w	Richmond 12	2	2.0		4
1737/43	Leighton Buzzard 42	7½	2.1		A78, 17

1738	Newport Pagnell 52	10	2.3		A12
1738w	Harrow 13	2½	2.3		4
1741	Abingdon 59	10	2.0		A12
1748	Salisbury 84	18	2.6*		A12
1750	Ipswich 70	12	2.1*		A35
1750	Harwich 73	12	2.0*	n17	A35
1750	Sudbury 57	9	1.9*		A35

(e)

1725w	Yarmouth-Norwich 23	3	1.6		12
1726w	Do	4	2.1		12
1727	Norwich-Bury St Edmunds 41	7	2.0		12
1728ws	Oxford-Gloucester 50	12	2.9	n10	11
1730	Bath-Exeter 84	21	3.0		A36
1732	York-Scarborough 40	6	1.8		18
1733	Bristol-Gloucester 35	6	2.1		31
1737	Stapleford-Bath 31	10	(3.1)	n18	32
1740/5/50	Hereford-Gloucester 35	8½	2.9		A48
1743w	Norwich-King's Lynn 42	6	1.7	n7	12
1744	Do	7	2.0		12
1747	Bury St Edmunds-Norwich or King's Lynn 41-3	8	2.2-2.3	n19	12
1750	Bristol- Bath 13	2	1.8	n20	33

(f) Coach-waggons, caravans etc.

1657	Coventry 93	10	1.3		A3
1657	Ipswich 70	10; 8	1.7; 1.4	n21	A3
1657	Colchester 52	5	1.2		A3
1657	Norwich 110	12	1.3		A3
1710w	Gosport 82	9	1.3	n22	A11
1718	Reading 42	3½	1.0	n23	A40
1722/3	Bury St Edmunds 72	9	1.5	n22	A82
1743w	Northampton 67	6-7	1.1-1.3	n24	A78
1749	Devizes 91	9	1.2	n22	A12
1750w	Bath-Bristol 13	1½	1.4	n22	33
1750	Salisbury 84	11	1.6	n25	10

(g) Waggons

1650ws	Ingatestone 24	2½	1.3		34
1674-1703ws	Oxford 58	4	0.8	n10	15, A70
1678w	Ampthill 46	5½	1.4		35
1697ws	Peterborough 79	8	1.2		36
1720ws	Per 100 miles	7-8	0.8-1.0		30
1720	Northampton 67	6	1.1	n26	17
1724	Dorchester 129	10	0.9		37
1735	Norwich 110	10	1.1	n27	14
1737/44	Frome 108	8	0.9	n26	38
1740/50	Stowmarket 74	5	0.8	n5	7
1743w	Stamford 93	8	1.0	n28	16
1743	Huntingdon 60	4	0.8	n28	16
1743	Oundle 78	4	0.6	n28	16
1743	Spalding 98	8	1.0		A49
1747w	Bristol 122	10	1.0		39
1750w	Norwich-King's Lynn 42	3	0.9	n29	7
1750	Salisbury 84	5	0.7	n26	A33

Notes

'Sh.' is shillings. 'ppm' is pence per mile. 'w' next to the date indicates winter; 'ws' indicates both winter and summer; all other entries are summer. Italics in the first column indicates that the source is an advertisement. An asterisk in the ppm column indicates a flying coach (defined here as covering over 54 miles per day), whether or not the source describes it as such and even if only one of several references indicates a flying coach.

1. Possibly increased to 45s. in winter (1672). **2.** 25s. here is assumed to be a misprint for 27s., as all the other fares are the same as later. **3.** In 14-seater coach; includes 4d. per stage to the coachman. **4.** Only York-Durham in 1706, but apparently charged the full York-Newcastle fare. **5.** Fare reduction. **6.** Fare increase. **7.** Outsiders ½ price, Beccles 1734-43, Worcester 1747, Yarmouth 1741, Ipswich 1734-43, Norwich-King's Lynn 1743. **8.** Footmen behind ½ price (1744-5). **9.** Only four passengers. **10.** Maximum fare specified by Oxford Vice-Chancellor, Gloucester 1713, Oxford 1669-1703, Oxford-Gloucester 1728, Oxford waggons 1674-1703. **11.** One-day service. **12.** Fare reduction to defeat a new competitor. **13.** Fare reduction until 21 Aug. **14.** Doubtful. **15.** 'it is in some places less than a shilling for every five miles'. **16.** 'For riding behind 6s.' **17.** Outsiders 7s. 6d. (1.2 ppm). **18.** Assumed to be the full Salisbury-Bath fare (39 miles). **19.** 'Stage post chaises'. **20.** Landau with four horses. **21.** 'Wagon coach ... In the coach 10 shillings, and 8 shillings behind'. **22.** Caravan. **23.** 'Berlin coach'. **24.** 'Ge-hoe coach', carrying 8; up 7s., down 6s.. **25.** 'Flying cart'. **26.** Flying waggon. **27.** 'Double-breasted waggon'. **28.** Probably a flying waggon (began 28 Mar to Huntingdon). **29.** Covered cart.

References ('A' indicates references in Appendix 8)

1. McGrath, vol. 44, p. 415; Symson, Nos. 573, 1161. **2.** SP 29/319, No. 200; *ibid.*, No. 202. **3.** Blundell, vol. 110, pp. 314-15; vol. 112, p. 289. **4.** LEP, 6 Nov 1735, 24 Oct 1738. **5.** Thoresby, vol. 2, p. 148. **6.** *Leeds Mercury*, 7 Jan 1735. **7.** *Ipswich Journal*, 5 Apr 1740, 6 Jan 1750. **8.** J. Latimer, *The annals of Bristol in the seventeenth century* (1900), p. 302. **9.** *Daily Post*, 1 Feb, 13 Mar 1725, 20 Mar 1728. **10.** *Salisbury Journal*, 2 Apr 1750. **11.** Bodleian Library, University Archives, Chancellor's Court, 134/1/1. **12.** *Norwich Gazette*, 27 Nov 1725, 12 Nov 1726, 18 Mar 1727, 20 June 1741, 22 Jan 1743, 5 May 1744, 18 Apr 1747. **13.** *Post-Boy*, 6 & 13 June 1699. **14.** *Norwich Mercury*, 22 Mar 1735. **15.** Pawson, p. 42. **16.** *Stamford Mercury*, 17 & 24 Feb, 17 Mar 1743. **17.** *Northampton Mercury*, 9 May 1720, 11 Apr 1743. **18.** *York Courant*, 25 July 1732. **19.** Harper, vol. 1, pp. 78-9. **20.** Dugdale, p. 109. **21.** Pepys, vol. 4, 14 June 1663. **22.** Delaune 1681, p. 346. **23.** *Harleian Miscellany*, vol. 8 (1746), p. 539. **24.** A2A entry for Northamptonshire RO, QSR 1/79/1; Edward Maunde Thompson (ed.), *Correspondence of the family of Hatton*, Camden Society, 2nd ser., vol. 22 (1878), pp. 141-2. **25.** Guy Miège, *The new state of England* (1691), part 2, p. 47; *ibid.* (1701), part 2, p. 23. **26.** Christopher Morris (ed.), *The journeys of Celia Fiennes* (1947), p. 134. **27.** E 112/726/106, Fisher's schedule; E 133/62/37, pp. 2, 9. **28.** James E. Thorold Rogers, *A history of agriculture and prices in England*, vol. 7 (1902), p. 533. **29.** C 114/172, Thresher v. Thresher, pp. 3-4, 12 at back. **30.** G.J. Gent, *Great Britain's Vade Mecum* (1720), p. 351. **31.** *Farley's Bristol News-Paper*, 27 Jan 1733. **32.** Wiltshire RO, 492/269. **33.** *Bristol Weekly Intelligencer*, 27 Jan, 28 Apr 1750. **34.** Essex RO, D/DP A172. **35.** Earl of Cardigan, 'Domestic expenses of a nobleman's household', Bedfordshire Historical Record Society, vol. 32 (1952), p. 119. **36.** Fitzwilliam, p. 11. **37.** C 11/1189/64, 2nd schedule. **38.** *Sherborne Mercury*, 19 July 1737, 10 Apr 1744. **39.** John Latimer, *The annals of Bristol in the eighteenth century* (1893), p. 269.

ABBREVIATIONS USED IN THE NOTES

Albert	William Albert, *The turnpike road system in England 1663-1840* (1972).
Aston	Diary of Sir Willoughby Aston, Liverpool RO, 920 MD 172 to 175.
Blundell	*The great diurnal of Nicholas Blundell of Little Crosby, Lancashire,* Record Society of Lancashire and Cheshire, vols. 110, 112, 114 (1968/70/2).
C	Chancery records in the NA.
CJ	*House of Commons Journals.*
Crofts	J. Crofts, *Packhorse, waggon and post* (1967).
Davies	Richard Caulfield (ed.), *Journal of the Very Rev. Rowland Davies, LL.D,* Camden Soc., 1st ser., vol. 68 (1857).
Defoe	Daniel Defoe, *A tour through the whole island of Great Britain* (1971 Penguin edn.).
Delaune 1681	Thomas Delaune, *The present state of London* (1681).
Delaune 1690	Thomas Delaune, *Angliae metropolis: or, the present state of London* (1690).
Dugdale	William Harper (ed.), *The life, diary, and correspondence of Sir William Dugdale* (1827).
Dugdale (2)	Sir William Dugdale's diary, Warwickshire RO, MI 318.
E	Exchequer records in the NA.
Eaton	Joan Wake and D.C. Champion (eds.), *The letters of Daniel Eaton to the third Earl of Cardigan 1725-1732,* Northamptonshire Record Society, vol. 24 (1971).
Fitzwilliam	D.R. Hainsworth and Cherry Walker (eds.), *The correspondence of Lord Fitzwilliam of Milton and Francis Guybon his steward 1697-1709,* Northamptonshire Record Society, vol. 36 (1990).
Gerhold	Dorian Gerhold, *Road transport before the railways: Russell's London flying waggons* (1993).
Hainsworth	D.R. Hainsworth, *Stewards, lords and people* (1992).
Harper	C.G. Harper, *Stage-coach and mail in days of yore* (2 vols., 1903).
Henry	Diary of Matthew Henry, Bodleian Library, MS. Eng. Misc. e.330.
Herbert	Nicholas Herbert, *Road travel and transport in Gloucestershire 1722-1822* (1985).
Hey	David Hey, *Packmen, carriers and packhorse roads* (1980).
Jackman	W.T. Jackman, *The development of transportation in modern England* (1916).

JTH	*Journal of Transport History.*
LEP	*London Evening-Post.*
Lowther	D.R. Hainsworth (ed.), *The correspondence of Sir John Lowther of Whitehaven 1693-1698* (1983).
McGrath	J.R. McGrath (ed.), *The Flemings in Oxford*, Oxfordshire Historical Society, vols. 44, 62, 79 (1904/13/24).
NA	National Archives.
Newcome	Richard Parkinson (ed.), *The autobiography of Henry Newcome, M.A.*, Chetham Society, vols. 26-7 (1852).
Nicholson	Transcript of William Nicholson's diary (in Carlisle Library).
Nicholson (2)	*Transactions of the Cumberland & Westmorland Antiquarian & Archaeological Society*, vols. 1-4, 35 (1901-4, 1935).
'Packhorses'	Dorian Gerhold, 'Packhorses and wheeled vehicles in England, 1550-1800', *Journal of Transport History*, 3rd ser., vol. 14 (1993), pp. 1-26.
Pawson	Eric Pawson, *Transport and economy: the turnpike roads of eighteenth century Britain* (1977).
Pepys	Robert Latham and William Matthews (eds.), *The diary of Samuel Pepys* (11 vols., 1970-83).
POB	*The Proceedings of the Old Bailey*: database at http://hri.shef.ac.uk/db/bailey
PROB	Prerogative Court of Canterbury records in the NA.
'Productivity'	Dorian Gerhold, 'Productivity change in road transport before and after turnpiking, 1690-1840', *Economic History Review*, vol. 49 (1996), pp. 491-515.
Rawdon	Robert Davies (ed.), *The life of Marmaduke Rawdon*, Camden Society, 1st ser., vol. 85 (1863).
RO	Record Office or Archives Office.
Schellinks	M. Enwood and H.L. Lehmann (ed.), *The journal of William Schellinks' travels in England 1661-1663*, Camden Society, 5th ser., vol. 1 (1993).
SP	State papers in the NA.
Symson	S.D.Smith (ed.), *'An exact and industrious tradesman': the letter book of Joseph Symson of Kendal 1711-20*, Records of Social and Economic History, n.s., vol. 34 (2002).
Thoresby	Joseph Hunter (ed.), *The diary of Ralph Thoresby* (2 vols., 1830).
VCH	*Victoria History of the Counties of England.*
Wood	Andrew Clark (ed.), *The life and times of Anthony Wood*, Oxford Historical Society, vols. 19, 21, 26 (1891/2/4).

Newspapers with covering dates are cited by the later of the two dates.

NOTES

Notes on miles

Miles throughout this book are taken from John Cary, *Cary's new itinerary* (1802), measured from the General Post Office or (for Kent) London Bridge. For coaches, whose routes are usually known, the actual route is followed (by measurement on a modern map in the few cases where Cary does not cover the full route), but otherwise Cary's shortest route is used. For carriers, whose routes are rarely known, Cary's shortest route is normally used (except for Bristol and Exeter). Mileages for carriers and coaches to the same place may therefore differ. (Six miles are added for both in the exceptional case of Exeter via Dorchester, where a new road established in the 1750s between Salisbury and Blandford replaced a longer route.)

Cary's measurements were of course made long after the period covered here, but by 1802, despite the Salisbury-Blandford example, turnpikes had created relatively few wholly new stretches of road, and turnpike improvements were as likely to lengthen a route (by seeking to reduce gradients) as to shorten it. For example, for 18 major coach routes between 1798 and 1828, a period when many roads were significantly improved, the change in mileage in *Cary's new itinerary* in no case exceeded 1.125 miles. Taking the comparison back to 1771, using Daniel Paterson, *A new and accurate description of all the direct and principal cross roads in Great Britain* (1771), the change between 1771 and 1828 exceeded two miles in only one case (3.3 miles to Exeter via Yeovil). Changes of route are not a problem (at least for coaches) because stage-coach routes in 1650-1750 are usually known in reasonable detail. Cary's miles in 1802 are therefore a sound basis for examining stage-coach and carrier services in 1650-1750.

Notes to Introduction (pp. xi-xvii)

1. For a summary see Theo Barker and Dorian Gerhold, *The rise and rise of road transport, 1700-1990* (1993).
2. Gerhold.
3. *Oxford dictionary of national biography.*
4. Delaune 1681, p. 478.
5. For London directories, in which most of the carrier and coach lists were published, see Charles W.F. Goss, *The London directories 1677-1855* (1932).
6. Peter Earle, *The making of the English middle class* (1989), p. 17; L.D. Schwarz, *London in the age of industrialisation: entrepreneurs, labour force and living conditions, 1700-1850* (1992), p. 105.
7. Roger Finlay and Beatrice Shearer, 'Population growth and suburban expansion', in A.L. Beier and Roger Finlay (eds.), *London 1500-1700: the making of the metropolis* (1986), p. 39.
8. Below, pp. 8-9, 53-5, 62, 194-6.
9. See Dorian Gerhold, 'Searching for justice: Chancery records on the internet', *Ances-* tors, issue 13 (April/May 2003), pp. 35-40; also the National Archives' leaflets, Legal Records Information 19 and 22, on Exchequer and Chancery records respectively; both are on the National Archives website. Other works include Henry Horwitz, *Chancery equity records and proceedings 1600-1800* (1995) and Henry Horwitz, *Exchequer equity records and proceedings 1649-1841* (2001). Most of Series C 6 (part of the Chancery proceedings from 1649 and earlier to 1714) is indexed in the equity database, giving full personal names, place names and, for some suits c.1680-1714, the subject of the suit; it is at www.nationalarchives.gov.uk/equity. The National Archives' main catalogue (at www.nationalarchives.gov.uk/catalogue) includes some of the Chancery suits from 1386 to 1800 (but after 1558 giving only title of suit, e.g. Smith v. Smith, and sometimes the county) and a large proportion of the Chancery depositions taken in the country (as opposed to in London).

10. http://hri.shef.ac/db/bailey

11. See Jeremy Gibson and Else Churchill, *Probate jurisdictions: where to look for wills* (5th edn., 2002), which is also useful for inventories. A.J. Camp, *Wills and their whereabouts* (4th edn., 1974) is old, but is more helpful about which collections of probate records include inventories.

12. e.g. Appendix 3, No. 34. See also C 8/651/1. In the case of Thomas Bass of Abbotsley, both inventory and will record four packhorses, whereas for George Glover of Orrell the figures are 17 and 22 respectively, but Glover's will and inventory were ten months apart (Appendix 3, Nos. 7 and 25).

13. Available in the Thomason Tracts (for the 1650s) and the Burney Collection at the British Library. Microfilms of some or all of these are available at major libraries. The Burney Collection will soon be available on the internet.

14. The most accessible list is the British Library's Newspaper Library catalogue, indexed by title and place of publication, at www.bl.uk/catalogues/newspapers.html. The Newspaper Library has microfilms or originals of the majority of pre-1750 provincial newspapers, but there are significant gaps. For a fuller list, see R.M. Wiles, *Freshest advices: early provincial newspapers in England* (1965), though the locations given there have often changed, and the British Library's *Newsplan*, parts of which have been published. Despite its title, Jeremy Gibson, *Local newspapers 1750-1920* (1989) is useful for locations of pre-1750 newspapers.

15. Including William Matthews, *British diaries: an annotated bibliography of British diaries written between 1442 and 1942* (1950); Heather Creaton, *Unpublished London diaries*, London Record Society, vol. 37 (2003); Edward Geoffrey Cox, *A reference guide to the history of travel*, vol. 3 (1949); Robin Gard (ed.), *The observant traveller: diaries of travel in England, Wales and Scotland in the County Record Offices of England and Wales* (1989); C.S. Handley, *An annotated bibliography of diaries printed in English* (3rd edn., 2002), vols. 2 and 3.

16. Those in the British Library are indexed in www.bl.uk/catalogues/manuscripts.html. The Bodleian Library has a typescript list of its unpublished diaries. The A2A database (www.a2a.org.uk) is increasingly useful.

17. Many of them gathered together in NA, SP 29/316, Nos. 194-5 and SP 29/319, Nos. 200-2.

18. See Appendix 3.

19. Figs. 12 and 13; *A compleat history of the famous city of Norwich* (1728), p. 38.

20. e.g. Symson; Fitzwilliam; Lowther, Eaton.

21. Below, pp. 153-4.

22. Philip S. Bagwell, *The transport revolution from 1770* (1974), p. 36.

23. Thoresby, vol. 1, p. 295; Lord Macaulay, *The history of England from the accession of James the Second* (1913 edn.), vol. 1, pp. 365-6.

24. Defoe, pp. 429-44; John Ogilby, *Britannia* (1675), *passim*.

Notes to Chapter 1 (pp. 3-18)

1. Delaune 1681, 1690. These figures take no account of Delaune's omissions; see Appendix 1. The tonnage is capacity rather than actual loads, but again ignores omissions.

2. Egremont in west Cumberland had a direct London service, apparently only briefly, in the 1670s, and an attempt was made to start one from Whitehaven in 1697 (Hainsworth, pp. 77-8; Lowther, p. 434). Newcastle upon Tyne had London waggons by 1739 (*Newcastle Courant*, 1 Sept 1744).

3. The number of hearths in 1664 per carrying service in 1681 was: Devon 22,200, Yorkshire 17,600, Norfolk 14,800, Lancashire 4,700, Shropshire 4,300 (C.A.F. Meekings (ed.), *Dorset hearth tax assessments 1662-1664* (1951), pp. 108-10).

4. J.E.T. Rogers, *A history of agriculture and prices in England*, vol. 2 (1866), p. 605; E.M. Carus Wilson, 'The overseas trade of Bristol', in E. Power and M.M. Postan (eds.), *Studies in English trade in the fifteenth century* (1933), p. 189; H.S. Bennett, *The Pastons and their England* (1922), pp. 159-63; NA on-line catalogue for series C 1; VCH, *Gloucestershire*, vol. 4 (1988), pp. 45, 49. There was a possible Gloucester to London carrier by cart in 1381 (*ibid.*, p. 45). See Peter Spufford, *Power and profit: the merchant in medieval Europe* (2002), pp. 196-8 for the (apparently) slightly later development of long-distance carrying in western Europe.

5. Pamela Nightingale, 'The growth of London in the medieval economy', in Richard Britnell and John Hatcher (eds.), *Progress and problems in medieval England: essays in honour of Edward Miller* (1996), pp. 100-1, 103-4; Chrisopher Dyer, 'A summing up', in James A. Galloway (ed.), *Trade, urban hinterlands and market integration c.1300-1600* (2000), p. 106; A.L. Beier and Roger Finlay (eds.), *London 1500-1700: the making of the metropolis* (1986), pp. 12-15.

6. Gerhold, pp. 6, 248 n. 7.

7. J.F. Willard, 'Inland transportation in England during the fourteenth century', *Speculum*, vol. 1 (1926), pp. 361-74; John Langdon, *Horses, oxen and technological innovation* (1986), *passim.*, especially p. 227; B.D.M. Bunyard (ed.), *The brokage book of Southampton from 1439-40*, Southampton Record Society, vol. 40 (1941), pp. xvii, xxi; Hey, pp. 91-6.

8. e.g. Jackman, p. 43; Pawson, pp. 31, 282; Philip Bagwell and Peter Lyth, *Transport in Britain: from canal lock to gridlock* (2002), p. 39.

9. C.L. Kingsford (ed.), *Stow's survey of London* (1908), vol. 2, p. 282; 'Packhorses', pp. 3-9.

10. Packhorses are indicated by 'carrier' or 'carri-

ers' (as opposed to 'waggon' or 'waggoner') in Delaune's lists, though a few waggoners are wrongly recorded as carriers in 1690. Twenty-one inventories of Delaune's carriers clearly indicate packhorses, and Delaune records 17 as carriers and four as unspecified; of the latter, three relate to the Kendal service, which was certainly a packhorse one (and recorded as such in 1690), and the fourth to a Lincoln service in which the packhorse user, a waggon user and a third man were partners. Twenty-nine inventories clearly indicate waggons, and Delaune records 22 of these as waggon services, four as unspecified and three as carriers (two of the latter being clear errors, but the third possibly reflecting change in the means of carriage).

11. C 8/404/18; C 6/345/13; Appendix 2, Nos. 3, 10, 11; Richard Trappes-Lomax (ed.), *The diary and letter book of the Rev. Thomas Brockbank 1671-1709*, Chetham Society, n.s., vol. 89 (1930), p. 43; *Intelligencer*, 27 Feb 1665; Fig. 13; Symson, Nos. 26, 313, 839, 890, 1058.

12. C 8/404/18; C 24/1256, No. 7; Symson, Nos. 26, 580, 804, 839, 1466, 1571.

13. Delaune 1681, 1690; Fig. 13; Symson, No. 890; Gerard Turnbull, 'State regulation in the eighteenth-century English economy: another look at carriers' rates', JTH, 3rd ser., vol. 7 (1985), p. 35, n. 24.

14. Delaune 1681, 1690; M.L. Armitt, *Rydal* (1916), pp. 451, 453; Hainsworth, p. 78n; Jane M. Ewbank (ed.), *Antiquary on horseback* (1963), pp. 60-1; Pawson, pp. 38-9; Symson, Nos. 944, 1332, 2046.

15. Symson, Nos. 580, 1466. Only two carriers' inventories record watches (Appendix 2, Nos. 8 and 27). Twenty-one out of 60 record clocks.

16. C 7/237/28; I.S. Leadam (ed.), *Select cases in the King's Council in the Star Chamber ... 1477-1509*, Selden Society, vol. 16 (1903), pp. 80-8. For Morris's business, see Gerhold, pp. 9-16.

17. C 6/381/3; Fig. 39.

18. Assuming each gang set off from Exeter every three weeks (below, p. 64).

19. Appendix 2, No. 68. Hales was agent and then husband to Elizabeth Turner (C 5/355/1), probably the widow of John Turner, listed as Trowbridge carrier in 1690.

20. C 5/244/9. See also C 22/533/15; C 7/656/27; C 7/661/20; C 5/355/1; C 10/392/23.

21. Apart from one week with 13 and three with nineteen. Extra teams, of five to seven horses, were accommodated five times. The account apparently covers only some of Hales's 45 horses, but some teams could have been accommodated at a different inn in Staines, and some may have been employed collecting and delivering at towns around Trowbridge. Hales did not provide ponies for his waggoners.

22. Below, pp. 53-5.

23. Horses could be kept at grass, usually for 1/6 to

2/6 per week (apparently less in winter: e.g. *London Gazette*, 30 Aug 1688, 20 May 1689, 22 Oct 1691, 12 Dec 1692; *Evening Post*, 9 Oct 1725; *Oxford Gazette and Reading Mercury*, 30 May 1748), but this is unlikely to have been worthwhile for any length of time. Only one inventory lists horses at grass (Appendix 2, No. 29), although some could have included horses at grass not listed as such.

24. Lancashire RO, WCW, John Hilton 1698; Cheshire RO, wills, Edward Lee 1713.

25. C 112/92, No. 335; Gerhold, p. 171; C 6/393/27; Symson, Nos. 1690, 1943; C 8/434/92; C 8/227/119.

26. Gerhold, pp. 18-19, 32-3; *Evening Post*, 25 Apr 1727; *Norwich Mercury*, 29 Mar 1729.

27. At Stonehouse and Gloucester, Hinckley and Leicester (two cases) and Shaftesbury and Yeovil (Appendix 2, Nos. 35, 38; George Larkin, *A true relation of a great number of people frozen to death near Salsbury* (1685)).

28. Appendix 2, No. 36; PROB 11/395, q. 66; Wiltshire RO, Archdeaconry of Wiltshire, will and inventory of Barnard Keene 1690. A fourth partner, Philip Woodroffe, may have been based at Tetbury (John Houghton, *A collection for improvement of husbandry and trade* (1692-1703), 6 July 1694).

29. An Oxford carrier at Woodstock and a St Albans carrier at Barnet (Oxfordshire RO, 170/3/130; Appendix 2, No. 57).

30. C 5/67/33. See below, p. 56.

31. C 6/393/27; C 24/1108, No. 35, Roger Hurst; Appendix 2, No. 19; C 8/216/59; C 10/146/26; Hampshire RO, 1690 A 40/1-2; Oxfordshire RO, 136/4/14; PROB 11/446, q. 145, Alexander Moone; C 10/234/47; C 8/434/92;

32. Leicestershire RO, ID 41/4/99 to 101; C 8/404/18; Fig. 5.

33. See also *Post-Man*, 10 Apr 1705; *Evening Post*, 30 Dec 1725; *Leeds Mercury*, 5 Aug 1729, 10 Apr 1739; LEP, 23 Oct 1735. A Frome carrier in 1700-10 was said to serve the area 20 miles around Frome (C 24/1325, No. 16, John Horseman).

34. C 8/434/92; C 10/392/23. John Goldring of Petersfield's stock in 1717 was valued at £135 and sold for £250 (C 11/1983/24). For other sales, see C 6/345/13 (a share in the Kendal business for £150, c.1705); C 8/487/28 (ditto, £130, 1706); C 10/288/63 (the Devizes business, £80, 1693); C 7/656/27 (the Trowbridge business, £480, 1710); C 11/475/66 (the Exeter business, £410, 1704).

35. C 24/1325, No. 16, John Horseman. See Gerhold, pp. 167-70, 178. For two carriers dividing territory between them in 1619, see Devon RO, DD 2625.

36. Dorian Gerhold, 'The Whitmash family, carriers and coachmasters of Taunton and Yeovil, 1685-1848', *Proceedings of the Somerset Archaeological and Natural History Society*, vol. 143 (2001), pp. 117-31; VCH, *Gloucestershire*, vol. 11 (1988), pp. 223, 230. A possible third example is the family of James Jackson, Leeds

and Wakefield carrier in 1690 (Turnbull, 'State regulation', especially p. 35 n. 24).

37. See Gerhold.

38. But see Lowther, p. 434; *Worcester Post-Man*, 8 Apr 1715.

39. Rogers, *History of agriculture*, vol. 1, p. 660; C 1/46/60; catalogue entry for C 1/61/499. See also Bodleian Library, Twyne Langbein MS, vol. 4, pp. 28-9.

40. For Bristol, Defoe, p. 362; H.E. Nott (ed.), *The deposition books of Bristol ... 1643-1647*, Bristol Record Society, vol. 6 (1935), pp. 69, 77, 82, 140, 165, 203; H.E. Nott and Elizabeth Ralph (eds.), *The deposition books of Bristol ... 1650-1654*, Bristol Record Society vol. 13 (1948), pp. 95, 163, 194. For Norwich, *A compleat history of the famous city of Norwich* (1728), p. 38. For Oxford, Fig. 12; Bodleian Library, University Archives, Chancellor's Court, 134/1/1; Pawson, p. 36. For Cambridge, Cambridge University Library, T IV 1 to 4; *ibid.*, TX 19, ff. 18, 26, 32; *ibid.*, VC Ct III 22, No. 7. For Exeter, Gerhold, p. 9; *The Post-Master or, The Loyal Mercury* [Exeter], 29 Sept 1721, 9 Feb 1722. For Kendal, Fig. 13; Joseph Nicolson and Richard Burn, *The history and antiquities of the counties of Westmorland and Cumberland* (1777), vol. 1, p. 66.

41. Fig. 12; McGrath, vol. 44, pp. 241, 250-7.

42. *Leeds Mercury*, 3 Oct 1727; Gloucestershire RO, Inventories 1689 (161), 1692 (30 and 59), 1695 (236), 1696 (216), 1703 (174), 1705 (83), 1706 (116); J.A. Chartres and G.L. Turnbull, *A pilot study of source materials for an economic history of British inland transport and communications, 1600-1850*, SSRC Research Report HR 2674 (1975), pp. 35-6.

43. John Taylor, *Carriers cosmographie* (1637), preface.

44. Lowther, pp. 219, 379; C 5/236/25.

45. See e.g. C 6/380/36; C 7/379/44.

46. C 7/379/44; Fitzwilliam, pp. 89, 182.

47. Hey, pp. 119-23.

48. Lowther, p. 549.

49. Pawson, pp. 28-9; Crofts, p. 5; Defoe, pp. 53, 84, 554.

50. Anne Buck, 'Middlemen in the Bedfordshire lace industry', Bedfordshire Historical Record Society, vol. 57 (1978), pp. 37, 39. See also Defoe, pp. 502-3.

51. Fitzwilliam, p. 122; Eaton, pp. 13, 15, 30, 133; CJ, vol. 21, 1727-32, pp. 463-4; C 5/548/60; *London Gazette*, 15 Jan 1683; C 5/459/119.

52. i.e. with a driver sitting on one of the horses.

53. C 11/326/32.

Notes to Chapter 2 (pp. 19-30)

1. C 8/404/18. See also below, p. 60; Symson, No. 823.

2. *London Gazette*, 21 Jan 1689; C 8/227/119. See also C 8/651/1, Patterson's schedule 2; C 5/613/14; C 9/6/137; POB, t17370706-32.

3. C 11/2/7; C 8/358/186; C 8/556/7; C 7/237/28. See also C 8/434/92.

4. C 22/182/32, Edmund Cobbe (for complainant).

See also C 24/1325, No. 16, John Horseman.

5. C 11/2383/38; C 11/475/66; C 8/626/9. See also C 11/677/35, Fry's answer.

6. George Larkin, *A true relation of a great number of people frozen to death near Salsbury* (1685); CJ, vol. 11, 1693-7, p. 514. See also POB, t17481207-23.

7. Appendix 2, No. 14; 2 Kings 9. 20.

8. Appendix 2, Nos. 22, 40; C 11/2383/38; C 11/475/66. See also C 22/654/34, Joseph Holbrooke; C 10/484/13; C 10/392/23.

9. C 5/603/77; C 8/385/48. See also E 112/782/90.

10. *Brice's Weekly Journal*, 10 Apr 1730; C 8/385/48.

11. C 11/2282/59. Hence the many inventories of Delaune's carriers which do not include any carrying stock.

12. i.e. all those with ploughs and four others (Appendix 2, Nos. 40, 57, 60, 67).

13. Three packhorse users' inventories distinguish their packhorses from other horses (though one waggon user also differentiated his waggon horses and 'plough horses').

14. Counting only the 32 as farmers, and excluding cases where the type of carriage is uncertain or was mixed (hence based on 21 packhorse users and 29 waggon users).

15. Among the nine inventories (five of them waggon users) taken in August, September or October, in five cases animals were less than 20 per cent of the total value of the farming stock (Andrew Hart of Cambridge having no farm animals at all), even after hay, oats and beans have been disregarded; only in two cases (both packhorse users) did the figure exceed 35 per cent.

16. C 8/630/34.

17. E.J.T. Collins, 'The farm horse economy of England and Wales ... 1900-40', in F.M.L. Thompson (ed.), *Horses in European economic history: a preliminary canter* (1983), pp. 78-9.

18. Below, p. 105.

19. C 10/483/282 with C 5/371/39; C 8/216/59; C 5/237/28; C 11/2410/12; PROB 11/383, q. 47, Michael Minchen; Essex RO, D/A BR 12/34. See also Hertfordshire RO, A25/4664; C 11/2750/14, Edward Jaques. For an innkeeper purchasing a carrying business, see *London Gazette*, 17 Sept 1691.

20. C 8/163/79; Delaune 1681, 1690; Essex RO, T/A 44 Colchester 51.

21. C 6/258/47; PROB 11/383, q. 48, Richard Mills; C 11/1404/10; PROB 11/472, q. 170, John Lockett.

22. Essex RO, D/A BW 65/176; Essex RO, Quarter Sessions transcript, 400/17 and 108; PROB 11/431, q. 53, John Peacock.

23. C 6/392/107; Kent RO, PRS/I/8/28; *Norwich Gazette*, 1 May 1725, 26 Nov 1726; *Stamford Mercury*, 15 Mar 1733, 23 Nov 1738; C 7/585/20; C 7/95/52; C 10/421/48; Norfolk RO, Norfolk Archdeaconry 1693 wills p. 127. See also C 5/237/28; C 11/1174/30; Lincoln-

shire RO, INV 190/132; PROB 4/7099.

24. Excluding domestic offices. Based on inventories in Appendix 2.

25. Lichfield Joint RO, will and inventory of Richard Merchant 1690; C 5/461/86; PROB 11/457, q. 135, William Clark; C 11/1404/10; C 11/478/10; PROB 4/9544; above, pp. 23-4; PROB 4/12579. Warren's inventory also lists £4,700 for leases, bills and bonds. Robert Long of Monmouth had £300 of ready money in 1694, and Thomas Edwards of Grendon £350 of ready money and good debts in 1683 (C 5/126/4; PROB 4/9995). For other carriers with substantial property, see C 8/651/1 (Robert Ridgwell); PROB 11/507, q. 49, Robert Brookes; PROB 11/560, q. 208, John Goldring; PROB 11/421, q. 157, Robert Long; PROB 11/395, q. 66, Thomas Keene; Herefordshire RO, Deanery of Hereford wills, 1687, John Lane; PROB 11/639, q. 244, Nicholas Rothwell.

26. e.g. Elizabeth Yeats in 1687 had assets totalling £184.9s. 6d, but after deduction of debts and funeral expenses only £30.2s. 10d (Lancashire RO, WRW.K). See also Oxfordshire RO, 88/3/23; Lancashire RO, WRW.K, Richard Greenwood 1682, account.

27. Hainsworth, pp. 78-9.

28. Totals here exclude debts and leases. Carrying and farming stock cannot always be completely separated; stocks of hay, oats and beans have been excluded from the carrying stock where possible. Probate inventories do not of course include real estate and debts owed by the deceased.

29. Peter Earle, *The making of the English middle class* (1989), pp. 107-9.

30. PROB 11/578, q. 18, William Woollett; Essex RO, D/A BR 14/423; E 112/782/90; C 5/603/77; C 8/626/9; Delaune 1681, 1690; Appendix 2, No. 15.

31. e.g. C 11/2303/30.

32. C 7/648/13. For discussion of these accounts, see above, pp. 8-9; below, p. 55.

33. Weare at Dorchester and Rothwell in London paid for ostlers, Want for his servants.

34. C 7/237/28; C 6/381/3; C 104/218, Cremer v. Rothwell, provender account.

35. C 11/1189/64.

36. e.g. C 6/381/3; C 11/1328/3; C 11/1189/64.

37. Gerhold, p. 12; C 5/189/16. For other examples, see C 8/651/1; PROB 11/482, q. 89, Roger Goldring; PROB 11/519, q. 3, John Barnes; Herefordshire RO, Deanery of Hereford wills, 5 Mar 1687/8, John Lane; Northamptonshire RO, Northampton wills, 3rd series, W88; PROB 11/639, q. 244, Nicholas Rothwell.

38. C 5/371/39; PROB 11/508, q. 127.

39. The best descriptions are in C 11/2536/65; C 8/401/82; C 24/1265, No. 36; C 11/677/35.

40. C 24/1265, No. 36, Richard Woodrofe; POB, t17350522-1.

41. C 6/53/96.

42. See the accounts in C 8/401/82; C 11/677/35.

43. e.g. C 8/401/82; C 5/603/77; C 11/677/35. For four-weekly accounts, see C 8/216/59.

44. C 5/603/77.

45. Gerhold, pp. 28, 32, 77-8.

46. C 11/326/32; CJ, vol. 11, 1693-7, p. 513; Corporation of London RO, Misc. MSS.31.6. Porters sometimes acted as warehousekeepers (POB, t17370706-32, t17480115-14) or vice versa.

47. Corporation of London RO, Misc. MSS. 31. 6; C 24/1070, No. 50.

48. C 11/677/35.

49. C 10/234/47; C 8/410/82; C 8/359/27. See also C 11/677/35; C 8/216/59.

50. C 11/2303/30. 6s. per week was paid from 1707 to 1710.

51. Corporation of London RO, Misc. MSS. 31. 6: C 24/1129, No. 23, Mary Glass; C 8/401/82.

Notes to Chapter 3 (pp. 31-45)

1. Albert, pp. 199-200.

2. John Armstrong, 'The significance of coastal shipping in British domestic transport, 1550-1830', *International Journal of Maritime History*, vol. 3 (1991), p. 83.

3. *Norwich Mercury*, 26 July 1729, 5 June 1736; LEP, 16 Nov 1728; *Daily Courant*, 4 Mar 1727.

4. Appendix 3. See Gerhold, chapter 7, for 19th-century parallels.

5. *Newcastle Courant*, 1 Sept 1744.

6. Total costs have been estimated using the following proportions: oats 47 per cent, beans 25 per cent, labour 17 per cent, industrial goods 11 per cent; see 'Productivity', pp. 512-13. Taking 1660-9 as 100, total costs were outside the range 83-123 in only two years between 1650 and 1750. By decade the averages were 110, 100, 99, 99, 100, 97, 104, 106, 98, 99.

7. The 50 per cent differential suggested in 1675 (Thomas Birch, *History of the Royal Society of London*, vol. 3 (1757), p. 207) does not accord with the other evidence.

8. T.S. Willan, 'The justices of the peace and the rates of land carriage, 1692-1827', JTH, 1st ser., vol. 5 (1962), p. 198; *The Oxford almanack* (1703), p. 16.

9. e.g. see Appendix 3, parts A and B for Leeds and the West Riding in the 1690s.

10. *Newcastle Courant*, 1 Sept 1744.

11. C 22/946/32.

12. Counting waggon and packhorse rates separately but otherwise each rate once only (even if there were separate summer and winter rates) each time a new rate was set.

13. Possibly in part because carriers could feed their horses on grass in summer, though there is no indication of this in carriers' accounts with innkeepers; Symson in April 1715 thought that rates of land carriage 'will not fall until carriers turn to grass which will be about 25 next month' (Symson, No. 1084).

14. Eaton, pp. 13, 15, 30, 133; J.D. Marshall (ed.), *The autobiography of William Stout of Lancaster 1665-1752* (1967), pp. 95, 98, 107-8, 138.

15. T.S Willan, *River navigation in England 1600-1750* (1936), p. 121; H.J. Dyos and D.H. Aldcroft, *British transport: an economic*

survey from the seventeenth century to the twentieth (1974 Pelican edn.), p. 43.

16. CJ, vol. 23, 1737-41, pp. 493-5; Stamford Mercury, 14 Mar 1745. See also T.S. Willan, The English coasting trade (1967), p. xv, for timber Weymouth-London at 8s. per ton (0.7 pence per ton-mile). The same mileages are used here as by road.

17. The Oxford almanack (1692), p. 130; John Haynes, A view of the present state of the clothing trade (1706), pp. 65-6; Albert, p. 8; Willan, River navigation, p. 121.

18. Symson, pp. l-li and Nos. 1268, 1323, 1397, 1943.

19. See Gerhold, chapter 5.

20. C 8/163/79; C 7/595/61. In 1709 Richard Hales, Trowbridge carrier, 'made up his accounts with the clothiers and others his customers' (C 7/656/27).

21. London Gazette, 18 Nov 1680, 18 Dec 1682; Flying Post, 4 Feb 1699; Worcestershire RO, b899/720.8541; E 134/9 Geo II Mich 21; C 104/218, Cremer v. Rothwell, Book N, 14 Nov 1735; CJ, vol. 24, 1741-5, p. 851; POB, t17480115-14.

22. Peter Earle, The making of the English middle class (1989), pp. 17, 19.

23. C 5/548/60; C 6/198/83; C 8/227/119; C 8/434/92; C 6/414/29 and 43.

24. Alan Everitt, Change in the provinces: the seventeenth century (1969), p. 40; C 8/401/82; Fitzwilliam, pp. 186, 274, 278, and passim for venison; POB, t17370706-32; C 11/1189/64, Pearse's schedule 2; C 5/371/39; Stamford Mercury, 14 Mar, 1 Aug 1728; C 8/354/24; Defoe, p. 373; POB, t17300228-12. See next note for oysters.

25. Post-Man, 17 Dec 1698, 6 Nov 1701; Post Boy, 3 Nov 1698, 26 Jan 1699; C 11/1174/30; C 5/237/28; Eaton, p. 133.

26. Hainsworth, p. 250.

27. Lowther, pp. 545, 549; Everitt, Change in the provinces, p. 40; Walter M. Stern, 'Cheese shipped coastwise to London towards the middle of the eighteenth century', Guildhall Miscellany, vol. 4 (1971-3), p. 209.

28. C 8/651/1, Patterson's schedule 2; C 22/182/32, Edmund Cobb (for complainant); C 11/1189/64, Pearse's schedule 2; C 5/516/12; C 7/600/27; C 7/379/44; C 11/15/5; C 24/1325, No. 16, John Horseman; CJ, vol. 13, 1699-1702, pp. 570, 783-4; Defoe, p. 263; POB, t17240708-35.

29. Domestick Intelligence, 16 Nov 1682; C 6/89/34; C 11/474/64; Flying Post, 12 Oct 1699; C 6/53/96; C 6/378/69; William Le Hardy and Geoffrey Reckitt (eds.), County of Buckingham – Calendar to the sessions records, vol. 2, 1694-1705 (1936), pp. 406-7; Worcester Post-Man, 3 Feb 1716. See also London Gazette, 22 Jan 1685; POB, passim.

30. Fitzwilliam, passim. See also W.J. Smith (ed.), Herbert correspondence (1963); McGrath; Lowther.

31. Symson, Nos. 401, 406, 459, 609, 775, 869, 996, 1852.

32. F.P. and M.M. Verney (eds.), Memoirs of the Verney family during the seventeenth century (1907), vol. 2, p. 276.

33. London Gazette, 26 Dec 1682, 25 Jan 1683, 29 Apr 1689; Ruth Bird (ed.), The journal of Giles Moore, Sussex Record Society, vol. 68 (1971), p. 241; Post-Man, 12 Apr 1705, 3 Apr 1707; POB, t17500425-52; C 8/374/150; C 6/53/96.

34. C 6/63/41; K.H. Burley, The economic development of Essex in the later seventeenth and eighteenth centuries, London DPhil 1957, p. 189.

35. Gerhold, pp. 5, 120-3; C 7/600/27; Symson, p. xlvii and Nos. 836, 1943. For cloth from Rochdale in 1652-3, when carriage cost 2.7 per cent of the value, see Eric Kerridge, Trade and banking in early modern England (1988), p. 47.

36. Gerhold, pp. 121-3; Map 5; CJ, vol. 24, 1741-45, p. 851.

37. Marshall, Autobiography of William Stout, p. 138.

38. W.B. Stephens, Seventeenth century Exeter (1958), pp. 117-18; Daniel Defoe, The complete English tradesman (1726), vol. 1, p. 397. See also Haynes, View, p. 65 for wool.

39. Above, p. 35; C 6/63/41; Keith Wrightson, Earthly necessities: economic lives in early modern Britain, 1450-1750 (2002), p. 246; John Latimer, The annals of Bristol in the eighteenth century (1893), p. 269; James H. Thomas, Petersfield under the later Stuarts (1980), p. 44n; Kendal Weekly Courant, 4 Mar 1732.

40. Above, pp. 20,21; Publick Adviser, 26 May 1657; City Mercury, 4 Nov 1675; A true relation of a great number of people frozen to death near Salsbury (1685); London Gazette, 4 Sept 1693; C 5/613/14; Symson, Nos. 1557, 2046; Chester carriers' handbill on wall of agent's office, Erddig.

41. POB, passim.

42. Appendix 10; below, p. 137.

43. C 5/597/95; C 10/146/26.

44. Crofts, pp. 53-4; Brian Austen, English provincial posts 1633-1840 (1978), p. 8; Norfolk RO, Norwich city records, Assembly Book 1613-42, f. 278.

45. James F. Larkin (ed.), Stuart royal proclamations, vol. 2 (1983), pp. 468-70, 594-7; 12 Cha II c.35; J.W.M. Stone (ed.), The inland posts (1392-1672) (1987), pp. 71, 79-80, 187.

46. Quoted in W.G. Stitt Dibden (ed.), The Post Office 1635-1720, Postal History Society, Special Series No. 10 (1960), p. 32.

47. Roy R. Morgan, Chichester: a documentary history (1992), p. 60; Dibden, Post Office, p. 23.

48. London Gazette, 19 July 1686; 9 Anne c.11.

49. NA on-line catalogue for series C 1, e.g. C 1/302/50.

50. C 8/216/59; C 5/603/77.

51. Hainsworth, pp. 75, 77.

52. See Kerridge, Trade and banking, especially

chapter 4.

53. C 22/182/32, John Hamond.

54. C 24/1092, No. 37, Michael Oatway; C 8/262/77; C 6/319/57; C 24/1265, No. 36, p. 6. See also C 11/677/35; C 9/6/137; *London Gazette*, 2 Mar 1693; POB, t17350522-1.

55. C 8/529/69; C 11/15/5. See also C 7/595/61; C 5/164/81, schedule 2, 25 July & 2 Aug 1682.

56. Hainsworth, p. 81; *London Gazette*, 31 Oct 1695. See also POB, t17261012-38, t17370706-32.

57. Hainsworth, p. 79.

58. Eric G.M. Fletcher, *The carrier's liability* (1932), pp. 29-34, 120, 141, 145-6, 180, 183.

59. C 8/587/35; C 22/182/32.

60. *English Reports*, vol. 90, pp. 879-80, 903.

61. LEP, 11 Mar 1738; C 24/1086, Petty v. Travell, Anthony Rush; C 6/345/13; Lowther, pp. 126, 159; Smith, *Herbert correspondence*, p. 326; C 5/603/77. For tax receipts sent by carrier with an armed guard, see NA, T 1/7, f. 38; NA, T 1/28, f. 70; *English Reports*, vol. 83, pp. 723-4.

62. Hainsworth, p. 83.

63. Fitzwilliam, pp. 186, 259; C 5/310/16.

64. C 11/1189/64. See also Symson, Nos. 779, 941, 1091. For accounts of returns of money, including conveyance of cash to London, see C 11/677/35, schedules.

65. C 24/1092, No. 37; E 112/782/82.

66. C 11/472/31; C 11/474/47.

67. C 5/213/33; *English Reports*, vol. 90, pp. 879-80, 903; C 11/677/35; C 11/587/9, Iliff's schedule 1; C 22/182/32; Hainsworth, p. 81; McGrath, vol. 44, pp. 377-8; *Stamford Mercury*, 14 Mar 1728. See also Essex RO, D/DP A172 (8s. per £100 from Ingatestone in 1650) and Hainsworth, p. 81 (10s. per £100 reckoned enough from Peterborough in 1697, and 2s. 6d. per £100 paid in 1708).

68. *Post Boy*, 25 Feb 1699.

69. C 22/182/32, John Hamond.

70. Thomas Baddeley of Newcastle-under-Lyme in 1694 had a musket and a fowling piece, and John Frost of Lightcliffe near Halifax in 1713 had two pistols and a gun (PROB 4/7099; Borthwick Institute, Pontefract, inventory of John Frost). There is no evidence of dogs being used by carriers in this period.

71. POB, t17230828-69, t17261012-38, t17350522-1, t17370706-32.

72. POB, t17350522-1, t17560225-45.

73. POB, t17261012-38.

74. C 5/459/119.

75. e.g. *Calendar of State Papers Domestic*, 1675-6, pp. 20, 219; *The great robbery in the west: or, the inn-keeper turn'd highway-man* (1678); *London Gazette*, 18 Nov 1680, 18 Dec 1682, 13 Mar 1690, 12 Mar 1691, 2 Mar 1693; *Post-Man*, 22 May 1697.

76. C 24/1265, No. 36, answers to Q. 5.

Notes to Chapter 4 (pp. 46-58)

1. C 8/651/1, Patterson's schedule 2. Omitted items, added on the same basis as for the Oxford carrier (see below), assuming the Ridgwell accounts to have covered nine days, are 12s. 11d. for depreciation of horses, 1s. 8d. for depreciation of waggons and 1s. 6d. for rent, bringing the total to £16 3s. 1d. (on which the percentages in the text are based). The comparative percentages for Ridgwell and the Oxford carrier are provender 60/69, harness & shoeing 14/7, horses 4/2, waggoners 8/6, horsekeepers, bookkeepers & porters 10/7, waggons 4/8, rent 0/1.

2. The fact that 'the tole' amounted to only 4d. out of £7 15s. 2d. indicates that it was made soon after 1715 (the date of the first Turnpike Act on the Oxford road) or before 1715 (referring to a bridge toll pre-dating the turnpikes).

3. The main curiosity is the small cost of corn compared with hay and straw, and the apparent replacement of oats by bran at Oxford.

4. 3s. 8d. for depreciation of horses (assuming seven horses, six-year working life, £8 5s. 0d. per horse; see below p. 52 and Gerhold, p. 136); 1s. 3d. for depreciation of waggons (assuming £10 per waggon – based on inventory evidence – and three-year working life); 1s. 6d. for rent (assuming £4 per annum – little more than a guess – for warehouses in the provincial town and London).

5. John Clark (ed.), *The medieval horse and its equipment c.1150-c.1450* (1995), pp. 22-9, 169. A hand was four inches.

6. Joan Thirsk, *Horses in early modern England: for service, for pleasure, for power* (1978), pp. 10, 26-7; Keith Chivers, *The shire horse* (1976), pp. 15, 21; P.R. Edwards, *The horse trade of Tudor and Stuart England* (1988), pp. 50-1.

7. Of 505 horses aged five or more recorded in the horse toll books of Oxford 1673-1720, the average height was 13.9 hands, and only two were more than 15 hands (both 16 hands). At Warwick in 1686-9, out of 158 horses (excluding the nags), the average was 14.2 hands, and none was more than 15 hands. None of the 49 horses listed with sizes in the book for Bristol market in 1705-14 was over 14¾ hands. I am grateful to Peter Edwards for allowing me to use his notes on these sources (from Oxford Reference Library, Oxford City records, F.4.4; Warwickshire RO, Warwick borough records, W13/1; Bristol RO).

8. See e.g. *Stamford Mercury*, 1714-17. For larger horses, *ibid.*, 15 Nov 1716, 26 Sept, 19 Dec 1717; *Evening Post*, 27 Sept 1716.

9. e.g. *Stamford Mercury*, 10 May 1716; *Daily Post*, 23 Mar, 29 Apr 1728, 11 & 12 Apr 1729; LEP, 13 Feb, 13 Mar, 3 Apr 1746.

10. London Metropolitan Archives, X88/1, p. 200.

11. Based on 12 inventories of coachmasters (1672-1723) and 17 inventories of carriers by waggon (1663-1718), in Appendices 2 and 7. Harness is excluded where possible.

12. House of Lords Record Office, Main Papers, 2 Feb 1718/19.

13. Appendix 2, Nos. 40, 54, 60, 68, 71.

14. A proclamation of 1635 and later statutes

limiting waggon teams to a certain number of horses or horses and oxen were probably seeking to close a loophole, and are anyway not evidence that *carriers* were using oxen (Thomas Rymer, *Foedera* (1967 edn.), vol. 9, part 1, pp. 26-7; 7 & 8 Will III c.29; etc.).

15. David R. Ringrose, *Transportation and economic stagnation in Spain, 1750-1850* (1970), pp. 45, 48; John Langdon, *Horses, oxen and technological innovation* (1986), pp. 21, 160-4; Malcolm Kennedy, *Hauling the loads: a history of Australia's working horses and bullocks* (1992), pp. 2, 18, 22, 25.

16. E.E. Rich and C.H. Wilson (eds.), *Cambridge economic history of Europe*, vol. 4 (1967), p. 216; Langdon, *Horses, oxen*, p. 155. For the introduction and spread of waggons, see 'Packhorses'.

17. Jackman, pp. 60-1, 68-9.

18. J. Geraint Jenkins, *The English farm wagon: origins and structure* (1972), pp. 34, 83; Anthony Bird, *Roads and vehicles* (1973), pp. 75-6; C 6/233/32; C 11/587/9, Iliff's fourth schedule, 27 June 1739.

19. CJ, vol. 24, 1741-5, p. 798; below, p. 148.

20. PROB 5/4898.

21. Below, p. 58.

22. William L. Sachse, 'The journal of Nathan Prince, 1747', *American Neptune*, vol. 16 (1956), p. 84. I am grateful to John Armstrong for this reference.

23. Joseph Lucas (trans.), *Kalm's account of his visit to England ... 1748* (1892), p. 11.

24. 7 & 8 Will III c.29; 6 Anne c.56; CJ, vol. 12, 1697-99, pp. 682-3; CJ, vol. 15, 1705-08, pp. 531, 562-3; Somerset RO, 192 (1) 118. Pepys thought double file for waggons might be worthwhile 'where there is breadth enough' (Pepys, vol. 3, 1 Nov 1662). See also *Gloucester Journal*, 19 Feb 1760 (advertisement for sale of waggon).

25. Jackman, pp. 60, 64, 66-8; 6 Anne c.56; 9 Anne c.23.

26. C 7/579/80; *London Gazette*, 26 May 1687; Essex RO, Quarter Sessions typescript, 457/28; London Metropolitan Archives, MJ/SP 1689 Aug/8; C 7/214/135; *The case of John Littlehales* (British Library, 816 m. 14); CJ, vol. 11, 1693-97, pp. 511-14; CJ, vol. 12, 1697-99, pp. 682-3; CJ, vol. 15, 1705-08, pp. 531, 562-3.

27. C 5/244/9.

28. Anchitell Grey, *Debates of the House of Commons from the year 1667 to the year 1694* (1769), vol. 1, p. 232.

29. Parliamentary Papers 1808 vol. 2, *Reports from the Committee on the highways of the Kingdom*, pp. 411-13, 416-17, 420, 435-6; William Youatt, *The horse; with a treatise on draught* (1831), p. 414.

30. CJ, vol. 11, 1693-97, pp. 511-12.

31. C 11/587/9, Iliff's third schedule.

32. Appendix 2, Nos. 29, 40, 55, 70, 72.

33. Above, p. 50. Other references are to six horses in 1663 and 1684, four horses at length and three abreast in 1691, and five horses at length

or seven abreast in 1707 (Harper, vol. 1, p. 127; C 5/371/39; C 7/214/135; CJ, vol. 15, 1705-08, pp. 562-3).

34. David Loggan, *Oxonia illustrata* (1675); ibid., *Cantabrigia illustrata* (c.1690); Sir Robert Atkyns, *Ancient and present state of Glostershire* (1712), Ampney Park and Bradley Court; Bowles' engraving of Cheapside, c.1750.

35. 'Packhorses', p. 12.

36. PRO, STAC 8/28/5.

37. 'Packhorses', p. 12.

38. C 5/371/39; C 10/238/80; C 5/93/65; C 5/613/14.

39. See Appendix 2. In 1730 there were said to be seven waggons at a time leaving Frome (John Pinkerton, *A general collection of the best and most interesting voyages and travels* (1808-14), vol. 2, p. 29).

40. See Appendix 5 for further discussion.

41. Above, p. 9.

42. C 8/556/7.

43. C 8/556/74; C 10/288/63.

44. Below, p. 74.

45. C 11/1189/64.

46. C 6/381/3; above, pp. 8-9.

47. C 104/218, Cremer v. Rothwell, provender account. Cremer's inn is identified in LEP, 6 June 1741.

48. *Aris's Birmingham Gazette*, 12 Mar, 4 June 1744, 11 Mar, 13 May 1745

49. Twice on Friday, twice on Sunday and once on Tuesday.

50. Fitzwilliam, p. 41; Thoresby, vol. 2, p. 14; *Leeds Mercury*, 20 Dec 1726.

51. e.g. Helen Stocks (ed.), *Records of the Borough of Leicester ... 1603-1688* (1923), pp. 222, 496; Pepys, vol. 6, 30 Nov 1665.

52. Only Barry's account has weeks without a waggon, when it is theoretically possible that waggons lodged at different inns.

53. C 5/67/33; C 5/93/65.

54. Hampshire RO, 1690 A 40/1-2; C 11/2750/14, Edward Jaques.

55. e.g. the Norwich and Bury St Edmunds services in 1735 were travelling late at night and early in the morning (Appendix 4).

56. James Masschaele, *Peasants, merchants, and markets: inland trade in medieval England, 1150-1350* (1997), pp. 203-4; Peter Spufford, *Power and profit: the merchant in medieval Europe* (2002), p. 200. See also Henri Dubois, 'Techniques et coûts des transports terrestres dans l'espace bourguignon aux XIVe et XVe siècles', *Annales de Bourgogne*, vol. 52 (1980), p. 73.

57. In this case Delaune mistakenly records only one partner, and gives the destination as Exeter.

58. See p. 247 below, note 23.

59. Under 40 miles, 4; 40-49, 3; 50-59, 2; 60-69, 5; 70-79, 4; 80-89, 1; 90-99, 7; 100-109, 3; 110-119, 3; 120-129, 3; 130-139, 0; 140-149, 2; 150 or more, 1.

60. Appendix 2, Nos. 33, 43, 50.

61. The teams hauling Russell's Exeter waggons in

1816-21 covered 106 to 122 miles per week (Gerhold, p. 59).

62. Gerhold, p. 57.
63. Hampshire RO, 44M69/G2/497.
64. Below, p. 74.
65. C 6/92/56; C 24/1127, No. 4; C 5/548/60.
66. C 8/556/7; C 11/2303/30; C 10/238/80. See also C 5/388/62; C 11/677/35, Fry's answer. Daniel Want usually paid 2s. per horse per day's work at Maidenhead, bearing the cost of provender himself.
67. Based on Hales's horses in Appendix 5 (oats 2s. per bushel, beans 4s. per bushel).

Notes to Chapter 5 (pp. 59-68)

1. Hey, p. 87; Henry Bracken, *The traveller's pocket-farrier* (1701), p. 5. For Exmoor ponies, averaging about 12 hands, see *Exmoor Review*, No. 2 (1960), unpag. See also J.R. Chanter, 'Devonshire lanes', *Transactions of the Devonshire Association*, vol. 6 (1873-4), p. 190.
2. Thomas Blundeville, *The fower chiefyst offices belongyng to horsemanshippe* (1565), f. 13r; Gervase Markham, *A way to get wealth* (1683 edn.), p. 4. I am grateful to Peter Edwards for these references.
3. Based on 21 packhorse inventories 1680-1718 and 17 waggon inventories 1663-1718 (Appendix 2); research on horse toll books and other sources by Peter Edwards.
4. Appendix 2, Nos. 14, 19, 25, 67; Blundeville, *Fower chiefyst offices*, f. 13r.
5. Roderick J. Barman, 'Packing in British Columbia: transport on a resource frontier', *JTH*, 3rd ser., vol. 21 (2000), pp. 143, 153.
6. Smoke Elser and Bill Brown, *Packin' in on mules and horses* (1980), pp. 1-4.
7. Hey, pp. 90-1, 98; Ronald E. Zupko, *A dictionary of weights and measures for the British Isles* (1985), pp. 270-1; Symson, p. xlvii; above, p. 52. At Wakefield in 1704 an English pack weighed about 16 to 18 stone (224-252 lb), though a Scotch pack was about 24 stone (336 lb) (C 24/1256, No. 7, Isaac Kirby).
8. Hey, p. 90; POB, t17520914-25.
9. Figs. 4 and 35; David Loggan, *Cantabrigia illustrata* (c.1690); Herbert, pp. 4, 72. For varying American practice in this respect, and the reasons, see Elser, *Packin' in*, pp. 114-16.
10. POB, t17520914-25.
11. Appendix 2, Nos. 3, 22, 28, 29, 73; *Weekly Courant* [Nottingham], 25 June 1724; *Leeds Mercury*, 6 July 1725, 11 June 1728, 19 Apr 1737, 22 May 1739; *Adams's Weekly Courant*, 3 Apr 1750; *Orion Adams's Weekly Journal*, 17 Mar 1752; Crofts, p. 3. For drifts, see also *Exeter Flying Post*, 24 Jan 1757.
12. C 22/654/34, Joseph Holbrooke; *Chester Courant*, 5 Dec 1749, quoted in *Cheshire sheaf*, 3rd ser., vol. 10 (1913), p. 90; *Whitworth's Manchester Advertiser*, 19 Apr 1757; *Manchester Magazine*, 7 Apr 1747. I am grateful to Chris Lewis for the Manchester reference. Richard Hatton's 20 packhorses were described by

Delaune as two gangs (Appendix 2, No. 4; Delaune 1681).
13. Excluding doubtful cases. In some cases horses kept chiefly for farm work may not have been listed separately, and one horse will usually have been for the carrier to ride on himself, such as the 'hackney horse' of Edward Miles of Ludlow.
14. Naylor's 101 horses would raise the average to 19 horses and capacity to 41 cwt.
15. Possibly, however, more than one of the three Lewes partners came to London every week.
16. Above, pp. 8-9.
17. C 104/218, Cremer v. Rothwell, provender account; above, p. 55.
18. C 24/1325, No. 16, John Williams.
19. Henri Dubois, 'Techniques et coûts des transports terrestres dans l'espace bourguignon aux XIVe et XVe siècles', *Annales de Bourgogne*, vol. 52 (1980), p. 73. See also Peter Spufford, *Power and profit: the merchant in medieval Europe* (2002), p. 200.
20. Appendix 4; above, pp. 16, 18.
21. Though Exeter packhorses managed 42 miles in one day of their journeys, between Egham and London (Appendix 4).
22. E.M. Carus Wilson, 'The overseas trade of Bristol', in E. Power and M.M. Postan (eds.), *Studies in English trade in the fifteenth century* (1933), p. 189; H.S. Bennett, *The Pastons and their England* (1922), pp. 159, 162.
23. e.g. if one carrier had several gangs travelling separately, if two or more carriers sent their gangs out together, if the main destination is unclear, if the horses were also used for local deliveries, or if Delaune mistook the number of partners.
24. The figures are: under 40 miles, 5; 40-49, 0; 50-59, 3; 60-69, 5; 70-79, 3; 80-89, 2; 90-99, 4; 100-109, 12; 110-119, 7; 120-129, 20; 130-139, 14; 140-149, 8; 150-159, 6; 160-169, 2; 170 plus, 3.
25. C 6/258/53; Appendix 2, Nos. 7, 15, 20. For a local carrier using horses both as packhorses and cart-horses, see *York Courant*, 28 Sept 1756.
26. See also Appendix 2, No. 2, with both gears and packsaddles in 1680.
27. C 6/381/3; C 11/677/35; C 11/587/9; above, pp. 62-3; *Gloucester Journal*, 22 Nov 1737; Appendix 2, No. 29; *LEP*, 26 Apr 1737; *Sherborne Mercury*, 11 Dec 1739; C 104/218, Cremer v. Rothwell, provender account; handbill framed on wall of agent's office, Erddig, Clwyd; Robert Dymond, *Exeter and neighbourhood under George the Third* (1879-80). See also Wiltshire RO, 1195/27, reference to Henry Norman, probably a Bristol carrier, 1714.
28. J.D. Marshall (ed.), *The autobiography of William Stout of Lancaster 1665-1752* (1967), pp. 95, 98, 107-8, 114, 138.
29. 'Packhorses', p. 8; *A complete guide to all persons who have any trade or concern with the City of London* (1758); Bristol RO, Deposition

Books, 1650-4, f. 301.
30. Delaune 1681, 1690; CJ, vol. 11, 1693-97, p. 511.
31. See 'Packhorses' for more detail. The main differences here from that article are some of the figures on Map 7, the figures for provender in Table 4, and (in chapter 6) additional evidence for the last London packhorses and the relationship with the introduction of flying waggons.
32. Sir John Lowther in 1698 could not 'imagine you should think a single chest of 220 or 230 lbs can lye upon any horse without wounding him to pieces' (Lowther, p. 624). See also *A collection of the state papers of John Thurloe, Esq* (1742), vol. 3, pp. 91-2.
33. For the inflexibility of pack sizes, see Symson, Nos. 2, 1385, 1438.
34. Above, p. 59.
35. Above, pp. 52, 60.
36. Above, pp. 57, 64.
37. 'Packhorses', pp. 13-14, 17.
38. Above, pp. 57, 63. An Exeter carrier informed potential customers in 1705 'that they may be accommodated for expedition by pack-horse carriage' (*Daily Courant*, 3 Mar 1705).
39. Above, pp. 32, 34; Appendix 3.
40. Above, p. 49.
41. The percentage of all services conducted by waggon (averaged for 1681 and 1690 together) declined from 85 per cent for 11-20 miles to 46 per cent for 41-50 miles, then rose from 45 per cent for 51-60 miles to 79 per cent for 81-90 miles, then declined (not smoothly) to 12 per cent for over 150 miles.

Notes to Chapter 6 (pp. 69-75)

1. 'Productivity', pp. 505-6.
2. See below, pp.
3. They did however later make high-speed vans feasible by reducing the additional cost of greater speed for the most urgent goods; see Gerhold, pp. 188-94.
4. Gerhold, p. 129. In 1719 the carriers and others of Lancashire and Cheshire claimed that tolls on a waggon from there to London and back amounted to 12s. 8d., equivalent to only about 0.5 pence per mile and about 0.25 pence per ton-mile of capacity, but there were then few turnpikes (House of Lords Record Office, Main Papers, 2 Feb 1718/19).
5. John Pinkerton, *A general collection of the best and most interesting voyages and travels* (1808-14), vol. 2, p. 8; Defoe, p. 433; Gerhold, pp. 197-8; M. Postlethwayt, *Universal dictionary of trade and commerce* (1755), vol. 2, p. 617; CJ, vol. 28, 1757-61, p. 140; 5 Geo III c.38; 14 Geo II c.42.
6. Gerhold, pp. 29-30.
7. Below, p. 'Packhorses', p. 8; Pym Yeatman (ed.), 'The diary of Benjamin Granger, of Bolsover, 1688-1708', *Journal of the Derbyshire Archaeological and Natural History Society*, vol. 9 (1887), p. 67; POB, t17350522-1; *Newcastle Courant*, 1 Sept 1744; CJ, vol. 24, 1741-45,

pp. 804, 812; *York Courant*, 3 Jan 1749. Only the Sheffield date is known to be when the service started. There was possibly a Liverpool waggon in 1713 (Symson, No. 719). The 1719 reference relates to various places in Lancashire, apparently including Manchester and Warrington.
8. Gerhold, pp. 27-8.
9. Twenty-four per cent comparing Rothwell's horses with Hales's (Appendix 5). Rothwell and Hales paid the same per peck for oats and beans; expenditure on hay is taken as constant, at Hales's price to eliminate the effect of dear hay in London.
10. On some routes better roads may have made use of stronger horses possible (above, p. 49).
11. 'Productivity', pp. 502-3.
12. Appendix 2, No. 31; Gerhold, p. 143.
13. 'Productivity', pp. 400, 408.
14. C 10/392/23; C 7/656/27.
15. C 8/626/9.
16. Based on London directories.
17. Dorian Gerhold, 'The growth of the London carrying trade, 1681-1838', *Economic History Review*, 2nd ser., vol. 41, pp. 400, 408, together with the carrier lists used there; C 11/587/9, Iliff's third schedule. Firms covering over 100 miles from London numbered 97 in 1681 and 85 in 1690 and 1765. Exclusion of services covering less than 20 miles accounts for the difference from figures elsewhere in this book.
18. *Gloucester Journal*, 22 Nov 1737; LEP, 26 Apr 1737; Gerhold, pp. 17, 19; *Sherborne Mercury*, 11 Dec 1739; above, p. 62; A.P. Wadsworth and J. de L. Mann, *The cotton trade and industrial Lancashire, 1600-1780* (1965), p. 220; LEP, 18 Mar 1749; *Adams's Weekly Courant*, 3 Apr 1750; LEP, 2 Mar 1751; Joseph Nicolson and Richard Burn, *The history and antiquities of the counties of Westmorland and Cumberland* (1777), vol. 1, p. 66; *The Liverpool memorandum book ... for the year MDCCLIII* (1753); *Whitworth's Manchester Advertiser*, 19 Apr 1757; *A complete guide to all persons who have any trade or concern with the City of London* (1758).
19. Above, pp. 61, 62-3, 65.
20. e.g. Chard and Exeter 'flying waggons' taking five days in 1746-59 and 5½ days in 1757 (33 and 29 miles per day) respectively and lodging overnight in both cases (Appendix 4; *Sherborne Mercury*, 24 Oct 1757). See also Gerhold, p. 29.
21. Fitzwilliam, p. 274; *Northampton Mercury*, 9 May 1720; *Sherborne Mercury*, 10 May 1737; *Gloucester Journal*, 2 May 1738. See also Fig. 26.
22. *Sherborne Mercury*, 10 May, 21 June, 19 July, 9 Aug 1737, 4 Apr 1738, 3 Apr 1739; Gerhold, pp. 3, 56.
23. 'Packhorses', p. 22; *Stamford Mercury*, 17 Feb, 28 Apr 1743; *York Courant*, 13 Dec 1748.
24. *Sherborne Mercury*, 4 Apr 1738, 3 Apr 1739, 6 Apr 1742, 19 Apr 1743, 10 Apr 1744; above,

pp. 55, 62; *Gloucester Journal*, 5 Apr 1748, 28 Mar 1749, 27 Mar, 23 Oct 1750; *Complete guide* (1758, 1760).

25. In the West Country in the 19th century carriage by flying waggon was about 15 per cent dearer than by ordinary waggon (Gerhold, p. 151).

26. Defoe, p. 441. Postlethwayt claimed in 1755 that carriage was 30 per cent cheaper than 'before the roads were amended by turnpikes', but the earlier rates of carriage seem much too high (compared with examples in Appendix 3), and one is a rate paid by the government (Postlethwayt, *Universal dictionary*, vol. 2, p. 617). The rates in Appendix 3 compared where possible with Postlethwayt's later rates suggest little or no change.

27. Albert, pp. 180-1.

28. R.G. Wilson, 'Transport dues as indices of economic growth, 1775-1820', *Economic History Review*, 2nd ser., vol. 19 (1966), p. 111.

29. Albert, pp. 260-2; 'Productivity', p. 494. Taking costs in 1693-1702 as 100, they were 100 in the 1730s, 110 in the 1740s and 111 in the 1750s (*ibid.*).

30. 'Productivity', pp. 494-7, 513.

31. Gerhold, pp. 23, 181-2; Gerhold, 'Growth', p. 400.

32. Gerhold, 'Growth', p. 400.

Notes to Chapter 7 (pp. 79-90)

1. Based on 0.5 horses per double mile (below, p. 149) and the mileage in Table 7.

2. Appendices 6 and 8.

3. National Library of Wales, Ottley/Pitchford 2615, 2617.

4. Jackman, p. 115.

5. Above, p. 4; 'Packhorses', pp. 3-4, 10, 19.

6. NA, STAC 8/61/1; British Library, Add MS 15828, f. 25; E.A. Pratt, *A history of inland transport and communication* (1912), p. 38; Joan Parkes, *Travel in England in the seventeenth century* (1925), p. 80. Fares were similar to those later, i.e. Ipswich 0.9 pence per mile in 1613 (W.H. Richardson (ed.), *The annalls of Ipswiche ... by Nath. Bacon ... 1654* (1884), pp. 453-4), and Colchester 1.2 pence per mile in 1630 (SP 46/76, f. 270).

7. SP 29/319, No. 200.

8. SP 29/316, No. 194; SP 29/319, No. 202, p. 6.

9. Appendix 2, No. 32.

10. Crofts (p. 111) suggests that they had slung compartments within them for passengers, but this is based on mid-18th-century evidence.

11. Below, pp. 82-3, 139-40.

12. Laszlo Tarr, *The history of the carriage* (1969), p. 203.

13. *Publick Adviser*, 26 May 1657; PROB 4/12579; Delaune 1681; PROB 11/367, q. 124; sources listed for Appendix 8, part C.

14. Historic Manuscripts Commission, 12th report, appendix, part 1, vol. 1 (1888), *The manuscripts of the Earl Cowper*, pp. 393-4.

15. Allowing one hour each day for dining and for feeding the horses.

16. Cambridge University Library, TX 19, f. 43v; Norfolk RO, Norwich City records, Mayor's Court Book, vol. 20, 1634-46, f. 124; *Publick Adviser*, 26 May 1657.

17. Historic Manuscripts Commission, 7th report, appendix (1879), p. 458a. The coach to St Albans used by Lady Mary Verney in 1647, cited by Parkes as a stage-coach (*Travel in England*, p. 82) appears to have been a hired coach (F.P. and M.M. Verney (eds.), *Memoirs of the Verney family during the seventeenth century* (1907), vol. 1, pp. 359, 362). But see J.T. Smith and M.A. North (eds.), *St Albans 1650-1700* (2003), p. 138.

18. SP 29/319, No. 200. For the difficulty of keeping coach horses in 1651, see *The memoirs of Sir Hugh Cholmley* (1777), p. 47.

19. John Chandler (ed.), *Travels through Stuart Britain: the adventures of John Taylor, the water poet* (1999), p. 209.

20. Dugdale, pp. 113, 145; Dugdale (2), 18 Sept 1682.

21. SP 29/319, No. 200.

22. *The trade of England revived* (1681), p. 28.

23. Paul Charbon, *Au temps des malles-poste et des diligences* (1979), pp. 12-15; Tarr, *The history of the carriage*, p. 234; Jan de Vries, *Barges and capitalism: passenger transportation in the Dutch economy, 1632-1839* (1981), p. 59.

24. *Mercurius Politicus*, 8 Apr 1658. See below, p. 112.

25. *A Perfect Diurnall: or Occurrences*, 21 Aug 1654; *Severall Proceedings of State Affaires*, 22 June 1654; *Severall Proceedings in Parliament*, 16 Nov, 28 Dec 1654; *Mercurius Politicus*, 29 Oct 1657, 8 Apr, 13 May 1658; York City Archives, Housebooks vol. 38, ff. 16-17.

26. *Severall Proceedings of State Affaires*, 5 May 1653; *Severall Proceedings in Parliament*, 28 Dec 1654; C.H. Firth and R.S. Rait, *Acts and ordinances of the Interregnum 1642-1660* (1911), vol. 2, p. 923; *Perfect Diurnall*, 28 Aug 1654; Fig. 48; Rawdon, p. 79; York City Archives, Housebooks vol. 38, ff. 16-17; SP 29/316, No. 194; Andrew Browning (ed.), *Memoirs of Sir John Reresby* (1991), pp. 169, 219, 288, 545. See also *Intelligencer*, 18 Apr 1664 ('a passage coach' to Ware).

27. *A Perfect Diurnall: or Occurrences*, 21 Aug 1654; *Severall Proceedings of State Affaires*, 24 Aug 1654; *Mercurius Politicus*, 8 Apr, 13 May 1658; International Genealogical Index, Yorkshire (Gardner); C 9/50/48; Guildhall Library, MS 6673/3, 9 Nov 1645; *A list of the 400 hackney-coaches licensed in July and August, 1662* (1664); C 9/50/48; PROB 11/334, q. 154, Henry Waters; *Severall Proceedings of State Affaires*, 5 May 1653.

28. *Mercurius Politicus*, 24 Mar 1659; Corporation of London RO, Repertories vol. 64, f. 51, vol. 65, f. 37; C 10/65/72; C 24/987, No. 61; SP 29/319, No. 200.

29. SP 29/319, No. 200; Corporation of London RO, Repertories vol. 64, f. 51, vol. 65, f. 37; Guildhall Library, London, MS 9052/19, will

of Thomas Biscabe; C 5/164/40.

30. *Publick Adviser*, 26 May 1657; *List of the 400 hackney-coaches*.

31. Bodleian Library, Bankes MS, 5/77; SP 29/319, No. 200.

32. *List of the 400 hackney-coaches*; SP 29/319, No. 200. The role of the hackney coachmen as pioneers is noted in Philip Warren, *The history of the London cab trade* (1995), chapter 4.

33. PROB 11/334, q. 154, Henry Waters; C 5/164/40; *The case of the hackney-coachmen* (n.d.).

34. Above; below, p. 103.

35. SP 29/319, No. 200. See *The Newes*, 10 Dec 1663 and Corporation of London RO, Court of Orphans inventories 294 (B) for a Rochester service run by a London innkeeper or innkeeper's son.

36. *Publick Adviser*, 26 May 1657.

37. However, they dominated services at Portsmouth and Norwich, and there were also individuals involved at Cambridge, Lincoln, Dorchester/Salisbury and Chelmsford.

38. *Publick Adviser*, 22 June 1657; *Mercurius Politicus*, 30 Sept 1658; NA, PC 2/62, p. 188.

39. *Mercurius Politicus*, 23 Apr 1657, 13 May 1658; C 5/558/57; C 5/558/58; Guildhall Library, MS 6667/4, 11 Apr 1672; SP 29/319, No. 200; PROB 4/14082.

40. Edward Chamberlayne, *Angliae notitia: or, the present state of England* (1671), part 2, pp. 405-6. Jackman, p. 120, misdates this passage to 1649.

41. See below, p. 145.

42. SP 29/319, Nos. 200 and 201; *Harleian miscellany*, vol. 8 (1746), p. 548.

43. *The Newes*, 1 June 1665; *Intelligencer*, 12 June 1665; *List of the 400 hackney-coaches*; Appendix 6. See G.C. Williamson, *Trade tokens issued in the seventeenth century* (1889/91), p. 820, for a possible Highgate service in 1669.

44. See SP 29/316, Nos. 194-5; SP 29/319, Nos. 200-2; *Stage-coaches vindicated* (1672); *Harleian miscellany*, vol. 8 (1746), pp. 538-48.

45. Corporation of London RO, Repertories vol. 78, f. 3; *House of Commons Journals*, vol. 9, 1667-87, pp. 192-3, 333, 479; Walter Rye, *Extracts from the Court Books of the City of Norwich 1666-1688* (1905), p. 129.

46. Chamberlayne, *Angliae notitia*, part 2, pp. 405-6.

47. The Northampton road was an unusually good one, at least in 1727 (Eaton, p. 90).

48. *Post Boy*, 23 May 1700.

49. Thoresby, vol. 1, p. 28; Bodleian Library, University Archives, Chancellor's Court, 134/1/1; C 7/270/74; *Norwich Gazette*, 11 Feb 1710; John Addy (ed.), *The diary of Henry Prescott*, Record Society of Lancashire and Cheshire, vol. 132 (1994), p. 462; *Exeter Mercury*, 24 Aug 1716. Thomas Eldridge of Oxford (the man licensed in 1701) claimed in 1735 to have kept the Bath and Bristol stage-coach there for nearly 40 years (LEP, 29 Apr 1735). An Oxford-Gloucester coach licensed in 1713 functioned in practice as a London service

(Bodleian Library, *ibid*; *Gloucester Journal*, 11 June 1722).

50. *Post-Man*, 27 July 1706; LEP, 29 Apr 1735; *Evening Post*, 19 Oct 1721 (advertisement for *King's Head*, Gloucester); *Farley's Bristol News-Paper*, 9 Apr 1726; *Gloucester Journal*, 18 Mar 1740, 14 May 1745, 10 Apr 1750; Edmund Hobhouse (ed.), *The diary of a West Country physician* (1934), p. 97; *London Gazette*, 15 Mar 1730.

51. *Evening Post*, 19 Oct 1721; *Farley's Bristol News-Paper*, 9 Apr 1726, 4 Apr 1730; *Norwich Gazette*, 27 Nov 1725, 12 Nov 1726, 18 Mar 1727; *York Courant*, 23 June 1730; *Norwich Mercury*, 15 Jan 1737, 14 May 1737.

52. e.g. Pratt, *History of inland transport*, p. 51; John Copeland, *Roads and their traffic 1750-1850* (1968), p. 85; Philip Bagwell and Peter Lyth, *Transport in Britain: from canal lock to gridlock* (2002), p. 39. Pawson, pp. 292-3, is only slightly more cautious.

53. *London Gazette*, 10 Nov 1684, 10 Dec 1688, 12 Jan 1691, 11 Dec 1693, 27 Jan 1696, 7 Dec 1702; *Post-Man*, 30 Nov 1697, 24 Dec 1700, 12 Dec 1702; *Post Boy*, 14 Jan 1701; *Daily Courant*, 12 Dec 1702.

54. E 112/598/541; E 112/726/106; C 104/218, *Cremer v. Rothwell*. But see p. 150 below for the Birmingham coach.

55. Gerhold, p. 80. See pp. 149-50 below.

56. Below, p. 150.

57. Below, pp. 115, 119, 142-3, 149-50.

Notes to Chapter 8 (pp. 91-102)

1. Diaries etc. of Aston, Blundell, Calverley, Cartwright, Davies, Dugdale, Henry, Lauder, Newcome senior and junior, Nicholson, Pepys, Rawdon, Reresby, Skipwith, Thoresby, Whitley and Wood, and works of Dryden (see Appendix 8 for detailed references); Lawrence's diary, Halkett's autobiography and Whyman on the Verneys (see notes to this chapter); Bodleian Library, MS Rawl. D1114; John Addy (ed.), *The diary of Henry Prescott*, Record Society of Lancashire and Cheshire, vol. 127 (1987); *A full and true account of an horrid and barbarous robbery ... upon the body of the Cambridge coach* (1728); *Post-Man*, 19 Nov 1698; *Worcester Post-Man*, 3 Dec 1714; *Evening Post*, 12 Mar 1723; Eaton, p. 63.

2. John G. Nichols (ed.), *The autobiography of Anne Lady Halkett*, Camden Soc., n.s., vol. 13 (1875), pp. 96, 104; Pepys, vol. 4, 14 June 1663; vol. 9, 23 May 1668; Blundell, vol. 110, pp. 108, 319; Henry, ff. 103, 128; British Library, Add MS 27418, 14 Oct 1717.

3. Blundell, vol. 112, p. 289; Rawdon, p. 85; below, pp. 98, 102.

4. Bodleian Library, MS Eng. Hist. *c*.711, 28 Apr 1687; Harper, vol. 1, pp. 63-4.

5. Diaries of Aston, Blundell, Calverley, Rawdon, Reresby and Whitley (see Appendix 8 for detailed references). Calverley provides an example of London to Yorkshire on horseback (16 May 1708), and Blundell Cheshire to

London on horseback (vol. 112, pp. 152-3).

6. Andrew Browning (ed.), *Memoirs of Sir John Reresby* (1991 edn.), p. 214. Lord Ossulston used the Uxbridge stage-coach in 1712, but hired the whole coach (C 104/113, part 2, diary, 28 Oct 1712).

7. Pepys, vol. 10, p. 451; Michael Reed, 'London and its hinterland 1600-1800: the view from the provinces', in Peter Clark and Bernard Lepetit (eds.), *Capital cities and their hinterlands in early modern Europe* (1996), p. 70, with information from Derbyshire RO. See also Eaton, p. 63. Misson almost certainly exaggerated when he stated of waggons that 'only a few poor old women make use of this vehicle' (– Ozell (trans.), *M. Misson's memoirs and observations in his travels over England* (1719), pp. 331-2).

8. G.E. Aylmer (ed.), *The diary of William Lawrence* (1961), pp. 27-8.

9. George Farquhar, *The stage-coach* (1728), p. 11; Pepys, vol. 4, 15 June 1663; Blundell, vol. 110, p. 114.

10. Below, p. 99; Pepys, vol. 9, 26 May 1668; Matthew Henry Lee (ed.), *Diaries and letters of Philip Henry, M.A.* (1882), p. 339; Symson, Nos. 1305, 1310, 1557.

11. See John Taylor, *Carriers cosmographie* (1637); John Armstrong, 'The significance of coastal shipping in British domestic transport, 1550-1830', *International Journal of Maritime History*, vol. 3 (1991), pp. 78-9. For Norwich-Yarmouth vessels see *Norwich Mercury*, 2 July 1726, 27 Apr 1728.

12. *Weekly Worcester Journal*, 1 May 1747.

13. British Library, Add MS 34788, p. 21. For 6d. between Yarmouth and Norwich (0.3d. per mile), see *Norwich Mercury*, 2 July 1726.

14. Walter Macleod (ed.), *Journal of the Hon. John Erskine of Carnock 1683-1687*, Scottish History Society, vol. 14 (1893), p. 104; Bodleian Library, MS Rawl. D1114, 9-11 and 20-2 May 1676.

15. Schellinks, pp. 45, 63, 65, 69; Bodleian Library, MS Eng. Misc. e.218, p. 1; Bodleian Library, MS Don. d.115, p. 337; Beverley McAnear, 'An American in London, 1735-1736', *The Pennsylvania Magazine*, vol. 64 (1940), p. 370.

16. E.S. de Beer, *The diary of John Evelyn* (1955), vol. 3, pp. 588, 597, vol. 4, p. 592.

17. Below, pp. 151-2.

18. i.e sometimes five days Chester-London, and once three days Lichfield-London.

19. MS Eng. Hist. c.711, *passim*. The summer speed is based on 18 days from April to September in 1684-95; distances on all but three were 30-36 miles, and speeds on all but five were from 3.7 to 4.6 miles per hour. See also Lambeth Palace Library, MS 1770, 14-16 May 1706 (three days London-Stamford, like the York stage-coach in winter); and David Robertson (ed.), *Diary of Francis Evans, Secretary to Bishop Lloyd, 1699-1706*, Worcestershire Historical Society (1903), p. xviii (generally

five days London-Worcester).

20. Ronald Stewart-Brown (ed.), *Isaac Greene – a Lancashire lawyer of the 18th century* (1921), pp. 33, 46-7, 62.

21. Guy Miège, *The new state of England* (1691), part 2, p. 46; Nicholson, *passim.*; Dugdale, *passim.*

22. Dugdale, *passim.* (usually 32-47 miles per day); SP 29/319, No. 200 (York-London at 40 miles per day); McGrath, vol. 44, p. 247n (Rydal-London at about 42 miles per day); S.H. Scott, 'Letters from a Westmorland man in London: 1719-1734', *The Antiquary*, vol. 41 (1905), pp. 328, 382 (Preston-London at about 44 miles per day).

23. Pepys, vol. 10, p. 452; British Library, Add MS 27418, 16-19 May 1708 (York-London in 3½ days, or 58 miles per day).

24. Manchester Local Studies Unit, microfilm 136, pp. 118, 175.

25. Pepys, vol. 10, p. 452; Wiltshire RO, 161/170, 12 Sept 1720.

26. Symson, No. 2046.

27. Richard Trappes-Lomax (ed.), *The diary and letter book of the Rev. Thomas Brockbank 1671-1709*, Chetham Society, new ser., vol. 89 (1930), pp. 43, 45; Hainsworth, p. 78n; Symson, No. 2046. 12s. to Rye in 1657 (2.3 pence per mile) seems untypically expensive (*Publick Adviser*, 26 May 1657).

28. *Public Intelligencer*, 6 Apr 1657; Bodleian Library, University Archives, Chancellor's Court, 134/1/1; Appendices 8 and 10; Robert Dymond, *Exeter and neighbourhood under George the Third* (1879-80), 1728.

29. Joan Parkes, *Travel in England in the seventeenth century* (1925), pp. 52-3; *Mercurius Politicus*, 1 July 1658; *London Gazette*, 14 Apr 1670, quoted in William Salt Library, 307/viii/1, p. 178; Jackman, pp. 110-11; Delaune 1681, p. 346; *The case of the deputy post-masters* (1749).

30. Pepys, vol. 10, p. 452; Schellinks, p. 178; Northamptonshire RO, I.L. 2686, 9 June 1713; Dugdale, p. 105; D Laing (ed.), *The diary of Alexander Brodie of Brodie, MDCLII-MDCLXXX* (1863), pp. 253-4.

31. NA, PRO 30/24/7, No. 532.

32. SP 29/319, No. 200; Harper, vol. 1, pp. 78-9 (two London-Salisbury fares 30s. plus 4s. 6d. 'to gratify coachmen' in 1684). Cressett's comparison of the total costs of stage-coach and horse travel from York to London plus two weeks in London includes what appears to be a very low charge for horse-hire (by comparison with the York-London charge in 1657).

33. Edward Chamberlayne, *Angliae notitia: or, the present state of England* (1671), part 2, pp. 405-6.

34. Thoresby, vol. 1, p. 28; SP 29/316, No. 194, p. 3; *Harleian miscellany*, vol. 8 (1746), p. 539; *Stage-coaches vindicated* (1672), p. 5; Warwickshire RO, MI 213, 21 Dec 1654; Newcome, vol. 26, p. 179; Susan E. Why-

man, *Sociability and power in late-Stuart England: the cultural world of the Verneys 1660-1720* (1999), pp. 100-7. In May 1712 Mr Samuel Kirks rode on horseback while his wife and son were in the Chester coach (Henry, f. 113).

35. e.g. Blundell, vol. 110, p. 314-15; British Library, Add 27418, 13 Oct 1712; Rawdon, pp. 79, 81, 85, 88; Browning, *Memoirs*, p. 219; Mary Carbery (ed.), *Mrs. Elizabeth Freke her diary 1671 to 1714* (1913), p. 43; Bodleian Library, MS Eng Hist *c*.711, 7 June 1684, 28 Apr 1687; LEP, 21 June 1750.

36. *Stage-coaches vindicated*, p. 5.

37. Nicholson, 25 Mar, 22 Dec 1707; Wiltshire RO, 161/170, 28 June 1718; Thoresby, vol. 2, p. 382.

38. *Stage-coaches vindicated*, p. 2.

39. SP 29/319, No. 200.

40. Yorkshire Archaeological Society, MS 21-5, 19 Feb 1683; Nicholson, 5 Apr 1711; Newcome, vol. 27, p. 239; above, p. 91; Farquhar, *Stage-coach*, p. 2; Whyman, *Sociability and power*, p. 102; Wiltshire RO, 161/170, 23 & 27 June 1718.

41. Carbery, *Mrs. Elizabeth Freke her diary*, p. 49; Rawdon, pp. 70-1.

42. Aston, 920 MD 173, 27 Jan 1686.

43. Symson, No. 1557.

44. Nichols, *Autobiography of Anne Lady Halkett*, p. 104; Rawdon, p. 85; Parkes, *Travel in England*, p. 214; *Post-Man*, 19 Nov 1698; Lambeth Palace Library, MS 1770, 4 Oct 1709; Nicholson, 6 Apr 1711; *Evening Post*, 12 Mar 1723; G.D. Henderson and H.H. Porter (eds.), *James Gordon's diary 1692-1710*, Third Spalding Club (1949), p. 176.

45. *Stage-coaches vindicated*, p. 2. See Manchester Local Studies Unit, microfilm 136, 1670, 1675, 1683, 1689, 1692, 1698, 1700.

46. Newcome, vol. 26, pp. 183-4, vol. 27, pp. 220, 239; Nicholson, 6 Apr 1711; Dugdale, pp. 108-47; Aston. Twenty-three of Dugdale's journeys were only between St Albans and London.

47. Rawdon, p. 85. Some of the less full diaries, such as Dugdale's, may have omitted minor mishaps, but it is unlikely that any significant accident would have been left out.

48. *Post Boy*, 18 June 1698. See also *London Gazette*, 6 June 1681, 19 June 1682, 10 Nov 1684, 11 Apr 1689, 16 Nov 1693; *Post-Man*, 17 May 1698, 21 Mar 1704, 27 July 1706; *Post Boy*, 4 Jan 1700, 16 Oct 1701; *Flying Post*, 31 Aug 1699; Henry, f. 110; POB, *passim*.

49. J.M. Beattie, *Crime and the courts in England 1660-1800* (1986), p. 149.

50. Ralph Wilson, *A full and impartial account of all the robberies committed by John Hawkins, George Sympson ... and their companions* [1722], p. 17.

51. Dugdale, pp. 135-6; Carbery, *Mrs Elizabeth Freke her diary*, p. 43.

52. Below, p. 142; John Clavell, *A recantation of an ill led life* (1628), p. 35.

53. Wilson, *Full and impartial account*, p. 17; POB, t17400116-46.

54. Corporation of London RO, Orphans' inventories 2170.

55. LEP, 14 Mar 1738; *Salisbury Journal*, 10 Sept 1764.

56. Pepys, vol. 9, 26 May 1668; Newcome, vol. 27, p. 239.

57. Henry, ff. 85, 109; J.D. Humphreys (ed.), *The correspondence and diary of Philip Doddridge, D.D.* (1829), vol. 1, p. 139; Elizabeth Bergen Brophy, *Women's lives and the 18th-century English novel* (1991), p. 118; Donald Crawford (ed.), *Journals of Sir John Lauder, Lord Fountainhall*, Scottish History Society, vol. 36 (1900), p. 175.

58. Rawdon, p. 88; Nichols (ed.), *Autobiography of Anne Lady Halkett*, p. 104; Crawford, *Journals of Sir John Lauder*, pp. 168, 174; Wood, vol. 26, p. 318.

59. Below, p. 146.

60. Mrs Manley, *A stage-coach journey to Exeter* (1725). This purports to describe a real journey in 1694, but the days of the week do not match those of that year.

61. Aylmer (ed.), *Diary of William Lawrence*, pp. 27-8; Bodleian Library, MS Eng. Hist. *c*.711, 29 Apr 1687; Thoresby, vol. 2, p. 207.

Notes to Chapter 9 (pp. 103-11)

1. Delaune 1681; Gloucestershire RO, wills 1676/90, 1680/75; SP 29/319, No. 200; C 5/516/12; C 7/95/52; C 7/270/74; *Evening Post*, 4 Aug 1715.

2. E 112/598/541. Fleming had a hackney licence and was lessee of the *Axe* Inn in the parish of Allhallows on the Wall (not a coaching inn) (Corporation of London RO, Misc. MSS. 212. 7; PROB 11/384, q. 129).

3. Delaune 1690; PROB 11/393, q. 161, Henry Earle; C 10/65/72; C 24/987, No. 61; PROB 11/424, q. 4, William Fowler; Corporation of London RO, Orphans Inventories 2170. Another Londoner was John Payne, King's Lynn coachmaster (Centre for Metropolitan History, poll tax database, 1692).

4. SP 29/319, No. 200.

5. Borthwick Institute, York Deanery, Nov 1693, Margaret Gardner; *ibid.*, York City DAB, f. 34r; Lambeth Palace Library, MS 1834, f. 24; PROB 11/405, q. 102, Henry Molden.

6. Above, p. 87; below, p. 110.

7. Except to distinguish rival coaches, as at Oxford.

8. *Harleian miscellany*, vol. 8 (1746), pp. 547-8.

9. SP 29/319, No. 200.

10. Above, pp. 48-9.

11. Except one in 1681 and three in 1690.

12. SP 29/319, No. 200.

13. Delaune 1681, 1690; *London Topographical Record*, vol. 4 (1907), p. 98; E 112/598/541.

14. See *Post-Boy*, 21 Oct, 23 Oct 1707.

15. *London Gazette*, 11 June 1677, 20 Oct 1684; Hertfordshire RO, 9AR20r; PROB 4/17190; Essex RO, Quarter Sessions transcript,

415/67-8, 96; Essex RO, D/A BR 12/34; British Record Society, vol. 79 (Thomas Robinson); C 8/421/85.

16. Corporation of London RO, Misc. MSS. 212.7; PROB 11/437, q. 54, Elias Gliss. At least two and probably six of the Windsor coachmen in Delaune 1681 had hackney licences.

17. *The humble petition of a great number of the licenced hackney coachmen* (n.d; *c*.1663) (British Library, 816.m.12, No. 151).

18. Mr Earl is stated, but Cressett must have meant Fowler.

19. SP 29/319, No. 200; Anne Buck, 'Middlemen in the Bedfordshire lace industry', Bedfordshire Historical Record Society, vol. 57 (1978), p. 36; Wiltshire RO, Dean & Chapter of Salisbury, 1678 Roll J, 52; PROB 4/9544; Appendix 7, Nos. 18 and 23; PROB 31/231, No. 816; above, p. 24.

20. E 134/1 W & M Mich 23, William Deacon. See also E133/62/37, p. 8.

21. Fig. 65. See also PROB 4/5871.

22. *Norwich Gazette*, 11 Feb 1710; C 11/2287/35; *Evening Post*, 28 June 1720; Bodleian Library, University Archives, Chancellor's Court, 134/1/1; *York Mercury*, 24 Dec 1728.

23. C 24/1233, part 1, No. 9; London Metropolitan Archives, AM/PI 1705/7.

24. *English Reports*, vol. 92, p. 478; POB, t17490405-13; *London Gazette*, 23 July 1691.

25. *The case of the hackney-coachmen* (n.d.; British Library, 816 m.12, No. 154); PROB 11/334, q. 154, Henry Waters; *Flying Post*, 21 Dec 1699. Also, *Post-Man*, 9 June 1702, for a hackney coachman of Richmond, Surrey.

26. John Houghton, *A collection for improvement of husbandry and trade* (1692-1703), 19 July 1695.

27. Harper, vol. 1, p. 80.

28. Margaret Galor of the Epping coach in 1690 is not described as a widow, but had succeeded Richard Galor.

29. SP 29/319, No. 200; Appendix 7; James H. Thomas, *Petersfield under the later Stuarts* (1980), pp. 12, 53; PROB 11/367, q. 119, Andrew Hart; Norfolk and Norwich RO, Norfolk Archdeaconry, 1693 wills, p. 127; Charles John Palmer, *The perlustration of Great Yarmouth* (1872-5), vol. 1, p. 209; PROB 11/393, q. 161, Henry Earle.

30. 'Mr' may sometimes have been used because the forename was unknown.

31. *Evening Post*, 24 Nov 1715; C 5/624/78; Browne Willis, *The history and antiquities of the town, hundred and deanry of Buckingham* (1755), p. 50; Susan E. Whyman, *Sociability and power in late-Stuart England: the cultural worlds of the Verneys 1660-1720* (1999), pp. 153-6.

32. Appendix 7; Peter Earle, *The making of the English middle class* (1989), pp. 106-8.

33. *A list of the 400 hackney-coaches licensed in July and August, 1662* (1664); SP 29/319, No. 200.

34. *The Newes*, 24 Mar 1664; Wiltshire RO, Dean &

Chapter of Salisbury, 1678 Roll J, 52; Appendix 7, No. 22; *Evening Post*, 21 May 1724; LEP, 23 Apr 1734, 15 Feb 1735, 14 Mar 1738, 17 Apr 1746.

35. E 112/598/541; Delaune 1681; PROB 4/17640; E 112/795/54; LEP, 15 Feb 1733, 18 Apr 1738.

36. *Gloucester Journal*, 24 Mar 1741.

37. *Norwich Gazette*, 21 Jan 1710, 20 June, 24 Oct 1741, 1 May 1742; *Norwich Mercury*, 5 Apr 1729, 18 Oct 1735, 20 Mar 1736, 27 Nov 1756.

38. Dorian Gerhold, 'The Whitmash family, carriers and coachmasters of Taunton and Yeovil, 1685-1848', *Proceedings of the Somerset Archaeological and Natural History Society*, vol. 143 (2001), pp. 119-20; LEP, 26 Apr 1737, 2 May 1738; PROB 31/231, No. 816; above, p. 55; *Kentish Post*, 17 Mar, 4 Apr, 22 Sept 1750.

39. *York Courant*, 11 Apr 1732; *Stamford Mercury*, 23 Aug 1733; LEP, 10 Oct 1730, 15 July 1735; PROB 11/669, q. 21, Thomas Yonick.

40. Below, p. 160; *Daily Post*, 13 May 1724; LEP, 1 May 1731, 2 Dec 1732, 8 May 1735, 24 Apr 1736.

41. *Suffolk Mercury*, 7 Feb 1737; *Norwich Mercury*, 7 Apr 1739, 14 Mar 1741; LEP, 4 June 1741; *London Gazette*, 15 Mar 1730.

42. C 11/2086/35.

Notes to Chapter 10 (pp. 112-18)

1. Fig. 46; Rawdon, p. 70; above, p. 85. A Cambridge coach with six passengers in 1728 was as 'as full as it could cram' (*A full and true account of an horrid and barbarous robbery ... upon the body of the Cambridge coach* (1728)).

2. G.A. Thrupp, *The history of coaches* (1877), pp. 40, 42, 102; Appendix 7; *A Perfect Diurnall: or, Occurrences*, 29 May 1654; William Youatt, *The horse* (1866), pp. 566-9; Ned Ward, *The London spy* (1955 edn.), p. 132; below, p. 158; E 134/8 Geo III Easter 10.

3. Thrupp, *History of coaches*, pp. 40, 102.

4. Quoted in Harper, vol. 1, pp. 63-4. See also Blundell, vol. 112, p. 289. The six passengers presumably did not include those in the boots.

5. Wood, vol. 21, p. 155; *Archaeologia*, vol. 20 (1824), p. 472; PROB 4/14082.

6. e.g. *London Gazette*, 10 Dec 1688, 23 Mar 1691, 6 & 13 Aug 1694; *Post Boy*, 10 Nov 1702; *Post-Man*, 12 Dec 1702, 29 June 1704; *Evening Post*, 11 Dec 1712; POB, t17200303-15. Also *Worcester Post-Man*, 18 Nov 1720 ('a notorious cutter of the backs of coaches').

7. Figs. 45 and 58; Herbert, p. 45; POB, t17490405-13; Rawdon, pp. 70-1.

8. Rawdon, p. 85.

9. PROB 4/14082; Fig. 64; PROB 11/363, q. 106, John Freckleton.

10. See Herbert, p. 50.

11. Joan Parkes, *Travel in England in the seventeenth century* (1925), p. 71; Pepys, vol. 9, 10 July 1668; PROB 4/14082; Fig. 64; *Daily Courant*, 3 Apr 1721; *Stamford Mercury*, 23

Aug 1733; *Narrative of the journey of an Irish gentleman through England in the year 1752* (1869), p. 60.

12. *Northampton Mercury*, 18 Mar 1728; LEP, 26 Nov 1734, 6 Nov 1735; *Adams's Weekly Courant*, 19 June 1750. Rowe's principle was apparently 'friction wheels' between main wheels and axle (Jacob Rowe, *All sorts of wheel-carriage, improved* (1734), p. 6). Other new terms seem to have been for caravan-type services, e.g. the 'berlin coach' to Reading in 1718 and the 'ge-hoe coach' to Northampton in 1743, both with very low fares (Appendix 10). There were 12-seater flying coaches to Oxford in 1720 (Bodleian Library, University Archives, Chancellor's Court, 134/1/2-2).

13. See Appendices 8 and 10.

14. Appendices 8 and 10.

15. *London Gazette*, 17 July 1682, 30 Sept 1689, 23 Jan 1690; *Flying Post*, 7 Oct 1699; *Post-Man*, 19 Oct 1706, 4 Feb, 17 May, 27 Nov 1707, 27 & 29 Jan 1708, 21 Aug 1714, 30 June, 18 Oct 1715; *Daily Courant*, 11 Feb 1706, 12 May 1707, 27 Mar 1708, 22 Apr 1727; *The General Remark on Trade*, 4 Aug 1707; *Evening Post*, 11 Aug 1716, 5 Dec 1717, 24 Nov 1719, 23 Aug 1720, 20 July 1721; *Stamford Mercury*, 15 Nov 1716, 11 Oct 1733, 26 Sept 1734; *Daily Post*, 6 May 1723, 4 May 1726, 18 Mar 1727, 26 Mar 1728, 12 May 1729; *Daily Journal*, 7 May 1728; LEP, 22 Oct 1728, 13 Aug 1730, 31 Mar 1737, 22 Aug 1741; *Norwich Mercury*, 2 Nov 1728; *Newcastle Courant*, 8 Apr 1738, 24 May 1744, 16 May 1745; *Daily Advertiser*, 28 May 1744. Of the five exceptions, two were an inch under 15 hands, one near 15 hands and two over 16 hands. See also above, pp. 48-9. The law required hackney coach horses to be at least 14 hands high (9 Anne *c.*16).

16. Defoe, pp. 255, 409.

17. *Stage-coaches vindicated* (1672), p. 5 (confirmed in London Metropolitan Archives, X88/1, p. 200).

18. *Daily Post*, 14 Apr 1727.

19. Some inventories may use 'horse' in the early 19th-century sense of a gelding more than six years old (R.W. Dickson, *An improved system of management of live stock and cattle* (n.d.), vol. 2, p. 108).

20. *Mercurius Politicus*, 23 Apr 1657, 24 Mar 1659; *Publick Adviser*, 2, 16 & 22 June 1657; *The Newes*, 1 June 1665; LEP, 16 May 1732.

21. John G. Nichols (ed.), *The autobiography of Anne Lady Halkett*, Camden Society, 2nd ser., vol. 13 (1875), pp. 95, 104; F.P. and M.M. Verney (eds.), *Memoirs of the Verney family during the seventeenth century* (1907), vol. 2, p. 9; Rawdon, p. 70; *Mercurius Politicus*, 29 Oct 1657; *Post-Man*, 19 Nov 1698, 24 Jan 1706; advertisement reprinted in Ann H.G. Cottingham, *The hostelries of Henley* (2000), p. 250; Blundell, vol. 114 (1972), p. 116.

22. The less frequent services sometimes advertised at the beginning or end of the period of summer schedules suggest this (e.g. *Weekly Worcester Journal*, 26 Mar 1742).

23. PROB 4/14082; PROB 4/5871.

24. POB, t17371207-18. See also below, p. , for Henley and Stanmore coaches. Waterson's Cambridge coach in December 1681 possibly had four-horse teams, but the inventory does not assign all the horses to teams (Appendix 7, No. 3).

25. Thomas Pennant, *The journey from Chester to London* (1782), p. 137; Northamptonshire RO, IC 1719.

26. Above, pp. 50-1.

27. E 134/8 Geo III Easter 10.

28. Figs. 45 and 58; Warwickshire RO, CR 1368/4, Nos. 1-2; David Loggan, *Cantabrigia illustrata* (c.1690); Herbert, p. 45. See also John Harris, *The artist and the country house* (1979), *passim*.

29. Nichols, *Autobiography of Anne Lady Halkett*, p. 104.

30. From 59 to 80 for horses and 20 to 41 for coaches. Crosland's stock (Appendix 7, No. 21) is omitted because the horses were clearly in a poor state.

31. Again varying widely, from £2.10.0 to £8.2.0 for horses and £6.0.0 to £20.10.0 for coaches.

32. Parliamentary papers, 1831-32 vol. 7, *Report from Select Committee on the observance of the Sabbath Day*, p. 378; E.W. Bovill, *The England of Nimrod and Surtees 1815-1854* (1959), p. 139; Institution of Civil Engineers, *Minutes of Proceedings*, vol. 2 (1842-3), p. 115. These sources are not explicit about whether daily meant seven days a week rather than six; if the former, the figures given here for the earlier coaches would need to be multiplied by 1.17.

33. The sum 'disburst for horses' is assumed here to include the £76.10.0 paid for both horses and coaches.

34. E 112/726/106, Fisher's schedule. For the two periods (18 Sept-26 Oct and 26 Oct-29 Dec) the percentages were: provender 83.0 and 82.1, ostler 8.6 and 7.6, coachman 2.8 and 1.8, smith 2.5 and 3.5, coach (i.e. repairs and greasing coach wheels) 2.0 and 2.9, harness 0.8 and 0.8, horse-hire 0 and 0.7 and tolls 0.4 and 0.7.

35. E 134/8 Geo III Easter 10.

36. *Harleian miscellany*, vol. 8 (1746), p. 542.

37. SP 29/319, No. 200; E 134/1 W & M Mich 23, William Deacon; *Evening Post*, 21 May 1724.

38. Borthwick Institute, York Deanery, Margaret Gardner 1693; C 8/216/59.

Notes to Chapter 11 (pp. 119-40)

1. E 112/598/541; E 134/1 W & M Mich 23; E 126/15, ff. 298-9.

2. Rawdon, pp. 70-1; *The Mercury: or Advertisements concerning Trade*, 7 Mar 1677; E 112/598/541.

3. E 112/598/541, William Morris's schedule. See also Appendix 7, No. 14.

4. E 112/598/541.

5. Above, pp. 5-6, 56.

6. LEP, 2 Sept 1740.

7. E 134/1 W & M Mich 23; Gerhold, pp. 8, 26.

8. *Mercurius Politicus*, 8 Apr 1658; E 134/1 W & M Mich 23; Mrs Manley, *A stage-coach journey to Exeter* (1725).

9. A jointly owned team hauling all the coaches between Bridport and Dorchester (apparently operated separately from the Dorchester-Salisbury stretch in the late 1680s) would have covered 89 miles a week, compared with the average of 84.

10. *Stage-coaches vindicated* (1672), p. 5; Rawdon, pp. 70-1; E 112/598/541, William Morris's schedule; C 7/305/8. With only two services per week, load factors in 1688-9 would have been higher in winter than in summer.

11. *Mercurius Politicus*, 9 Apr, 29 Oct 1657, 8 Apr, 13 May 1658, 24 Mar 1659.

12. It is assumed here that Pennant in 1740 substituted the Welsh Harp for the Four Crosses in error. Dining places were only sometimes stated. The variations were: in summer, between Crick (1690) and Northampton (1700-23), and between the Four Crosses (1713) and the Welsh Harp (all other dates); and in winter, between Coleshill (1686), Castle Bromwich (1689 and 1712) and the Welsh Harp (1690 and 1693, in the latter case during heavy snow), and between St Albans (1712) and Barnet (all other dates).

13. Holloway's four teams could have covered the first two stages out of London of the Chester, Lichfield and Shrewsbury coaches.

14. Delaune 1690. The days recorded in 21 diary etc. entries suggest three services per week, but, for up journeys, the four Friday departures are from 1700 or earlier, the five Wednesday departures from 1701-13 and the four Monday ones from 1712-23. For down journeys, there are two Wednesday departures, from 1709 and 1717, two Fridays, from 1709 and 1718, and four Mondays, from 1711-23. In 1738 there were three services a week (below, p. 149).

15. *Mercurius Politicus*, 9 Apr 1657.

16. Blundell, vol. 114, p. 116. Aston's stops at Crick (close to Hillmorton) in May 1690 and July 1701 (in 1690 dining there instead of at Northampton) may have had a similar purpose.

17. Joseph C. Bridges, 'The diary of Nehemiah Griffith, Esq., of Rhual, Mold, for the year 1715', *Journal of the Architectural, Archaeological and Historic Society for ... Chester*, n.s., vol. 15 (1909), p. 31; Symson, No. 1305 (July, but clearly referring to winter timings). Of 14 references to winter journeys between 1669 and 1731, the up departures were on Monday (5) and Thursday (3); the down departures were on Monday (2), Tuesday (1) and Thursday (3).

18. Pepys, vol. 9, 23 and 26 May 1668.

19. In 1690 those to Chester were mistakenly described as waggons.

20. Dugdale, pp. 140, 144.

21. Dugdale, pp. 139, 140, 144, 146, 147.

22. Bodleian Library, MS Eng. Hist. *c*.711, 4-10 June 1686, 21-23 July 1687, 2-4 July 1689; John Addy (ed.), *The diary of Henry Prescott*, Record Society of Lancashire and Cheshire, vol. 127 (1987), p. 247; *Weekly Intelligencer*, 9 Jan 1655.

23. *Post-Man*, 18 Mar 1703, 30 Jan 1705; Henry, ff. 85-6; Blundell, vol. 110, p. 138, vol. 112, pp. 208-9; Nicholson, 24-29 Nov 1707; LEP, 4 June 1737; C 11/2086/35.

24. John Ogilby, *Britannia* (1675), p. 41; VCH, *Staffordshire*, vol. 2 (1967), p. 277; NA, WO 30/48; Bodleian Library, MS Eng. Hist. *c*.711, *passim.*; *Intelligencer*, 16 Nov 1663, quoted in William Salt Library, 307/viii/1, p. 165; C.L.S. Linnell, *The diaries of Thomas Wilson, D.D. 1731-37 and 1750* (1964), pp. 240-1.

25. Ogilby, *Britannia, passim*. For coach routes, see Appendix 8.

26. Appendix 6; Nicholson, 14-16 June 1714; *Severall Proceedings in Parliament*, 28 Dec 1658; SP 29/319, No. 200; Delaune 1681.

27. Diaries of Lauder in 1667, Thoresby in 1683 and Nicholson in 1702-11 (see Appendix 8); *Severall Proceedings of State Affaires*, 5 May 1653; *Mercurius Politicus*, 8 Apr 1658; also Rawdon, pp. 81, 83 for winter.

28. In 1653 the lodging place that night was at Tuxford. The lodging place for the first night out of London is not given in 1658.

29. In 1712-23 it dined at Grantham instead of Newark and Doncaster instead of Ferrybridge, probably indicating where the extra change of horses took place for both Wakefield and York coaches on those days (Thoresby, vol. 2, pp. 207, 382; Nicholson (2), vol. 4, p. 57).

30. Changing the daily distances on the first three days to 32, 33 and 27 miles. Dining in 1667 was at Hatfield, Wansford and Long Bennington instead of Barnet, Stilton and Grantham respectively.

31. Thoresby, vol. 2, p. 355.

32. PROB 4/5871.

33. PROB 11/546, q. 109, Edward Bray; C 11/2/7, depositions.

34. Davies, pp. 28-30, 55-7, 63-5, 81-2.

35. Matched only by the one-day Sudbury coach in 1738.

36. LEP, 6 Apr, 5 Oct 1717, 18 Sept 1735; *Suffolk Mercury*, 25 June 1722, 5 June 1727, 7 & 28 Feb 1737; *Norwich Mercury*, 14 Mar 1741; *Norwich Gazette*, 24 Sept 1743; *Ipswich Journal*, 10 Mar 1750; C 11/2222/12; C 11/2287/35. The westernmost of the two teams in 1741 may have been able to do other stage-coach work.

37. LEP, 11 Apr, 27 June 1738, 2 Oct 1739; *The intelligencer: or, merchants assistant* (1738). The 18 hours is based on coach speeds discussed later; below, p. . In 1753 the proprietors were innkeepers at Egham and Farnham (LEP, 5 Apr 1753).

38. LEP, 23 June 1730; *Intelligencer: or merchants assistant*; Appendix 8.

39. See Appendix 8.

40. *English Reports*, vol. 88, pp. 49-50.
41. Dining places divided the winter journey on each day into one section of 16 to 19 miles and one of 8 to 12 miles, but the significance of this is unclear.
42. Delaune 1681; *Worcester Post-Man*, 22 Mar 1717; Blundell, vol. 112, p. 153; PROB 11/522, q. 155, Thomas Winslow; fire insurance certificate, 1715, for the *Red Lion*, High Wycombe (information from Wycombe Museum); Gloucestershire RO, wills 1714/269; C 11/1782/54; C 11/382/38; *Worcester Journal*, 5 May 1738, 25 May 1744; Appendix 8.
43. E 112/726/106. Also E 133/62/37; E 134/2 Anne Mich 22; E 134/2 & 3 Anne Hil 12; E 126/18, f. 385.
44. SP 29/319, No. 200; Delaune 1681; *London Gazette*, 21 May 1694; E 133/62/37, p. 9.
45. The numbers left at Colnbrook or Maidenhead (usually four) suggest two-horse teams, but only if the total number remained six. The harness consisted of two sets each for four horses. The coaches appear to have held six passengers (E 112/726/106, Fisher's schedule).
46. Ann H.G. Cottingham, *The hostelries of Henley* (2000), p. 250.
47. E 112/570/10. Adams was later innkeeper at the *White Hart* (*Daily Post*, 8 Apr 1724).
48. *Post Boy*, 18 Apr 1699; LEP, 24 Oct 1738; Defoe, pp. 170-1; *Intelligencer*, 12 June 1665; *Impartial Protestant Mercury*, 26 May 1682; British Museum, Prints & Drawings, Heal Collection, 42.17 (no date, but John Towers, the advertiser, also offered a Farnham coach in 1697 – *Post-Man*, 15 July 1697); *Daily Courant*, 6 May 1725; *Evening Post*, 1 Apr 1718; *Daily Post*, 15 May 1721; SP 29/319, No. 202, p. 15.
49. *Daily Post*, 2 May 1726, 17 Mar 1729; LEP, 6 Nov 1735; *The traveller's and chapman's daily instructor* (1705); *Daily Journal*, 16 Feb 1728. See also POB, t17371207-18.
50. Based on an index of costs 1650-1750, comprising 57 per cent oats, 26 per cent beans, 8 per cent labour and 9 per cent industrial products (see 'Productivity', p. 513); oat prices are taken from J. Thirsk (ed.), *The agrarian history of England and Wales*, vol. 5, 1640-1750 (1985), pp. 828-31. Taking costs in 1654-63 as 100, costs ranged from 75 in 1691 to 124 in 1675, but were outside the range 80-115 in only 16 years. High-cost periods were 1650-3, 1657-63, 1674-6, 1682-6, 1693-1700, 1708-11, 1714-15, 1724-5, 1728-30 and 1741-2; low-cost periods were 1672-3, 1679-80, 1689-91, 1702-5 and 1744-8.
51. Exeter 1728.
52. Oxford 1672, Banbury 1690, Yarmouth 1743.
53. Nottingham and Wallingford 1699, Norwich 1741.
54. Some relationship is visible in 1657-63 (high), 1689-91 (low) and 1724-5 and 1728-30 (high), but there is sometimes none even when the fare information is relatively good, notably during the low-cost period of 1744-8.
55. e.g. to Bristol in 1658, Reading in 1672, Banbury in 1690, Henley in 1699-1703, Windsor in 1707, Newbury in 1727, Bury St Edmunds in 1722-50.
56. *Norwich Gazette*, 20 June, 3 & 24 Oct 1741, 1 May 1742.
57. Peter J. Bowden (ed.), *Economic change: wages, profits and rents 1500-1750* (1990), pp. 210-13.
58. Except in 1682-4 but these were fares set by the Vice-Chancellor.
59. Advertised as in the Exeter coach (*Brice's Weekly Journal*, 21 June 1728), but probably a separate service.
60. Other than (according to a pamphleteer) for York, Chester and Exeter in 1672 (Appendix 10).
61. *Suffolk Mercury*, 7 & 28 Feb 1737; Bodleian Library, University Archives, Chancellor's Court, 134/1/1, 28 Dec 1713/5 Apr 1728; LEP, 20 Apr 1736. This perhaps explains the two examples of passengers paying the full fare but travelling only part of the way (Appendix 10).
62. Blundell, vol. 110, p. 314-15; *Daily Courant*, 24 Apr 1725; LEP, 25 Feb 1749.
63. *Post Boy*, 26 Jan 1699; Nicholson, 22 Dec 1707; Fitzwilliam, pp. 16, 18, 38, 39, 40, 52, 90, 127; *Post Boy*, 10 Nov 1702; LEP, 21 Nov 1730; *Ipswich Journal*, 1 Sept 1739; *London Gazette*, 13 Apr 1693; LEP, 15 May 1744.
64. *Publick Adviser*, 26 May 1657; Appendix 3; R.C. Tombs, *The King's post* (1905), p. 24; *Post-Man*, 23 June 1728; Charles G. Harper, *The Great North Road* (1922), vol. 1, p. 35; Warwickshire RO, CR 1368/4, Nos. 1-2; *Newcastle Courant*, 13 Oct 1712. Twenty-four examples from 1723-50 ranged from 17 to 41 pence per ton-mile and averaged 29 pence.
65. E 133/62/37, p. 4; E 112/726/106, Fisher's schedule.
66. NA, PC 2/62, p. 188; above, p. 41.
67. Appendix 7; *Post-Man*, 23 June 1698.
68. E 112/598/541. Three coaches per week are assumed, and a 40s. fare. No account is taken here of additional income, e.g. from parcels or passengers in the boot. The figures cover individual expenditure on horses as well as partnership expenditure. Morris's expenditure in purchasing his coaches and horses is disregarded as capital expenditure (above, pp. 116-17). The longer period is 10 May 1688 to 22 April 1689.
69. John Smead, who also had an interest in downplaying his earnings, stated that from 1679 to 1684 he had made not more than £40 per year profit from his quarter-share in the coach (C 5/164/40). He claimed to have spent £350 on new stock.
70. *Stage coaches vindicated* (1672), p. 5.
71. Fares taken at intermediate places may have been applied directly to payment of expenses, in which cases the loadings would have been slightly higher than stated here.
72. E 112/598/541. John Smead claimed to have re-

jected an offer of £300 in 1684 (C 5/164/40).

73. C 7/270/74; E 133/62/37, p. 9; E 112/777/62. The Gloucester figure here does not take account of any horses required between Gloucester and Hereford.

74. E 112/726/106, Fisher's schedule. The two periods were 18 Sept-26 Oct and 26 Oct-29 Dec. The number of weeks of receipts do not exactly correspond to the stated dates; receipts have been related here to the actual number of weeks and the last week in the account for the second period omitted.

75. E 112/726/106; E 133/62/37, p. 2.

76. E 112/777/62.

77. Above, pp. 81-2.

78. Six of the ten in 1681 were at a single inn, the *Bell Savage*, and two (including the Coventry coach-waggon) reappear as waggons in 1690 following their transfer to a different inn. One of the latter, at the same inn, is recorded as a coach-waggon in 1694 (*London Gazette*, 16 Aug 1694). The Newcastle-under-Lyme coach-waggon is omitted both in 1681 and 1690.

79. Appendix 8, part C. The 'Ware Long Coach' is mentioned in 1704 and an inventory may record the Newcastle-under-Lyme coach-waggon in 1707 (*Post-Man*, 1 July 1704; Appendix 2, No. 26).

80. *Whitehall Evening-Post*, 24 Apr 1725 (London-Bath waggon carrying 36); Harper, vol. 1, p. 119 (Shrewsbury long coach for 12-18 in 1750); *Hampshire Chronicle*, 28 May 1792 (Southampton coaches for 10-16 insiders).

81. A caravan to carry 18 persons was offered for sale in 1689 (*London Gazette*, 6 May 1689).

82. Appendix 8; *Post-Man*, 21 Mar 1706; *A complete guide to all persons who have any trade or concern with the City of London* (1765). See also LEP, 27 Mar 1739; *Norwich Gazette*, 28 Mar 1741; C 24/1644, No. 22, Richard Foster.

Notes to Chapter 12 (pp. 141-50)

1. Northamptonshire RO, I.L. 2686, 7-8 June 1725. For a coach-waggon halted by floods, see Newcome, vol. 27, p. 241.

2. A2A entry for Northamptonshire RO, QSR 1/79/1.

3. Above, p. 90; York City Archives, Housebooks, vol. 38, ff. 16-17.

4. C 104/218, Cremer *v.* Rothwell, provender account.

5. Only three out of 34 advertisements in the 1650s, and only a further eight to the end of the century.

6. Nicholson (2), vol. 35, p. 95, vol. 4, p. 57; *Harleian miscellany*, vol. 8 (1746), p. 545. Only two coachmasters recorded in inventories (John Holloway and Humphrey Richards) had watches.

7. Above, pp. 121, 127-8; Edmond Malone (ed.), *The critical and miscellaneous prose works of John Dryden* (1800), vol. 1, part 2, pp. 87-8. See also Davies, p. 57.

8. The only example found of Sunday travel is the Chester coach in April 1701, which rested on Good Friday and travelled on Easter Sunday instead (Aston, 920 MD 174, 18-20 Apr 1701). The lifting of the prohibition in 1710 applied only to hackney coaches (9 Anne *c.*16).

9. e.g. Lincoln in two days from May in 1732/4 (but April in 1743) and Birmingham in two days in May or June 1744-6 (but April in 1750) (Appendix 8).

10. Appendix 8; above, pp. 132-3.

11. Above, pp. 132, 135.

12. *Lewes Journal*, 13 Dec 1762, quoted in Charles G. Harper, *The Brighton road* (1906), p. 34.

13. Above, p. 131. The Norwich coaches, for fast journeys before Christmas to carry fowls to London, had three fresh teams of six horses, indicating four teams and stages of 28 miles (*Norwich Mercury*, 15 Dec 1739; *Norwich Gazette*, 18 Dec 1742, 15 Dec 1744, 3 Oct 1741).

14. In the 1730s and 1740s, flying coaches which started relatively early in the year generally covered 61 miles a day or less (except those to East Anglia, Northampton, Cirencester and those which departed around midnight); those starting relatively late generally covered 63 or more miles (except those to the West Country, Worcester and Birmingham).

15. But one Oxford coach announced in advance changes between summer and winter at Lady Day (25 March) and Michaelmas (29 September) (*Oxford almanack* (1692, 1703).

16. Henry, f. 99.

17. However, the Cirencester, Gloucester and Worcester coaches had a reduced frequency in the first two or three weeks of flying (e.g. *Gloucester Journal*, 20 Mar, 3 Apr 1739; *Weekly Worcester Journal*, 26 Mar 1742).

18. Counted only once if they appear both in 1681 and 1690.

19. *Ipswich Journal*, 10 Mar 1739, 10 Mar 1764, etc.; *Mercury: or Advertisements concerning Trade*, 7 Mar 1677; Appendix 7, No. 14; above, p. 126.

20. There are only four possible examples of more than one coach at a time (Thoresby, vol. 2, p. 233; Pepys, vol. 9, 23 May 1668; Nicholson (2), vol. 35, p. 95; Rawdon, p. 79), in two cases relating to Cambridge.

21. Also, it is assumed here that in the two cases in which travellers specified a time of getting up but not of setting off, the coach departed an hour later, as it did in Nicholson's case in 1709, though Pepys in 1668 took two hours (Nicholson (2), vol. 35, p. 95; Pepys, vol. 9, 23 May, 26 May 1668).

22. Schellinks, p. 45. See also Aston, 920 MD 175, 12 July 1701; Blundell, vol. 114, p. 105.

23. *Narrative of the journey of an Irish gentleman through England in the year 1752* (1869), pp. 60-82, 126-39; LEP, 3 Feb 1753. Just breakfast and dinner seems to have become common later (e.g. *Northampton Mercury*, 17 Oct 1763; *Ipswich Journal*, 8 Sept 1764; *York Courant*,

26 Feb 1765, 18 Mar 1766).

24. Davies, pp. 57, 65 (including a one-hour breakfast stop at Bury St Edmunds); Bodleian Library, MS Eng. Hist. *c.*711, 29 Apr 1687.

25. Though William Byrd took two hours with the Maldon and Tunbridge Wells coaches in 1718-19 (Louis B. Wright and Marion Tinling (eds.), *William Byrd of Virginia – the London diary (1717-1721) and other writings* (1958), pp. 187, 300).

26. Albert, p. 34.

27. National Library of Wales, Ottley/Pitchford 2615.

28. John G. Nichols (ed.), *The autobiography of Anne Lady Halkett*, Camden Society, 2nd ser., vol. 13 (1875), pp. 95-6.

29. *Norwich Mercury*, 22 Sept 1739.

30. Assuming a one-hour stop and a half-hour stop.

31. Thoresby, vol. 1, pp. 154, 162; Lambeth Palace Library, MS 1770.

32. Above, pp. 57-8.

33. Above, p. 52. Based on evidence cited in 'Packhorses', p. 12.

34. Above, p. 50.

35. The coach wheels alone could weigh 6 to 7 cwt (Crofts, p. 119).

36. In William Youatt, *The horse; with a treatise on draught* (1831), pp. 403-52. Note that Brunel's figures were for horses' work on good roads, and some of the 17th-century variables are unknown.

37. Youatt, *Horse*, p. 416.

38. When Rothwell's Birmingham coach switched from its three-day schedule to its two-day one in June 1744 and May 1745, the horses were compensated by larger rations in London, costing 11 per cent more (Appendix 5).

39. Gerhold, p. 80.

40. Above, pp. 117, 120-1, 132.

41. For services covering 11-40 miles and over 40 miles respectively, 5 and 5 were summer only, 7 and 11 were thrice-weekly in summer and twice-weekly in winter, 7 and 5 varied their frequency in a different way, 9 and 15 had the same frequency but different times or days, and 32 and 12 did not change.

42. Appendix 7; above, p.

43. E 112/598/541; C 104/218, Cremer *v.* Rothwell, book N. In 1737-9 Rothwell's London receipts rose from an average of 43 shillings per week in April to 69 in June and then declined to 29 in October.

44. Fitzwilliam, p. 186; Appendix 2, No. 74; *The intelligencer: or, merchants assistant* (1738). With his stock in 1742 and his timings in 1738 (Fig. 75), Blackbourne could have had four teams of four or five horses in summer each handling one coach and one waggon journey per fortnight.

45. LEP, 18 Oct 1716.

46. C 104/218, Cremer *v.* Rothwell, Book N and provender account; *Aris's Birmingham Gazette*, 5 Dec 1743, 5 Nov 1744, 11 Feb, 18 Nov 1745; *Warwickshire and Staffordshire Journal*,

20 July 1738. Delaune lists one summer-only coach to Bath and Bristol in 1681 and 1690 and one to Tamworth and one to Stanmore in 1690.

Notes to Chapter 13 (pp. 151-64)

1. E.A. Wrigley and R.S. Schofield, *The population history of England 1541-1871: a reconstruction* (1981), pp. 209-10; below, p. 169.

2. In two cases (Norwich and Gloucester) this is documented, mainly through advertisements; in others the continued existence of a single service, often using the same London inn, indicates a continuing partnership.

3. Above, p. 89.

4. LEP, 30 Sept 1742, 22 Sept 1744, 26 Jan 1751; *Northampton Mercury*, 6 Feb 1744; Ralph Straus, *Carriages and coaches: their history and their evolution* (1912), p. 170; *The case of the deputy post-masters* (1749).

5. Gerhold, pp. 34-5, 131-4, 143; 'Productivity', pp. 502-6.

6. Only a single Bristol firm is recorded in the first half of the 18th century, a single Worcester firm from 1738 and a single Canterbury firm from 1737.

7. 'Productivity', pp. 509-11.

8. Map by Arthur Cossons in H.C. Darby (ed.), *An historical geography of England before A.D. 1800* (1951), p. 428; Peter Wade-Martins (ed.), *An historical atlas of Norfolk* (1994), maps 4 and 69; above, pp. xvii, 126-7, 130.

9. Based largely on information in Albert, pp. 202-5, 224-9, but miles from John Cary, *Cary's new itinerary* (1802). The 18 routes are Birmingham, Bristol, Canterbury, Chester, Cirencester, Exeter, Gloucester, Ipswich, Northampton, Norwich, Nottingham, Oxford, Portsmouth, Salisbury, Taunton, Worcester, Yarmouth and York, counting the whole of each route even where several coaches used the same road.

10. e.g. only 6d. in the 1720s for a coach on the Shenfield-Harwich road, and not more than 6d. from 1696 for a coach on the Wymondham to Attleborough road (Defoe, p. 433; Arthur Cossons, 'The turnpike roads of Norfolk', *Norfolk Archaeology*, vol. 30 (1952), p. 199).

11. LEP, 18 Sept 1735, 4 Dec 1736, 4 June 1737; C 11/2086/35; *Daily Post*, 28 Mar 1730; *Warwickshire and Staffordshire Journal*, 20 July 1738. The Warrington coach in 1737-8 may have been a new venture after a break in service (Appendix 6).

12. There is no evidence of shorter timings masked by later departure times; e.g. the York coach was leaving York in summer 1753 at the same time (5 a.m.) as it had done since 1653, and London an hour earlier than formerly ((LEP, 12 Apr 1753). The pre-1750 speeding up in Pawson, p. 288, does not appear to be supported by evidence.

13. Appendix 8; above, p. 133. The Newbury departure was at about 3 a.m. (Appendix 9).

14. Appendix 10; *Salisbury Journal*, 7 May 1753. Some coaches may have carried outsiders without advertising the fact.
15. Below, p. 164.
16. Defoe, p. 434; above, p. 132; *Ipswich Journal*, 31 Mar 1764; *Suffolk Mercury*, 23 Sept 1734; *Norwich Mercury*, 7 Apr 1739; *Norwich Gazette*, 20 June, 3 & 24 Oct 1741, 1 May 1742.
17. Arthur Cossons, 'Roads', in VCH, *Wiltshire*, vol. 4 (1959), pp. 256, 258.
18. P. Russell, 'Roads', in VCH, *Leicestershire*, vol. 3 (1955), pp. 79, 81.
19. Defoe, p. 434.
20. e.g. 7 & 8 Will III c.9.
21. Albert, pp. 97-100, 136-40; R.G. Wilson, 'Transport dues as indices of economic growth, 1775-1820', *Economic History Review*, 2nd ser., vol. 19 (1966), pp. 112-13; A.D.M. Phillips and B.J. Turton, 'The turnpike network of Staffordshire, 1700-1840', *Collections for a history of Staffordshire*, 4th ser., vol. 13 (1988), pp. 64, 66.
22. Brenda J. Buchanan, 'The Great Bath Road, 1700-1830', *Bath History*, vol. 4 (1992), pp. 81, 85, 87.
23. William Albert, 'The turnpike trusts', in Derek Aldcroft and Michael Freeman, *Transport in the Industrial Revolution* (1983), pp. 34-5.
24. Though the Yarmouth coach in 1689-90 managed 61 miles on one of its days.
25. *Salisbury Journal*, 28 May 1753. Also the Boston coach in 1759 (London to Peterborough – 79 miles – in one day), on some shorter routes and a few coaches covering mileages achieved on other routes much earlier (*Northampton Mercury*, 23 Apr 1759; Table 8, Dover and Exeter). The Trowbridge vehicle was 'like a post chariot, and the greatest part of the road with four horses; carries four passengers face to face'; the fare was 2.5 pence per mile.
26. Table 8; *Sherborne Mercury*, 29 Mar 1762; *Derby Mercury*, 23 Mar 1764.
27. LEP, 5 May, 11 July, 18 Aug, 16 Sept 1752, 1 & 3 Feb, 24 Apr 1753.
28. Several did not carry outsiders (e.g. *Derby Mercury*, 18 May 1764; *Northampton Mercury*, 22 Apr 1765).
29. LEP, 3 Feb 1753; *Felix Farley's Bristol Journal*, 9 Feb 1754.
30. Above, p. 115; Appendix 9. Steel springs are not mentioned. For the Blandford 'flying stage-berlin', with description, see *Salisbury Journal*, 7 May 1753.
31. From the newspapers used in compiling Table 8. Only London services are included, and only one fare per season per coach. The five highest fares were from 3.2 to 3.5 pence per mile. Costs, estimated as in 'Productivity', p. 513, but using London pea prices as a proxy for beans and with a cost breakdown derived from Leeds and Manchester coaches in 1760-1 (E 134/8 Geo III Easter 10) in decades from the 1720s to the 1760s were 100, 91, 90, 97 and 100.
32. Thirteen of these were on East Anglian routes (1.5 to 1.9 pence per mile), two were the first vehicles on steel springs (1.7) and two were uncharacteristically low fares to Taunton (1.8) and Bath (1.7).
33. British Library, Add MS 27971, 26-7 Aug, 9-10 Oct 1761. The fare in this case was 3.2 pence per mile but soon fell to 2.7 (*Adams's Weekly Courant*, 31 Mar, 6 Oct, 3 Nov 1761).
34. *Salisbury Journal*, 10 Sept 1764; *York Courant*, 26 Feb 1765; *Sherborne Mercury*, 16 July 1764; *Northampton Mercury*, 18 Feb 1765. A coach could of course have proprietors 20 miles apart running 10-mile stages in both directions.
35. *Ipswich Journal*, 8 Sept 1764. See also *ibid.*, 14 Jan, 3, 10 & 31 Mar 1764; *Sussex Weekly Advertiser*, 30 May 1757; *Salisbury Journal*, 9 Apr 1753, 4 Apr 1754, 1 Mar, 1 Nov 1762; etc.
36. e.g. B. Keith-Lucas, 'Kentish turnpikes', *Archaeologia Cantiana*, vol. 100 (1985), pp. 363-4; Arthur Cossons, 'Warwickshire turnpikes', *Birmingham Archaeological Society, Transactions and Proceedings*, vol. 64 (1946), p. 60.
37. Buchanan, 'Great Bath Road', pp. 81-3, 87; *Felix Farley's Bristol Journal*, 23 Feb 1754.
38. David Harrison, *The bridges of medieval England: transport and society 400-1800* (2004), p. 71; LEP, 14 Oct 1752; Russell, 'Roads', pp. 81-2; VCH, *Gloucestershire*, vol. 4 (1988), p. 129; Pawson, pp. 241-2.
39. Appendix 9. Steel springs are not specifically stated for the Northampton berlin coach, the Trowbridge 'vehicle' and the Cambridge 'fly' of 1756-9.
40. e.g. Bristol in 1754 and Gloucester in 1756 (*Felix Farley's Bristol Journal*, 9 Feb 1754; *Gloucester Journal*, 6 Apr 1756), though use of steel springs was not necessarily always successful and continued.
41. *Salisbury Journal*, 1 Mar 1762.
42. Their impact on these was slight earlier, e.g. the Gloucester flying machine on steel springs set off at 5 a.m. in summer 1756, instead of the former 3 a.m. or 4 a.m. (Appendix 8: *Gloucester Journal*, 6 Apr 1756).
43. *Sherborne Mercury*, 7 Apr 1754, 12 Nov 1764; Oliver W. Holmes and Peter T. Rohrbach, *Stagecoach East: stagecoach days in the East from the colonial period to the Civil War* (1983), pp. 105, 137. Steel-sprung coaches also charged high fares (except in 1752-3), ranging from 2.6 to 3.4 pence per mile in 1754-65 and averaging 2.9, but this partly reflected their high speeds.
44. C 54/6036, No. 6; C 54/6097, Nos. 2 and 3; C 54/6137, No. 4; C 54/6208, No. 8; C 12/822/36.
45. Count Frederick Kielmansegge, *Diary of a journey to England in the years 1761-1762* (1902), pp. 135-6, 270.
46. Appendix 6; *Salisbury Journal*, 3 Dec 1764.
47. LEP, 1 Feb 1753; *Manchester Mercury*, 2 Sept 1760.

48. e.g. *Lewes Journal*, Nov 1762, quoted in Charles G. Harper, *The Brighton road* (1906), p. 33.
49. *Norwich Mercury*, 16 Feb 1771.
50. 'Productivity', p. 508; above, p. 116. But see below, p. 254, note 32.
51. B. Austen, 'The impact of the mail coach on public coach services in England and Wales, 1784-1840', in Dorian Gerhold (ed.), *Road transport in the horse-drawn era* (1996), p. 215; Parliamentary papers, 1831 vol. 8, *Report from Select Committee on Steam Carriages*, p. 56.
52. M.J. Freeman, 'The stage-coach system of south Hampshire, 1775-1851', *Journal of Historical Geography*, vol. 1 (1975), pp. 277-9.

Notes to Chapter 14 (pp. 165-73)

1. Above, p. 4.
2. Above, p. 6.
3. e.g. Defoe, pp. 144, 171; Jackman, pp. 92-3, 296; Hey, p. 113; G.G. Hopkinson, 'Road development in South Yorkshire and North Derbyshire, 1700-1850', *Transactions of the Hunter Archaeological Society*, vol. 10 (1971), pp. 17-18; CJ, vol. 21, 1727-32, p. 438.
4. Above, pp. 14-16.
5. Thoresby, vol. 2, p. 206.
6. John Langton, 'The industrial revolution and the regional geography of England', *Transactions of the Institute of British Geographers*, new ser., vol. 9 (1984), pp. 145, 162-3.
7. Michael Reed, 'London and its hinterland 1600-1800: the view from the provinces', in Peter Clark and Bernard Lepetit, *Capital cities and their hinterlands in early modern Europe* (1996), p. 65.
8. Defoe, p. 261.
9. Maxine Berg, *The age of manufactures 1700-1820* (1985), p. 31.
10. Rick Szostak, *The role of transportation in the Industrial Revolution: a comparison of England and France* (1991), pp. 53-4, 60-8, 73-7; David R. Ringrose, *Transportation and economic stagnation in Spain, 1750-1850* (1970), *passim*; Jan de Vries, *Barges and capitalism: passenger transportation in the Dutch economy (1632-1839)* (1981), pp. 128-9.
11. Xavier de Planhol, *An historical geography of France* (1994), pp. 233-5.
12. G.L. Turnbull, 'Provincial road carrying in England in the eighteenth century', JTH, 2nd ser., vol. 4, No. 1 (1977), p. 28.
13. L.D. Schwarz, *London in the age of industrialisation: entrepreneurs, labour force and living conditions, 1700-1850* (1992), pp. 31, 34-9; Reed, 'London and its hinterland', p. 56; Gerhold, pp. 100-1; Szostak, *Role of transportation*, p. 196.
14. Roger Finlay and Beatrice Shearer, 'Population growth and suburban expansion', in A.L. Beier and Roger Finlay (eds.), *London 1500-1700: the making of the metropolis* (1986), p. 39; Jan de Vries, *European urbanization 1500-1800* (1984), pp. 270-1; Keith Wrightson, *Earthly necessities: economic lives in early modern Britain, 1470-1750* (2002), p. 236.
15. De Vries, *European urbanization*, p. 82.
16. Lawrence Stone and Jeanne C. Fawtier Stone, *An open elite? England 1540-1880* (1984), pp. 258-9.
17. Donald Crawford (ed.), *Journals of Sir John Lauder, Lord Fountainhall*, Scottish History Society, vol. 36 (1900), p. 173.
18. *Harleian miscellany*, vol. 8 (1746), p. 541; *Stage-coaches vindicated*, p. 5.
19. Szostak, *Role of transportation*, pp. 32-3, 173; Richard Wilson and Alan Mackley, *Creating paradise: the building of the English country house 1660-1880* (2000), pp. 58-60.
20. Above, p. 75; 'Productivity', pp. 494-5.
21. Above, pp. 38-9.
22. Dorian Gerhold, 'The growth of the London carrying trade, 1681-1838', *Economic History Review*, vol. 41 (1988), p. 403.
23. Szostack, *Role of transportation*, pp. 14-16.
24. Peter Spufford, *Power and profit: the merchant in medieval Europe* (2002), pp. 179-87; David Harrison, *The bridges of medieval England: transport and society 400-1800* (2004), pp. 12-29, 143-5, 221.
25. John Langdon, *Horses, oxen and technological innovation* (1986), pp. 61, 204-5, 270; Christopher Dyer, *Everyday life in medieval England* (1994), p. 302; above, p.4.
26. James Masschaele, 'Transport costs in medieval England', *Economic History Review*, vol. 46 (1993), pp. 275-6, with *The agrarian history of England and Wales*, vols. 2-5 (1988/91/67/85-6) for provender prices. However Masschaele's costs are for substantial loads and not for scheduled services, which would have been dearer. Each horse hauled about eight bushels of wheat in a cart, or 3.4 to 4.5 cwt (depending on assumptions about the weight of a bushel of wheat), compared with about 6 cwt for waggon horses in the 17th century (above, p. 52).
27. Above, p. 3; NA, on-line catalogue for C 1.
28. 'Packhorses', pp. 9-12.
29. There is a little evidence of irregular London waggon services in the 1620s and 1630s, but only at two very small places: Stanton Fitzwarren, Wiltshire, and Great Bardfield, Essex, neither of which had carriers in 1681-90 (NA, STAC 8/34/13; Bodleian Library, Bankes MS 19/2, 63/40). Delaune lists a waggon to Chester, Oswestry and Wrexham in 1681 on Wednesdays 'not constantly'.
30. Wrightson, *Earthly necessities*, p. 231.
31. Peter Clark (ed.), *The Cambridge urban history of Britain*, vol. 2, *1540-1840* (2000), pp. 181, 188-9, 316, 326, 386, 650; Wrightson, *Earthly necessities*, pp. 231, 237-8, 241, 248.

INDEX

Page numbers in **bold** refer to illustrations or maps;
'car' indicates carriers; 'co' stage-coaches.